Lawyers and the Making of English Land Law 1832–1940

LAWYERS AND THE MAKING OF ENGLISH LAND LAW 1832–1940

J. STUART ANDERSON

CLARENDON PRESS · OXFORD

*This book has been printed digitally and produced in a standard specification
in order to ensure its continuing availability*

OXFORD
UNIVERSITY PRESS

Great Clarendon Street, Oxford OX2 6DP

Oxford University Press is a department of the University of Oxford.
It furthers the University's objective of excellence in research, scholarship,
and education by publishing world-wide in

Oxford New York

Auckland Bangkok Buenos Aires Cape Town Chennai
Dar es Salaam Delhi Hong Kong Istanbul Karachi Kolkata
Kuala Lumpur Madrid Melbourne Mexico City Mumbai Nairobi
São Paulo Shanghai Taipei Tokyo Toronto

Oxford is a registered trade mark of Oxford University Press
in the UK and in certain other countries

Published in the United States
by Oxford University Press Inc., New York

ISBN 0-19-825670-1

Printed in Great Britain by
Antony Rowe Ltd., Eastbourne

Preface

THIS is a study spanning three sorts of concern. One is law-making. The land law in my title is predominantly land transfer law, with a good dash of ownership thrown in. Legal change came through statute, and this book addresses the conception, formulation, frustrations, and enactment of that form of legal process. Land use law is wholly omitted because its genesis was different; judges played an important part there. Here they are virtually absent, just an occasional extra-judicial pronouncement reminding us of their existence. It is planned and purposive legal change (and resistance to it) which features here, not the outcomes of the accidents of litigation, however significant the pattern they can be made to fit.

A central concern is thus with the law-makers themselves. The law of real property was tough law, always the preserve of specialists. Its reformulation, for whatever purpose and at whosesoever behest, had to involve them. The book looks at them and their kin, but within an examination of the structure of the legal professions and its effect upon law-making. Shortly before the start of my chosen period it would have been legal profession, singular; and the bar would have been meant. Attorneys were tradesmen; and for some quite long time after they had constituted themselves a profession the name stuck. Whether it was just a derogatory name, or whether there was something in the claim that solicitors' 'qualifications', and hence their entry to the hall of the professions, applied to just part of their work is a theme running throughout the book. If Harold Perkin's *The Rise of Professional Society* had appeared before the bulk of the text had been completed I would have pointed some of my arguments more than I did. I hope that what I have to say about the formation of the solicitors' profession as such, the tensions within it between London and the north of England, its relation to barristers (as will be seen, 'barristers' is more apt than 'the bar') in co-operating and competing over the management of legal change will add to his analysis. This is the book's second sort of concern.

One small corner of professional formation needs early mention. The body that ends this book under the grand name of The Law Society first appeared in the 1820s as the Law Institution, but from 1833 called itself the Incorporated Law Society, or, more formally, but very rarely, The Incorporated Law Society. It was managed by a committee which at first was called just that, but which later became the Council, especially to its members. To some outsiders and to critics it became instead 'the council', the small 'c' denoting unwillingness to accept that oligarchic group's pretensions to professional leadership. In writing of it I have used the formal name consistently for the later period, when its position was generally accepted, but more usually the descriptive small 'c' for the earlier, in an attempt to capture more accurately the contemporary nuances. On the other hand, since nothing turned on it, I have have simplified to 'the Incorporated Law Society' until 1903, with The Law Society thereafter.

I have divided the text roughly in the 1870s because thereafter the presence of the state was much more obviously felt, which is at least suggestive of a qualitative change. I am inclined to think that that was not permanently so, and that that is what at root divides me from Avner Offer's pioneering work on the period after 1870.[1] I admire his vision and owe him a great debt, not in any way reduced by what must seem like congenital inability to agree with him. At times this may seem wilful, since in his text itself there are numerous counter-indications which could be used to construct conclusions quite different from his own. Yet what he means as his conclusions cannot be mistaken, so forcefully are they drawn. It is these that I have used. If I have misrepresented his analysis, I am sorry. The earlier section of the book is new territory.

Like Dr Offer I have relied in part upon Departmental papers in the Public Record Office, though only for the later chapters, where much of the significant activity happened in private. My

---

[1] 'The Origins of the Law of Property Acts, 1910–1925', (1977) 40 *MLR* 505; *Property and Politics, 1870–1914* (1981).

main source however cannot easily be classified in historians' terms as either primary or secondary. It is the professional press. This is a massive archive of professional activity and opinion, containing details by the hundred not available elsewhere and in the aggregate conveying an unrivalled picture of a profession in the process of self-formation. It cemented loyalties, purveyed values, relayed news, caused disputes, resolved them, and made things happen. It itself was a constitutive agent of the profession, for solicitors in particular. Sadly its indexes were never meant to bear that burden, and the volumes must be read entire, advertisements and all, and in sequence if their value is to be realized. I have found the *Solicitors' Journal* the most fruitful, with The *Law Times* an honourable second.[2] Each ran at about 800 pages of text per year, indexes and advertisements extra. The *Law Journal*[3] was of similar size. There may be private correspondence and diaries which will illuminate murky corners left by these three, but they will certainly be few and the light scarcely needed. This study only just begins to exploit the richness that historians of the professions can find there. Lawyers, academic lawyers in particular, who believe that the scholarly periodical tradition began with the *Law Quarterly Review*[4] should think again—there is a wealth of material in these weekly professional papers that is quite indistinguishable from the later journals.

Some small fragment of it is discussed when this study reaches its third major concern, addressed particularly to students of modern land law inquisitive about the origin of their texts. Towards the end of the book I offer an account of the compilation of the 1925 legislation which covers many of the problems with which they will be familiar. Before that, however, they will find discussion of a much wider range of possibilities strung over a long period—indeed, for virtually the entire span covered by this book there were far-reaching proposals for systematic rewriting of real property law extant. They came to very little, and I offer explanations of why. Non-lawyers will no doubt skip much of my discussion of

---

[2] The *Solicitors' Journal* began in 1857, replacing the *Legal Observer*, which first appeared in 1830. See further pp. 98–106 below. The *Law Times* was first published in 1843.

[3] First published 1866.

[4] First published 1885.

texts. At one point in particular that would be a mistake. The Conveyancing Acts of the early 1880s are no doubt technical stuff, but they are the very ideal-type of law-making by and for a profession, carrying a significance far beyond their dry appearance.

Much of the book concerns title registration, reflecting its dominance of professional and political thinking over long periods. I have tried to show that it was not one issue but many, a point which I think Dr Offer rather missed. Like him, however, I found that its origin lay not in 'the land question' but in 'law reform', which I analyse at some length and relate to the evolution of the legal professions. This sets up the central tension: law reform is a good for the professions, but reform of these particular laws is, as it were, reflexive—they concern not just land but lawyers too; every reform of the land laws by lawyers was also self-reform. Every reform of the land laws from 'outside' was a reform of the profession from outside and a diminution of its claims over law reform itself. But the land laws were from time to time a matter of high political controversy. So how was change to come, and whose changes were they to be?

Contents

List of Abbreviations

A.-G.	Attorney-General
APLS	Associated Provincial Law Societies
BLL	Bodleian Law Library
DNB	*Dictionary of National Biography*
EHR	*English Historical Review*
HCD	House of Commons Debates
HCP	House of Commons Papers
HLD	House of Lords Debates
HLP	House of Lords Papers
Hist. Jo.	*Historical Journal*
ILS	Incorporated Law Society
Jo. Leg. Hist.	*Journal of Legal History*
LA	Law Association
LAS	Law Amendment Society
Law Jo.	*Law Journal*
Law Mag. & Law Rev.	*Law Magazine and Law Review*
Law Rev.	*Law Review*
Law Soc. Gaz.	*Law Society's Gazette*
Leg. O.	*Legal Observer*
LQR	*Law Quarterly Review*
LS	Law Society
LT	*Law Times*
Manchester LA	Manchester Law Association
M&PLA	Metropolitan and Provincial Law Association
MLR	*Modern Law Review*
PD	Parliamentary Debates
PRO	Public Record Office
Proc. Brit. Acad.	*Proceedings of the British Academy*
S.-G.	Solicitor-General
Sol. Jo.	*Solicitors' Journal*
SR&O	Statutory Rules & Orders

Table of Cases

Table of Statutes

PART I

1832–1875

1

Lawyers and Law Reform

1. Prologue

1.1.   As Henry Brougham began his great six-hour speech on law reform to the Commons in February 1828,[1] the speech that declared open season for assault upon all the densest thickets of the common law, he promised to skip lightly past real property law. He had been beaten to the post by James Humphreys, whose visionary proposals for systematic reform[2] he compared with the pioneering work James Mackintosh had done for penal reform a decade before. Home Secretary Peel was believed to be about to introduce legislative proposals in response, so he, Brougham, need add little. He was being disingenuous. Humphreys's work and Brougham's own pre-scriptions represent visions of law reform so different that they have next to nothing in common save the name. Humphreys had written a code, working outwards from basic principle to construct a system. Brougham proposed a medley of *ad hoc* statutes to right individual nonsenses—each one much needed, but each one quite independent of the others; laws reform, not law reform. And so for all his tribute to Humphreys, Brougham did turn to real property law, urging there the same sort of incremental changes as he had for other areas of law: the abolition of local tenures, rationalization of the machinery of fines and recoveries, abolition of trusts to preserve contingent remainders, the simplification of words of limitation, and so on.

Brougham claimed, pretended perhaps, that some of this

---

[1] 18 PD (2nd ser.) 127; see esp. 131, 171, 181–6, 223–4, 227, 233.
[2] James Humphreys. *Observations on the Actual State of the English Law of Real Property, with the Outlines of a Code* (1827).

would frighten the conveyancers, the conveyancing barristers[3] of Lincoln's Inn whose treatises, precedent books, and opinions on title established them as the lords of their segment of the lawyers' professions. Perhaps he was teasing. Tinney, Hodgson, Duckworth, Brodie, Sanders, Duval, Tyrell—their temperaments differed of course, so that what to one would be an unacceptable risk would to another be unjustifiable timidity, but as a group they were not reactionary.[4] Their very skill lay in adapting the underlying law to the property dispositions of the wealthy, devising documents to achieve the precise ends of their clients, resorting to creative private statutes where necessary. Controlled innovation, limited incrementalism, this was why these men had gained the eminence they had. They were recognizably the same species as Brougham, but though Humphreys was by profession a conveyancer, intellectually his Code owed nothing to that tradition.[5]

The father of systematic law reform in England, grandfather perhaps, was Jeremy Bentham. He greeted Humphreys's Code with an enthusiasm so ecstatic as at times to be incoherent, chiding him here and there for not going further, criticizing bits and pieces in Humphreys's book, but emphatically endorsing his scheme, overcome by admiration for its breadth and by wonder that its author was not some raw young iconoclast but a 60-year-old Chancery junior.[6] One particular element in Humphreys's scheme had for long been urged by the more adventurous of the incremental reformers among the conveyancers, a scheme for the general registration of deeds and assurances.

---

[3] These were barristers specializing in drafting, and giving opinions on, conveyancing documents. They were distinct from 'certified conveyancers' who, though licensed by the Inns of Court, were not barristers; for them see Harry Kirk, *Portrait of a Profession* (1976), 134 ff.

[4] Obituaries: P. B. Brodie: (1855) 21 *Law Rev.* 348; Lewis Duval: (1844) 1 *Law Rev.* 139, partly reprinted at (1844–5) 29 *Leg. O.* 78; W. H. Tinney: (1871) 51 *LT* 126, F. Boase, *Modern English Biography*; John Tyrell: (1840) 20 *Leg. O.* 449. For Samuel Duckworth see M. Stenton, ed., *Who's Who of British Members of Parliament*, i, 1832–45. F. W. Sanders wrote *An Essay on Uses and Trusts . . .* (1791, 4th edn. 1824), and Tyrell published his *Suggestions Sent to the Commissioners Appointed to Inquire into the Laws of Real Property* in 1829.

[5] Bernard Rudden, 'A Code too Soon', in P. Wallington and R. M. Merkin, eds., *Essays in Memory of Professor F. H. Lawson* (1986).

[6] (1826) 6 *Westminster Review* 446; attribution from the *Wellesley Index to Victorian Periodicals, 1824–1900*, ed. Walter E. Houghton (1966–). My interpretation differs from Professor Rudden's, n. 5 above.

Such a proposal had been made long ago, by a law reform committee established during the Commonwealth and headed by Matthew Hale.[7] But though it had been revived from time to time, and though Middlesex and Yorkshire had acquired their own local variants on the theme, nothing had come of it nationally. Here Bentham had, as he put it, a present for Humphreys—though it would be more accurate to describe it as an idea of a present: carbon paper, which, as Bentham described it, would greatly ease the clerical side of registration. Bentham's interest lay primarily in getting ideas into practice, so he had an avid interest in practicalities—witness the panopticon, for example. Schemes for registration tended to founder on practical difficulties, so here was Bentham's own stab at solving one of them, the cost and delay involved in the copying necessary if registration was to work. Assuming that Humphreys too would want to see his proposals in operation, the old man was willing to make a gift to him of this technological idea.

Contrast such enthusiasm with the vitriol directed at Brougham's speech by the Benthamite *Westminster Review* in an article now attributed to Bentham himself.[8] Brougham, it said, was anti-democratic where Bentham was not; Brougham wanted to preserve the corrupt system of payment by fees, where Bentham wanted salaries; Brougham's deliberate omission of real property law, equity, and commercial law would make true, systematic law reform impossible; Brougham's was a mere tinkering with the present system, which, as any true disciple of Bentham would have learned, existed only to foster the interests of lawyers, interests wholly congruent with Brougham's own vainglorious nature.

Here, then, are three characteristics tending to separate Bentham's own vision of law reform from that of incrementalists, even ambitious incrementalists such as Brougham. First, law reform should start, not with the existing state of the law, but from an investigation of the present needs of society, constructing whatever new concepts and vocabulary are neces-

---

[7] Sir W. S. Holdsworth, *A History of English Law*, vi. 416.
[8] (1829) 11 *Westminster Review* 447; attributed in *Wellesley Index* to Jeremy Bentham with assistance from George Bentham. See also Jeremy Bentham, *Lord Brougham Displayed* (1832).

sary; secondly, necessarily, the enterprise should be systematic; thirdly, perhaps optionally, 'judge and co.' cannot be trusted with the task themselves. Humphreys fitted the bill, though an exception to the third desideratum; Brougham failed.

1.2.   The Real Property Commissions established in the wake of Brougham's address were staffed by judge & co.: Tinney, Hodgson, Duckworth, Brodie, Sanders, Duval, Tyrell. Apart from their chairman, the Scottish common lawyer, John Campbell, this was a selection from the élite conveyancers. They occupied a peculiar position at the bar. If they were purely chambers counsel they could not be promoted to the ranks of the KCs, ostensibly because bar etiquette prohibited silks from drawing documents or taking pupils—the one the mainstay of conveyancers' work, the other the means of transmitting their skills.[9] The status of Conveyancing Counsel to the Court, invented in 1851 as a by-product of Chancery reform, went some way towards recognizing their achievement—their centrality, indeed, since many of them drafted the private statutes and company documents which formed the legal basis of nineteenth-century capitalist investment. But even this élite ranked below the silks, and the bench was firmly closed to them unless they could combine conveyancing with general Chancery practice. Though none could hope for immortality through the law reports, in their own sphere they were tantamount to judges. An opinion on the validity of a title by Charles Butler, or Lewis Duval, or Brodie, or Bellenden Ker was as near to being final as makes no difference.[10]

Their concern was usually with how things could be done, rather than with what it was to be achieved. The wonderful flexibility of the doctrine of estates, of trusts, of powers, made everything possible that anyone could want; it was just a question of finding a way. The Real Property Commissioners wanted the substantive law left quite alone, it was well suited to the temper of the times, allowing everything sensible to be done and prohibiting nothing important. But as was common

---

[9] See Joshua Williams, *Letters to John Bull on Lawyers and Law Reform* (1857), reviewed in (1857–8) 4 *Law Mag. & Law Rev.* 139.
[10] (1844) 1 *Law Rev.* 39.

among conveyancers they objected to the roundabout way in which many transactions had to be conducted. Their prescription[11] was very much the same as Brougham's; the Fines and Recoveries Act 1832, the Real Property Limitation Act 1833, and the Wills Act 1837 were just their more conspicuous achievements. It was a daring work, as Maitland put it,[12] but it was also a characteristic work. Peter Brodie's clever Fines and Recoveries Act did its job well enough, thought the reformist *Law Review* on his death in 1855, but it would have been much better to have achieved the reform far more directly.[13] As Charles Butler, the father of that generation of conveyancers, would have said approvingly, it had been a pruning and grafting of the ancient stock.[14] Humphreys's Code was praised by the Commission, but it was not taken seriously.[15]

2. The Dauntless and Experimental Advocates of Law Reform[16]

2.1. After 1832, young barristers with connection enough to win a seat in the Commons could reasonably hope to make a name through law reform of the Brougham variety. One such man was James Stewart, a conveyancer and equity draftsman who sat for Honiton as a reforming Liberal in 1837.[17] In the following year he was a member of the Select Committee on Copyhold Enfranchisement,[18] along with Campbell and Duckworth from the now defunct Real Property Commission. Then in 1841 he piloted through the Commons a bill to remove the

---

[11] Reports of the Real Property Commissioners, (1829) HCP x; (1830) HCP xi; (1831–2) HCP xxiii; (1833) HCP xxii.

[12] F. W. Maitland, *Collected Papers*, ed. H. A. L. Fisher, i (1911), 198–9.

[13] (1855) 21 *Law Rev.* 348.

[14] (1845) 2 *Law Rev.* 114.

[15] See Rudden, 'A Code too Soon'.

[16] (1851–2) 43 *Leg. O.* 1.

[17] Stenton, ed., *Who's Who*. Boase, *Modern English Biography* confounds him with one John Stewart. He wrote *The Practice of Conveyancing* (1827, 3rd edn. 1846–7), and edited *Blackstone's Commentaries* from 1839 to 1854. Suitably for the Secretary of the Copyhold Commission ((1852) 16 *Law Rev.* 225) he also wrote *How to Enfranchise your Copyhold under the Copyhold Acts of 1841 and 1852*. See further, Ch. 2 below.

[18] Select Committee on Copyhold Enfranchisement, (1837–8) HCP xxiii. 189.

necessity for the lease when conveying land by lease and release—a modest and useful incremental reform that had been advocated in the *Edinburgh Review* as long ago as 1821.[19] Even here, as the writer had foretold, vested interests bit. Though not a word was said about it during debate, the bill had been carefully drafted so as not to upset the Crown, which was thereby enabled to continue levying pro rata stamp duty on the lease as though nothing had changed. So though on Stewart's estimation about £50,000 a year had been saved on land trans-action costs, about the same amount was still being levied by the Stamp Office on documents which no longer existed.[20] Stewart's second effort, a bill to reform the administration of charitable trusts, ran headlong into Church opposition and sank with all hands.[21] His third, a bill to provide Parliamentary short-form conveyances for transactions worth less than £300, was presented to the Lords by Lord Campbell in 1843, Stewart having left Parliament in 1841. It was condemned as incompe-tent by liberal and conservative alike, and Stewart himself was dubbed a dilettante law reformer by the Lord Chancellor.[22]

Looking back in 1852 Stewart acknowledged the defects of his bill. Yet, he wrote, it was better to try but make mistakes than not to try at all. For out of the mistakes came progress, as had even been the case with his conveyancing bill, which had led to ideas which culminated (not very happily in fact) in two Acts successfully promoted in 1846 by Lord Brougham, providing optional short-forms for conveyances and leases.[23] What Stewart did not say was actually much more important than this rather feeble self-justification: in 1844 with Brougham and others, to reduce amateurism and to provide continuity, he had launched the Society for Promoting the Amendment of the Law.[24]

[19] Conveyance by Release without Lease Act 1841, 4 & 5 Vict., c. 21; see (1841) 56 PD (3rd ser.) 726; (1821) 35 *Edinburgh Review* 190—the attribution to Bellenden Ker in *Wellesley Index*, i is deleted in iv. 784.

[20] James Stewart, *Suggestions as to Reform in Some Branches of the Law* (1842), p. xi; see also (1844) 28 *Leg. O.* 225, 285.

[21] (1841) 57 PD (3rd ser.) 569, 1513 ff.

[22] (1843) 68 PD (3rd ser.) 1015f.; cf. C. H. Bellenden Ker's 'Letter' in Charles Davidson, *Concise Precedents in Conveyancing* (2nd edn. 1845), 26 ff.

[23] James Stewart, *Suggestions* (2nd edn. 1852), p. x, citing 8 & 9 Vict., cc. 119 and 124.

[24] (1872) 53 *LT* 304 (misspelt), and see below, sect. 2. 4.

2.2. Bentham, Humphreys, and the Real Property Commissioners all agreed that a general registry of deeds should be instituted. The Commissioners' elaborate investigation of the question was matched by an equally elaborate legislative proposal.[25] Mainly the work of Lewis Duval, it claimed to solve one of the practical problems that always beset deeds registration— how to construct the index of names necessary for the searching of the register in such a way as to be complete, accurate, and, above all, reasonably speedy in operation.[26] But its impeccable pedigree got it nowhere. Registration bills habitually fell in the Commons, giving rise to a belief among some reformers that unless the law-making system itself were reformed, necessary amendment of the law would always be thwarted by entrenched vested interests or short-sightedness.

A major theme of the teachers of the Scottish Enlightenment had been that the primary function of modern government was to provide a system of modern law conducive to the development of the nation.[27] They sketched out how this should be achieved, with the stress on the systematic nature of the enterprise. Their students became the founders of the *Edinburgh Review*, they went south to become lawyers, administrators, politicians, all well placed, so they thought, to put theory into practice—Henry Brougham was one. Something like the same inspiration arose independently in England from the work of Bentham, who likewise stressed that the key to the enterprise was system. Such ambition could be realized only if the legislature acknowledged both its own importance as a general lawmaker and also the over-riding constraints imposed upon it by the systematic nature of the reforms needed. This was hardly to be expected from a legislature itself unreformed, but after 1832 the great task would surely be put in hand? It seemed not. In 1833 the Benthamite Arthur Symonds raged in the *Westminster Review* against the lack of progress made on the Real Property Commissioners' bills:

The government which ought to have lent its utmost aid to give weight to these measures has held back, and these improvements have had to

[25] (1830) HCP xi.

[26] See n. 10 above; also (1844) 28 *Leg. O.* 300, and Ch. 2 below.

[27] Stefan Collini, Donald Winch, and John Burrow, *That Noble Science of Politics* (1983), esp. ch. 1.

struggle with all the ignorance, and the repugnant selfishness and apathy, which characterises the English gentry.[28]

Ten years later solicitor Edwin Field also criticized government inactivity, and repeated Symonds's view that even when government did establish commissions to make reform proposals they operated 'without relation to the general principles of jurisprudence and each other'.[29] But his conclusion was broader: that the unreformed legal profession was itself scarcely capable of the task:

Not only have we had the patient set to cure himself, but our very statesmen believe he can do it best. We ourselves heard Mr Brougham . . . ridicule Lord Eldon . . . We have since seen Lord Brougham pursue pretty much the same principle which Mr Brougham then so happily exposed.

It was all very well for James Stewart's law reform book to claim this to be the century of law reform, but only

if he means individual attention—granted. Bentham may be said to belong to this century, and many have followed him. If he means attention by the State, we trust he is a prophet, for we cannot say much in commendation if he speaks as a historian.

Where is our registry Act, demanded Field? Still merely an aspiration. Has the state shortened conveyances? Not at all. Solicitors had, to their honour, but the state did nothing.

With this disappointment that government should ignore its responsibility for law reform came anger that the country was being held back, since all sound theory demonstrated that law reform based upon the scientific principles of political economy[30] is an essential prerequisite of national development. Further though, these charges contained an unarticulated claim for the hegemony of the legal profession, for nobody could imagine any other source of sound law reform. Which bit of that profession? Field's argument was not that there was no current legal change—on the contrary, much of his article

---

[28] (1833) 19 *Westminster Review* 54; attribution from *Wellesley Index*.
[29] (1843) 39 *Westminster Review* 205; Thomas Sadler, *Edwin Wilkins Field* (1872), 33.
[30] See Collini, Winch, and Burrow, *Politics*, ch. 4; J. S. Mill on John Austin, (1863) 118 *Edinburgh Review* 39.

proclaims his feeling of vicarious shame for yet another inept bankruptcy Act recently passed into law. But not all statutory change counted as Law Reform, only that according with the principles of jurisprudence, which could not be expected from blinkered coteries of leading barristers, however well meaning. Who then? And which jurisprudence?

One answer to these questions located the centre of operations in the mind of a great analytical thinker—Bentham pre-eminently, Austin perhaps.[31] Such scientific amateurs, as their opponents characterized them, would then devise schemes from a priori propositions by methods that were essentially deductive. There is exaggeration in this, for Bentham used both factual data and foreign analogies in constructing his schemes, but there is enough basic truth in it to stand.[32] If Bentham was to be queen bee, the workers would be disciples steeped in his writing, usually young men with leanings that we would now call academic and which 'practical' men then called 'theoretical'. Logical system was the key, and its ideal was the legislative code. Field praised Bentham as the only truly philosophical analyst of our 'heterogeneous medley of laws', preferring science to random incrementalism. But he criticized him for excessive reliance on deductive method. For Field the science of law was inductive, in that true legal principles could be inferred from a scientific study of the laws of civilized nations on a particular question, bearing in mind, of course, the principles of political economy. Though he did not say so, this shift had advantages for a man like Field, a self-taught, successful, city solicitor. He did not have to sit at anyone's feet. He could turn at once to legal matters in which he had considerable practical experience, without having to develop an all-embracing system first. This was equally true of Brougham, whom Field condemned. Field saw 'science' as the differentiation[33] which provided a cloak

---

[31] Enid Campbell, 'German Influences in English Legal Education and Jurisprudence in the Nineteenth Century', (1959) 4 *University of Western Australia Law Review*, 357; Raymond Cocks, *Foundations of the Modern Bar* (1983), esp. 44–51.

[32] See e.g. Austin on the Criminal Law Commission: *Lectures on Jurisprudence* (5th edn. 1885), 10; but contrast Lecture 39 and 'Notes on Codification and Law Reform', which were first published in 1885 in the 5th edn. of his *Lectures*.

[33] Cf. R. C. J. Cocks, *Sir Henry Maine* (1988), 14–19; contrast Richard L. Abel, *The Legal Profession in England and Wales* (1988), 9.

behind which a claim to participation in the law-making process could be made by an outsider—for Field, as a solicitor, could not assert that mixture of practical experience and authority which was the hallmark of the incrementalist barristers who monopolized the high places.

Many of the systematic law reformers shared this belief, fostered by Bentham himself, that the key to progress lay elsewhere than in the accumulated professional knowledge of the legal élite, and that the possession of such knowledge by itself brought no pre-eminent status. Young barristers armed with theory could leapfrog their elders. Solicitors could outflank the bar. Just as the Law Reformers' insistent attempts over a long period to move the process of law formation out of the chambers of the Houses of Parliament and into standing commissions of enlightened lawyers represent the clearest claim for lawyers' hegemony over law and legislation, so the equally unsuccessful efforts to establish a law university to train those enlightened lawyers away from the grip of the Inns of Court represent an internal challenge to the power relations of the barristers' profession.[34] That university would teach jurisprudence, political economy, Roman and foreign law; it would school legislators in whose hands the development of the law would henceforward lie. In 1849 a visionary writer on 'The State of the Profession'[35] called upon the bar to cast aside its petty jealousy of fellow for fellow and raise itself in public esteem by embracing the cause of law reform. With a law university to provide enlightenment, systematic law-reporting to record the wisdom of judges, a law club open to all lawyers, and a Ministry of Justice to carry the profession into the heart of government, there were no limits to what might be achieved. With a profession as elevated as that it was conceivable, he thought, that a body of practitioners might be withdrawn from their practice, at state expense, to draft the body of jurisprudentially sound legislation the modern world demanded. Perhaps a

---

[34] (1845) 2 *Law Rev.* 243; (1845) 3 *Law Rev.* 362; (1848) 8 *Law Rev.* 122, 379; (1849–50) 11 *Law Rev.* 201, 347; (1850–1) 13 *Law Rev.* 143; (1851) 14 *Law Rev.* 306; Helen Beynon, (1981) 2 *Jo. Leg. Hist.* 62. See generally Cocks, *Foundations*, esp. chs. 4 and 5; Brian Abel-Smith and Robert Stevens, *Lawyers and the Courts* (1967), 68–78.

[35] (1849) 10 *Law Rev.* 148.

Society for Promoting the Amendment of the Law could take a similarly broad approach?

2.3 Among cautious lawyers, the Real Property Commission was regarded as something of a model for law reform.[36] It comprised a small group of non-political experts, whose bills, drafted by themselves, if they passed at all passed unamended. But it fell far short of the Utopian vision just quoted. 'Our Commission is all confusion,' wrote John Campbell, chairman of the Real Property Commission, 'the conveyancers insist on being paid.'[37] Although £1,200 a year was found for each of them, one at least, Peter Brodie, draftsman of the Fines and Recoveries Act, gave himself so entirely to the Commission's work that he lost his practice thereby and had to rebuild it in the following years, and John Tyrell fared little better.[38] Further, once the Commission was wound up, there was no institutional base to apply pressure for implementation. Yet in formulating its proposals the Commission had consulted widely within its own peer group, so that its plans represented something approaching a consensus among the knowledgeable. Enactment, however, depended upon individual effort by members of Parliament, with the result that the Commission's good-housekeeping recommendations lived on as statutes, but its major innovative scheme had made no progress at all. One did not need to be a zealot for law reform to see the need for the Society for Promoting the Amendment of the Law.

2.4. The Law Amendment Society (LAS), as it soon became known, was founded in 1844, with Lord Brougham as its president and James Stewart its treasurer. It drew membership from all the groups outlined above, with barristers predominating. Field joined, one of rather few solicitors identifiable in the membership list published after the society had been under way

---

[36] (1844–5) 29 *Leg. O.* 116, 176.

[37] Mrs Hardcastle, *Life of John, Lord Campbell* (1881), i. 459, 464.

[38] (1854–5) 21 *Law Rev.* 348; (1840) 20 *Leg. O.* 449; (1830) HCP xviii. 497; and see C. H. Bellenden Ker, *On the Reform of the Law of Real Property* (1853), 40. The payment was unusual but not unique: J. M. Collinge, *Officials of Royal Commissions of Inquiry, 1815–1870* (1984), 4, 14, 15.

for about a year,[39] though more joined later. Other solicitors in that list were Robert Wilson, whose plan for title registration is of great importance, J. Meadows White, who gave evidence in its support to the 1857 Commission on Land Title Registration, and Samuel Amory, who was a member of the Council of the Incorporated Law Society (ILS). Indeed, although the identified solicitors were relatively few, perhaps only fourteen out of 119, all but one were members of the ILS, which marked them out from the general run of solicitors. Wilson, Germain Lavie, and Joseph Maynard eventually served on its Council. Field and Harvey Gem were on the first council of the Metropolitan and Provincial Law Society,[40] founded in 1847. Joseph Parkes was another of the solicitors, joint author of Brougham's law reform speech in 1828, Whig party agent; his *History of the Court of Chancery* was a polemic for reform of that court, an interest he shared, incidentally, with Edwin Field. Parkes was soon afterwards himself rewarded by the Whigs with a Mastership in Chancery, like Nassau Senior, another member.

Others can be identified as part of the Benthamite inheritance. Walter Coulson was Bentham's protégé from youth, working for a time as his amanuensis.[41] John Herbert Koe QC, another child protégé, had been his hard-worked secretary.[42] Koe edited the second edition of a book on bankruptcy by another member, Basil Montagu QC. Montagu[43] was a campaigner for bankruptcy law reform, but he had also worked with Romilly against the death penalty and with Koe, Mill, and Ricardo on a committee investigating juvenile crime. He had sometimes been used by Bentham as an intermediary, having once been engaged to translate into English some of the work of Étienne Dumont, himself Bentham's translator and publisher. From 1848 another

---

[39] (1844) 28 *Leg. O.* 365. The very first list, contained in an advertisement in the *Morning Chronicle*, 12 Apr. 1844, is reprinted in (1843–4) 27 *Leg. O.* 484. It includes Field, Gem, Coulson, Koe, Montagu, Duckworth, Christie, and Kelly. Membership of the first Council is reported at (1844) 28 *Leg. O.* 52.

[40] See below, pp. 30–33.

[41] *The Collected Works of Jeremy Bentham: Correspondence*, viii, ed. Stephen Conway (1988), 66 n., 432; obit. (1860–1) 36 *LT* 96.

[42] *Collected Works: Correspondence*, vi, ed. J. R. Dinwiddy (1984), 365 n.; viii. 4 n.; 432, and *passim*; ix, ed. Stephen Conway (1989), *passim*.

[43] *Collected Works: Correspondence*, vii, ed. J. R. Dinwiddy (1988), 450 n.; viii. 15 n., 95, 537 n.; (1852) 37 *Gentleman's Mag.* 410; (1851–2) 18 *LT* 237.

Benthamite, Arthur Symonds, was the Society's joint secretary.[44] Equally, however, names appear of the reforming conveyancers discussed above: Duval and Samuel Duckworth, both members of the first Real Property Commission, J. H. Christie,[45] James Stewart of course; and the rising star of the next generation, W. D. Lewis,[46] then only recently called to the bar.

The LAS was from the beginning an amalgam of different interests in law reform, grand or restrained, with tensions that would have to be resolved. Yet its breadth of opinion gave it every promise of influence. If it did no more than serve as a rallying-point round which law reformers might gather and find mutual encouragement it would do well—but it also furnished weapons for the fight, its Council boasted in 1848.[47] Its potential was recognized by the ambitious: Fitzroy Kelly and Edwin James were both members.[48]

3. The Virtues of Caution

Conservative reaction to these developments was complex and to some extent confused. Its voice is best heard in the *Legal Observer*, a journal founded in 1830 by Robert Maugham, who at about the same time was instrumental in establishing the Incorporated Law Society, whose secretary he became.[49] It tended to be the mouthpiece for the ILS council,[50] but the occasions on which that body had anything much to say were few, and Maugham's main objective seems rather to have been the encouraging of the professional ethic among solicitors of

---

[44] (1848) 8 *Law Rev.* 233; Beynon, (1981) 2 *Jo. Leg. Hist.* 62.

[45] Christie was in the first promotions to the rank of Conveyancing Counsel to the Court, (1852) 44 *Leg. O.* 199.

[46] For the prodigious energy of this neglected man, who died aged only 38, see (1861) 5 *Sol. Jo.* 242 and below, p. 38. His lectures were sometimes reprinted in the professional press, e.g. (1851–2) 43 *Leg. O.* 107, and see (1848–9) 9 *Law Rev.* 221. He is noticed by Cocks, *Foundations*, 115.

[47] (1848) 36 *Leg. O.* 242.

[48] For Kelly and James see Cocks, *Foundations*, index entries; also for James, (1858) 31 *LT* 78, 93.

[49] Kirk, *Portrait*, 26–30; and, on the early history of the ILS, (1844) 29 *Leg. O.* 421, (1848) 36 *Leg. O.* 185.

[50] (1870) 49 *LT* 236; Kirk, *Portrait*, 59, 132; cf. (1856) 28 *LT* 182.

all sorts. He was hampered by his own close association with the élite metropolitan solicitors, and was correspondingly ignorant of provincial practice, but though he had less success in reaching out to provincial practitioners than did the more strident *Law Times*[51] he shared its general ethos that all solicitors from all areas and of all sorts of business should be united into a single profession. Consistently with this value, the *Legal Observer* supported law reform that would increase business coming to attorneys and solicitors: reform of Chancery procedure, for example, reduction in court fees generally, reform or abolition of the ecclesiastical courts.[52]

Similarly, Maugham did not seek to defend the accumulated absurdities that made land transaction law such a complicated business. He recognized that 'perhaps the most remarkable feature of the reformed Parliament is its love of altering the law', even though that drove 'respectable old lawyers almost out of their wits'.[53] Defensively, however, he justified a position of extreme caution:

The administration of the law, as the government of the State, is now subject to general discussion. This is no fault of the *Legal Observer*. Our existence commenced with the new order of things, and we are willing to lend our aid in giving a right direction to the changes which are going forward.[54]

There were three problems, however.[55] The first was that although the great men now seemed to agree that change was needed, they often failed to agree on what that change should be, each one jockeying with the other for his own scheme. Secondly, all Maugham's instincts inclined him to reform 'bit and bit'. But if one tried to do that with land transaction law one often found that change actually created so much new

---

[51] Cocks, *Foundations*, 64–5.

[52] e.g. (1843–4) 27 *Leg. O.* 1. Cf. its favourable reception of Lord Campbell's Fatal Accidents Act: 'some of the profits of railway carelessness and mismanagement will therefore pass into the pockets of the injured survivors and their legal advisors . . .' (1846) 32 *Leg. O.* 1.

[53] (1843–4) 27 *Leg. O.* 17.

[54] Ibid. 211.

[55] For the following analysis see (1843–4) 27 *Leg. O.* 81, 208, 211, 307 ('bit and bit'), 369, 401, 420, 422, 443, 445; (1844) 28 *Leg. O.* 49; (1845–6) 31 *Leg. O.* 201.

uncertainty that matters became worse, not better. The alternative might be to pass the whole subject over to a commission
of experts, but, on the other hand, if change were simply going
to beget more change it might be better just to put up with the
present law—at least men knew how to work it. Thirdly, since
there was no permanent law reform institution in government,
proposals arose at the whim of individual lawyer-politicians,
who drafted their bills as best they could but often without
expert help. These were frequently amended in their passage
through Parliament, yet, he thought, the profession at large
only started to think seriously about the question after the bill
was enacted, at which stage all its deficiencies became apparent.
Take, for example, Lord Lyndhurst's Transfer of Property Bill,
1844,[56] initially an ambitious attempt to abolish or reform a large
miscellany of outdated real property rules. Lyndhurst circulated
it to conveyancers for private comment, but seems not to have
paid anyone for expert advice. Consequently perhaps, response
was erratic, but Lyndhurst let himself be chivvied by Lord
Campbell into continuing with those parts of the bill that
professional opinion had not yet criticized. Shorn of about half
its clauses it whistled through Parliament with little discussion.
While it did so the *Legal Observer*, which welcomed its general
tenor, began to find difficulties with one of its most important
clauses. The bill passed. The difficulties were real. The Act had
to be repealed in its entirety in the following session, the
offending clause being dropped, its object attempted by a
different method, and all the other clauses being substantially
redrafted before re-enactment in the Real Property Amendment
Act. And this was a law reform sponsored by the Lord Chancellor—the same Lord Chancellor, incidentally, who had dubbed
James Stewart a dilettante.

So the *Legal Observer* gave the Law Amendment Society a
cautious welcome, thinking it might be 'serviceable as much in
restraining crude and inconsiderate changes as in forwarding

---

[56] For the following account see (1843–4) 27 *Leg. O.* 369, 420, 422; (1844) 28
Leg. O. 225, 259, 285, 375, 446; (1844–5) 29 *Leg. O.* 76, 237, 297, 497; (1845) 30
Leg. O. 449. The statutes are Transfer of Property Act 1844 (7 & 8 Vict., c. 76), of
which s. 8 was the main offender, and Real Property Act 1845 (8 & 9 Vict., c.
106). Campbell's chivvying and Lyndhurst's use of conveyancers are at (1844)
75 PD (3rd ser.) 224.

useful and advisable improvements'.[57] The LAS itself had made
a distinct bid for this sort of support in its very first announcement. Reforms, it said, were clearly needed, but

that they should be proceeded with in the most cautious spirit, and
that no further change should be made without all possible investigation, will not be disputed. Many of the recent alterations in the law,
however beneficial in intent, have, it is conceived, been carried into
operation in a defective form. Public attention is not always directed to
them, and they frequently rest too much on individual responsibility
in their passage through parliament.[58]

On the other hand, the *Legal Observer* was not suddenly going
to espouse law reforms which might harm its readership's
economic interests. In 1844 it reminded its readers of its successful role ever since its foundation in opposing the establishment
both of local courts (a reform which would have harmed London
solicitors) and of a general register of deeds (which might have
harmed provincial solicitors).[59] Its opposition would continue,
notwithstanding the formation of the LAS and the establishment of the *Law Review*, a new journal favourable to law reform.
Nor would it stray far from cautious incrementalism. It lampooned young barristers who invoked 'the aid of that last-
created goddess *Utility*' and who 'sacrificed whole hecatombs'
of old learning at her altar.[60] Its ideal Prime Minister would be a
man who 'entertained a high respect for our ancient laws and
institutions, and was exceedingly slow and cautious in altering
them.'[61] It could see no use at all for the study of modern
civilian legal systems; even classical Roman Law should be kept
from English students until they had grasped the essentials of
their own law.[62] The council of the ILS was equally unenthusiastic. 'Notwithstanding the extensive alterations in the law . . .
which have been carried into effect during the last sixteen
years,' its annual report for 1847 complained, '. . . further
projects of change in our judicial code continue to be brought
before the legislature!'[63]

One problem that the *Legal Observer* saw with statutory law

---

[57] (1843–4) 27 *Leg. O.* 462.   [58] Ibid.
[59] (1844) 29 *Leg. O.* 16.   [60] Ibid. 277.
[61] (1845–6) 31 *Leg. O.* 141.
[62] (1846) 32 *Leg. O.* 237, reviewing *Spence's Equity.*   [63] (1847) 34 *Leg. O.* 191.

reform was the uncertainty it induced. Optional short-forms for conveyances, introduced by statute, failed, it thought, because there was no 'decisive authority' able to tell ordinary practitioners that they were safe to use.[64] Now some of the men who could provide this sort of leadership, men at the top of their segment of the bar, had joined the LAS. Perhaps safe law reform was a possibility from a society whose membership after a year[65] contained seventeen Queen's Counsel, three Serjeants at Law, and one member of the ILS Council itself:

We wish to speak with all due respect of the labours of that learned body, composed as it is of many members of all branches of the profession, who are highly competent to weigh and consider any proposal for the improvement of the law; albeit, there are others associated with them who, to our thinking, are far too wild in their theories, and possess not enough practical experience, to justify the profession in trusting to their guidance.[66]

Nothing was ever going to convert the *Legal Observer* to the cause of deeds registration—in 1851 it kept the fires burning by reprinting Oliver Cromwell's scheme for registration of assurances[67]—but its first editorial article for that year of the Great Exhibition recognized with only the gentlest lament that 'it would be vain in these days to claim any merit, or expect any indulgence on the ground of antiquity.'[68] In the next year its anxiety was not so much that reforms were coming, more that they would turn out to be individuals' 'pet projects',[69] a theme which it amplified in 1853 by condemning piecemeal change, calling for systematic plans,[70] and encouraging the Lord Chancellor to adopt the role of Minister of Justice in co-ordinating reforms. No doubt some of this was tactical, and it is certainly true that the *Legal Observer*'s favourite law reformer remained Lord St Leonards. But still, the ostensible values propounded and the language in which they were discussed are identical with those of the reformers proper. Further, just as the LAS had adopted a pattern of committees, with published reports

---

[64] (1844) 29 *Leg. O.* 178; also (1845) 30 *Leg. O.* 409, (1845–6) 31 *Leg. O.* 517, (1848–9) 37 *Leg. O.* 306.
[65] See n. 39 above.
[66] (1845) 30 *Leg. O.* 369.
[67] (1851) 42 *Leg. O.* 377.
[68] Ibid. 1.
[69] (1852–3) 45 *Leg. O.* 20.
[70] (1853–4) 47 *Leg. O.* 1.

and open discussion meetings as the vehicle for law reform, so the *Legal Observer*, in reprinting those reports, discussing their faults, and urging consideration of them by local law societies contributed to the dissemination and ultimate acceptance of many of the new ideas. Indeed by 1850 it had even become reconciled to the *Law Review*,[71] the mouthpiece, as it saw it, of the LAS, frequently recommending its readers to study its many 'able articles' on particular topics, sometimes listing the contents of the review by way of advertisement, and even finding a good word to say for the visionary article cited above on 'The State of The Profession'.[72]

4. Utopia Denied

The LAS was dominated by lawyers, though open to all-comers with an interest in law reform. By subdividing into subject-area committees from its very beginning,[73] areas defined by the divisions in legal practice, it made its real character clear. Its ideology was that law reform was a non-party matter, or put another way, that control over law reform should be vested in lawyers. This is one explanation of its attraction for conservatives.[74] A major plank of its programme was that something like a Ministry of Justice was needed to provide continuity of officials, pay for legal researchers and legislative draftsmen, oversight of a systematic programme of reform, and authority to push it through.[75] It would, moreover, scrutinize all other departments' bills to ensure congruence with basic legal principles. This is a manifesto for lawyers. A version of the plan was submitted to Home Secretary Peel,[76] Lord Langdale spoke in

---

[71] (1850) 40 *Leg. O. passim*; contrast, however, (1851–2) 43 *Leg. O.* 1.

[72] (1849) 38 *Leg. O.* 160, commenting on (1849) 10 *Law Rev.* 148.

[73] Ibid. 421, cf. 67; (1845) 30 *Leg. O.* 153.

[74] Ibid. 421, cf. 67; (1845) 30 *Leg. O.* 170.

[75] e.g. (1844–5) 29 *Leg. O.* 116; (1845) 30 *Leg. O.* 197; (1845) 2 *Law Rev.* 243; (1848) 8 *Law Rev.* 122; (1849–50) 11 *Law Rev.* 79, 201; (1850) 12 *Law Rev.* 93; (1850–1) 13 *Law Rev.* 143; (1851) 14 *Law Rev.* 306; (1851–2) 15 *Law Rev.* 300; and esp. (1862) 13 *Law Mag. & Law Rev.* 357; A. H. Manchester, *Modern Legal History* (1980), 106 ff.

[76] (1845) 30 *Leg. O.* 197.

favour of it to a Select Committee in 1848,[77] and Lord John Russell said it was being considered in 1850.[78] But though it was accepted that the Lord Chancellor was too heavily worked to be an effective overseer of all legal process, the reform that emerged did not create the Ministry of Justice that the LAS wanted. Instead the Lord Chancellor's judicial duties were reduced by filling the vacancy among the Vice-Chancellors and instituting Lords Justices of Appeal, to free him for legislative work. However, a permanent department of government was not created for him.[79] Lawyers were not to gain a departmental foothold in Whitehall, far less were they to be the mediator of other departments' claims.

Recognizing the defeat the cause had suffered, the LAS announced that it itself was performing some of the functions of a Ministry of Justice by originating considered measures of law reform, emanating from within the profession itself.[80] In 1851 not only did it send its various reports on real property reform unsolicited to the Home Department, but a meeting chaired by James Stewart sent its reports on Common Law and Equity Procedure too. For good measure the LAS sent a questionnaire to every County Court judge concerning an aspect of the law of evidence, and duly forwarded the replies to the Home Department. All were then printed by order of the House of Lords.[81]

Real power was to rest where it always had. In 1853 the new Lord Chancellor, Lord Cranworth, not a notably radical figure, gave what came to be known as his 'law reform speech'. Nodding in the direction of Bentham and Romilly he acknowledged that his predecessors had not regarded responsibility for law reform as being part of their office, but nowadays any Lord Chancellor had to maintain an overview of the entire legal system, in which reform was a major element. In effect he was to be the Minister of Justice. There was to be a statute law

---

[77] Select Committee on Fees in Courts of Law and Equity, (1847–8) HCP xv, questions 1427–30, 1491–1500. Contrast John, Lord Campbell, *Lives of the Chancellors*, vii (1847), 724.

[78] Select Committee on Official Salaries, (1850) HCP xv. 179, questions 1339 ff.

[79] Sir C. Schuster, (1937) *Politica* 239, 337; esp. 241–2, 347–9.

[80] 8th Annual Report of the Council of the LAS, (1851) 42 *Leg. O.* 476.

[81] (1851) HLP xvi. 329, 349, 425.

commission, there would be changes in Chancery procedure, something would be done about courts of probate, there would be better regulation of charities, and, above all, there would be reform of land transfer.[82] Cranworth was a Whig, but a year earlier Lord Derby's Conservative government had proclaimed that it would make law reform a major item of its business. As the *Law Review* underlined, the parties were now competing for Law Reform.[83] As spokesman for the LAS, it looked forward to reading an annual 'law reform budget' from the government of the day. But its own part in shaping it would remain informal.

5. The Services of a Liberal and Learned Profession; The Zealous Vindication of the rights of Professional Men[84]

Contemporaneously with the institutionalizing of law reform, solicitors consolidated themselves into professional organizations. The vast bulk of day-to-day land transfer work was in their hands, though, as already discussed, conveyancing barristers were the ultimate source of authority and reference in difficult cases or, one supposes, where the affairs of the very wealthy were involved. The solicitors had acquired a statutory monopoly of this work in 1804 as solace for the imposition of severe taxation upon them, taxation which was still extant in the mid-century.[85] It rankled, particularly because with income tax becoming permanent solicitors faced double taxation compared with rival occupations, including the bar.[86] As with all aspects of their work solicitors did face some competition from unauthorized rivals, against whom they did use the penal provisions of the statutory monopoly. But so far as can be seen

[82] 14 Feb. 1853, 124 PD (3rd ser.) 41. For reception see (1853) 18 *Law Rev.* 1 (enthusiasm), (1855) 21 *Law Rev.* 248 (disappointment), (1855–6) 23 *Law Rev.* 29 (despair).

[83] 119 PD (3rd ser.) 1, 27–8; (1852) 16 *Law Rev.* 1; (1852–3) 40 *Leg. O.* 264.

[84] Annual Report of the committee of Manchester Law Association, (1851–2) 43 *Leg. O.* 248; (1846–7) 33 *Leg. O.* 216.

[85] Abel, *The Legal Profession*, 140–1.

[86] e.g. (1844) 28 *Leg. O.* 444; (1844–5) 29 *Leg. O.* 256, 316; (1848) 35 *Leg. O.* 425; Address of the M&PLA to the Profession, (1847) 34 *Leg. O.* 46, favourably received at (1847) 6 *Law Rev.* 392, 401.

from the pages of the legal press these competitors were low-level and unorganized, and it is certainly not the case that solicitors thought that they had won a good deal in 1804. Nor, however, did any questions of the conveyancing monopoly bulk large in the mid-century. Solicitors' worries were very much more with aspects of litigation and semi-contentious work such as the administration of bankruptcy, and the competition that frightened them came from the bar.[87]

Before the establishment of the Incorporated Law Society, solicitors' professional organization in London was fragmented.[88] The Society of Gentlemen Practisers still existed in a rump form, and was usually referred to as the Law Society. There was a Northern Agents Society, comprising those London firms doing substantial agency work for northern solicitors in the central London courts. Robert Maugham saw both these as precursors of the ILS, existing to secure honourable professional conduct and standards, a euphemism for cartel-like behaviour that reduced competition between the dominant partnerships. In addition, however, a Metropolitan Law Society was founded in 1819 with the main function of procuring prosecutions against unqualified persons trespassing on solicitors' monopolies, which usually meant debt-collectors who diversified into issuing and managing court process.

The ILS got under way in 1825, taking form as a deed of settlement company in 1827, then acquiring a charter in 1831.[89] It differed from its precursors in having independent legal personality, its own premises, centring on a library, and permanent staff. To the objects espoused by the Gentlemen Practisers and the Northern Agents it added control over entry to the occupation of solicitor by working for progressively higher entrance standards and the introduction of examinations, an aim it achieved by gaining superintendence of the entry roll, which it managed under supervision of the judges.[90] Though,

---

[87] e.g. Address of the M&PLA to the Profession, (1847) 34 *Leg. O.* 46; see generally, Kirk, *Portrait*, ch. 9.

[88] For this paragraph see (1844) 28 *Leg. O.* 421; (1847–8) 34 *Leg. O.* 492; and generally, Kirk, *Portrait*, ch. 2. The Northern Agents cartel evidently continued: (1860–1) 5 *Sol. Jo.* 291.

[89] Kirk, *Portrait*, ch. 2; (1844–5) 30 *Leg. O.* 475; (1848) 36 *Leg. O.* 246.

[90] e.g. Solicitors Act 1843 (6 & 7 Vict., c. 73), s. 21.

reinforcing the common perception of the ILS as an élite organization, Maugham never included the Metropolitan Association among the inspirations for his society,[91] it none the less found itself pushed by practitioners into adopting such a policing role. Its committee of management—later its council—clearly found that job uncongenial, and its lack of vigour in the task caused nearly constant friction with more lowly solicitors who felt more keenly threatened by unlicensed competition. As a consequence every now and again solicitors who felt excluded from the ILS would establish a Legal Protective Society, leading to acrimony in the lawyers' press and a revival of interest in the job by the ILS Council.[92] One such society was operating with loud fanfare in the formative period of the mid-1840s.[93]

The founders of the ILS had set its entry fee deliberately high to encourage exclusiveness. Its council tended to be a closed oligarchy with a penchant for complacent self-congratulation. Almost entirely London run, and, within that, the preserve of the prosperous élite, it met constant criticism for passivity in the face of changing times.[94] Its structure was that of a social club; its legal form that of a commercial enterprise, since the major features of the 1827 joint venture had been carried forward into the first charter; but its function was increasingly regulatory, supervising the admission of men to the roll and policing their subsequent conduct. By 1843 contradictions in its legal structure had become intolerable.[95] It could not at one and the same time have a joint stock format, with heritable shares, yet be restricted to solicitors. It could not have a form that required it to distribute a dividend, and yet be a semi-public regulatory agency. So, with strife and much communal soul-searching, a new charter was obtained, shedding the remnants of the joint-stock form and embodying the professional ethics outlined above.

Similar processes for similar reasons occurred in the big northern cities at much the same time. Liverpool's law society

---

[91] (1844) 28 *Leg. O.* 421.
[92] e.g. (1844–5) 29 *Leg. O.* 82.
[93] (1843–4) 27 *Leg. O.* 421, 424, 457–8, 488; (1844) 28 *Leg. O.* 421, 480; (1844–5) 29 *Leg. O.* 15, 152; (1844) 3 *LT* 441, 477; (1844–5) 4 *LT* 78, 147, 244, 500.
[94] Kirk, *Portrait*, 33, 42 ff.
[95] (1845) 30 *Leg. O.* 475, where the new charter is reprinted.

was founded in 1827, initially as the Liverpool Law Library Association.[96] Like the ILS it initially set high entrance fees, reducing them in 1851 to attract a broader membership, a move partially copied by the ILS in 1854. A particularly entrepreneurial society, Liverpool soon acquired meeting-rooms for use as a 'Law Exchange', formed a limited liability company in 1865 so as to operate a property auction business for solicitors, cajoled local solicitors into adopting standard conditions of sale so as to facilitate its work, did deals with local accountants and auctioneers over division of professional labour, and in 1867 led the way among provincial law societies by shedding its status as an unincorporated association and acquiring permanent legal capacity. The Manchester Law Association[97] was a relative latecomer, established only in 1838, but again with a library and meeting-premises, and with a particularly active honorary secretary who was to pioneer the extension of the professional ethic on a national scale. Leeds, the third important base of the northern axis, had had a law society since 1805, though the Yorkshire attornies had been co-operating from time to time on professional matters long before that.[98]

The structure of legal practice in these northern cities was similar to that in the Lincoln's Inn and City areas of London, whence came the members of the ILS council. Whereas nationally the overwhelming number of solicitors operated as sole practitioners, these big, permanent, law societies originated in areas dominated by partnerships, commonly of three solicitors, sometimes of four or even five.[99] To that extent they shared the value of professional respectability—the reduction of competition between the dominant suppliers in the market. But the legal communities in the northern cities were much smaller than in London, which seems to have reduced the friction

---

[96] For this account of Liverpool LS see (1851–2) 43 *Leg. O.* 60; (1854) 48 *Leg. O.* 328; (1860–1) 36 *LT* 97; (1861–2) 37 *LT* 84; (1870–1) 50 *LT* 30; (1871–2) 52 *LT* 34; (1877–8) 22 *Sol. Jo.* 625; Peter Howell Williams, *A Gentleman's Calling: The Liverpool Attorney-at-Law* (1980), 184, 266, 269; its records for 1829 to 1859 are missing, ibid. 252.

[97] Abel, *The Legal Profession*, 246; (1839) 17 *Leg. O.* 445; (1845) 29 *Leg. O.* 260; (1846) 31 *Leg. O.* 266; its rules are reprinted at (1843–4) 2 *LT* 300.

[98] Abel, *The Legal Profession*, 246; Lawton, (1986) 83 *Law Soc. Gaz.* 3074–5, 3081–2.

[99] *Law List* for 1845, *passim*; cf. Abel, *The Legal Profession*, ch. 13.

between sole practitioners and the commercial partnerships that
is so much a feature of the history of the London solicitors.
Perhaps shared local identity was the key. From the very
beginning, for example, the Manchester Law Association, when
considering its reaction to proposed law reforms, actively
sought the co-operation of the Manchester Chamber of Commerce,[100] perceiving an interest as 'Manchester', in distinction
from the purely professional self-perception of the ILS. Liverpool Law Association similarly took account of local interests
when formulating its policies.[101]

In 1844 the Manchester Law Association took the lead in the
formation of the Provincial Law Societies Association, to which
societies from all parts of the country adhered.[102] It is not known
whether the founders had hoped for a national federation
including the ILS; probably not,[103] since at that time there was
fierce division over the desirability of establishing county courts,
with provincial societies much in favour and the ILS allied with
the bar against. The Association's objects, however, suppressed
any hint of antagonism against London, being 'chiefly to promote the interests and watch over all legislative and other
interference with the just rights of the profession; to assist in
obtaining all useful and practical amendments of the law; and
to adopt measures for preserving the respectability of the
profession'.[104] This reference to law reform as a separate object
from resistance to legislative onslaughts against the profession
marks a further stage in the developing professional ethnic of
solicitors: that their professional organizations had an interest
in legal change for its own sake, and the status and expertise
for their views to warrant consideration by the powerful.[105] In
that same year the Manchester Law Association, considering
that Lord Lyndhurt's ill-fated Transfer of Property Bill made

[100] (1848) 35 *Leg. O.* 288; (1848–9) 37 *Leg. O.* 228.
[101] (1846–7) 33 *Leg. O.* 64.
[102] (1845) 29 *Leg. O.* 224, 260, 302; (1844) 3 *LT* 406; (1844–5) 4 *LT* 302, 305.
Constituent societies were widespread but not numerous: (1845–6) 31 *Leg. O.*
238, 267; cf. the attendance at the 1st annual dinner, (1845–6) 6 *LT* 307.
[103] Cf. (1844–5) 4 *LT* 483.
[104] (1845) 29 *Leg. O.* 260.
[105] Cf. the rules of Manchester LA, (1843–4) 2 *LT* 300. Model rules proposed
by the *Legal Observer* for country law societies in (1840–1) 20 *Leg. O.* 458, repr.
in (1847) 34 *Leg. O.* 122, do not include law reform as an object.

'great improvements upon the old system without at the same time trenching upon any important principles', had signified its presence by lodging a petition in favour of the bill's passing.[106] That aside however, the Provincial association was founded defensively to resist further advances by the bar. Its mood is well caught by one speaker at the Manchester association's annual dinner, an especially important occasion that year since it marked also the foundation of the Provincial association. Law societies he saw as 'a beleaguered citadel, assailed on all sides, and their members as the selected victims of that erratic legislation, which, seizing the subjects of its experimental philosophy rather for its own amusement than for their improvement or for the public necessity, required every vigilance in order to avert the evils of its most mischievous activity'.[107]

Initially ILS reports sounded a tone both defensive and patrician towards involvement in law reform. Its 1845 prospectus for new members explained that its council 'examine all bills brought into Parliament which relate to the law, and state in the proper quarter such objections to them, and also suggest such additions and alterations as appear to them necessary for improving and perfecting the proposed enactments; and in these and such like instances they take all such measures as seem best calculated to promote the general interests and respectability of the profession . . .'[108] The committee of the Provincial Law Societies Association habitually consulted its constituent associations about bills before Parliament,[109] but the object was much the same—to determine whether opposition was needed. In 1846–7, for example, it co-ordinated resistance to a deeds registration bill introduced by Lord Campbell.[110] Like the ILS, however, it involved itself in constructing national standards for a national profession by 'assisting on disputed

---

[106] (1844) 29 *Leg. O.* 260. Cf. its 'new and valuable suggestions' for ecclesiastical court reform, (1843) 1 *LT* 113, and see its work on local courts, (1845–6) 31 *Leg. O.* 266, and bankruptcy reform, (1849–50) 39 *Leg. O.* 256. It aimed to be 'an important auxiliary in effecting wise and comprehensive measures of legal reform', (1852–3) 45 *Leg. O.* 337.

[107] (1844) 29 *Leg. O.* 302.

[108] (1845–6) 31 *Leg. O.* 169.

[109] Ibid. 238; but see n. 105 above.

[110] (1846–7) 33 *Leg. O.* 273.

points of practice'.[111] The LAS council acknowledged the growing importance of solicitors' organization when, in 1846, it reported to its members that it was 'desirous that the society should act in harmony with the feelings and interests of the profession; and we believe that these are in this case [of conveyancing reform], as in most others, identical with the community at large'.[112] In practice this meant that the LAS would join the search for a method of professional remuneration for conveyancing more fitting to the times than payment by the item. Perhaps more importantly, the LAS signalled to solicitors' organizations that it did not regard them as upstarts, but rather as partners. The *Law Review* and, later, reports from the LAS and from committees on which some LAS members sat, frequently contained statements accepting the indispensibility of solicitors in land transactions, the need for proper professional standards to be maintained, and hence for professional remuneration to be guaranteed.[113] The *Legal Observer* was gracious in its acknowledgement.[114]

Campbell's bill aside, however, conveyancing reform took second place to reform of local courts. The Provincial Law Societies Association was well pleased with the structure of new county courts introduced in 1846, but dismayed by the general tone of Parliamentary debate.[115] Hitherto offices in many local courts had been open to solicitors. Henceforward they would be reserved for barristers, on the pretext that they alone could handle the increasingly difficult law of modern society.[116] It had been the same with other reforms—bankruptcy administration and commissionerships in lunacy had both recently been captured from solicitors by the bar. It had taken an Act of Parlia-

[111] (1846–7) 33 *Leg. O.* 64. Cf. the ILS, e.g. (1845) 30 *Leg. O.* 303—again, perhaps, rather more patrician.
[112] (1846) 32 *Leg. O.* 218.
[113] (1844) 1 *Law Rev.* 158; (1845) 2 *Law Rev.* 405, 431–2; (1847–8) 7 *Law Rev.* 386, 401; (1849) 10 *Law Rev.* 172; (1853–4) 19 *Law Rev.* 166, 177; and below, Ch. 2, sect. 6.
[114] (1845) 30 *Leg. O.* 369.
[115] (1846–7) 33 *Leg. O.* 273.
[116] 9 & 10 Vict., c. 95, s. 9. The exclusion was sudden and unexpected, contrast 8 & 9 Vict., c. 127, s. 9, and see discussion at (1845) 30 *Leg. O.* 269, 331. See generally, Cocks, *Foundations*, ch. 4, and Abel-Smith and Stevens, *Lawyers and the Courts*, 53–7.

ment in 1828[117] to enable barristers to accept office as Solicitor to government departments or boards, but once eligible they came to dominate. So, true to form, when the Solicitors Act 1843 introduced new regulations for the profession, including disqualifying solicitors from the magistracy, Solicitors to government boards were exempted.[118] Throughout the country solicitors were losing rights of audience in inferior courts hitherto enjoyed.[119] The bar, untaxed, unqualified, overstocked, virtually unregulated, was expanding. Solicitors, who had high entry costs, modern qualification tests for entry, annual taxation, regulation both internally and through subordination to taxing masters empowered to vet their bills of costs, felt squeezed and belittled by the bar from above, and threatened by advocates of cheap law from below. In the litigation business, fee scales in the new county courts were so low as to make the work unremunerative. Conveyancing reforms seemed set to retain itemized charging as the only permissible system of remuneration, while abolishing many of the items for which charge could be made. The *Legal Observer* could see the prize of professional status slipping away:

The interests of all other professions are admitted to be entitled to some consideration, but the body of legal practitioners, who pay in admission stamps and yearly certificates a much larger sum than any other class, are regarded as a set of persons whom it is not simply allowable, but decidedly laudable, to victimise. It has, therefore, become the fashion to believe that the best way to improve the law is to degrade, and, as far as possible, exterminate its professors, until every man, acting as his own lawyer, has, in the words of the proverb, a 'fool for his client'.[120]

'Whilst the bar, as congregated in its several Inns of Court and each Circuit mess, and numerously represented in Parliament, possesses ample means of securing the independence of the general body, and promoting the interests of its members,'[121] solicitors, a notorious rope of sand in which each

---

[117] 9 Geo. IV, c. 25.
[118] 6 & 7 Vict., c. 73, ss. 33–4, 47.
[119] Address of the M&PLA to the Profession, (1847) 34 *Leg. O.* 41.
[120] (1847) 34 *Leg. O.* 557.
[121] (1846–7) 33 *Leg. O.* 363; cf. Manchester LA, (1846–7) 33 *Leg. O.* 272.

member competed fiercely with each other, had no defences.[122]
So as the Manchester Law Association advocated,

it is by the aid of a cordial union among ourselves alone that we can
hope to prevent the high, the honourable, the important, profession of
an attorney sinking irretrievably in caste, and becoming no longer a
pursuit, which can consistently be embraced or followed by men of
education, standing or character.[123]

The initiative in seeking a 'comprehensive union' between
London and provincial law societies came from Manchester and
Leeds solicitors active in the Provincial Law Societies Association.[124] In late 1846, smarting from the snubs received in
Parliament during the county courts debates, they opened
negotiations with the ILS. The immediate outcome was not
encouraging. '[T]he great difficulty was to obtain the co-operation of the London solicitors, whose interests did not exactly
agree with the interests of the country solicitors. However, by
leaving out the points of difference, the desired union was
effected . . .' Not, however, by merger with the ILS, since its
council, which had recently obtained a new charter for the
organization, fitting more precisely its regulatory role under the
1843 Act, said that some of the objects proposed by the
Provincial Association's emissaries would be *ultra vires* the ILS.
Accordingly a new society was established, the Metropolitan
and Provincial Law Association, whose management committee
was about equally balanced between London and provincial
solicitors.

Though the universal union had failed to happen, initial links
between the ILS and the M&PLA were very close. Every
London member of the M&PLA management committee
belonged to the ILS, three of them were on its council.[125] At first

---

[122] See e.g. (1846) 32 *Leg. O.* 544; the metaphor was common, see e.g. (1853)
46 *Leg. O.* 137. The developments described in these paragraphs did not reduce
feelings of disunity—(1854) 48 *Leg. O.* 492, (1854–5) 49 *Leg. O.* 1.

[123] (1846) 33 *Leg. O.* 272.

[124] For this and the next paragraph see (1846–7) 33 *Leg. O.* 272, 273, 508;
(1847) 34 *Leg. O.* 41, 69, 92, 116, 141, 169 ('the great difficulty'), 294, 375, 392,
437, 457, 502, 562, 583. For a different analysis, heavily influenced by the view
from London, see Kirk, *Portrait*, 38–9.

[125] (1847) 34 *Leg. O.* 41; *Law List*, 1847. The ILS council members were
Coverdale, Grant, and Gregory; John Young was elected to it in the following
year—*Law List*, 1848.

the M&PLA operated from ILS premises, and Robert Maugham, ILS secretary, acted as its secretary too,[126] using his *Legal Observer* aggressively in the cause. The association's objects appear rather narrowly professional; its address to the profession consisted of a long elaboration of grievances which, by massing evidence for presentation to Parliament, the management committee hoped would lead to a public inquiry into the profession and the ultimate righting of wrongs.[127] Its initial methods were trade union-like too. From the start the *Legal Observer* preached constantly that its readers should join local associations, or found them if none existed, printing model rules as encouragement.[128] When Robert Maugham was replaced as secretary by William Shaen, the new man travelled the country to apply direct persuasion where the printed word had hitherto failed.[129] Then, as M&PLA committees got to work, circulars, questionnaires, and letters flowed back and forth between centre and localities, as the M&PLA tried to operate as a national body in a way that the ILS never had.[130] To crown this attempt at integration there was the annual provincial meeting, at which speeches were made, learned papers read, and business done—all well covered by the regional newspapers and the lawyers' press.

Listed second of the grievances in the association's address to the profession was

Crude legislation [which] has fastened upon our already overburthened legal code, many ill-digested and ill-constructed statutes, the fertile source of perplexity to judges and practitioners, and of litigation and expense to the suitor. We have seen a great deal of our ancient polity either altered or destroyed, and yet little substantial good effected, and

[126] (1848) 35 *Leg. O.* 406. He was also a member of the M&PLA, but not of the ILS (*Law List*).

[127] (1847) 34 *Leg. O.* 41.

[128] Ibid. 122.

[129] (1849) 38 *Leg. O.* 26. He was still travelling in 1854, though without much success: (1854) 48 *Leg. O.* 141. For this remarkable man see Joseph O. Baylen and Norbet J. Gossman, eds., *Biographical Dictionary of Modern British Radicals*, ii, *1830–1870* (1984); Margaret Josephine Shaen, *William Shaen: A Brief Sketch* (1912).

[130] e.g. (1849) 38 *Leg. O.* 45; (1853) 46 *Leg. O.* 137 (continues at 156, 173); (1854) 48 *Leg. O.* 141, 492. The ILS Council followed, e.g. (1855) 50 *Leg. O.* 286.

all recourse to the court is nearly as expensive, dilatory and oppressive as ever.[131]

Though this paragraph degenerated into a grumble about the establishment of new courts, and can be read simply as a plea in solicitors' own self-interest, the M&PLA's leaders did realize the importance of occupying a place on the high ground of law reform for its own sake. John Hope Shaw, solicitor and sometime Lord Mayor of Leeds, who had been the M&PLA's main founder, announced the establishment of committees to consider the present state of court procedure and conveyancing, and to suggest what should be done.[132] An important ally for him was Edwin Field, one of the two London members of the M&PLA management committee who had also been founder members of the LAS.[133] Though initially the M&PLA announced that its policy towards law reform should be one of constructive reaction to other men's proposals, by the early 1850s Field had steered it towards a more creative role.[134] Through a joint initiative with the ILS he achieved a measure of Chancery reform for Ireland blaming lack of positive support from English solicitors for lack of similar progress in England. In 1851 he was even jockeying the M&PLA towards drafting its own proposals for title registration, a reform which the Manchester Law Association had also endorsed—though both bodies always vigorously opposed bills for deeds registration.[135]

The outcome was that by the early 1850s the ILS and the

---

[131] (1847) 34 *Leg. O.* 41, 45.

[132] (1848) 35 *Leg. O.* 286, 406; cf. (1849) 37 *Leg. O.* 412, but contrast (1851) 42 *Leg. O.* 40; (1852–3) 45 *Leg. O.* 420. For Hope Shaw see Richard Vickerman Taylor, *The Biographia Leodiensis* (1865), 520–3 (British Biographical Archive fiche 990/227); E. P. Hennock, *Fit and Proper Persons* (1973), 204–7 and pl. 22.

[133] See n. 29 above. He was particularly interested in partnership law—see (1855) 22 *Law Rev.* 138 and his evidence to the Select Committee on the Law of Partnership, (1851) HCP xviii. 1, which also heard James Stewart. Field also published *Observations of a Solicitor on the Right of the Public to Form Limited Liability Partnerships, and on the Theory, Practice and Costs of Commercial Charters* (1854). The other man was Harvey Gem, for whose interest in ecclesiastical law reform see his *Considerations on Ecclesiastical Courts' Reform . . .* (1844).

[134] (1849) 38 *Leg. O.* 43; (1851) 42 *Leg. O.* 300; (1851–2) 43 *Leg. O.* 234; (1852) 44 *Leg. O.* 77, 501. Field's counterpart in the ILS was W. S. Cookson, for whom see (1877) 21 *Sol. Jo.* 728, and below, n. 155.

[135] (1850–1) 41 *Leg. O.* 291. It was generally hostile to deeds registration, (1851–2) 43 *Leg. O.* 248, though it would probably have accepted a scheme instituting local registries, ibid. and (1853–4) 47 *Leg. O.* 277.

M&PLA both had committees considering all the important areas of law reform and specific bills on them, the major provincial law societies had likewise, smaller provincial law societies considered some of those matters *ad hoc* and forwarded their conclusions and suggestions to one or other of the national societies, and the *Legal Observer* printed much of the discussion and urged more societies to play their part.[136] Talk among solicitors had become less defensive, with their ability to make positive contribution to law reform increasingly stressed.[137] In 1853 the LAS wrote to all law societies asking for representatives to attend a three-day meeting on the amendment and consolidation of commercial law.[138] Only in Parliament did it remain politic to paint solicitors as arch-reactionaries whose self-interest would always work to block progress. Here, though, another analysis is possible. Many, most, law reform bills before Parliament resulted from individual effort by a member, with whatever professional help he happened to muster. Opposition and criticism from law societies, self-interested or not, was premissed upon the belief that law reform should be a professional business channelled through lawyers' associations. In this, law societies and the LAS could make common cause: 'a friend and ally'.[139]

6. Retrospect

6.1. 'In most societies . . . scholars and other learned men have been able to contribute significantly to the development of law. They have accomplished this by the force of their ideas . . . which they have successfully communicated to the law-making institutions in the system.'[140] In the England of the 1840s and

---

[136] e.g. (1848) 36 *Leg. O.* 246; (1849) 38 *Leg. O.* 345; (1852) 44 *Leg. O.* 275. It tended to be conservative—e.g. (1849) 38 *Leg. O.* 345; and see (1851–2) 43 *Leg. O.* 29, 72. Manchester LA also established sub-committees—(1846) 32 *Leg. O.* 315; (1848–9) 37 *Leg. O.* 228. M&PLA committees considered 59 bills in 1848, (1849) 38 *Leg. O.* 61 (the extracts begin at 43); it soon became short of money, (1855) 50 *Leg. O.* 109. (Cf. the LAS, (1845) 30 *Leg. O.* 197.)

[137] e.g. (1851–2) 43 *Leg. O.* 248; (1852–3) 45 *Leg. O.* 420.

[138] (1852–3) 45 *Leg. O.* 337.

[139] (1847) 6 *Law Rev.* 392, 403; cf. (1851–2) *Law Rev.* 1.

[140] H. M. Hart and A. M. Sacks, *The Legal Process* (tentative edn. 1958), 770.

1850s there was no shortage of forceful ideas. Practising lawyers and lawyer/politicians of various persuasions had come together in a Law Reform movement which was permanent enough to persuade government of the desirability and practicability of thoroughgoing law reform. Its committees, papers, meetings, newspaper articles, and delegations provided the schemes for adoption and pressure to do so. By about 1850 the leadership of both Whigs and Conservatives were giving public support to the concept, and promising legislation. But the next stage, translation into legal form, the 'communication to the law-making institutions', was much more difficult. Whereas in general responsibility for introducing legislation shifted from private member to government during the period 1830–55, the absence of a Ministry of Justice left private law and its reform as an exception.[141] Whenever anyone raised again the desirability of such a department, one reason given was bound to be that it could make systematic law reform a reality.[142] Instead, however, the big departments of state came increasingly to dominate Parliament, so that, as he looked back on legislative practices during the century, Sir Courtenay Ilbert could write that for 'lawyers' law Parliament has neither time nor taste.'[143] Indeed the very notion of lawyers' law reflects this institutional vacuum, since all that it can mean is that part of the private law in which politicians for the time being are uninterested. It was law which, in a sense, belonged to the lawyers; it was theirs to operate and change as best they could.

Only in the person of C. H. Bellenden Ker[144] can one sense the difference a Ministry of Justice would have made, since so far as he could he operated as though he were one. A convey-ancer by profession, and a good one, during the 1830s he gave up his work in order to draft several important and sensitive bills for the Whigs, for which he received no financial recompense.[145] When a Lord Chancellor was in need of empirical data

---

[141] Sir Courtenay Ilbert, *Legislative Methods and Forms* (1901), 212 ff.

[142] Abel-Smith and Stevens, *Lawyers and the Courts*, 131 and sources there cited; Manchester, *Modern Legal History*, 106 ff. Note the retort of Sir C. Schuster, (1937) *Politica* 239, 337 esp. at 354–5; and see below, p. 253).

[143] Ilbert, *Legislative Methods*, 212; for Ilbert see *DNB*, 1922–30.

[144] *DNB*; Sir C. T. Carr, *A Victorian Law Reformer's Correspondence* (Selden Society lecture, 1955).

[145] Henry Parris, *Constitutional Bureaucracy* (1969), 175.

to support a flagging case for a deeds registration bill, it would be to Ker that he would turn[146]—as though Ker were a freelance Edwin Chadwick, doing the job government did itself in other spheres. He thought like a Ministry of Justice too, continually urging that reform should be systematic, believing that if it were, statute could profitably be confined to statements of principle, with judicial decision and, particularly, administrative regulation filling in the gaps as need arose.[147] Alternatively, legislation could be accompanied by explanatory memoranda, as he himself demonstrated with his Real Property Amendment Act.[148] Entrusted with its composition in 1845 following the débâcle with Lord Lyndhurst's Act of 1844, Ker enlisted two other conveyancers, Hayes and Christie, and circulated drafts to the profession. When the final text had been agreed he wrote a long open letter to the Lord Chancellor explaining its purpose and its construction, which was then published by Charles Davidson, a quickly rising promulgator of conveyancing doctrine and precedents, as a guide to the Act's use. But this was unusual; in general complaints about the poor quality of legislation did not abate. As the House of Lords always held several lawyers regarded as their profession's leaders, and the House of Commons held more who would like to be—in 1852 it contained ninety-eight qualified lawyers, of whom eighty-three were present or former barristers[149]—the introduction and passage of law reform bills remained haphazard and unpredictable.[150]

So Law Reform was to be a function of the legal profession not of government, as the foundation and activity of the LAS

---

[146] See below, Ch. 2 n. 131 and accompanying text.

[147] *On the Reform of the Law of Real Property*, 62; but contrast p. 31. See also *The Question of Registry or No Registry Considered* (1830), but contrast his insistence in *On the Reform*, 18, 23, that registration of deeds was the keystone without which there would be no reform of real property law for twenty years. See also below, Ch. 2, sect. 9, and cf. (1851–2) 15 *Law Rev.* 300.

[148] 8 & 9 Vict., c. 106. For what follows see Davidson, *Concise Precedents in Conveyancing* (2nd edn. 1845) 10f.; (1845–6) 31 *Leg. O.* 183. His publications began when he edited *Martin's Practice of Conveyancing* in 1844.

[149] (1852) 44 *Leg. O.* 279; (1852–3) 45 *Leg. O.* 20.

[150] For one of many complaints see (1849–50) 11 *Law Rev.* 201. Lack of continuity was a serious problem: see (1855–6) 23 *Law Rev.* 65; cf. (1853–4) 19 *Law Rev.* 111. Lack of payment was often mentioned as a cause: e.g. (1853–4) 47 *Leg. O.* 61; (1851–2) 15 *Law Rev.* 300, 307–8.

demonstrated. But the structure of the LAS militated against systematic law reform. Though it had a guiding council, its mode of operation allowed each of its committees to take up whatever proposals it wanted.[151] Moreover, while a Ministry of Justice might perhaps have provided a home for a lawyers' Edwin Chadwick, the LAS could not. It had no method of assessing the social or economic need for a particular reform, no way of measuring its costs against its promised benefits. Its reforms originated in ideas, not in social needs. So far as real property law reform was concerned, apart from routine exercises in simplification and rationalization, its favoured intellectual approach was not investigative but emulative of foreign systems. For these reasons it ought not to be seen as a 'Benthamite initiative on the part of young lawyers'[152]—it was both much more than that and much less. Indeed, from time to time Benthamite lawyers tried unsuccessfully to reorient the LAS towards exactly the systematic law reform that would have met with the master's approval.[153]

On the other hand, in the mid-century history of land law reform the LAS is more important than the Social Science Association, which has recently been identified as the main testing-ground for liberal reform.[154] That would be to overstate its importance for the reform of lawyers' law, even for those reforms of lawyers' law that had political significance. The annual meetings of the Social Science Association were indeed very grand affairs, at which the great men signalled their readiness to promote reforming causes and the ambitious made claims for attention. But so far as its Jurisprudence section was concerned, the papers it heard were very much the same as those presented to the LAS. The difference lay in what happened next: LAS papers were submitted to close scrutiny, leading perhaps to adoption by the committee concerned and ultimately by the LAS itself, with the possibility that the LAS

---

[151] See e.g. (1851–2) 15 *Law Rev.* 409; (1855) 22 *Law Rev.* 124.

[152] Lawrence Goldman, 'The Social Science Association (1857–1886): A Context for mid-Victorian Liberalism', (1986) 101 *EHR* 95, 98.

[153] e.g. Symonds, (1860) 35 *LT* 226, (1860–1) 36 *LT* 51. See also his *Papers Relative to the Obstruction of Public Business and the Organisation of the Civil Service* (privately printed, ?1853), reviewed at (1853) 18 *Law Rev.* 358.

[154] Goldman, 'The Social Science Association', 95, 98.

would have a bill drafted for presentation to Lord Chancellor or Attorney-General. This was not the case with the Social Science Association, which reacted far more passively to the papers it heard. If it played the role of shadow 'Parliament of Social Causes', it could not have done without the Law Amendment Society's mirroring of a ministry of justice to give it detailed and practical direction. Men active in the one, however, tended to crop up in the other as well. Most conspicuous for our purposes was the solicitor William Strickland Cookson, who was to be found on LAS committees, as Social Science Association Treasurer, as ILS President, and on the 1857 Royal Commission on registration.[155] And, at the end of 1863, he was one of the three LAS members who negotiated the Heads of Agreement by which the LAS, badly in debt, merged into the Social Science Association and thereafter lost its separate identity—and the law reform movement lost much of its distinctive thrust.[156] Unlike the LAS the Social Science Association originated no major reforms of real property law. Cookson, however, is important to our theme for other reasons, since it was he who led the ILS in its opposition to deeds registration. But it was a version of his title registration scheme that was enacted in 1875.

This returns us to the solicitors, whose claims to participation in the law reform process were a function both of the consignment of law reform to the legal profession and of their own growing self-awareness. Cookson and Field were tenacious and imaginative law reformers who both occupied senior positions in solicitors' national organizations. It was common for local law societies to pronounce their allegiance to law reform, and to be active in the cause. One reason was no doubt defensive, that if solicitors opposed every mooted change their ability to

---

[155] See (1877) 21 *Sol. Jo.* 728, and generally, below, Ch. 3. sects. 2 and 3. For examples of his involvement with the LAS see (1857) 1 *Sol. Jo.* 82, (1859–60) 4 *Sol. Jo.* 64, 126; also 'On the Means of Elevating and Improving the Profession, and Increasing its Usefulness,' (1856) 27 *LT* 29.

[156] (1863–4) 8 *Sol. Jo.* 55, 74; (1863–4) 16 *Law Mag. & Law Rev.* 374. The latter's friendly obituary of the LAS contrasts sharply with the brutality of the *Law Times* ((1864) 39 *LT* 97), though that journal had previously thought the LAS more useful than the Social Science Association ((1860–1) 36 *LT* 525). There is a favourable comparison of the Social Science Association with the Juridical Society at (1860) 9 *Law Mag. & Law Rev.* 75. For earlier optimism see (1855) 22 *Law Rev.* 392, 398; (1856) 23 *Law Rev.* 226.

resist attacks on their most important interests would be reduced. Further, though, their leaders had an obvious pride in their own work, and a feeling that they could do a better job honing legislative proposals than did the individualistic barristers who introduced them into Parliament. Most important was the drive for respectability and acceptance by the establishment, the urge to prove that they were better educated, better organized, more useful than the bar; that it was they, not the barristers, who had the virtues of practical men of business. Participation in law reform was a crucial element in their construction of professionalism. So much for the leaders. For the led, for many of the sole practitioners who had learnt 'the law' in their youth and who now practised across a much wider range of business than did either their leaders or the typical barrister, the pace of change could be simply a nuisance. When it affected their remuneration it would be a threat to their continuing livelihood. Yet their leaders believed that the profession would achieve the status it deserved, and would fight off the power of the bar on the one hand, the 'encroachments' of accountants, auctioneers, Parliamentary agents, and myriad freelance advisers and agents on the other, only if local law societies existed in every area, and only if they encompassed the bulk of all respectable solicitors. Tensions between leaders and led were as unavoidable as those between London and provinces.

The bar as such had no collective organization through which law reform could be promoted. W. D. Lewis's Juridical Society was founded only in 1855, as a forum for the study of the science of law, mainly in that historical and comparative mode which eschewed analytical jurisprudence—Maine was one of its first speakers. Only barristers could take full membership, though others could be associates. The *Law Magazine and Law Review* welcomed its intention to provide a forum where barristers could discuss projected law reform, but was glad that it had no ambition to *press* for changes; that was the job of the LAS.[157] Judges and barristers on their own, it thought, were too busy to give enough time to that sort of enterprise and professionally

---

[157] (1857) 3 *Law Mag. & Law Rev.* 1. For the Juridical Society's passivity see Bethell in *Papers read before the Juridical Society, 1858–63*, 129, 130.

too introverted to succeed.[158] The law-reform enterprise should be neither exclusive nor individualistic.

6.2. Into the mid-1840s land was a political issue but, for the most part, real property law was not. Some utilitarians did make the law of primogeniture an object of attack, but with little impact. One reason was that the law was only a small part of primogeniture, which in the main rested upon the customary behaviour of the aristocracy through their wills and their settlements, rather than upon the publicly imposed legal norms concerning intestate succession. At best the law was a symbol. Further, to deny landowners their custom would be to limit their freedom to deal with their property, which at this stage of the argument would have contradicted one of the critics' own dearly held values. Instead middle-class hostility crystallized into the single issue of Corn Law reform, which dominated politics until its achievement in 1846 and then faded away leaving no organization or philosophy in place to continue a struggle.[159]

Nor is there any sign of agitation from collective land-holding organizations. Permanent building societies date only from the mid-1840s, and freehold land societies were insignificant before about 1849. Terminating building societies were capable of concerted action, but it seems to have been *ad hoc* and defensive, usually only in response to threats to remove their exemptions from stamp duty. No doubt many of them had negotiated special prices for their land transactions with a solicitor anyway—there is evidence of that at all periods.[160] Perhaps they would support initiatives brought by others—reformers sometimes hoped that they would—but in so far as legal rules caused problems for them their solution was traditional in the first half of the nineteenth century, sectional legislation.[161]

---

[158] (1860) 9 *Law Mag. & Law Rev.* 75. This was an accurate prediction, see (1874–5) 58 *LT* 239.

[159] David Martin, 'Land Reform', in Patricia Hollis, ed., *Pressure from Without in Early Victorian England* (1974).

[160] See Seymour J. Price, *Building Societies: Their Origins and History* (1958), 40, 108, 109, 142; E. J. Cleary, *The Building Society Movement* (1965), 70, 80–1.

[161] e.g. Building Societies Act 1836, s. 3, whereby an endorsement of repayment on a building society mortgage deed worked as a reconveyance without need for the usual formal transfer.

In 1821 the *Edinburgh Review* noted how uninterested the public was in whether there should be a registry of deeds.[162] In 1852 James Stewart, surveying the period since he first published his own law reform proposals, concluded that

within the last ten years great progress has been made, not, I am afraid, in facilitating the transfer of land in this country, but in bringing home to the public the importance of this subject.[163]

He forbore to say how much this owed to his own efforts on behalf of the Law Amendment Society.[164] The main movers of change in the law of land transactions thus saw themselves as 'law reformers', and the category into which they are best placed is 'law reform', not yet 'land reform'.

[162] (1821) 35 *Edinburgh Review* 190.
[163] *Suggestions as to Reform in Some Branches of the Law* (2nd edn. 1852), p. vii, and cf. p. v.
[164] See below, Ch. 2, sect. 7.

2

Conveyancing Reform

1. Prologue

Typically, James Stewart's modest and useful reform of lease and release conveyancing had been shoddily executed. When Bellenden Ker rescued conveyancers from the mischievous effects of Lyndhurst's Act in 1845, he put Stewart's right as well.[1] In particular the Real Property Act allowed all interests in land henceforward to be transferred by simple deed of grant, abolishing much technicality and enabling us to speak of a 'conveyance' of land without anachronism.[2] This sort of reform, comparable to new precedents set by the higher courts in its strengths, its randomness, and its chronic incompleteness, continued the job of simplifying land transfer started by the Real Property Commissioners. However, for mid-century reformers the institution of a general register of deeds was the greatest prize within their reach, and for John Campbell, chairman of the Real Property Commissioners, failure to grasp it was a continuing disappointment.[3] Twenty years after their report he was still vying with Lord Brougham for the honour of being the man finally to introduce the system into England, and they were both still blaming shabby tactics by country solicitors for thwarting them. While Arthur Symonds had placed the blame instead on the conservatism of the gentry in the Commons, such different voices of the solicitors' profession as the *Legal Observer* and the Manchester Law Association accepted

[1] See above p. 35; C. Davidson, *Concise Precedents in Conveyancing* (4th edn. 1852), 54. The anomalous stamp on the non-existent lease was abolished by 13 & 14 Vict., c. 97, s. 6.

[2] 8 & 9 Vict., c. 106, ss. 2, 3.

[3] Mrs Hardcastle, *Life of John, Lord Campbell* (1881), i. 478–85, 494–5; ii. 3, 5, 13, 19, 29–30.

Campbell's attribution of responsibility, save that they saw their tactic as being the promotion of reasoned argument and their success as the triumph of truth over reformers' self-interest.[4]

2. The Case for Deeds Registration

'It is obvious', the Real Property Commissioners rightly if tautologically thought, 'that a documentary title cannot be complete unless the party to whom it is produced can be assured that no document which may defeat or alter the effect of those which are shown to him is kept out of sight'.[5] An apparent owner in fee simple might subsequently have mortgaged his land or put it into family settlement. Or one of the links in the chain of title might be false, because a will had been suppressed, or the exercise of a power of appointment on which its validity turned might have been revoked. Fraud might be to blame, though the Commissioners made much less of this than some advocates of registration did, but the effect of accident or mistake would be just as devastating. And that the effects were actually devastating was a matter on which the Commissioners had no doubt; there was 'abundant evidence', they wrote, though for various reasons it was 'difficult to produce many instances well documented.'[6] These various reasons boiled down to just one: that the Commissioners were lawyers, unequipped for social inquiry. Law reports gave them little help since cases were reported only if they raised novel legal issues, whereas fraud, accident, and mistake were usually clear-cut, they thought. They fell back, then, on a general feeling among conveyancers that they had been asked often enough to adjudicate in private on such cases for them to be confident of the existence of a real problem.

However, it was not actual loss caused by incomplete title that concerned them most, rather the fear of it. In order to be safe against the risk, they thought, purchasers had to make elaborate investigations into title, occasioning expense and

---

[4] See above, pp. 9, 27, 32, 33, 41.
[5] Second Report of the Real Property Commissioners, (1830) HCP. xi. 1, 4.
[6] Ibid. 6.

delay. Further, in seeking to provide assurance for purchasers—
insurance, perhaps—conveyancers had developed the system
of 'attendant terms', which added further to the costs.[7] This
system made use of a long lease which had initially been
granted over the land in question, quite genuinely, as security
for some temporary purpose. It might have been part of a
mortgage, but more often it would have formed part of a family
settlement, when it would be granted to the trustees of the
settlement to safeguard the rights of children or grandchildren
in the family who had not yet been born. It provided a safeguard
because it was a legal estate, and as such entitled its owner to
take possession of the land or its rents. Further, its priority
dated from its creation, so it would trump any inconsistent
interests of later date—other leases, say, mortgages, powers of
appointment, and so on. Its purpose would end, in technical
language it would be 'satisfied', when the children were born
or, in a mortgage, when the loan was repaid. If it was then
assigned back to the fee simple owner it would 'merge' into the
fee simple, and vanish as a separate entity. But if it were not, it
would be held on trust for the fee simple owner, in technical
language it would be 'attendant on the inheritance'. He could
then deal with it as he saw fit. Conveyancers developed the
habit of keeping these terms alive long after they had been
satisfied, in order to have them assigned to subsequent purchasers of the fee simple as security against undiscovered
intermediate dealings which might detract from the value ·or
validity of the title they were offered. Up to a point this worked.
But the Commissioners thought that it added great expense—
each attendant term had its own title to be investigated, its own
trustees to track down, and so on—and that there were enough
exceptions to the protection it offered for it to be a very
inefficient system. Further, of course, it worked only so long as
the purchaser acquired the oldest extant attendant term, a
matter which generated its own uncertainty. If instead all deeds
and assurances had to be recorded in a centralized registry the
necessity for attendant terms would disappear.

Some problems could not be cured by attendant terms. For

---

[7] Ibid. 7–13. The theory and practice is well explained by Joshua Williams,
Principles of the Law of Real Property (2nd edn. 1849), 396 ff.

example, where a large plot of land had been sold off in smaller portions only one purchaser would have the original title-deeds covering the period up until that sale. The others would have copies, but copies were not good enough in strict law. So they would also receive covenants from the holder of the title-deeds that he would produce them for inspection when required. But there were numerous technical problems here and again much expense. A registry would solve the problem. In passing, the Commissioners acknowledged that in practice it had already been solved.[8] Special conditions in contracts of sale were used to prevent purchasers calling for the original deeds. Here the Commissioners displayed a trait extremely common among law reformers. Having no knowledge of the market themselves, and lacking means of systematic inquiry, they assumed that because such contractual conditions might tend to reduce the value of land by exposing purchasers to a risk against which they could not insure, then in practice prices actually were depressed.

In sum: titles are insecure; this is bad in itself because it sometimes leads to loss; it is also bad because the fear of insecurity causes generally high conveyancing costs in assessing just how secure a particular title is; it is also bad because it has encouraged the development of an expensive, and as it happens, inefficient, insurance device. Registration will remove the underlying insecurity, thus removing the risk of loss, reducing costs generally, and obviating the need for attendant terms.

3. The Case for Deeds Registration Denied

The arguments against deeds registration varied a little depending upon precisely what scheme was proposed, but their outline was much the same whenever the question was raised.

Opponents, who normally were solicitors, would start by denying the premiss: the great Lincoln's Inn conveyancers might think that purchasing land was dicing with financial death, but that was because they were only ever consulted about the tiny percentage of transactions where something had gone wrong. Ordinary country practitioners, who had a far

---

[8] Second Report of the Real Property Commissioners, (1830) HCP xi. 15–17.

more intimate knowledge of the actual operation of property markets, would tell quite a different story, of thousands of purchases going through with a minimum of fuss and never a complaint afterwards. Even for titles which were less than perfect the opponents of deeds registration had their answer: the market. Special conditions could be inserted into any contract and were ubiquitous at property auctions.[9] They bound the purchaser to accept the title stipulated by the vendor. In practice, so it was said,[10] they did not push the price down, though in theory they should have done. There are obvious difficulties of quantification to these arguments, on both sides, which were not resolved at the time nor have they been since. Readers might agree, however, that there is the whiff of the ivory tower to a law reformer's article that begins:

> No persons experience more surprise than owners of landed estates, when they are informed that the property which they have enjoyed for a long course of years, either by descent from an ancestor, or by undisturbed transfer from a former owner, is in point of law totally unmarketable.[11]

Having established that the problem was much less than the reformers claimed, the next move was to argue that their diagnosis of what remained of it was wrong. It was not failure to *discover* deeds that caused insecurity, but difficulty in *understanding* them. The correct solution was to reform the substantive law, especially the intricacies of successive interests, and only afterwards to think about registering deeds. To move straight to the second step would simply avoid the issue. Worse than that, it would exacerbate it, since out of abundance of caution lawyers would register all sorts of deeds unnecessarily, which would simply clutter up the register and cause even more perplexity to purchasers' lawyers, who would have to struggle to understand them before they could conclude that they need not have bothered. This was a clever argument since it was calculated to divide the reformers, attracting those who believed

---

[9] e.g. Williams, *Principles* (3rd edn. 1852), 342.
[10] Bristol LS, (1859) 33 *LT* 67.
[11] 'On the Law Relating to Conditions of Sale', (1845) 2 *Law Rev.* 81, repr. in (1845) 5 *LT* 137, 185, 210, 229, 257, 277. The *Law Times* proposed its own set of standard conditions, ibid. 45. This flurry of interest suggests that the use of special conditions may have been on the increase.

that substantive changes of settlement and entail really were needed.[12]

Then opponents would argue that registration would bring its own problems. Depending on the precise terms of the scheme proposed it was often argued that registration threatened landowners' access to short-term credit.[13] As things stood a landowner could borrow money with ease by depositing his title-deeds with the lender. The resulting equitable mortgage was less safe to the lender than a formal legal mortgage, but from the borrower's point of view had the advantage that it required no documentation. A legal mortgage by contrast necessitated the full transfer of the title, with a re-transfer when the debt was cleared. But since that transaction affected the title it remained subject to inspection by subsequent purchasers, strictly speaking for up to the full sixty years of the limitation period. Equitable mortgages were secret, quick, and cheap to operate. Later they were often called 'bankers' mortgages', with banks developing standard procedures for granting them on demand. How would this work if deeds and assurances had to be registered? Would there be anything to deposit with the lender. If there was, because only duplicates were registered, then the register was telling a silent lie to a potential purchaser because it did not disclose all that he needed to know. Perhaps, then, registration of a *transaction* ought to be a condition of its validity? But that would deprive bankers' mortgages of all the advantages everyone thought they had. Perhaps these problems could be overcome if subtle enough procedures could be devised. But the more subtle the procedure the more expensive it would be—and equitable mortgages had minimal transaction costs.

A second problem that registration might cause was unwelcome publicity. Was the register to be open to public inspection? This was the rock on which the bills of the 1830s foundered, because the gentry certainly did not want public access to their mortgages to disclose to any busybody the extent of their indebtedness, nor did they want to expose their daughters'

---

[12] See e.g. J. Moore, n. 127 below; (1845–6) 31 *Leg. O.* 356 (J. Park), 397, 458; (1849–50) 40 *Leg. O.* 313; (1850–1) 41 *Leg. O.* 429, 431, 450; (1851) 42 *Leg. O.* 5, 24, 41, 133.
[13] e.g. (1845–6) 31 *Leg. O.* 1.

inheritance to fortune-seeking bachelors. On one occasion even a Solicitor-General, Sir John Romilly, raised the spectre of an Heir-at-Law Society, existing solely for the purpose of enabling true heirs to claim their rightful inheritance under long-forgotten dispositions.[14] Local law societies knew well of the activities of trade protection societies, which circulated names of debtors, gleaned from court records, sometimes with ruinous results. What would there be to keep them from similar use of the deeds registry?[15] A closed register then? But how would the landowner know what was going on? Any forger might lodge a false deed at the registry, sell or mortgage the land to the innocent purchaser and make off with the proceeds. The first that the landowner would know about it would be when he was dispossessed.

Perhaps the solution was that adopted in the Middlesex and Yorkshire deeds registries, that the register was open, but that only a 'memorial' of the deed was registered, not the whole thing. But if such a device was unhelpful to the trade protection societies, so would it necessarily be for conveyancers. Experience suggested (and this time it really did) that the most that memorials told the inquiring solicitor was that there might be something of which he perhaps ought to be aware. It did not gather all the relevant information into one place, so scarcely improved matters at all. And it certainly would do nothing to reduce costs. Searches in the Middlesex and Yorkshire registries were known to be expensive.[16] If on the other hand the whole deed were to be registered, then costs would certainly increase, because two versions of every instrument would be needed— an original to be registered, and a duplicate to be kept in the landowner's office for everyday use, or vice versa. Bentham had hoped technology would solve this problem, but it had not.

This argument has drifted from a claim that registration would bring new problems to one that it would increase general costs, not reduce them as its proponents claimed. In addition to the points made above, opponents tried to tabulate the additional direct costs of registration. Lodging each document,

[14] (1849) 103 PD (3rd ser.) 330.
[15] e.g. Wolverhampton LS, (1851–2) 43 *Leg. O.* 250.
[16] The Middlesex Deeds Registry was very profitable for its sinecure office-holders; see e.g. (1849) 38 *Leg. O.* 238.

searching each index, getting copies made—all could be made the occasion for Registry fees. Even if some of these exercises did not carry official fees, someone was going to have to make a journey to the Registry to do the work, and that would have to be reflected in the bill to the client. This is where country solicitors' opposition really did focus, because if the Registry were to be centralized, no doubt in London, then this work would probably have to be done by using London solicitors as agents, and they were far from cheap. Further, if the Registry were centralized, and if registration were to be of the whole deed, it was not clear that London agents would be competent to conduct the search. How could someone without local knowledge know which land deeds covered, at a time when conveyances usually described it by physical feature or by traditional field and lane names? How could they know enough about the pedigree of the people involved to tell whether questions of identity had been satisfactorily answered? But if registration were to be local, how were transactions covering large estates in several areas to be handled? A mortgagee would have to register his mortgage in every county, increasing the cost of borrowing. Any of these alternatives, it was argued, would add significantly to the time taken to conclude a land transaction.

4. Rejoinder

These were powerful arguments. No deeds registration bill passed either House of Parliament until after 1850, and none ever passed the Commons. Yet they were not unanswerable. It was easy enough to claim that solicitors were actually motivated only by self-interest, and that their supposed concern for their clients' bills was false. It was significant that opposition originated with solicitors out of London.[17] A registration scheme could hold costs down for the client, yet redistribute the work between London and the provinces so that the loss, if any there

---

[17] Yorkshire, West Riding: (1851) 42 *Leg. O.* 5: Manchester LA. ibid. 24; Northamptonshire, ibid. 25; Kent, ibid. 60. See generally ibid. 133. Yorkshire Registrars, (1851–2) 43 *Leg. O.* 229.

was, would fall on the country practitioner. This argument was often made, and contrasted with the selflessness of the reformers. Further, registration could be presented as a benefit even if the costs point were conceded, since reformers did not concede that reform would end with the accomplishment of deeds registration. Other reforms could accompany it, bringing savings big enough to outweigh the additional costs.

In particular the length of conveyancing documents could be reduced. Deeds of conveyance did sometimes contain endlessly repetitive clauses and inordinately long covenants against extremely remote contingencies, but the fact that most of these were in common form, having been polished by leading conveyancers over the generations and included in their precedent books, encouraged reformers to believe that such clauses could be put into statutory form, to be incorporated into a conveyance by simple reference to the appropriate section of the statute. Even without statutory shortening of deeds, registration would tend to reduce their length by eliminating the need for 'recitals'—clauses which reiterated the contents of previous deeds as a safeguard against their loss or destruction. Since solicitors' charges for reading or writing a conveyancing document were directly proportional to its length, the costs of achieving the additional security that registration would bring would thus be carried by the solicitors, not by the landowners.

5. Battle Joined

It was an unpromising site for a battle. The Real Property Commissioners had not asked whether savings to clients would be at solicitors' expense, but it now seemed that only if that were so would registration actually cheapen conveyancing—and then it would only do so in part because of other reforms that it would facilitate. Solicitors had defeated Campbell in 1830. They said they won because their arguments were good; Brougham said they won through reminding landowners that they controlled the mortgage market.[18]

---

[18] (1845) 80 PD (3rd Ser.) 497, 507; he particularly blamed Yorkshire. Only Lord Campbell heard the speech out, ibid. 515.

There are difficulties in drawing a clear link between solicitors' resistance to deeds registration and their promotion of
their own economic self-interest. Many reformers, including the
LAS, espoused the causes of deeds registration and short-form
conveyancing while at the same time unequivocally asserting
the right of solicitors to a level of remuneration befitting a liberal
profession.[19] When solicitors' organizations really did feel that
livelihoods were at stake they said so, but that was not often
the case with their opposition to deeds registration. Centralization was vehemently opposed by provincial solicitors, but even
that need not have reduced their emoluments—it would
depend how the costs scales were constructed: and the argument that centralization would cause clients delay and result in
an inferior service is perfectly plausible in itself. Further, though
in the mid-1840s Lords Brougham and Campbell tended rather
to bunch their conveyancing reform bills, to that bills instituting
short-forms and abolishing satisfied terms were introduced at
much the same time as their revival of deeds registration bills,[20]
and though all of these might be thought to have threatened
solicitors' emoluments, only registration bills received sustained
opposition. To understand these difficulties we must consider
the problem of solicitors' remuneration.

6. The Problem of Solicitors' Remuneration

Lack of empirical evidence makes the question of solicitors'
remuneration particularly difficult to analyse. Virtually nothing
is known about how their bills for conveyancing were calculated
or what range of prices there was. We do not know whether
clients searched around for competitive pricing, whether they
paid willingly, or whether they paid only after insisting that a
bill had been vetted by a Taxing Master. No quantitative
evidence existed at the time, nor was there much discussion of
how the system did behave in practice. Yet one supposes that
their day-to-day experience of extracting money from clients
was at least one factor influencing solicitors in their reception of
proposals for conveyancing reform.

[19] See below, pp. 54–55; (1846) 7 *LT* 217; (1846) 31 *Leg. O.* 565.
[20] (1845) 80 PD (3rd ser.) 497, 515.

The law was that solicitors could charge only by the item of work done, only for items authorized by statute, and only to the amount authorized by statute. A bill would then list all those items. From 1843 Taxing Masters could disallow anything unauthorized.[21] Charges concerning documents ran at so much per folio of 72 words: 1s. for drawing, 8d. for engrossing, 6d. for attested copying, 5s. for perusing a skin of 15 folios.[22] One would thus expect solicitors to oppose reforms which directly or indirectly would reduce wordage. Further, once a new measure had passed into law, reformers habitually costed the savings it made for the landed interest, announcing the result as evidence of the progress being made. The Fines and Recoveries Act, James Stewart's Act abolishing the lease element in lease and release conveyancing, and, in due course, the Act abolishing satisfied terms all received this treatment.[23] If each itemized element in a solicitor's bill contained a profit element, however small, one would suppose that these Acts would be perceived as a threat to livelihood, unless perhaps the land market was expanding quickly enough to offset the loss.

Lord Brougham acted as though he did believe that solicitors opposed his reforms simply out of this sort of self-interest—registration and short-form conveyances in particular. But his tirades against solicitors were so obviously exaggerated that even Lord Campbell dissented from them. Brougham was given to this sort of rhetoric; his innuendo that if his land transfer reforms were instituted the value of land would increase from 30 to the 50 years' purchase habitual in another country was plainly ridiculous.[24] In this instance it was James Stewart who tried to redress the balance for reformers. It was not the costs of land transfer, he thought, that deterred purchasers from entering the market, but uncertainty of title, causing delay and general anxiety. Some countries, he said, with high transaction costs had vigorous markets, other with low costs seemed

---

[21] Solicitors Act 1843, s. 37.

[22] G. W. Greenwood, *A Manual of the Practice of Conveyancing* (1856), 360–3.

[23] Fines and Recoveries Act: (1844–5) 29 *Leg. O.* 178; lease/release: James Stewart, *Suggestions as to Reform in Some Branches of the Law* (2nd edn. 1842), xi; satisfied terms: Davidson, *Concise Precedents*, 73 n.

[24] (1846) 88 PD (3rd ser.) 145; (1846) 31 *Leg. O.* 516.

stagnant.[25] This was in line with LAS policy. And for all Brougham's pronouncements it does not seem that a simple fear of fee reduction influenced solicitors very much. When, for example, the *Law Times* criticized the passage of one short-forms Act, its grouse was only on the allied point, that it was unfair to reduce emoluments of solicitors alone while retaining onerous annual certificate duty for solicitors alone.[26] Similarly, one fear of short-term conveyancing was that it was part of a trend towards de-skilling solicitors, since if statute made certain forms mandatory, clients would no longer need professional advice on choice of methods.[27] These are principally arguments about status, not about emoluments.

The question then arises, what resemblance did the run of actual conveyancing bills bear to the lawfully authorized list? If the statutory form were simply that, a form into which figures arrived at by some other calculation were slotted for law's sake, it would be easier to understand why the opposition to statutory short-forms was muted. Further, it would explain how solicitors' organizations and spokesmen could so cheerfully boast of the voluntary efforts solicitors had themselves made to reduce the length of conveyances.[28] Otherwise we are left only with the possibilities that they were being altruistic or untruthful, since whereas Lord Brougham's short-form Acts explicitly acknowledged the difficulty by enacting that charges under them were to be based not upon length but upon the skill, labour, and responsibility shown in the work done,[29] charges for deeds voluntarily shortened should, in legal theory, necessarily have resulted in reduced bills. Yet it was commonly asserted that while Brougham's Acts were dead letters the shortened forms of conveyance developed by Charles Davidson were widely used. Again the quantitative evidence needed to test these hypotheses is lacking. None the less, sufficient indications exist for them to be plausible. First, Davidson's

---

[25] James Stewart, *On the Means of Facilitating the Transfer of Land* (1848); 3rd lecture, (1848) 36 *Leg. O.* 244.

[26] (1846) 7 *LT* 312.

[27] Cf. (1843–4) 27 *Leg. O.* 273, 275.

[28] Field, p. 10 above; Cayley Shadwell, (1845) 31 *Leg. O.* 165; (1844–5) 29 *Leg. O.* 276.

[29] 8 & 9 Vict., c. 119, s. 4 and c. 124, s. 3.

Concise Precedents was an immediate success from its first appearance in 1845, reaching its third edition in 1848, its sixth in 1865, and ultimately expiring only after its twenty-first edition was published in 1921. His much fatter book, *Precedents and Forms*, ran only from 1839 into the 1880s. Davidson himself brutally dismissed Brougham's Acts as pitifully amateurish,[30] a verdict which true or false would have been quite enough to warn solicitors off using them.[31] There is a grumpy article in the *Law Review* for 1845–6 justifying reformers' tactics in pushing Acts through without proper professional consultation: 'mere *bills*, as all know who have had any experience in the matter, lawyers *will not read*. But Acts they will and must read.'[32] It therefore did not surprise the author that it was often the amending Act that won acceptance. In this instance however Davidson read Brougham's Acts and thought that he could do the job better without legislation. Brougham's Acts had been pushed through at the end of a Parliamentary session, and without professional consultation.[33]

The acceptance of Davidson's forms—if acceptance there was—still needs explanation. The *Law Times* acknowledged Brougham's gesture to solicitors, but thought his formula unworkable. Taxing Masters, it predicted, would find themselves measuring 'skill' by drifting back towards payment by length.[34] The right solution would be to adopt an *ad valorem* scale, giving official recognition to the principle already tacitly adopted in practice of basing the charge on the value of the land concerned. How else could 'responsibility' be assessed? This opinion was reasonably common, and opposition on the grounds that an *ad valorem* scale might prevent a solicitor from charging a client what he thought he could pay does not weaken the argument advanced here, that the statutory rules about bills dictated only form, not content. James Stewart said that some

---

[30] Davidson, *Concise Precedents*, 3 n.

[31] Cf. (1845) 30 *Leg. O.* 409.

[32] (1845–6) 3 *Law Rev.* 183, 208, and cf. 192 n. This attitude more than any upset conservatives, e.g. (1844) 29 *Leg. O.* 116.

[33] (1846) 31 *Leg. O.* 516.

[34] (1846) 7 *LT* 216–17; and cf. (1845–6) 30 *Leg. O.* 272, 291, 369, 409; (1845–6) 31 *Leg. O.* 517, 564.

London solicitors were already using their own *ad valorem* scales, whatever the law might be.[35]

Of course, conveyancing bills were liable to official taxation. It is not known how frequently this happened. There are assertions that it was rare, but it cannot have been unknown.[36] However, even if it did happen it is possible that Taxing Masters relegated fidelity to the statute behind the need for fair remuneration. Lord Langdale, who as Master of the Rolls heard appeals from Taxing Masters, did exactly that in *Lucas* v. *Peacock*[37] in 1844:

Services of very great value are rendered for which no direct remuneration at all is given by the ordinary rules of taxation, but for which compensation is made in a manner which I can never speak of with satisfaction, but always with very great regret. It is notorious, that in numerous instances compensation for real services *bona fide* rendered, is not given by paying for this real and *bona fide* service, but is alone obtained through payments, to a considerable amount, for services which are really of little or no value at all to the client.

Until a system could be devised which enabled solicitors to be paid according to the real value of their services he would not deprive them of 'any lawful fees . . . on the notion that the business charged for might have been of no practical benefit'. Though *Lucas* v. *Peacock* did not concern conveyancing, Langdale's analysis was thought to apply equally there, as the LAS recognized in its report on solicitors' remuneration.[38]

If this is right, so that for one reason or another taxation did not greatly influence the amount a client was charged and if, as was the case, coercion through law societies and their disciplinary powers was only in its embryo, one would tentatively conclude that though bills had to be presented in a standard form, individual solicitors filled in the figures to suit their own perception of their value to their clients, tempered by the value

[35] (1848) 36 *Leg. O.* 244.

[36] e.g. (1846) 31 *Leg. O.* 564; and cf. the itemized scale approved by the Plymouth LS; (1843–4) 27 *Leg. O.* 165, which is generally higher than that in Greenwood, *Manual*. None the less, Greenwood's remark that some of his items are 'always made but will be disallowed in taxation' implies that taxation did sometimes happen.

[37] (1844) 8 Beav. 1.

[38] (1857–8) 2 *Sol. Jo.* 353.

of the property concerned and the amount the solicitor thought the client could bear.[39] Such an analysis fits the general tone of discussion of remuneration in the solicitors' press, and also the initiation of local scales, which can then be seen as part of a developing ethic that internal price competition had no place in a profession.

Certainly, nobody in the 1840s and 1850s defended the system of payment by item. It was common ground that an alternative should be found. Finding one was quite a different matter. Payment by item seems perhaps to rest on two foundations. The first is that it simply mirrors the rules for litigation costs, where detailed formulas plus the facility for appeal to a Taxing Master prevent abuse of the principle that losers pay winners' costs. The second is that both sets of rules, which in appearance look very similar to the lists of fees chargeable until the mid-nineteenth century by court officials, are distant echoes of solicitors' original status as officers of the court. The first foundation is clearly inappropriate for conveyancing costs, but the second does seem to raise the issue that was at the heart of a search for a substitute system: what was the proper status of the mid-nineteenth-century solicitor? Among law reformers the first part of the answer was easy: he was a member of a liberal and respectable profession. The second part of the answer was very much more difficult to find: what is the appropriate system of remuneration for a liberal profession?

Three alternatives presented themselves: free contract between solicitor and client; assessment of a charge by reference to the care, skill, and responsibility demonstrated in the work, with appeal to a Taxing Master; and payment of a fixed fee calculated by reference to the value of the land—the *ad valorem* scale. This interesting question of political economy was important enough to attract J. S. Mill to the Law Amendment Society's long and acrimonious discussion of the issue.[40] Free contract had its attraction. It was best fitted to the political climate of the time, and it freed solicitors from any demeaning subordination

---

[39] Cf. (1857–58) 2 *Sol. Jo.* 369; (1867–8) 12 *Sol. Jo.* 131; and see (1864–5) 9 *Sol. Jo.* 322.

[40] (1857–8) 2 *Sol. Jo.* 446, 590; (1857–8) 30 *LT* 332, 344; (1858) 31 *LT* 9, 36, 138; cf. (1858–9) 3 *Sol. Jo.* 428. For explicit links with the question of status see (1858) 31 *LT* 95.

to state officials, a burden borne by no other profession. But it would necessarily lead to internal price competition and perhaps even to the horror of advertising;[41] to say nothing of exposing the vulnerable to sharks. We need not linger with this interesting and intractable debate (which in the long run concerned the question whether a solicitors' cartel would be established sooner or only later). It is enough to record that no stable answer was forthcoming, so that law societies were free to develop their own *ad valorem* scales as a function of the development of professionalism. They did so by reference to whatever division of labour they had each negotiated with other professional organizations in their locality, based upon the particular legal forms usual in their local land transactions. Since both these elements varied considerably from place to place, consolidation of local scales into regional ones, and then into a single national scale, was a lengthy business involving, inevitably, further questions about the distribution of power between regional and central law societies.

Thus, probably, so long as the question rested within the circle of law reformers, direct reduction of solicitors' income from land transactions was neither seriously advanced nor seriously feared. It will be recalled that as part of their advocacy of deeds registration the Real Property Commissioners pointed to the costs clients had to bear from the use of attendant terms as an insurance against insecure title. These costs stemmed from the fact that each attendant term had its own independent title, needing investigation and assignment in the same way as title to the fee and, in theory, carrying the same sort of itemized bill. Yet when statute abolished satisfied terms in 1845 there was not a murmur from solicitors about loss of income.[42] Were attendant terms much rarer than the conveyancers thought? Perhaps—perhaps rare enough that the sort of solicitors who habitually came across them could absorb the loss by dismissing a couple of copying clerks. But perhaps that was true of short-forms as well; perhaps we can reconcile the evidence discussed in these paragraphs with assertions to be found later in the

---

[41] (1858) 31 *LT* 95; cf. 'underselling', (1869–70) 14 *Sol. Jo.* 12 ff.

[42] 8 & 9 Vict., c. 112. It had a precedent in the standard terms of Railway Acts: (1845–6) 3 *Law Rev.* 183, 190. It seems that several reforms were pioneered in this way: (1848–9) 9 *Law Rev.* 102; and cf. below, pp. 89–90.

century that conveyancing prices had fallen steadily over the years by positing that the loss fell on menial clerks rather than on solicitors;[43] or that where it did fall on solicitors, that they were the weakest members of the profession, already struggling at its bottom end, whose voice was unheard in law societies and unrecorded in the legal press. Alternatively, perhaps, after all, forms and contents of conveyancing documents influenced fees and profits to such a small extent that they were insignificant in law reform debates. In all probability resistance to short-form Acts on the grounds of their technical inadequacy can be taken at face value, and resistance to deeds registration likewise, except for provincial solicitors' opposition to centralized registration, which might have compelled them to share their fees with their London agents[44]—whose cartel would have had views on how the division would be made.

Only when pressure for change came from outside law reform circles might there be real risk to solicitors' emoluments. For a moment it looked as though this might happen during the 'burdens on land' debates in the late 1840s. But the law reform implications turned out to be under the control of law reformers and the moment passed. Of course, politicians, including lawyer-politicians, often made grand public claims that reforms would reduce attorneys' bills; and when they did the solicitors' organizations had to make appropriate reply. But those arguments concerned status, not the reality of solicitor–client relations.

7. Conveyancing Reform: the Law Amendment Society

The Real Property Committee of the Law Amendment Society was chaired by Samuel Duckworth, former Real Property Com-

---

[43] Cf. (1857–8) 2 *Sol Jo.* 369, and Raymond Cocks, *Foundations of the Modern Bar* (1983), 91–2.

[44] (1857–8) 30 *LT* 177: 'forcing the country firms into a conveyancing partnership at half profits with some fifteen or twenty of the London houses'. But for the *Law Times's* interest in preventing this see below, Ch. 3, sect. 5. Similar problems arose with searches in district Probate Registries, (1863–4) 8 *Sol. Jo.* 963.

missioner.[45] A 'sound law reformer and worthy man',[46] he promptly launched it into updating proposals for the sort of piecemeal changes which the Commission had considered in its day. Its first report recommended giving trustees powers *ex officio*, shortening deeds, incorporating standard covenants by reference, and so on. The *Law Review*, not yet committed to the wider perspectives of Law Reform, strongly approved this 'highly conservative' scheme.[47] Of a pamphlet by solicitor Robert Wilson suggesting that more radical reforms were possible, all the *Law Review* could find to say was how commendable it was that a solicitor could show himself to be such a learned gentleman.[48] With a promise to return to his pamphlet later (not kept), it moved condescendingly on. The Real Property Committee recognized that shortening deeds would not be acceptable unless the basis of solicitors' remuneration were changed, but rather than investigating *ad valorem* scales it suggested that fees somehow be made dependent upon the skill needed to perform the particular task in question.[49] Next it recommended the abolition of attendant terms. The harvest from these seeds came in the form of Brougham's short-form Acts and in 1845 an Act which did abolish satisfied terms, also introduced by Brougham.[50] Campbell, remembering the link the Commissioners made between insecurity of title, attendant terms, and deeds registration thought this latter bill premature.[51] But Brougham, whose attitude to law reform was like that of a boastful Don Juan recording conquests for conquest's sake, pressed on regardless. Then in 1846 the LAS tackled deeds registration. Not to be outdone, Campbell, now in the Lords, reintroduced Duval's deeds registration bill that had been

[45] (1847–8) 7 *Law Rev.* 154. Its reports are conveniently reprinted in (1851) HLP xvi. 349.

[46] (1851–2) 15 *Law Rev.* 409.

[47] (1845) 2 *Law Rev.* 405.

[48] (1844) 1 *Law Rev.* 158; Robert Wilson, *Outlines of a Plan for Adopting the Machinery of the Public Funds to the Transfer of Real Property: Respectfully Inscribed to the President and Council of the Society for Promoting the Amendment of the Law* (1844).

[49] (1844) 1 *Law Rev.* 158.

[50] Satisfied Terms Act 1845, 8 & 9 Vict., c. 112.

[51] (1845) 80 PD (3rd ser.) 497 ff.

rejected in 1830. And, just as before, the solicitors mobilized against it.[52] *Plus ça change.*

There could never have been any doubt that the Real Property committee of the LAS would recommend adoption of deeds registration.[53] The details of the scheme were, however, matters of some argument, with particular difficulty in devising an index that would enable quick, accurate, and complete searching to be achieved. Solving this problem had been Duval's contribution in 1830, when the Commissioners had reluctantly concluded that the optimal scheme, a map-based index, was unobtainable because of the cost of conducting the national survey necessary to produce the maps. A simple index by grantor's name would have been hopelessly unmanageable, even if subdivided by geographical region, so Duval combined both these elements with a novelty of his own: indexation by root of title. That is to say, that document would be identified which conveyancers would accept as the oldest necessary, in any particular case, to investigate as part of the proof of title; it would be allocated a reference number, and then all other subsequent documents deriving from it would be indexed by the same number.[54] It was good, but it was complicated. The Real Property Committee adopted a recommendation rather like this too, but noted that a map-based index would be far preferable. Now that the Tithe Commissioners had produced some good maps perhaps a system could be devised; but as that question was beyond the terms of reference given to the Committee by the LAS it made no further recommendation. The LAS promptly extended its terms of reference, and in the meantime, in response to recommendations of a Select Committee of the House of Lords, passed a resolution in favour of deeds registration and short-forms of documents.[55] In due course the Committee reported optimistically on the cost and feasibility of a national mapping survey.[56]

It seems that there was nothing in any of this that could not have been predicted in 1830. Yet there was, and it led to great

---

[52] (1845–6) 31 *Leg. O.* 1, 397, 458; (1846) 32 *Leg. O.* 1.
[53] (1846) 4 *Law Rev.* 336; and see n. 45 above.
[54] Second Report of the Real Property Commissioners, (1830) MCP xi. 1.
[55] (1846) 4 *Law Rev.* 384.
[56] (1846–7) 5 *Law Rev.* 385; and see n. 45 above.

complications. Two things in fact, leading in different directions. The first was that the LAS, through James Stewart in
particular, took advantage of the political climate of the mid-
1840s to sell the idea of conveyancing reform to the landed
interest—especially deeds registration. He even managed to
persuade them that the matter was urgent. The second was that
Robert Wilson's pamphlet persuaded Law Reformers, including
Stewart, that deeds registration was not the best way forward,
and that title registration was. Unfortunately title registration
was such a novelty, at least so far as anything other than the
mere concept was concerned, that the moment its principle
became accepted the reformers shattered into splinters, each
with its own scheme, all of them radically different. But though
they had convinced *themselves* of the superiority of title registration, through Stewart's efforts they had persuaded the gentry
of the necessity for deeds registration, and there were plenty of
the old guard left who would sponsor such a bill. To make
matters worse the first title registration scheme in the field,
Wilson's, was based on principles which were wholly incompatible with Duval's deeds registration bill.

James Stewart was the sort of man no reform movement can
do without. One of the original founders of the LAS, in 1846 he
was a member of the steering committee to consider the
direction of its law reform efforts.[57] He was always in the
vanguard of conveyancing reform. It was he who wrote the
LAS report that led to the Satisfied Terms Act,[58] then he moved
smartly on to champion deeds registration, dropping that
within a year or two to espouse registration of title. Wherever
the frontier was, Stewart was there. Further, he was a particularly energetic polemicist for the cause, especially among non-
lawyers, where he was instrumental in raising conveyancing
reform as a national issue. Taking advantage of the sensitivity
of the landowners in 1846 as the Corn Laws were finally
repealed, he wrote in the *Law Review* likening conveyancing
costs to tithes, the poor rate, the highway rate, and so on, as

---

[57] (1846) 4 *Law Rev.* 446.
[58] (1845) 3 *Law Rev.* 175. The *Legal Observer* regarded him as a guiding light of
conveyancing reform, (1845–6) 31 *Leg. O.* 564.

burdens falling peculiarly upon land.[59] He was accordingly called to give evidence to the House of Lords Select Committee on the Burdens on Land,[60] and rounded the year off by initiating a correspondence debate in *The Times*, with a letter headed 'To Members of Agricultural Societies and Others interested in Land', urging them to demand conveyancing reform.[61]

The gist of his case was very simple. The moral of the repeal of the Corn Laws was that if landowners were to be forced into accepting free trade in the produce of land, and therefore the reduction of their previous privileges, they were entitled to free trade in land itself, with the reduction of the present disadvantages it suffered in relation to personalty. There was no intrinsic reason why funds should stand at thirty-two years purchase but land at only twenty-seven; the law must be to blame. Stamp duty was a problem, of course, so too was the length of deeds, and the apparatus of tenure and estates. But that the problem really was the absence of a central deeds registry could be proved by looking to foreign states which did have one. Land there habitually fetched well over thirty years purchase, and even in Scotland it usually went for between one and five years more than in England.[62] He was anxious to reassure landowners that he meant no threat to their familiar pattern of land transactions. Entail and settlement could easily be accommodated within a system of registration. He was not always so clear in distinguishing between registration of deeds and registration of title. His evidence to the Select Committee concentrates heavily on the former,[63] and he seemed not to notice that the foreign comparison concerned the latter. When he was questioned about transfer of title by book entry, he was rather inclined to say that the principle of copyhold conveyancing

---

[59] (1846) 4 *Law Rev.* 164. (I identify him as the author of this anonymous piece from its style and from the similarity of its content and phraseology to his evidence to the House of Lords Select Committee, see n. 60 below.)

[60] (1846) HLP xxii. 1: Stewart's evidence is from p. 441.

[61] *The Times*, 22 and 30 Oct. 1846; repr. in (1846–7) 5 *Law Rev.* 214 and, with replies, (1846–7) 33 *Leg. O.* 48.

[62] (1846) 4 *Law Rev.* 164; evidence to the House of Lords Select Committee on Burdens on Land, (1846) HLP xxii. 1, *Report*, q. 5309. Note his acknowledgement of a probable increase in costs at q. 5310, and his link between deeds registration and short-forms at q. 5311. Cf. editorials in (1846) 7 *LT* 20 and 217.

[63] (1846) HLP xxii. 1, *Report*, qq. 5272, 5275, 5311.

could be extended to freehold, and drifted into title registration that way.[64] It is probable that at that time he was not very clear about the difference, though by the end of the year he had come out strongly in favour of registration of title.[65]

None the less, he persuaded the Select Committee—which of course is what it wanted. In among its analysis of all the taxes and excises burdening land is the single sentence, 'the committee are convinced that the marketable value of real property is seriously diminished by the tedious and expensive process attending its transfer.'[66] So Stewart had said. He had been supported by Nassau Senior, also a member of the LAS, whose rather more subtle opinion was that it was the uncertainty of the cost of conveyancing, keeping potential purchasers out of the market, that depressed the price of land. A register would cure this, and though the questions put to him by the Select Committee again reveal a confusion between the two sorts of registration, Senior himself meant title registration.[67] But he refused to speculate about the usual run of costs in ordinary cases, though he had his own horror story to tell, as all the eminent conveyancers always did, saying that the committee should ask a solicitor about usual costs.[68] It had, hearing a solicitor from Doncaster called Robert Baxter. Alas, he told it what it did not want to hear and was alternately bullied and ignored. His estimate of law costs on a £20,000 sale worked out at 1.25 per cent; he thought the price of land was most affected by the returns offered by railway company shares; he thought that the Yorkshire deeds registry increased costs for no additional security of title. When beaten over the head with the names of Duval, Brodie, Butler and all, he stood firm against the extension of deeds registration, though he did not rule out some form of guaranteed title which, he thought, would be particularly useful for small lenders who wanted the security of a full legal mortgage.[69] The

---

[64] (1846) HLP xxii. 1, *Report*, qq. 5312, 5315.

[65] *The Times*, 23 Oct. 1846.

[66] (1846) HLP xxii. 1, *Report*, p. viii.

[67] Ibid., qq. 5417–18, 5425, 5436; for questioners' confusion see q. 5444.

[68] Ibid., q. 5460.

[69] Ibid., esp. qq. 2675, 2684, 2698–702, 2711–39, 2772, 2774. Note the Committee's incredulity that equitable mortgages required an actual deposit of title-deeds, ibid., q. 2704.

Law Review later edited his evidence shamelessly to suit the reformers' case.[70]

The report gave the LAS all that it could have hoped for. The committee

> earnestly request the attention of the House to the important evidence of Mr Stewart on the evils proceeding from the length of deeds connected with real property . . . they are anxious to impress on the House the necessity of a thorough revision of the whole subject of conveyancing, and the disuse of the present prolix, expensive and vexatious system. . . . The committee, however, limit themselves to the expression of their opinion, that a registry of title to all real property is essential to the success of any attempt to simplify the system of conveyancing.[71]

At about the same time Lord Beaumont, chairman of the Select Committee, seconded a resolution at an open meeting of the LAS calling for registration of deeds.[72] He was not alone in confusing the two ideas. By now the LAS Real Property Committee had approved both a plan for registering deeds and an amended version of Wilson's scheme for registering title, indexing both reports under the common heading 'As to a general register of titles'.[73] As a result of all this activity a new Real Property Commission was established in 1847, to be chaired by Lord Langdale, with Lord Beaumont also a member, as were C. H. Bellenden Ker and Walter Coulson, LAS members. It did not report until 1850.

8. The New World: Title Registration

Robert Wilson, solicitor, joined the LAS at its inception in 1844 and at once presented it with a reasoned case for the superiority of title registration over deeds registration, including an outline scheme for its achievement. It was noted, and as we have seen, ignored, by the *Law Review*.[74] It seems similarly to have been ignored by the LAS Real Property Committee, for not until 1846

[70] (1846) 4 *Law Rev.* 384, 391.
[71] (1846) HLP xxii. 1, *Report*, p. xii.
[72] (1846) 4 *Law Rev.* 364.
[73] (1846) 4 *Law Rev.* 336; the heading is in (1851) HLP xv. 349.
[74] (1846) 4 *Law Rev.* 336; Wilson, *Outlines*.

did that committee consider it, perhaps because by then the
Westminster Review had declared that by contrast with deeds
registration Wilson's plan afforded the only means by which
'the infinitely varied modifications of enjoyment to which real
property becomes subject in an advanced state of society may
be made consistent with its free alienation'.[75] Wilson always
claimed to have been the first to work out a scheme for title
registration, and also to have originated the idea independently,
though he acknowledged that the principle had been suggested
to the first Real Property Commissioners by Mr Fonnereau, a
solicitor, and by Mr Hogg, a barrister.[76] Of these two suggestions, Fonnereau's was the more detailed, though it was
scarcely more than an argument for registration of the legal fee
simple, with other interests being hidden behind trusts. He
had volunteered his scheme to the Commission without being
asked and, like Wilson in his turn, was ignored by the conveyancing barristers. In 1846 a young solicitor from the Isle of
Wight, Henry Sewell, also published a scheme for real property
reform in which title registration played a major part, again
seemingly independently.[77] The *Legal Observer* pronounced
rather sniffily that his scheme would not work, though it did
not bother to say why.[78] Sewell's scheme was more far-reaching
than Wilson's, but his proposals for registration less detailed.
His preface is illuminating. First he stressed his awareness of
his relatively lowly position: only barristers could claim to be
authorities on the subjects he was considering. Secondly,
though, he stressed solicitors' closeness to clients. It is they
who see clients' frustration at lawyers' inability to predict how
long it will take to prove title, with consequent uncertainty over

[75] (1845) 43 *Westminster Review* 373, 383.

[76] Second Report of the Real Property Commissioners, (1830) HCP xi. 97, 52.

[77] Henry Sewell, *A Letter to Lord Worsley on the Burdens Affecting Real Property,
with Reasons in Favour of a General Registry of Title* (1846); repr. in 1850 as *A Letter
to the Earl of Yarborough, etc.* Sewell migrated to the Canterbury settlement in
New Zealand in the hope of implementing his proposals there, soon becoming
a prominent politician. In 1860 he helped pass New Zealand's first title
registration statute, the (non-Torrens) Land Titles Act, principally to speed
extinguishment of Maori title, and himself became Registrar-General: *The Journal
of Henry Sewell, 1853–7*, ed. W. David McIntyre, i (1980), 26–7: *Dictionary of New
Zealand Biography*, i (1990), 391.

[78] (1846) 32 *Leg. O.* 386. It was more favourably inclined in 1850: (1850) 40 *Leg.
O.* 135.

costs and inability to plan accurately the financing of the transaction. It is they who have to try to explain to clients the mysteries of a bill of conveyancing costs. Solicitors, in seeing the system as a whole, were more likely than barristers to be able to suggest reforms of it as a whole.

He had seen what nobody else had seen, that deeds registration served the interest of the conveyancing barristers. Their search for defects in titles, their construction of special contractual conditions[79] to immunize vendors against weak links—all their work, in short—turned on their access to detailed documentation. A register would be the sole and complete depository of all the information relevant to a title. They could then be confident that they had all the information available, and would be able to give their opinions safely. This was the essence of deeds registration—it was to be an enormous data bank from which the validity of any title could be inferred by study of the information it contained. Title registration was utterly different. It was a register of conclusions, not of information from which conclusions might be drawn. A register of title stated that a particular vendor was indeed the owner of the land he claimed; the information on which that conclusion had been reached was suppressed, it was irrelevant, it was obsolete. This was so clear to Sewell that he mentioned it only in a final footnote: registration of deeds is about disclosure of their contents, registration of title is not.

In contrast to the conveyancers, who tended to think in terms of identifying a problem and then devising a technical solution, Sewell and Wilson had arrived at general conclusions by beginning with general principle. For Wilson[80] conveyancing was based upon three interlocking ideas. First, proof of title was retrospective—it was achieved by looking back through previous transactions, rather than starting with the present fact of possession, as was in reality what happened for transactions concerning chattels or stock. Secondly, the onus of proof was on the vendor to show affirmatively that there was no flaw in the title, rather than it being for the purchaser to demonstrate

---

[79] Cf. Evidence of Nassau Senior to the House of Lords Select Committee on Burdens on Land, (1846) HLP xxii, *Report*, qq. 5410–13.

[80] *Outlines*. Quotations are from pp. 6, 6, 13, 15, 18 (emphasis original), 45 (leases), 27 (mortgages.)

the invalidity—as it would be in general litigation. Thirdly, legal title was intrinsically fragmented, because of what he called the 'theory of estates'. By this theory each 'derivative interest'—a term of years, say, or a life estate—'is an integral portion of the right of property; and, by consequence, the title to the fee simple is usually a *complex title*, made up of a combination of independent parts'. By contrast, under the theory

which prevails with regard to personal property, derivative interests are subordinate contracts or trusts, affecting an entire and indivisible right of legal property. This theory may be called . . . the theory of representation of a *simple title* representing subordinate interests. The public funds are held in this way.

Successive interests in themselves were not a problem, he thought, since they existed to meet real needs.

The evil complained of is not that complicated transactions complicate the title while they last, and so far as they operate; but that the complication continues after the occasion for it has ceased . . . even the expiration of the estates created by [a] settlement does not restore the title to its former state of unity. It is cemented together, but the marks of the previous fracture remain.

The title 'includes the limitations which the settlement created, and the collateral evidence [births, marriages, deaths] by which these limitations are proved to have become inoperative.' The solution was to separate derivative interests from the right of property, leading to a simple and indivisible title. Derivative interests

might be secured by controlling . . . the exercise of a simple and uniform power of alienation belonging to the indivisible legal title. That is to say, although derivative interests must and ought to occasion complication when and so far as they intervene, each particular title might be reduced, in their absence, to a state of simplicity resembling that to which all titles would be reduced if they were wholly abolished.

So it was with stock:

title to stock is always free, *so far as it does not remain, at that time, subjected to a continuing external restraint*. The machinery is only clogged *when and so far as there is a continuing necessity to modify its action*: it is ready to effect an instant and absolutely secure transfer, as soon as the clog is withdrawn.

How? Stock stood registered in a book in its owner's name—several names if trustees were involved, though they would never be expressly identified as such. Transfer was effected by book entry, that mere action passing title. But if there were some claim against the owner, the claimant could enter a *distringas*, a sort of stop-notice, which would give him a short time in which to make his claim in the event of a proposed transfer. Whilst that *distringas* was on the books, the derivative interest behind it was protected, though the books did not disclose what it was. But as soon as it was removed the stock could again be safely transmitted. So it should be with land, argued Wilson. Successive interests should be created only by trusts, and they should be protected only by stop-notices of one sort or another. So long as there was no stop-notice, the trustees would pass good title. The law of notice would be abolished, though a transferee implicated in fraud would hold as constructive trustee for so long as he held the land—if he passed the title on to someone not so implicated, then that person would get a clear title. Whether there had or had not been fraud would be a question with which a jury could be trusted.

A real property register would need some refinements not necessary for stock. Leases, for example, would have to be notified to the Registrar and protected by some sort of reservation on the title-certificate. A transferee of the fee simple would then take subject to the lease, as he would with any incorporeal hereditament created by deed and similarly protected. Wilson was willing for incorporeal hereditaments arising by prescription or usage to bind without entry on the register, and perhaps also 'short leases in possession, at rack rent, though founded on contract, might properly be included in the class of notorious facts to be investigated by enquiry' and hence not needing protection via the register. On the other hand the register could also be used as a convenient place on which to note 'permanent charges' against the land, such as an adverse right to minerals. For those things which did need protection on the register in order to retain continuing validity against transferees of the fee simple a separate certificate could be provided—for leases in particular. One would expect Wilson to have suggested something similar for mortgages, but he was hazy on this subject, seeming rather to think that equitable mortgages by deposit of the title-certificate would be adequate and should become the norm, given that a code of statutory rights for the mortgagee could be enacted. Apart from that his scheme will not seem unfamiliar to any reader who knows anything about the Land Registration Act 1925.

Changes would be needed to inheritance procedure to maintain the integrity of the register. Wilson suggested that someone akin to an intestate's personal representative through whom personal property devolved be instituted to do the same job for realty. Moreover, the system would need good maps if it was to work. But Wilson thought that tithe maps provided a start and that anyway the country should afford a proper national mapping survey. The major remaining problem was how to get the scheme started, how to make it attractive from the beginning. Here he would give landowners a choice. They could have their title certified by some government agent, in which case it would no longer be open to challenge, and henceforward subject only to whatever interests were protected on the register, or they could register simply the fact of their present possession. In the latter instance they could upgrade their title after a short time by advertising their intention to do so; if there were no objections, then the title would become certified. He thought that a maximum of three years would do for that. The easiest way to get all this started would be for an assistant registrar to visit each parish in turn (with due advance notice given), receive evidence from landowners wishing to take advantage of the scheme, and enter their titles on the register accordingly. It would all be optional, though perhaps in due course the few recalcitrant landowners would have to be brought into line by compulsion. There would be a central registry, in London.

When the LAS Real Property Committee recovered from its unwillingness even to consider such a novelty it gave Wilson's scheme its blessing, though not without modifications.[81] The first filled in the major gap in the scheme by providing a

---

[81] (1846) 4 *Law Rev.* 336.

mechanism for legal mortgages. The borrower would surrender his title-certificate to the Registrar, who would issue a new one to him, subject to a mortgagee's interest. The mortgagee would get a charge certificate, transferable by simple book-entry. It is a little surprising that Wilson had not spelled this out himself, since he saw as one of the important advantages of title registration that it would enable 'transferable *land warrants* [to] take up and circulate the immense unemployed capital which so often clogs the London money-market', by analogy with 'dock warrants' which did the same job for bulky goods in transit.

The second modification altered Wilson's original design. There should be two registers, not just one. The second would be for equitable interests arising under settlements and trusts. The first register would disclose that there was a trust, but not its details. A copy of the settlement concerned would be lodged at the registry, where it would form the root of title for the derivative interests arising under it, which would then be registered in the second register. These would be assignable by deeds registered in accordance with Lord Campbell's plan for deeds registration. But such registration would not of itself necessarily bar transfer of the legal title. Instead registration of an equitable interest would entitle its holder to a short period of notice from the registrar if a dealing with the legal title were proposed; he could then consent, allowing the transaction to go through free from his interest, or he could refuse, or he could remain silent. The Committee's view on these latter two possibilities is unclear; it is probable that it left open the question of the effect of silence—it could be either that the transfer would take effect free from the equitable interest, or that silence was equivalent to refusal, so that the transferee would take subject to it. Obviously there was room for much future argument here.

The LAS Real Property Committee accepted Wilson's plan in June 1846, just a month after it had published its own scheme for the registration of deeds. It expressed no preference, indeed it does not seem to have seen any conflict between the two systems, so perhaps the Committee saw its second amendment to Wilson's scheme as bridging the gap between the two ideas, forming a hybrid. There was at least one other hybrid suggested at about that time, the Drummond/Page Wood bill in 1849,[82] and it is possible to read the Conveyancing Commission's report of 1850 in the same way. Indeed Duval's scheme encouraged the idea by using the notion of a root of title as an organizing principle of deeds registration.

James Stewart however abandoned deeds registration, so his proselytizing letters to *The Times* that October urged upon landowners the great advantages they would gain by adopting title registration as their goal.[83] And in December his own paper to the LAS Real Property Committee confidently asserted that most people now favoured registration of titles based upon a map.[84] The only remaining question, which he set himself to answer, was how to get such a system started. The difficulty was that the initial costs of getting land on to a register would fall upon the present owner, whereas the benefits would accrue mainly to subsequent sellers.

Stewart's solution was startlingly original: insurance. In a complete reversal of the premiss on which all plans for deeds registration had been based, he declared that the vast majority of present titles were completely safe, albeit not always up to the Chancery Court's 'marketable title' standard—but since hardly any title ever won that accolade, that did not matter very much. What happened in practice, he said, was that in cases of doubt an opinion on a title's safety was obtained from a leading conveyancer, which was very rarely later upset. If this conveyancer's opinion was then *insured*, the title could effectively be guaranteed, and hence registered with immediate benefit to the present generation of landowners. (He did not way so, but he must have doubted that Wilson's very short limitation period of two to three years for upgrading possessory titles would be acceptable.) The risk to be insured was the fallibility of the conveyancer's opinion which, he thought, insurance companies would agree to bear since it was well known that very few titles were ever invalidated as a result of litigation. The insurance companies could select their own expert to give the opinion,

---

[82] See n. 87 below, and text.
[83] See n. 61 above.
[84] (1847–8) 7 *Law Rev.* 154. Note also his almost contemporaneous lecture, 'A Plan for a Register of Titles', ibid. 386, repr. in 1848 as *On the Means of Facilitating the Transfer of Land*.

and there could be various classes of title certified in this way, with various specified risks stipulated. The Real Property Committee accepted the plan,[85] adding that it would work well in conjunction with title registration, because then the insurance costs could be borne by a public body. That would need legislation, it said; but the idea would also work without registration of title, as a form of private enterprise certification. The *Law Review* added that since some insurance offices already covered some conveyancing risks, such as the birth of issue, there was every hope that they would indeed enter this new business.[86]

After this great outburst of creative thought, and with Lord Langdale's Royal Commission deliberating, there was something of a lull in reformers' activity, there being plenty of other areas of law to which they could turn their attention. But expectations had been aroused, and as word leaked out that the Commission was divided, proposals again emerged. Most notable was a rather curious hybrid bill combining elements of deeds registration and title registration which was sponsored in the Commons in 1849 by Henry Drummond, a banker with such idiosyncratic political views that he was rarely taken as seriously as he took himself, seconded by W. Page Wood, the future Chancellor, Lord Hatherley.[87] Though opposed by the Home Secretary, the Attorney-General, and the Solicitor-General, it passed its second reading by 55 votes to 45.[88] The LAS and the *Law Review* thought it a poor bill, but credited their own educational efforts for this astonishing turnaround in opinion among the squirearchy.[89] A year later the *Legal Observer* reached the same conclusion, from the opposing point of view:

It has been conjectured that this recent effort to incorporate into the inquiry before Parliament a supposed relief to the landed interest arises from a conviction in the mind of the investigators that the frauds to be prevented are comparatively few; that the skill and diligence of

[85] (1847–8) 7 *Law Rev.* 154.

[86] Ibid.

[87] Real Property Transfer Bill, (1849) HCP vi. 135. It was greeted with incredulity by law societies, e.g. (1849) 38 *Leg. O.* 1, 345; (1849–50) 39 *Leg. O.* 256. For Drummond see *DNB* and (1860) 9 *Gentleman's Magazine* (3rd ser.) 657.

[88] (1849) 103 PD (3rd ser.) 323 ff.

[89] (1849) 10 *Law Rev.* 172; (1849) 38 *Leg. O.* 212.

conveyancers and solicitors prevent any extensive mischief; and that the new system, like all human contrivances will be equally liable, with the old, to error, and equally subject to ingenious frauds. It is surmised, therefore, that this attractive object of relieving the agricultural classes has been pressed into the service in order that a powerful section of the legislature in both Houses may be induced to favour the proposal.[90]

As in 1846, so in 1850: the imminence of an official report was heralded in the *Law Review* with an article headed 'What the landowner may demand and obtain',[91] with the intention of maintaining demand for reform. In addition to the now familiar saving of costs it stressed a further possibility: improved mechanisms for raising credit secured on land, a benefit of title registration that Wilson himself had claimed with his 'land warrant' suggestion. The indefatigable James Stewart duly got himself called as a witness before another committee, this time Robert Slaney's Select Committee on the Investments of the Middle and Working Classes, which was mainly concerned with savings banks, limited liability partnerships, and the like. It duly reported that the middle and working classes were anxious to invest in land or landed securities, or to lend on mortgages themselves, but that the uncertainty and complexity of land titles, the length and expense of conveyances, and the cost of stamps generally put this beyond their reach.[92] Stewart thought the solution lay with more easily transferable mortgages, which would have predictable transaction costs and little delay, as he had found in many continental jurisdictions.

Registration of title would result in a transferable certificate that would make borrowing easier, with advantages both to landowners and small capitalists, but as with title insurance the idea of simple land securities was not dependent upon registration. The LAS Real Property Committee explained in 1851[93] how they could be achieved in three ways: through title registration, with or without insurance; by an insured title, without registration; or by establishing Debenture Land Companies, based

---

[90] (1850) 40 *Leg. O.* 313.

[91] (1849–50) 11 *Law Rev.* 361, 440.

[92] House of Commons Select Committee on the Investment of the Savings of the Middle and Working Classes, (1850) HCP xix. 169. Stewart's evidence is at qq. 275 ff.; much of it concerns partnership—land is at qq. 275–91.

[93] (1851) 14 *Law Rev.* 336. See further, n. 92 to Ch. 3 below.

roughly upon the Prussian *Landsverein*. The idea was that shareholders would contribute capital to the company, which would lend it on mortgage to landowners; it would then sell 'land debentures', negotiable interest-bearing bonds, secured upon the fund of land it had acquired from the landowners. Debenture holders would not otherwise have easy access to such security, nor would they otherwise get such easy transferability; whereas landowners would know that the company would always be willing to lend, and so would apply to it before looking elsewhere. The difference between the interest rates would pay dividends to the shareholders. (The sums did work out, apparently.) Proponents of these land banks thought title registration would be advantageous, and so lent their voice to the campaign; and proponents of title registration used that support as an additional merit for their idea.

All this lobbying worked, so that by 1850 or 1851 there was opinion enough in the Commons and in the press for reform to be confidently predicted. That is not to say that all MPs were very sure what it was they were now favouring. In 1852 the committee of the Manchester Law Association reported to its members that a delegation sent to the Commons to lobby against Lord Campbell's deeds registration bill had found that

a general feeling existed . . . in favour of some plan of registration for facilitating the transfer of land, and reducing the expenses of conveyancing, yet that many were averse to the settlement of a question so grave and complicated at an advanced period of the Session, and that not a few were decidedly opposed to the centralising character of the scheme, whilst others were altogether in error or ignorance as to its objects and provisions.[94]

9. 1850: The Conveyancing Commission's Report

While the LAS busied itself advancing the frontier of conveyancing reform and educating the public in its necessity, the Conveyancing Commission itself was in a state of addled disagreement. As long ago as 1830 one member, conveyancer and law reformer

---

[94] (1851–2) 43 *Leg. O.* 248.

C. H. Bellenden Ker, had advocated deeds registration.[95] But though he still thought it essential, he now wanted it to be preceded by a general overhaul of the substantive law of real property.[96] Ker urged his plan on the Commission, but its chairman ruled that reforms of substantive law were beyond its remit.[97]

Langdale on the other hand was the one member of the Commission in favour of implementing Wilson's title registration scheme.[98] He was hoist with his own petard. The Report stated blandly that though the Commission would like to see that scheme considered, it would first need simplification of the law of titles, which was beyond the Commission's terms of reference.[99] According to Walter Coulson, another Commission member, the rest of the Commission were in fact opposed to Wilson's scheme under any circumstances. Coulson was on the way to becoming an influential man. He shortly afterwards became Home Office draughtsman, a post carrying rather more responsibility for legislation than the title implies.[100] When the next Select Committee wanted an expert to vet various plans for deeds and title registration, Coulson was their man. He had strong objections to Wilson's scheme, and in addition both he and Bellenden Ker thought it most unlikely that the landowners would accept it—indeed, Coulson did not see why they should.[101] For both the lawyer-bureaucrats on the Commission to oppose Wilson's scheme ruled it out for the time being.

With Ker's grand plan and Langdale's preference for title registration out of the way, the Commission was left with deeds

---

[95] C. H. Bellenden Ker, *The Question of Registry or No Registry Considered* (1830).

[96] See generally, *On the Reform of the Law of Real Property* (1853), esp. ch. 2. But in his *Shall we Register our Deeds?* (1853) he made the quite different argument that deeds registration was the necessary keystone without which there would be no real property reform for twenty years: pp. 18, 23.

[97] *On the Reform of the Law of Real Property* (1853), 91.

[98] Evidence of Walter Coulson to the House of Commons Select Committee on the Registration of Assurances Bill, (1852–53) HCP xxxvi. 397, qq. 959–60.

[99] Report of the Registration and Conveyancing Commission, (1850) HCP xxxii. 1.

[100] Sir Courtenay Ilbert, *Legislative Methods and Forms* (1901); (1860) 36 LT 96.

[101] House of Commons Select Committee, n. 98 above, qq. 959 ff., 986 ff., 1044: but cf. q. 1099. For Bellenden Ker see *On the Reform of the Law of Real Property* (1853), 89.

registration to consider. Here, too, it split. A majority recommended proceeding with a deeds registration scheme. They thought that since 1830 maps had become available which could be used to index the register, obviating entirely the remaining names element in Duval's scheme. His system of grouping deeds by their common root of title should be enacted with just that amendment. Francis Broderip, a solicitor, and Joseph Humphry, a conveyancer, thought that the existing tithe maps were not up to the job, that Duval's scheme could not be made to work without maps, and that therefore deeds registration should not now be recommended. It is unclear from the Report what the majority would have decided if they also had thought the maps inadequate.[102] It had taken more than three years for this report to be made.

At the time of the Commission's establishment there had been some Whig doubt that it was necessary at all: perhaps bills could simply be drafted to give effect to the House of Lords Select Committee on the Burdens on Land forthwith.[103] So in 1851 government reacted quickly to the Report by promising a bill, which was in fact introduced by Lord Campbell, then Lord Chief Justice, with government blessing. The predictable opposition from solicitors materialized, though the Manchester Law Association might have supported the principle of deeds registration if the bill had created local registries rather than just one in London.[104] Campbell, however, dismissed this as far too expensive.[105] Less expected was opposition from within the House of Lords itself, that is, from within the coven of law lords whose word on these things was usually decisive in that House. The bill was shunted into a Select Committee where the maps question was replayed, Bellenden Ker and Coulson appearing as witnesses for the Commission's conclusion, Humphry and Broderip for their dissent. This time the minority won, to the extent that the committee reluctantly agreed that the available tithe maps would not suit.[106] So they excised that part of the

---

[102] Contrast Beaumont, (1853) 124 PD (3rd ser.) 925, with Coulson and Bellenden Ker, n. 132 below and text.
[103] Henry Parris, *Constitutional Bureaucracy* (1969), 175, 177.
[104] (1851–2) 43 *Leg. O.* 248.
[105] (1851) 116 PD (3rd ser.) 1158.
[106] Ibid. 1311 ff.; Bellenden Ker, *Shall we Register our Deeds?* 4.

bill, leaving it to continue in more or less the same shape as the
Duval bill of 1830—to the great annoyance of the law societies.[107] In that form the Lords passed it, with a fair amount of
sniping at Lord Truro, the Lord Chancellor, who was held
responsible for the deletion of the mapping sections, and with
some grumbling by some of the landowners.[108] But it stood no
chance of passing the Commons. 1851 was a year of government
crisis and of interminable debates over re-establishment of
Catholic bishoprics in England. Registration of deeds and assurances would have to wait for another session.

When that session came there was a new administration and
a new Lord Chancellor, St Leonards. Since 1830 he had opposed
deeds registration,[109] so he occupied himself with Chancery
reform instead. When the next session came there was a new
administration and a new Lord Chancellor, Cranworth. In 1851
he had supported Campbell's bill, so with a grand flourish he
entered his new role of quasi-Minister of Justice by reintroducing that bill in much the same form in which it had passed
the Lords. It did so again, though this time in the teeth of
dogged opposition from St Leonards.[110] Petitions against the bill
flowed into the Commons from law societies, building societies,
and banks (perhaps more of a trickle in this case), causing it to
be referred to a Select Committee.[111] Lord John Russell wrung
his hands with anxiety lest the committee think it necessary to
receive evidence, the Commission having surely gone over all
that ground.[112] Alas for him, the committee turned itself into a
seminar on title registration and killed the bill stone dead. Two
of its eight voting members would have killed title registration
too.

[107] (1851) 42 *Leg. O.* 151, and see ibid. 24–5, 112–13, 133, 177, 213. Petitions of
landowners against the bill were duly reported in the *Legal Observer*, ibid. 94, as
support for lawyers' opposition.
[108] (1851) 116 PD (3rd ser.) 1311 ff.; 117 PD 255 ff.; and cf. (1851) 42 *Leg. O.* 73,
229.
[109] See e.g. Mrs Hardcastle, *Life of John, Lord Campbell*, i. 482.
[110] (1853) 124 PD (3rd ser.) 41 ff., 929 ff.; 126 PD 663 ff., 1223 ff.
[111] Report of the House of Commons Select Committee on the Registration of
Assurances Bill, (1852–3) HCP xxxvi. 397: the petitions are reprinted in appendix
4.
[112] (1853) 127 PD (3rd ser.) 714.

10. Epitaph for Deeds Registration

How is this sudden failure of a project long-mooted to be explained? On the face of it, the immediate causes were personal. Campbell wanted the glory because he had identified himself with deeds registration long ago.[113] But he was unfamiliar with the detailed problems, and lost time while deciding to accept amendments which a more expert promoter would have anticipated.[114] Campbell treated Truro as something of a joke, and Brougham, who was Campbell's ally on this bill, had for long belittled the man who was now Lord Chancellor. So although Truro was anyway much less of a law reformer than either of these men, one explanation for his weakening amendments in 1851, and the further delay they caused, may be that he was reacting against what he certainly saw as an attempt to rush the bill through by law lords whose acquaintance with the problems was no greater than his own, yet without involving him.[115] In 1853 there was a change of cast. Bethell, the new Solicitor-General, was a much more radical reformer than Cranworth, had an antipathy towards him, and according to Campbell hardly even tried to disguise his eagerness to 'clutch the Great Seal'.[116] Bethell attended all the Select Committee meetings and voted for the demise of Cranworth's bill, even though Cranworth was nominally his leader. John Vincent has pointed out in connection with Lord Chancellors' patronage that right into the 1860s the lawyers in Parliament operated as an enclave of *ancien régime* politics. In so far as personal factionalism was an attribute of that, his analysis can be extended into this aspect of law reform.[117] Indeed, the reformers' failure to establish a

---

[113] Mrs Hardcastle, *Life of John, Lord Campbell*, i. 494, 501, 522; ii. 30 n.

[114] These concerned the perennial problem of equitable mortgages: (1851) 117 PD (3rd ser.) 967, 1077.

[115] Mrs Hardcastle, *Life of John, Lord Campbell*, ii. 291–2; John Vincent (ed.), *Disraeli, Derby and the Conservative Party: The Political Journals of Lord Stanley, 1846–1869* (1966), 27–8; (1851) 116 PD (3rd ser.) 1312. For Truro see also (1856) 23 *Law Rev.* 349, where his antecedents as a solicitor and his lack of prowess as a law reformer are linked.

[116] Mrs Hardcastle, *Life of John, Lord Campbell*, ii. 315, 331, 336, 343 f., 357, 368; and cf. (1852–3) 45 *Leg. O.* 165.

[117] John Vincent, *The Formation of the Liberal Party 1857–1868* (1966), 45–7.

Ministry of Justice *necessarily* made the politics of private law personal.

The second factor, connected to the first, was the exclusiveness of the reformers. In the upper House the law lords provided most of the input. Some landowners did voice fears, or add general approval, but they were greatly overshadowed by the lawyers, who in some debates were the only speakers. It was as though the great men were talking among themselves, and then having reached some sort of accommodation, were relying upon their authority to browbeat a jury. At the conclusion of the Lords' debates in both 1851 and 1853 someone commented that the bill was safe to pass because it had been blessed by the whole legal establishment, with the rider in 1853 that only St Leonards stood out.[118] Bellenden Ker said the same in a pamphlet in 1853, 'only' St Leonards opposed.[119] What he meant was that of those whose opinions were entitled to carry weight, only St Leonards opposed: that is, of the law lords and the senior conveyancers, who were the only legitimate voice of law reform. The same exclusiveness pervaded his treatment of other critics. St Leonards had incorporated into one speech a letter he had received from John Greene, a solicitor in Bury St Edmunds, who had analysed 750 land transactions going through his office. He demonstrated that more than 70 per cent concerned values of less than £500, for which the legal fees had ranged between £1 and £7, exclusive of stamps. He calculated that registration of deeds would add at least £4.10s. to every bill, and cause significant delay.[120] This was the first quantitative evidence on the issue, but Bellenden Ker was not interested.[121] Since St Leonards could be labelled 'opponent' his endorsement of the letter could be discounted. Greene was too significant to answer directly, Bellenden Ker addressing only what he chose to see as his motives, not his arguments. The

---

[118] Marquis of Lansdowne, (1851) 117 PD (3rd ser.) 1137; Lord Overstone, (1853) 126 PD (3rd ser.) 1223.

[119] Bellenden Ker, *Shall we Register our Deeds?*, 6.

[120] For Greene (sometimes spelt Green) see (1853) 124 PD (3rd ser.) 956, repr. (1852–3) 45 *Leg. O.* 369. An unusually long and detailed letter in the *Solicitors' Journal* illustrates both Greene's enthusiasm for law reform and the tensions discussed so far in this book, (1859–60) 4 *Sol. Jo.* 193: for subsequent correspondence see ibid. 212, 256.

[121] *Shall we Register our Deeds?*, 6, 17–18.

thought that clients might indeed worry about their bill was not a point he needed to answer. To banks' petitions against Cranworth's bill he replied with authority rather than argument: Lord Overstone had supported it in the Lords. That Lord Overstone was to country banking practice what the Lord Chancellor was to country solicitors' practice was beside the point, no doubt.[122] Bellenden Ker could not escape quite so easily when faced with numerous petitions from building societies against the bill. This time his reaction was of patrician impatience. 'Is it to be supposed that the reform of real property law is to stop with the establishment of a registry?', he replied; if the uninformed would just wait until their betters had produced the whole package of reform, then they would see how they were to be benefited.

The *Law Review*, unofficial voice of the LAS, was inclined towards the same tone when later that year the radicals raised the issue of franchise reform:

The friends of Law Amendment considering that the cause to which their energies are devoted is the most important of all subjects within the cognizance either of the political philosopher or the practical politician, naturally feel no little anxiety at the announcement of a new plan of Parliamentary Reform.[123]

It was not just that their own concerns would be squeezed out for lack of time, but also that the experience of 1832 did not show that franchise reform improved the quality of MPs. It would be much better to eliminate corruption at elections, so that the Commons could begin to rival the Lords as a law-reforming chamber, or a Ministry of Justice be instituted to entrench the process of Law Reform. Lord Campbell, always anxious to blame someone else for the failure of his bill, wrote:

It is a curious fact that the Lords have become more rational and more liberal on all subjects of law reform than the Commons. That House is now infested with lawyers. It was said that the Reform Bill would exclude them altogether, but their number has since trebled, and they are no longer the quiet, silent nominees of borough proprietors. Nowadays they have numerous constituents whose prejudices they must try to flatter; and they hope for the office of Attorney General or

---

[122] For Overstone see *DNB*.   [123] (1853–4) 19 *Law Rev.* 94.

Solicitor General by obtaining notoriety in proposing bad Bills or opposing good ones.[124]

Campbell was deluding himself. While the veterans of the 1830s refought the causes of their youth in the comfortable belief that having reached the pinnacle of their profession they could at last put Lord Eldon to flight,[125] the next generation in the Commons was intent on bypassing them by espousing title registration instead. But Campbell and the *Law Review* were right to this extent, that the Commons was a rougher place than the Lords, one where law reform would not be treated as the private preserve of the Inns of Court. Indeed, opposition to Cranworth's bill first surfaced there not through the ubiquitous petitions from law societies but when John Bright complained that deeds registration threatened harm to Manchester building societies, which had done so much to develop his city.[126] As a country solicitor had written in opposition to Campbell's bill in 1851:

No doubt the advocates of the measure are high in influence, potent and persevering; but on behalf of small proprietors in general, and my poorer clients in particular, I hope and trust that we may still be able to congratulate ourselves, and to say,—thank God there is a House of Commons![127]

This solicitor believed that 'whatever doubts and difficulties may occur to the imagination of an acute and practised convey-ancer, the proprietors of land have no such feelings of insecurity [of title] as is represented to exist'. Walter Coulson also doubted that 'we in London' were fair judges of the complexity of the great bulk of titles.[128] Similarly, public reception of the Satisfied Terms Act changed Joshua Williams's opinion on what was important in real property law:

the saving of expense to the generality of purchasers seems greatly to counterbalance the inconvenience to which the very small minority

---

[124] Mrs Hardcastle, *Life of John, Lord Campbell*, ii. 343.

[125] For an explicit example see Brougham, (1845) 80 PD (3rd ser.) 497.

[126] (1853) 127 PD (3rd ser.) 714.

[127] [J. Moore], *Observations on the Proposed Registration of Deeds, with Reference more particularly to the Pamphlet of William Hazlitt, Esq., by a Country Solicitor* (1851), 18.

[128] Evidence to the House of Commons Select Committee on the Registration of Assurances Bill, (1852–2) HCP xxxvi. 397, q. 1096.

may be put . . . The public generally require that the expense of legal transactions shall be lessened, whilst they appear very little anxious that titles should be made secure. It is notorious that in sales by auction, conditions to accept defective titles have very little effect in deterring purchasers. These considerations seem to affect the question of a general registry of deeds, and to render it doubtful whether the increased certainty of title which the registry would confer in a few cases, would counterbalance the increase of expense to which every transaction, even the smallest, would inevitably be subject.[129]

Deeds registration had been devised by élite conveyancers as an aid to their sort of work.[130] Whatever other benefits were adduced in its favour were mere buttresses to a scheme that was not in fact based upon the needs of practical businessmen. Given a forum in which the latter's views could be heard it would be vulnerable to charges that it would make business more difficult—which is exactly what the petitions against the bill did say. Belated responses to the outside world were made. Bellenden Ker published a paper demonstrating how registration fees could be made much less than those charged by the existing Middlesex and Yorkshire registries.[131] Fees in Cranworth's bill were tapered, especially benefiting transactions worth less than £200. But neither stemmed the petitions. Just as the LAS democratized theoretical law reform, so the reformed House of Commons undermined whatever personal authority the law lords may have had on legal matters.

Advocates of deeds registration were not helped by the promoters of title registration's choice of an exactly opposite starting-point for their argument—that title was in the great bulk of cases perfectly secure. Further, and curiously, the support that Bellenden Ker and Coulson gave to the Commission's recommendations tended to be accompanied by doubts that weakened its case. By 1853 each had said in public that a map-based index was essential to the registry's working, notwithstanding that those excised clauses from Campbell's bill

---

[129] Joshua Williams, *Principles of the Law of Real Property* (3rd edn. 1852) 342; resiling from ibid. (2nd edn. 1849), 396 ff.

[130] Cf. Bellenden Ker, *On the Reform of the Law of Real Property*, 19: 'such then is the duty of the counsel who has to advise . . .'.

[131] C. H. Bellenden Ker, Letter to the Lord Chancellor on the Cost of Registration of Assurances, (1852–3) HLP xxv. 687; repr. (1853) 46 *Leg. O.* 63, 171, 196.

had not been restored.[132] The difference between them and the dissentients on the Commission was that whereas the latter believed that without maps the registry would fail, Coulson and Bellenden Ker believed that once a registry was established its imminent failure would prompt production of the required maps. Moreover, concern about the cost of deeds registration stimulated an argument that struck at its very heart. A conveyancer, J. Thomas Humphry, wrote that by identifying indexation of the register as the problem, and in devising solutions to make for easy searching, reformers from Duval onwards had created corresponding problems for the people who were to do the registering.[133] Indexation by root of title required judicial judgment in each case, he argued (note again the typical conveyancer's assumption of complexity). Yet calculations of the cost of registration and of the time needed for each transaction assumed that it would be a simple clerical task like indexation by name. A Bellenden Ker would be unimpressed by this argument, indeed Ker himself publicly conceded that Duval's scheme was too complicated—in the very same pamphlet that advocated its acceptance.[134] But that was because he thought the best approach was to appoint a Registrar who would then make whatever binding rules he thought necessary.[135] However, such an expansion of the administrative state was anathema to a man like Truro, one of whose objections to Campbell's bill had been that rule-making belonged in Parliament (that is to say, with him and his ilk) and not with appointed officials (to wit, Bellenden Ker and *his* ilk).[136]

[132] Bellenden Ker, *Shall we Register our Deeds?*, 11; Coulson, Evidence to the House of Commons Select Committee on the Registration of Assurances Bill, (1852–3) HCP xxxvi, 397, q. 1007.

[133] Joseph Thomas Humphry. *The Registration of Assurances Bill: Its Peculiar System and Practical Consequences Considered* (1853). It was cited with approval by the 1857 Registration of Title Commission, (1857, 2nd session) HCP xxi. 245, 266 and by his colleague William Hayes in his reply to the Select Committee on the Registration of Assurances Bill, (1852–3) HCP xxxvi, 397, appendix. See also the replies of Thomas Jarman and J. H. Christie, ibid. This Humphry is not the J. Humphry who dissented from the Report of the 1850 Commission.

[134] Bellenden Ker, *Shall we Register our Deeds?*, 12.

[135] Ibid.; and Bellenden Ker, *On the Reform of the Law of Real Property*, 45, 62.

[136] (1851) 116 PD (3rd ser.) 1312; cf. G. J. Johnson's description of a later bill as one 'to create an office of Land Registry and to confer on such office powers to construct a system to facilitate the transfer of land, subject to such directions (if any) as are herein contained', (1870–1) 15 *Sol. Jo.* 159. For Johnson see n. 124 to Ch. 3 below.

In truth, the Select Committee paid hardly any attention to deeds registration. At its first meeting it agreed a set of four questions it should address, as though it had all the time in the world, the first of which was whether title registration offered advantages over and above facilitating the transfer of land.[137] While the Conveyancing Commission had been deliberating, and in the three years since its Report, schemes for title registration had proliferated. In addition to the two versions of Wilson's scheme, James Stewart had one, W. Strickland Cookson had presented one to the LAS, and there was an outline by another active LAS member, the barrister Edward Webster.[138] Cookson together with his M&PLA colleagues Edwin Field and William Williams briefed conveyancer John Bullar to draft heads of a title registration bill, which they then presented to the Select Committee.[139] It turned out to lie somewhere between Cookson's own scheme and Wilson Mark I. Further, the Select Committee also had before it two bills introduced into the Commons. One was limited to Ireland, drafted by Irish barrister Vincent Scully, MP, the other was sponsored again by Henry Drummond, this time in conjunction with LAS member and active property-law reformer, Thomas Headlam, QC, MP.[140] It was again rather a curious bill, scarcely more than a fragment, and perhaps meant only to keep the question alive, but it was none the less a signal that deeds registration had had its day. In fact Cranworth's bill itself was more than a simple deeds registration bill, since by providing that beneficiaries under trusts would lose their interests on a transfer unless protected

---

[137] Report of the Select Committee on the Registration of Assurances Bill, (1852–3) HCP xxxvi. 397.

[138] Wilson, *Outlines*; Stewart, (1847–8) 7 *Law Rev.* 154, and *On the Means of Facilitating the Transfer of Land*; Cookson, (1852) 16 *Law Rev.* 361, (1852) 44 *Leg. O.* 348; and see Edward Webster's LAS paper, (1857–8) 2 *Sol. Jo.* 649. He was influential in the LAS at this time, see e.g. (1857–8) 2 *Sol. Jo.* 447, 649; (1858) 3 *Sol. Jo.* 395.

[139] See Report of the House of Commons Select Committee on the Registration of Assurances Bill, (1852–3) HCP xxxvi. 397, q. 678 and appendices 1 and 3.

[140] Scully's bill is reprinted in *Occupying Ownership: Ireland*, ed. V. Scully the younger (1881), and his evidence is at Report of the Select Committee, (1852–3) HCP xxxvi. 397, qq. 858 ff. For Scully see further below, pp. 91, 112 n, and his *The Irish Land Question, with Practical Plans for an Improved Land Tenure and a New Land System* (1851), and *Mutual Land Societies: Their Present Position and Future Prospects* (1851). For the Drummond/Headlam bill see (1853) HCP vi. 65.

in some way on the register, it had reversed the usual rules of notice and thus altered the substantive law. This enabled critics to say that if the substantive law were to be altered by a registration scheme, then it should be by a registration scheme that gave real advantages.[141] That these advantages might extend beyond issues of land transfer is shown by the Select Committee's first question, and by the presence among its members of Vincent Scully, who was to become the most active proponent of land debenture schemes.

There was far too much for the Select Committee to tackle in the time available. It heard Cookson, Field, and Williams, who gave rather different versions of their scheme;[142] it called in Walter Coulson for his verdict—unfavourable on everything; it appended Bullar's heads of a title registration bill; it reprinted the numerous petitions against Cranworth's bill; it reported that the principle of title registration was sound; and it recommended that a Commission be established to settle the details. And that is what happened.[143] The Commission had a membership of twelve. It included five of the six Select Committee members who had voted for its establishment, including Scully, but neither of the two dissenters. In addition Headlam, Cookson, and Robert Wilson himself were members. There was obviously no intention of reopening any question of principle.

[141] (1854) 20 *Leg. O.* 142.

[142] (1852–3) HCP xxxvi. 397: Cookson, qq. 1 ff.; Field, qq. 222 ff.; Williams, q. 285 ff.

[143] Royal Commission on Registration of Title, appointed 18 Jan. 1854; Report (1857, 2nd session) HCP xxi. 245.

3

Title Registration Achieved

1. Concepts and Problems

With the 1853 Report, as it happened, deeds registration was doomed. Even Lord Cranworth acknowledged as much in due course. Its theory was good, he thought, but its consequences for small transactions were unacceptable.[1] For a good long time any brave reformer raising the issue would be met with derision.[2] It had turned out to have only a specialist appeal, offering experts an improved mechanism for assessing complex titles at the probable cost of imposing additional expenses on ordinary practitioners in run of the mill transactions. Title registration claimed immunity from this defect; it would bring benefits across the board. Yet its principle was still far from being accepted either in Parliament or outside. The Report of the 1853 Select Committee and the backing of the subsequent Commission was only a beginning. Title registration was still an untested idea based on a priori assumptions about the way in which land transactions worked. Whether facts would form a more obliging fit than they had done for deeds registration remained to be seen.

Broadly speaking, and with every benefit of hindsight, three sorts of issue had to be resolved. They interlocked, their ramifications changed over time, and not all were given equal attention at any one time. First, a complex cost/benefit analysis had to conclude that registration was needed and worthwhile. Secondly, the proper role of the state in land transactions had

---

[1] (1862) 165 PD (3rd ser.) 898.

[2] e.g. Cairns, (1859) 152 PD (3rd ser.) 298. Edward Thomas Wakefield tried with his *The Feasibility of Constructing a New System of Registering Title Deeds* (1853), but in a long debate the LAS finally rejected his proposals: (1857–8) 2 *Sol. Jo.* 447, 689; see also ibid. 812, (1858) 3 *Sol. Jo.* 395.

to be delimited. Thirdly, a choice had to be made as to what
type of registration system was to be enacted.

(*a*) *Costs and benefits outlined.*   Most obviously, monetary costs
to landowners needed estimating both for initial registration
and for subsequent dealings. These would vary with the type
of system under consideration, as different systems offered
different sorts of registration and made different provisions for
subsequent dealings. They would also depend upon the role of
the state, which might subsidize costs in various ways. For
there to be a demonstrable saving, present costs also needed to
be calculated and a comparison made. Similar questions could
be asked about transaction speeds.

Landowners might face less tangible costs—loss of privacy
for example, greater scope for state intervention in their affairs.
Or should that be seen as a benefit to society? Similarly, and
again depending upon the type of scheme in issue, landowners'
freedom to shape their land transactions according to their own
fancy might be curtailed. Would this happen? Would it be a
cost or a benefit?

Then there was the issue of indirect costs, particularly to
solicitors. The assumption in these early years was that registered conveyancing would operate within their conveyancing
monopoly. But even so, since solicitors had a margin of profit,
or at least an allowable charge, on each particle of the conveyancing process, to streamline that process might cause monetary
loss. How big a loss, or even how big a profit, turned again
upon the contours of the particular scheme in issue, and also
on whether the introduction of the new system generated new
business. Some law societies thought it would, so that the books
would at least balance. They also hoped that *ad valorem* scales
would change the basis of charge, change also the residue of
their former image as semi-trustworthy tradesmen. Or perhaps
the way forward lay through freedom of contract with their
clients?[3]

On the other hand, some solicitors were quick to cry 'plunder'
from the very beginning. In the early years they found little

---

[3] See above, Ch. 2, sect. 6, and (1864) 8 *Sol. Jo.* 963, 980, 991, 994; (1864–5) 9
Sol. Jo. 277, 414, 812; (1866) 10 *Sol. Jo.* 815; (1869) 14 *Sol. Jo.* 12, 30, 349, 397; (1870)
15 *Sol. Jo.* 82; (1871–2) 16 *Sol. Jo.* 201; (1873) 18 *Sol. Jo.* 1, 64, 84, 324.

response in the formal arguments of their law societies, most of which were unwilling to take a public stance against progress for fear of losing the very respectability they craved. Further, the argument was first put in terms which presupposed a notion of professionalism that was contestable, that to be a solicitor was to hold an office, rather than being to engage in an occupation. Proof lay in the heavy taxation paid by solicitors in the form of stamp duty upon their articles of clerkship and in the cost of the certificate they had to buy annually to allow them to practise. Analogies were drawn with the holders of other judicial offices which had been abolished or seriously undermined by statutory change, where compensation had been paid by the state.[4] But law societies in the mid-century were engaged in long and determined efforts to abolish these imposts,[5] so at this time the 'dispossession' argument was made only by individual solicitors, not by law societies. For it to be taken up officially, as it were, would need changes both to professional organization and to the perception of professionalism itself.

(b) *The role of the state.* At the mundane level the argument was about money. Should the state subsidize fees directly? Should it do so indirectly, by requiring only that the registry recoup its actual expenditure, ignoring overheads such as the cost of the building or the making of maps, if the register were to be based on maps? Should it risk loss by creating district registries, in the hope of stimulating business? Should it risk loss by allowing indefeasible titles to be guaranteed against the Consolidated Fund in return for an insurance premium? Was it *proper* for the state to act as an insurance company, or should that function be left to private capital?

These issues turned in part on the answer to deeper questions. What was registration for? Was it just a facility for private owners, for which they should be expected to pay in full? Only recently, in the 1840s, had the principle been accepted that courts of law should be funded by the state through salaries, with suitors paying just part of the running costs through fees.

---

[4] e.g. (1858–9) 3 *Sol. Jo.* 293; cf. (1873–4) 56 *LT* 250, 453.
[5] Harry Kirk, *Portrait of a Profession* (1976), 132 ff., but see 209. (1860–1) 36 *LT* 53; (1861) 6 *Sol. Jo.* 501, 796; (1864–5) 9 *Sol. Jo.* 495, 498, 505, 536, 572, 637, 643, 673, 699, 749.

When Lord St Leonards reiterated this principle in 1852 he was careful to exclude Chancery's estate management function. That was a private matter, for which full costs should be charged.[6] Is that how registration should be seen? Or is there a state interest in smoothing the path for private owners? That might turn on what the alternatives are, a question of high politics. Alternatively, perhaps the state itself might find uses for registration, as an adjunct to taxation policy perhaps, or for land use planning purposes, or maybe just as an aid in gathering agricultural or population statistics? If so, then two sorts of conclusion might follow. First, that the state might justifiably carry some of the costs; secondly, that the state might justifiably impose on landowners whatever restrictions on their freedom of choice were necessary to make registration work—or not, according to one's politics.

Then there were issues of staffing and patronage. Who would have power of appointment to these new posts? To whom would registrars be responsible? What mix of functions was it constitutionally proper for them to have? These were difficult questions: constitutional bureaucracy was in its childhood. Were the posts to be judicial? In 1851 there had been a public squabble in the Lords between Campbell, Brougham, and Lyndhurst concerning appointments under Campbell's deeds registration bill, the underlying issue being whether and how the Lord Chancellor's patronage over minor judicial posts should be immunized from Treasury control. Was this a model for title registration? A decade later Westbury's use of patronage under his own (be it noted) Bankruptcy Act quickly caused rumour and criticism, while his Conservative counterpart, Lord Chelmsford, was not much better.[7] Both these men were proponents of title registration, so the issue was important.[8] It brought Westbury's downfall in 1865. Further, if the Lord Chancellor had the patronage, whether or not under Treasury

---

[6] (1852) 123 PD (3rd ser.) 170–1. For the general principle see Lord Langdale's evidence to the Select Committee on Fees in Courts of Law and Equity, (1847–8) HCP xv, q. 1473.

[7] Westbury: J. B. Atlay, *The Victorian Chancellors* (1908), ii ch. 12, 13. Chelmsford: e.g. (1858–9) 3 *Sol. Jo.* 261; (1859) 33 *LT* 49; (1860–1) 4 *Sol. Jo.* 511.

[8] See e.g. (1859–60) 4 *Sol. Jo.* 66, 179; (1862) 167 PD (3rd ser.) 1108.

control, would he use it to advance just barristers or would solicitors too be eligible?

Just as title registration raised issues of the nature of professionalism, so too it was inextricably involved with questions about state power and administrative organization.

(c) *Types of title registration.* Assuming, as its proponents originally did, that registration was part of private law, with no state interest other than the perfection of private law, then, still, what exactly was the function of registration? Was the aim to provide a system for subsequent dealings, with initial registration just an embarrassingly difficult first step? Or was the initial registration the real point, a sort of cleansing of title, a declaration of soundness, such that a landowner could get his title cleared by the registrar and then deal with it by non-registered transactions if he wished? Perhaps this turned on what one thought the problem was: repetitive examination of the root of title on the one hand, complicated settlements and mortgages on the other. It would matter to the cost/benefit equation though, since the essence of registered dealings was that they used standard short-form documents, with consequential threats to solicitors' emoluments. If, however, a trip to the registrar served only to clear away accumulated debris from the title, with the option thereafter of conducting transactions in the traditional way, perhaps nobody would lose by the innovation?

Does registration necessitate guaranteed titles? Or does one register whatever one has, leaving it to purchasers' private legal advisers to assess its legal worth? The cost/benefit equation will vary greatly with the answer, as will questions about types and levels of staffing in registries. If titles are guaranteed, who should guarantee them? Is there a risk of loss? It might seem that after years of preaching that titles were so insecure that deeds registration was essential, reformers would hesitate to tell the state and the insurance business that the risks were low enough for even small premiums to bring them a reasonable profit. Not so, because all of a sudden someone unearthed a new source of quantitative evidence. Railway companies had been acquiring numerous pockets of land for their lines, sidings, rolling-yards, and stations, providing thereby a sort of national sample of land titles, chosen solely by geographical distribution.

By the early 1860s the common estimate was that they had dealt in a million titles. Sometimes they used voluntary dealing, more often a form of compulsory purchase. But either way they were vulnerable to claims from owners of hidden interests whom they had failed to compensate. Yet wealthy though railway companies were thought to be, claims had been exceedingly few, perhaps only a dozen or so. Once this point had been made it was never disputed, though the conclusions drawn from it varied somewhat.[9]

Was registration to affect the substantive law? What powers, for example, should registered proprietors have? Whatever powers their particular title-deeds gave them? A set of standard powers applicable to all proprietors? That would mean some overreaching powers, presumably. Would they just be available to registered proprietors, or was this proposition one for general law reform? Would the powers be mandatory, or could one contract out of them? Put the other way about, was registration to abolish just constructive notice, or express notice as well? Or perhaps only those landowners whose powers had not been curtailed by their particular title-deeds would be eligible for registration? Similarly, would registration alter the mechanics of intestate succession? Would the heir need to register before coming into his inheritance? How would the registrar know he was the heir? Should land devolve instead through an administrator or real representative? If so, was this proposed just for registered land or generally?

Finally, depending upon the model of registration chosen and the reason for choosing it, the question of compulsion arose.

2. 1857: The Royal Commission's Report

The Commission reported in 1857.[10] From the treasury of schemes proposed to them the Commissioners had found

---

[9] Westbury, (1862) 165 PD (3rd ser.) 351 at 365; used by E. P. Wolstenholme, 'Simplification of Title to Land: An Outline of a Plan' (1862), in *Papers read before the Juridical Society*, ii (1862), 533, 534. The originator may have been James Stewart, see e.g. (1845–6) 3 *Law Rev.* 183 at 190.

[10] Report of the Commission on the Registration of Title with Reference to the Sale and Transfer of Land, (1857, 2nd session) HCP xxi. 245 (hereinafter referred to as 1857 *Report*).

common ground enough for ten of the eleven active members to sign the Report—the twelfth had been appointed to the bench in the meantime. The dissentient was Robert Wilson, whose booklet had begun the saga in 1844. He seems to have dissented because he regarded his own proposal as an integrated whole, so that the Report's acceptance of many of his substantive propositions did not reconcile him to its rejection of his machinery. But there were also three notes of partial dissent appended to the Report, including two from law-reforming MPs whose efforts on the 1853 Select Committee had led to the Commission's establishment. These were Thomas Headlam and Vincent Scully, each of whom had proposed a scheme to the Commission which, when rejected, they kept alive by this form of qualified dissent. The tally of lawyers on the Commission thus read: for the Report, without reservation: Bethell, Lewis, and Cookson; for the Report, but with important reservations: Headlam and Scully; against the Report (though in broad sympathy with much of its substance): Wilson.

The Commission's most important choices are best seen through what was rejected. Scully's proposal to create a Landed Estates Court modelled on the Irish experience fell because it misdiagnosed the problem. In Ireland perhaps complexity of title and accumulation of debt were so serious that the right solution was to let a court provide a fresh start, certifying a clear title which registration would then keep uncluttered. But in England neither debt nor complexity was the issue, only repetitive re-examination of title. Another element in Scully's plan, that for land debentures, seemed to the Commission to involve a monopolistic scheme, depriving landowners of existing choices. So it too fell, as did the Cookson/Bullar draft bill of 1853 which would have reduced registered proprietors' transaction powers below those presently available. The Commission rejected that bill for the further reason that it did not allow for registration of mortgaged land. A good registration scheme needed a wider ambit than that. Such was provided by Wilson's scheme, but the Commission could not accept the statism inherent in his notion of parochial visitation to inquire into title, which they also thought had the vice of making registration compulsory in practice. Wilson's reliance on compulsory public mapping made his scheme too expensive, they thought, and since the existing public maps were inadequate there would be too long a delay before his system became operative. Besides, to require adjudication on boundaries would provoke dispute and litigation, which was also a reason for rejecting the idea that registered titles necessarily be unimpeachable. On the other hand they saw advantages in a guaranteed title, that is, one that used a state insurance scheme to compensate for losses caused by registration. Even this element of statism was too much for Thomas Headlam, who dissented on principle from the proposition that it was proper for the state to enter into an insurance contract with one citizen to the possible detriment of another, or to enter into pecuniary arrangements of a speculative nature.

The approved machinery thus called only for a registrar, who would offer guaranteed titles after investigation by an approved conveyancer, and who would also allow the registration of possessory titles along the Cookson lines. Guaranteed titles would be insured on the Consolidated Fund, in return for a premium paid into it. All would be voluntary. The registry would be in London; but persuaded that a central registrar would have difficulty in ascertaining boundaries, they recommended also that there be branch offices in the localities. They concluded with strong criticism of the existing system of solicitors' remuneration, an unequivocal recognition of solicitors' importance and responsibility under their proposed scheme, and a call for the introduction of an *ad valorem* scale.

So much for machinery. What about the substance of registration? The Commission's major assumption was that title registration was a private law matter, designed to provide improved facilities for present and future patterns of land transaction within the present law. It should not make more difficult any common form of transaction currently in use, nor, save in a few specified cases, should it alter the substantive law. Given that it is obvious that fees simple should be registrable, how were lesser estates, leases, mortgages, and trusts to be treated consistently with the Commission's major premiss while yet resulting in a practicable system? At this point the Commissioners had to grapple with title registration's greatest intellectual challenge, though they did not do so explicitly. *Deeds* registration could be projected as simply adjectival law, a means whereby the substantive law would work as it was meant to.

Registration of deeds made no judgment about their effect, or their meaning; whatever transactions people had devised, all that registration did was ensure that they were not hidden from successors with a legitimate interest in the state of the title. It was unclear whether title registration could do just that, or whether the very classification of its registers, the arrangement of its stop notices and its binding notices, what it included and what it omitted, what it allowed to be registered and what merely noted, did not project a particular perception of what real property law was, how it typically operated, and how it ought to work.

The Commission solved this problem by looking to the actual operation of the present law: to the law in action, not to the law in books. A proposed registration system inconsistent with the latter but consistent with the former would not involve changing the law, since such a change would already have been achieved by tacit consensus among the conveyancers, whose common practice in the matter was authoritative. In this they followed the proponents of deeds registration (who, of course, were doing no more than declaring themselves to be authoritative, since proponents of deeds registration tended to come from the ranks of the declarators of best practice), who had met the same issue when considering the treatment of beneficiaries under trusts. Book law provided that beneficiaries could remain passive, reliant on the doctrine of notice to protect them against third parties, whereas even deeds registration schemes required them to be active to the extent of registering the documents under which they claimed. Save under the purest 'mirror of title' schemes, title registration demanded more, requiring at least the registration of caveats. Sometimes title registration proposals went further, requiring registration of equitable estates, or ordaining that beneficiaries must appear in response to advertisements by a proprietor with a registered possessory title now intending to upgrade it. Reformers had always replied that the law in action should be the yardstick, and they had equally no hesitation in asserting what that was. The Report of the Commission of 1850 summarizes their position:

There is a large class of arrangements under which land is vested in trustees . . . and provisions are studiously framed for rendering it unnecessary that purchasers, mortgagees and others dealing with the trustees should be concerned to see the circumstances under which the trust is to be performed. The result . . . is convenient to a purchaser, because he obtains a clearer and a simpler title; but as the advantage to the purchaser is not the motive which leads to the adoption of these expedients by the parties interested in the estates to be sold, their frequent adoption is evidence that they are convenient to the parties as well as to the purchaser.[11]

There was therefore no need for a registration scheme to give greater protection to beneficiaries than settlors habitually did, whatever the general law might say. The conclusion was usually butressed by the observation that although the doctrine of notice applied in theory to trusts of personalty, since there was no equivalent in practice of the rules concerning constructive notice beneficiaries were in fact reliant upon the honesty of their trustees. Yet this did not stop donors settling vast sums of money on such trusts, nor had lawyers developed mechanisms giving any greater protection to beneficiaries. These common-places among reformers[12] were adopted by the 1857 Commissioners, though it should be noted that there was no quantitative evidence for the supposed practices concerning trusts of land.

It followed that there should be no substantive registration for interests under trusts, which, the Commission concluded, would anyway be a bad thing because it would reintroduce the discredited regime of deeds registration and clog the register in no time. On the face of it, then, beneficiaries would be sacrificed to the general efficiency of the register, one of very few changes to the general law proposed.[13] But it was merely a nominal change, for the reasons described above. Besides, some protection would be available. Beneficiaries could lodge caveats to prevent transactions behind their back, and where beneficiaries were under a legal disability a court could issue an injunction or inhibition against dealings. Further, the system would provide that if an estate was registered in the name of several trustees the rule of survivorship would not apply, so the risk of fraud would be much reduced by avoiding the possibility of the land's coming into the hands of a sole trustee. If settlors wished to

---

[11] (1850) HCP xxxii, *Report*, para. 30.
[12] e.g. (1857) 1 *Sol. Jo.* 886.
[13] Perhaps their only major proposal was to institute real representatives.

cling to settlements creating successive legal estates instead of vesting the fee simple in trustees they would have to forgo the benefits of registration.

One Commissioner, Thomas Headlam, urged that this system be extended to all derivative interests, that a sale of a registered title should overreach *all* interests created or arising after registration, of whatever sort. Caveats alone would provide for their protection. The Commission passed this by without comment. For registration to confer its maximum possible benefits, and for it to facilitate all common and useful transactions, in addition to the register of proprietorship there would be a parallel register for leases and charges.

The effect would be that after registration the 'registered ownership will represent the fee simple', which, with the exception of charges and leases, 'will not thereafter be capable of subdivision or modification into particular or limited estates or interests'.[14] Trusts would either be overreached on a sale or, through the mechanisms outlined above, would prevent a sale altogether. A few interests would bind the title notwithstanding lack of registration: leases in possession, for example, which could best be ascertained on the spot, and whose title 'is generally so independent of the documentary title to the property that they necessarily form a partial exception'.[15] Most of these substantive provisions can be traced without difficulty back to Wilson's original pamphlet or to Cookson's later modifications of it. Two draft bills from Commission member W. D. Lewis were appended to show how the scheme would look in detail.[16] Once again it will seem familiar to students of our modern land registration system.

3. 1859: The Commission Confounded

By no effort of imagination could the Registration Commission be described as neutral. It was a pressure group purely and

---

[14] *1857 Report*, para. 35.

[15] Ibid., para. 36.

[16] Lewis died shortly afterwards. For him see above, pp. 15, 38, and (1860–1) 36 *LT* 149, (1860–1) 5 *Sol. Jo.* 247. He is credited with having written the report (together with Spencer Walpole), (1858–9) 32 *LT* 59.

simply. Its achievement lay in producing a scheme around which reformers could cohere, though Wilson's refusal to sign the report was meant to keep his alternative open, as were the politically more adept partial dissents of Headlam and Scully. So even the measure of agreement achieved by the Commission had its price. Further, one reason why that agreement had been possible lay in the homogeneous nature of the Commissioners, all sharing an intellectual commitment to the cause, with the lawyers among them drawn from narrow segments near the top of their respective branches of the profession. There were other intellectual strands among real property law reformers, which offered alternative visions of the future ignored by the Commission. A conveyancing barrister, E. N. Ayrton, for example, had proposed a system whereby private deeds would be abbreviated and all legal owners given wide overreaching powers.[17] This would obviate registration, he thought.

The élite lawyers influential in the political parties were unconvinced. They preferred Scully's diagnosis that complication of title was the evil to be addressed. Bethell was an exception, but then he had signed the Report. As Attorney-General he quickly drafted a bill along its lines, but in a neat reversal of their roles earlier in the decade he was blocked by his Lord Chancellor, Lord Cranworth.[18] When the Lords reassembled in February 1858 it was to hear Cranworth dissociating himself from the Commission's recommendations.[19] There would be no registry, the Irish Encumbered Estates Court was instead to provide the inspiration for reform. Owners wishing to clear their titles of accumulated tangles of doubt and subordinate interests could henceforward ask Chancery to sort it all out for them and issue a certificate of clear title. Then the government fell. Cranworth's bill was lost in the Commons,[20] and the Conservatives promised reforms more akin to the Commission's.[21] In 1859 their Solicitor-General, the Irishman

[17] 1857 *Report*, 503–6, 586–94; and cf. 'Title Books versus Title Deeds; or Public Registration of Titles superseded', (1858) 5 *Law Mag. & Law Rev.* 67. There is a short obituary of Ayrton at (1873–4) 56 *LT* 134.

[18] (1857–8) 2 *Sol. Jo.* 300; (1857–8) 148 PD (3rd ser.) 758.

[19] (1857–8) 148 PD (3rd ser.) 807; (1858) 149 PD (3rd ser.) 559.

[20] It had passed the Lords by 13 votes to 12: (1858) 150 PD (3rd ser.) 418 (Land Transfer Bill).

[21] Lord Chelmsford, (1858) 149 PD (3rd ser.) 570.

Hugh Cairns, introduced companion bills into the Commons.[22] They were not what was expected. The first instituted in England a Landed Estates Court with power to clear away accumulated complexity by awarding certified indefeasible titles, much as Cranworth's bill had done, but through the medium of a new court. The second established a registry in which those titles, but only those titles, might be registered if the owner wished. This second bill adopted the Commission's model for registration, enabling Cairns to claim at least partial fidelity to its Report. In truth it was far different, since the Commission had denied that complication of title was the problem, and Cairns in turn had rejected its plan for registration of possessory titles.

None the less his scheme attracted support from the middle ground of both parties and would have passed had this government not fallen too. Even so there was opposition, which was significant enough in the long run for it to be worth recording and analysing. Voicing an opinion shared with other conveyancing barristers, Richard Malins MP thought the emphasis on certification and indefeasibility futile: landowners confident of their titles would see no need for certification, those doubtful would not take the risk of rejection; there would be a court with nothing to declare and a registry with nothing to register.[23] This is what the reformist lawyer-bureaucrats Walter Coulson and C. H. Bellenden Ker had argued a decade earlier,[24] but now the usual response was only amused condescension.[25] In Parliament, solicitors aside,[26] only Lord John Russell, from the Liberal benches, supported Malins, and on grounds that indicate a second possible line of opposition: expense.[27] He thought it wrong to create a new court for which no demand had yet been proved. Since compensation would have to be paid to its judges and officers if it had to be wound up for lack of business, it would be better to try the jurisdiction experimentally in an

---

[22] Title to Landed Estates Bill, Registry of Landed Estates Bill, (1859, 1st session) HCP i; (1859) 152 PD (3rd ser.) 277, 153 PD (3rd ser.) 95.

[23] (1859) 153 PD (3rd ser.) 95.

[24] See above, Ch. 2, sect. 9.

[25] Walpole, (1859) 153 PD (3rd ser.) 109; Cardwell, ibid. 137.

[26] Bowyer, ibid. 104; Hadfield, ibid. 107.

[27] Ibid. 120.

existing court at first. His argument was diametrically opposed to the third line of opposition, pressed most strongly by solicitors outside Parliament and brought into it through their petitions and in the speeches of sympathetic members, that a fair and workable registration system required local registries for its operation, whereas Cairns had provided for just the one, in London.

Assessment of professional reaction from outside Parliament is clearly necessary, but it is problematic. There were several petitions to Parliament, to which we shall return. First we must consider the evidence of lawyers' activity to be found extensively in the pages of the professional press, which operated both to marshall support for opposition and also as a source of record. The problem is that the journals had become riven by personal antagonism, in which attitudes to title registration played a significant part. Their hostilities affected issues of professional organization beyond the immediate question of Cairns's bill, contributing indirectly to events as far distant as 1875. We must digress—and, besides, it is a good story. It starts in the early fifties when the *Law Times*, which regarded itself as the tribune of provincial solicitors, and the more narrowly London-oriented *Legal Observer* had shared a cautious pessimism towards title registration.[28] Their cosy relationship, however, was shattered in 1856 by the relaunching of the *Legal Observer* as the *Solicitors' Journal*, in direct rivalry to the *Law Times*. The newcomer generally favoured title registration; the *Law Times* became stridently opposed.

The seed of the new journal was sown at an M&PLA meeting in 1854 when Mr Hope Shaw, the Leeds solicitor prominent in founding the organization, suggested that solicitors could best combat the unfair and hostile treatment they received from the national press by establishing their own newspaper.[29] To a sceptical reply in the *Law Times* he responded that he had also in mind the need to reinvigorate and expand the solicitors'

---

[28] e.g. (1853) 21 *LT* 217; (1852–3) 45 *Leg. O.* 313; (1854) 48 *Leg. O.* 2, 4; (1854) 49 *Leg. O.* 2.

[29] (1854) 49 *Leg. O.* 1, 4, 14; (1854–5) 24 *LT* 57, 74. The question had been raised with the M&PLA in 1852, (1852) 44 *Leg. O.* 118. (For Hope Shaw see n. 132 to Ch. 1 above.)

professional press.[30] Two years later a Law Newspaper Company Ltd. announced its intention of launching the *Solicitors' Journal*. The *Law Times*, it said, tended too much to favour the bar at the expense of solicitors, and provincial solicitors at the expense of London. A new voice was needed to 'impress upon the attorneys and solicitors throughout England and Wales, that they all belong to one common body, having one common interest, one common character, and therefore all ought to unite to support that body, to promote that interest, and to elevate that character'.[31] Mr E. W. Cox, proprietor and editor of the *Law Times* responded angrily and with a sense of betrayal.[32] He was a man of wide publishing, writing, and business interests, something of a public figure, an energetic man who combined readiness to investigate any business opportunity himself with a touch of paranoia against anyone moving into his own territory.[33] Here the threat was very serious, and it was to the journal which was essential to his persona. Though he was a barrister he had once been a provincial solicitor himself,[34] and knew the problems and aspirations of provincial practitioners. Through the *Law Times* he had helped found solicitors' insurance companies, he had helped fight off challenges to solicitors' work from barristers and from armies of unqualified accountants, estate agents, and others, he had campaigned to improve standards, to set higher entrance requirements, to reduce fraud, and he had used his journal to help found the M&PLA itself, from which this attack on his very being now came. And it was an attack that hid behind the cowardly form of a limited liability company, an innovation thoroughly immoral.[35]

[30] (1854) 49 *Leg. O.* 14.

[31] (1857–8) 2 *Sol. Jo.* 312.

[32] See, for just a start, (1856–7) 28 *LT* 118, 125, 173, 182, 197, 238 . . .

[33] For Cox see *DNB* and Raymond Cocks, *Foundations of the Modern Bar* (1983), esp. ch. 3. The additional information is from (1857–8) 30 *LT* 161, (1859) 33 *LT* 145, 150; (1860–1) 36 *LT* 366, 373. He recorded his own professional progress assiduously, e.g. (1860–1) 36 *LT* 461; (1861) 37 *LT* 69, 370; (1869–70) 48 *LT* 377, 407, 427, 442; and he reprinted in his journal the papers he gave to the Jurisprudence section of the Social Science Association, e.g. (1871) 51 *LT* 440, continued at 52 *LT* 4.

[34] (1856–7) 28 *LT* 182.

[35] (1856–7) 28 *LT* 175; cf. (1857–8) 30 *LT* 29, 70, 103. But see his earlier proposal for a Solicitors Co. Ltd. to fight off 'encroachers': (1855–6) 26 *LT* 230, 267; (1856) 27 *LT* 79.

How, he asked, had it happened? Closer investigation revealed to him a plot.[36] The directors were solicitors from the big London agency houses, to whom provincial solicitors sent their work when something needed doing in London. They had infiltrated the M&PLA and perverted it to their private purpose. Their purpose? The name of one of them supplied the clue: he was W. S. Cookson; with him were Edwin Field and William Williams, law reformers all. Their purpose was obvious: to advance the cause of title registration with which Cookson was so prominently connected, to institute a London registry, and thereby capture the bulk of the entire country's conveyancing. The M&PLA was to be their base, the *Solicitors' Journal* their vehicle for propaganda. The survival of his journal and opposition to title registration became fused in his mind. For the next three years the *Law Times* poured out diatribes against Cookson and all his works, and against limited liability companies in general.[37]

The thesis looked plausible, especially to those who did not read the *Solicitors' Journal* or could not check through a local society the factual allegations Cox made. The *Solicitors' Journal* did advocate title registration, though never as energetically as Cox said it did, nor did it advocate a centralized system as he implied that it did, nor, for that matter, did Cookson himself.[38] Nor did they advocate compulsion, though Cox brushed that aside with the claim that once a registry was established compulsion was bound to follow.[39] The overlap between the directors of the company and the London members of the management committee of the M&PLA looked suspicious, though it was actually as consistent with the stated aims of the

[36] (1856–7) 28 *LT* 133, 175; (1857) 29 *LT* 42, 58, 70; (1857–8) 30 *LT* 3, 133, 139, 252, 257 . . .; and, especially, (1858) 31 *LT* 1.

[37] e.g. (1857) 29 *LT* 42; (1858) 31 *LT* 1; (1859) 33 *LT* 1; and, for limited liability companies, e.g. (1857–8) 30 *LT* 29, 70, 103; (1860–1) 37 *LT* 317.

[38] See e.g. (1858) 31 *LT* 18; (1858–9) 32 *LT* 253; (1858) 3 *Sol. Jo.* 241, 281, and cf. 341, 373.

[39] (1859) 33 *LT* 1. The *Solicitors' Journal* was unenthusiastic about the rival Torrens system, (1858) 2 *Sol. Jo.* 885, though see also (1861) 5 *Sol. Jo.* 121, 196; (1861–2) 6 *Sol. Jo.* 110. It is an indication of how strongly title registration was tied to individual and professional advancement in England that for all Robert Torrens's articles and lectures there was never more than the slightest possibility that his system would be adopted in England or Ireland.

new journal as it was with a self-interested plot.[40] None the less, their manipulation of some of the M&PLA's meetings gave colour to Cox's accusation.[41] If these men had joined the M&PLA as recently as Cox claimed, the charge of infiltration might have had some substance, but that was not the case—at least, not as applied to the men whom Cox expressly named.[42] However, some of the law societies' representatives at the M&PLA meeting in 1854 regarded the subsequent development of the plan for a journal as wholly out of keeping with what had then been mooted, and thought the attack on the *Law Times* quite unwarranted.[43] They forced an offer of resignation from William Shaen, who was secretary to both the M&PLA and the Law Newspaper Company Ltd. When that was refused they withdrew from the M&PLA, a particularly serious blow in the case of Hull, which had hitherto been a stronghold. This was of course fully reported in the *Law Times*.[44]

So taking an avowedly sectional approach to the issue,[45] the *Law Times* set out systematically to destroy title registration. The Commission's Report was subjected to damning analysis, week after week. Papers and reports in favour of title registration were either answered point by point or went unnoticed.[46] Country solicitors were urged to prepare for a life or death struggle, to use their power as party election agents to vet candidates at the General Elections of 1857 and 1859, to lobby,

[40] (1856–7) 28 *LT* 175; (1857) 29 *LT* 70; (1858) 31 *LT* 118; (1857–8) 2 *Sol. Jo.* 618, 671, 766.

[41] (1859) 33 *LT* 25.

[42] The *Law List* records membership of the M&PLA by the men accused by Cox. W. S. Cookson, T. H. Bower, H. Lake, and E. W. Field were members in 1850; F. H. Janson joined in 1853 and W. Trinder in 1856; W. Williams seems never to have joined. Cookson's interest in general law reform continued throughout this period, e.g. (1858–9) 4 *Sol. Jo.* 64, 126.

[43] (1857–8) 30 *LT* 161, 205, 212; (1858) 31 *LT* 118; (1857–8) 2 *Sol. Jo.* 134.

[44] (1858) 31 *LT* 118, 165; (1857–8) 2 *Sol. Jo.* 671. For Shaen see n. 129 to Ch. 1 above. He was associated with Cookson in at least one religious endeavour, Henry Solly, *These Eighty Years*, ii. 337–8.

[45] (1856–7) 28 *LT* 209.

[46] See e.g. the treatment of a report by Liverpool LS, (1859) 33 *LT* 13, 51, and by contrast Bristol (not party to the plot), ibid. 67; letter from 'H', (1860–1) 36 *LT* 213, 222. The *LT* printed E. T. Wakefield's paper against title registration (n. 2 above), but not the contrary argument by E. Webster. The *Sol. Jo.* published only Webster, (1857–8) 2 *Sol. Jo.* 649. Only the *Sol. Jo.* reported that the LAS had decided for Webster against Wakefield, (1857–8) 2 *Sol. Jo.* 447, 689, 812. See also (1858) 31 *LT* 25.

to petition, to write—and so on.[47] Meanwhile the *Solicitors'*
Journal praised the Report's general tenor, gave prominence to
the papers and reports ignored by the *Law Times*, and, while
never wholly suppressing the doubts and criticisms voiced by
some solicitors, did what it could to play down divisions
between London and provincial practitioners.[48] It did not
report, for example, a bitter meeting of leading solicitors at
Fendall's Hotel, Westminster, in April 1859, which had concluded against the Cairns bill then pending.[49] But a year or so
later it reported in detail a meeting of the Metropolitan and
Provincial Law Association at which, though irreconcilable
differences of opinion about registration were apparent, the
main protagonists agreed that the split was not between city
and country, and that to that extent the ghost of the Fendall's
meeting had been laid.[50] In turn the *Law Times* did not report
that later meeting; except when urging its dissolution it was
boycotting what it pointedly called the 'Metropolitan *etc* Law
Association'.[51]

The war did not last. Cox had the *Law Times Reports* as part of
his armoury.[52] He improved them still further, pegged the
price, and expanded his journal with ever more sections for
specialist interests. The *Solicitors' Journal* followed suit, but the
Weekly Reporter, which its parent company bought and amal-
gamated with the journal,[53] was a weak competitor. In 1861[54]
the Law Newspaper Company Ltd., heavily in debt to its

---

[47] (1858) 31 *LT* 105, 117; (1859) 33 *LT* 61, 74. See generally (1857–8) 30 *LT* 149;
(1858–9) 32 *LT* 241, 253, 265; (1859) 33 *LT* 49, 85; (1860–1) 36 *LT* 173.

[48] See n. 46 above; and (1857) 1 *Sol. Jo.* 49, 69, 77, 345, 386, 641, 661, 741, 886;
(1858–9) 3 *Sol. Jo.* 341, 373; (1859–60) 4 *Sol. Jo.* 42. It fiercely opposed registration
unaccompanied by change in the fee structure, (1858–9) 3 *Sol. Jo.* 241.

[49] (1859) 33 *LT* 33.

[50] (1859–60) 4 *Sol. Jo.* 263.

[51] (1857–8) 30 *LT* 69; (1858) 31 *LT* 105, 165; (1858–9) 32 *LT* 57; (1859) 33 *LT* 25;
(1859–60) 34 *LT* 37; (1860–1) 36 *LT* 306, 569. Cox had linked Liverpool, Leeds,
and Manchester to the plot, (1857–8) 30 *LT* 3, 222, 234. The brevity of the *LT*
reports of M&PLA meetings (e.g. (1859–60) 34 *LT* 67, 77; (1860) 35 *LT* 350)
deprived its readers of the wide range of papers on registration read at them.
They were reported in the *Sol. Jo.*, especially at (1859–60) 4 *Sol. Jo.* 66, 86, 183,
263.

[52] (1859–60) 34 *LT* 1, 69; (1860–1) 36 *LT* 25.

[53] (1858–9) 3 *Sol. Jo.* 321.

[54] For what follows see (1861) 37 *LT* 69, 89, 106, 125, 150, 161, 185, 193, 197,
205, 209, 241; (1861–2) 6 *Sol. Jo.* 81, 101, 121, 151, 231, 266, 267, 313, 353.

printers, had reached the end of its paid-up capital. Cox made a bid for the title, was rebuffed, and claimed outrage when it was secretly sold to the printers by the directors, though he gloried in the failure of the Cookson interest. Retrospective approval was sought from the shareholders, but a hostile winding-up action had first to be fended off before the company went into voluntary liquidation. An allegation that the petitioner in the hostile action was a man of straw acting on Cox's behalf seems to have been believed by the judge, but though Cox retaliated with a promise to lay a criminal information against those responsible for the claim, nothing came of it. The *Solicitors' Journal* continued under new ownership, eventually taking over from the *Law Times* as a forum for professional opinion of all shades and as the major source of reporting of professional reports, meetings, and debates. Cox, however, lost his antagonism to it;[55] he had been threatened by the big guns of the city and he had won. He even had a trophy to show for his victory, as in the midst of the battle the 'solicitors of England and Wales' had presented him with an expensive piece of silver, engraved in recognition of all his services for them.[56]

What effect then did Cox's campaign have? His readers were kept in partial ignorance by his selective reporting, as were the *Solicitors' Journal*'s from its side. But for all Cox's vehemence and for all the *Solicitors' Journal*'s self-interest, the letters from country solicitors to the professional press showed exactly the same range of opinion[57] that existed in all other groups of lawyers, from rejection of the very idea of registration through

---

[55] But see (1862–3) 7 *Sol. Jo.* 777; the libel action concerning the *Weekly Reporter* and the *Law Times*, (1863–4) 8 *Sol. Jo.* 41; and the delightful contretemps over Cox's Inns of Court Hotel Company Limited (!), (1862–3) 7 *Sol. Jo.* 561, 579, 617, 713; (1864–5) 9 *Sol. Jo.* 108.

[56] (1858–9) 32 *LT* 205.

[57] *Law Times*, e.g.: (1857) 29 *LT* 114, 157, 213, 237; (1857–8) 30 *LT* 103, 127, 169, 199, 212; (1858–9) 32 *LT* 270, 278, 294; (1859) 33 *LT* 17; (1860–1) 36 *LT* 213.

Solicitors' Journal e.g.: (1857–8) 2 *Sol. Jo.* 12; (1858–9) 3 *Sol. Jo.* 293, 314, 326; (1859–60) 4 *Sol. Jo.* 193, 212, 256; (1861–2) 6 *Sol. Jo.* 419; and see n. 48 above.

LAS: (1857–8) 30 *LT* 338; (1858) 31 *LT* 25; (1857–8) 2 *Sol. Jo.* 447, 649, 689, 812.

Juridical Society: Wolstenholme, 'Simplification of Title to Land'; Joshua Williams, 'On the True Remedies for the Evils which Affect the Transfer of Land', in *Papers read before the Juridical Society*, ii (1862), 589 (lampooned at (1861) 37 *LT* 576). When the *Sol. Jo.* reprinted these papers only Williams's drew comment, (1861–2) 6 *Sol. Jo.* 362, 502.

to acceptance of its need, mooting the same variants on the registration theme and the same range of alternative reforms to real property law that appear in the workings of the LAS, the Juridical Society, and in the papers presented to the Commission and the Select Committee before it. Similarly, papers given to M&PLA meetings, and replies to questionnaires issued by that organization or the ILS show agreement on most issues to have been impossible.[58] This is no different from the barristers, and no different from the situation as reported in the LAS annual report for 1858.[59] Cox's silver piece signifies something, of course, as does his weakening of the M&PLA. Total provincial membership, and its distribution, had been fluctuating in the preceding years, but it is probable that there had been a gentle increase in membership among solicitors away from the big population centres of the North and the Midlands. This increase stopped, going into a decline from which it never recovered. Hull was lost to it, Sheffield also. Membership in some smaller provincial centres disappeared, such as Taunton; but not, for example, Worcester or Wakefield or York. Birmingham's membership did not expand as one might have expected. The big centres, however—Leeds, Liverpool, and Manchester— were scarcely affected.[60] The M&PLA management committee

[58] Papers: (1859–60) 4 *Sol. Jo.* 66, 86, 183, 263.
Meetings and questionnaires: (1857–8) 2 *Sol. Jo.* 134, 240, 280, 326; (1858–9) 3 *Sol. Jo.* 341, 373, 960; (1857–8) 30 *LT* 227, 279; (1859) 33 *LT* 25.

[59] (1857–8) 2 *Sol. Jo.* 812.

[60] The *Law List* identifies adherents to the M&PLA and to the ILS. It is probably not wholly accurate, and I have not systematically combed it for solicitors entered under two or more different addresses, though I think that they are few. The numbers following are therefore approximate.
In 1856 572 provincial solicitors were listed as M&PLA members, of whom 155 had left it by 1861. Its total provincial membership declined to 492 in 1861, and to 427 in 1871. It had been 589 in 1853.
The aggregate membership for Leeds, Liverpool, and Manchester was: 1853: 172 (plus 39 at Hull); 1856: 146; 1861: 158; 1871: 172, of which Manchester had 99. By 1871 the M&PLA was virtually the northern equivalent of the ILS, which had only 43 members in these three cities, an improvement from the 15 it had had in 1861. ILS rural membership increased greatly during that decade. Birmingham was mixed:

1853	16 M&PLA,	8 ILS (some belonged to both)
1856	25 M&PLA,	10 ILS (some belonged to both)
1861	27 M&PLA,	16 ILS (some belonged to both)
1871	27 M&PLA,	20 ILS (some belonged to both)

For Birmingham and Hull's role in the foundation of the *Sol. Jo.* see (1857–8) 30 *LT* 161; (1858) 31 *LT* 118.

itself tended to support title registration, but weakened by Cox's onslaught took only a neutral view on most of Cairns's bill.[61] Yet as a means of forestalling title registration, the withdrawal of country members from the M&PLA as advocated by Cox was bound to fail. Whether or not the cause was that they were dominated by commercial lawyers rather than conveyancers,[62] the fact was that the big regional law societies took much the same pragmatic line towards title registration as did the *Solicitors' Journal*.[63] There were probably only about another dozen active local law societies in the whole country,[64] including those already listed, so country solicitors leaving the M&PLA had nowhere else to go. Even if they believed with Cox that the ILS had become more sympathetic to provincial needs, it was clear even to him that attempts to translate that sympathy into seats for provincial practitioners on the ILS council were still being rebuffed by the old guard, and that the only men who might one day force the door open were the Edwin Fields and John Hope Shaws against whom he had sworn enmity.[65] Thus although it is possible that Cox succeeded in generating a latent hostility to the concept of title registration among country practitioners, they had few outlets in which to express it. All that was left to them, individual action aside, was the oldest and least effective of political tools, the ad hoc petition to the Commons praying that a bill should not pass.[66]

These petitions, however, which were numerous, showed a pragmatism lacking in Cox's writing, focusing on the crux of their economic grievance: that Cairns's bills should not pass

---

[61] (1857–8) 2 *Sol. Jo.* 134; (1858–9) 3 *Sol. Jo.* 341, 373, 960; (1859) 33 *LT* 25. Hope Shaw himself retained a residual Yorkshire loyalty to deeds registration, (1859–60) 4 *Sol. Jo.* 263.

[62] (1857–8) 30 *LT* 133.

[63] Manchester: (1859) 33 *LT* 8; (1858–9) 3 *Sol. Jo.* 373; (1859–60) 4 *Sol. Jo.* 262. Liverpool: (1857–8) 30 *LT* 218, 222; (1859) 33 *LT* 13, 51. Bristol: (1859) 33 *LT* 67.

[64] Perhaps an underestimate: (1873–4) 18 *Sol. Jo.* 67. The problem is in identifying the continuously active societies from the nominal.

[65] See (1857–8) 30 *LT* 69; (1858) 31 *LT* 117; (1860–1) 36 *LT* 569; (1861) 37 *LT* 47, 70, 93; and cf. (1862–3) 7 *Sol. Jo.* 630, 638, 653. Further, the Manchester LA, a dominant voice in the M&PLA, actively supported provincial causes dear to the *LT*'s heart, e.g. local Probate registries—(1860–1) 36 *LT* 426, 495; cf. (1860–1) 5 *Sol. Jo.* 609.

[66] e.g. (1859) 33 *LT* 25, 38, 85, 141. But see also ibid. 74, for other political activity.

unless district registries were created. As district probate registries had recently been established, as the country had been divided into regions for the purposes of bankruptcy administration, and as every county court came equipped with a county court registry, this demand could not have seemed unreasonable, especially as it was consistent with the Commission's Report and was supported by the LAS.[67] It was easily justified by reference to clients' probable costs, practical difficulties in searching registers at a distance, and the need to make a voluntary scheme attractive if the experiment were to work. To this the *Solicitors' Journal* added a demand that the bills should not pass unless accompanied by an *ad valorem* scale of remuneration,[68] since for Parliament to insist upon payment by length of document and then to abolish that length was a gross unfairness—an argument that in due course Bethell accepted in principle.[69] The question of local registries, however, was not tested in Parliament, the government falling before that tabled amendment was reached.

Lawyers outside Parliament also agreed in regretting that Cairns's bill, unlike earlier proposals for substantial change to real property law and procedure, had not been circulated for professional review nor even sent out privately to a conveyancing expert for scrutiny.[70] One result was that the bill suffered almost continual amendment as it moved through its parliamentary stages, giving an impression that government was pushing the measure through without proper thought for what it was doing. A somewhat intemperate reformer blasted the Lord Chancellor for abandoning disinterested consensual law reform: 'we have, in fact, been experiencing the evils of a government too weak and incapable to adopt or institute any useful or

[67] (1858–9) 3 *Sol. Jo.* 395; (1859) 7 *Law Mag. & Law Rev.* 387.

[68] (1858–9) 3 *Sol. Jo.* 241; cf. (1861–2) 6 *Sol. Jo.* 353.

[69] Bethell's original scheme was weakened in passage, (1861–2) 6 *Sol. Jo.* 661, becoming merely the permissive section 131 of the Transfer of Land Act 1862. For continuation of the general issue see Westbury's Attorneys and Solicitors Bill 1864, 176 PD (3rd ser.) 5, (1863–4) 8 *Sol. Jo.* 667, 675, 691, 707, 721; and for M&PLA involvement, ibid. 980, 991, 994; Westbury again, (1864–5) 9 *Sol. Jo.* 34, 57, 227; M&PLA again, (1865–6) 10 *Sol. Jo.* 815.

[70] (1859) 7 *Law Mag. & Law Rev.* 187; A. B., *A Letter to the Solicitor-General on the Landed Estates Bill* (1859), repr. (1859) 33 *LT* 22; and cf., later, Liverpool LS, (1870–1) 15 *Sol. Jo.* 42.

practical measures themselves, but strong enough to barricade to others the proper avenues to legislative reform.'[71] Yet such was the heat that Cox had fanned, generating rhetoric in what were otherwise quite moderate and balanced reports from law societies,[72] which seemed to think that unless they matched his flamboyant language they would be letting their members down, that one anonymous barrister, said to have the most extensive conveyancing practice in the kingdom, felt unable to develop his criticisms or to even declare his identity when writing to Lord Cairns. 'Opposition to your bills,' he wrote, 'will be attributed to ignorance, or prejudice, or self-interest; never to the motive, which yet exists in many minds—an honest doubt whether they are not likely to produce more harm than benefit to the community.'[73] To test the validity of solicitors' fears, and to disarm their opposition for the future, he suggested a trial of the scheme in Middlesex, where it was bound to do some good if only by replacing the worse than useless deeds registry.[74] Such a modest suggestion was quite out of keeping with the benefits claimed for registration by its proposers.

4. Bethell Triumphant

Palmerston's new administration had no place for Cranworth, finally discredited by his Attorney-General.[75] But to Bethell's surprise nor was he to be Lord Chancellor, that place instead being filled by the veteran law reformer Lord Campbell. According to Campbell the Cabinet was unreceptive to ambitious plans for law reform.[76] At his urging the Queen's speech in 1860 did contain some general promises, but he did not think that they would come to much, nor did they. Expense was a major hurdle. The Treasury was unwilling to pay for professional help in the preparation of the necessary legislation; Bethell's pro-

---

[71] (1859) 7 *Law Mag. & Law Rev.* 187—and note the account of the sinking by the Treasury of St Leonards' bills concerning crown debts and succession duty.

[72] Manchester, (1859) 33 *LT* 8; Bristol, ibid. 67.

[73] A. B., *A Letter to the Solicitor-General*; (1859) 7 *Law Mag. & Law Rev.* 187.

[74] Cf. letter, (1857) 1 *Sol. Jo.* 386; Bristol LS, (1859) 33 *LT* 67.

[75] See Mrs Hardcastle, *Life of John, Lord Campbell* (1881), ii. 315, 331, 326, 343, 357, 368.

[76] Ibid. 375, 390, 398; but cf. ibid. 381, where Bethell is blamed.

posed chief judgeship in bankruptcy, a central part of his major
bankruptcy law reform, fell because of its cost; his plan to
compensate redundant bankruptcy officials for loss of office
was vetoed by his own party.[77]

In June 1861 Campbell died, Bethell at last achieving the rank
of Lord Chancellor. He wasted no more time. When Parliament
assembled in February 1862 Lord Westbury, as he had become,
finally introduced his long-promised Transfer of Land Bill. It
came as rather a shock, turning out to be not at all what the
Commission had recommended, so detailed and so ambitious
that even the staunchest advocates of title registration had
doubts that it would work. Seeing his chance Cranworth
relaunched a version of his previous proposal. It again
eschewed registration and used Chancery to purify complex
titles, but this time he took one more step, using the resultant
Chancery certificate as a private record of title on which all
further dealings with the land would have to be noted in order
to be valid. This would obviate the need for a purchaser to
inspect the underlying deeds. Not wanting to be left out, Lord
Chelmsford threw revised versions of Cairns's bills back into
the ring as well. As the journals acidly remarked, there was
now to be a competition for law reform between the noble
lords.[78]

In due course the whole lot was referred to a Select Committee, from which only Westbury's and Cranworth's bills
returned.[79] Chelmsford's were dropped, since their registration
provisions were incompatible with Westbury's. The difference
was fundamental. Chelmsford followed the Commission's
scheme, going back ultimately to Wilson, though much modified by Cookson, that saw title as a unitary thing, protection for
most subordinate interests being achieved through notices and
caveats. Only a few subordinate interests, long leases for
example, would qualify for separate noting on subsidiary regis-

[77] For the issues see (1861) 161 PD (3rd ser.) 499–513; and cf. (1860) 35 LT 181,
217.
[78] (1862) 13 *Law Mag. & Law Rev.* 357; Liverpool LS, (1861–2) 6 *Sol. Jo.* 669; cf.
(1860–2) 6 *Sol. Jo.* 288, 576.
[79] (1862) HLP xxix. Westbury: Transfer of Land Bill; Cranworth: Declaration
of Title Bill, Security of Purchasers Bill; Chelmsford: Title to Landed Estates Bill,
Registry of Landed Estates Bill; St Leonards: Real Property (Title of Purchasers)
Bill.

ters. The scheme would involve use of trustees with overreaching powers in many cases, though not in as many as in some of the other proposals made to the Commission. It was essentially a balance between the ambitious overreaching schemes proposed in their different ways by Ayrton and Headlam on the one hand,[80] and a register built upon the principle of a mirror of title on the other. It was this latter principle that Westbury adopted.

Westbury was a determined law reformer, but his innovations were procedural rather than substantive—both the divorce reforms of 1857 and bankruptcy reform, for example. Similarly with his later schemes: consolidation, codification, and statute law revision are aimed at changing the nature of the legal system without thereby altering much law, as he said himself in an address to the Juridical Society in 1870.[81] So it was with land titles. For Westbury, title meant simply evidence: evidence which proved entitlement to an interest.[82] Cookson's scheme was doubly flawed in his eyes. It provided the benefits of registered transfer for only some sorts of interest rather than all, and it introduced a fictitious and imaginary ownership of the land simply for the purpose of registration, leaving the real ownership to the system of caveats and notices. This was unacceptable because it altered the underlying substantive law. Such indeed had been a criticism of Cairns's bill in 1859, that since it would give certified title only where an applicant had been in possession of the fee simple for five years, owners of land in settlement would be ineligible for the benefit unless they first recast their settlements to take effect behind trusts.[83] This would upset the devices perfected by conveyancers for the benefit of the landed classes over a long period, and would involve practical difficulty in finding sufficient trustees to do the job, and then in getting them to rubber stamp the day-to-day transactions conducted by the life tenant. His own system therefore enabled the precise mirroring of whatever structure of interests existed in particular land, with substantive registration

[80] See above, pp. 95, 96.
[81] (1869–70) 14 *Sol. Jo.* 473.
[82] (1862) 165 PD (3rd ser.) 351.
[83] e.g. meeting of solicitors at Fendall's Hotel, Apr. 1859, (1859) 33 *LT* 33; cf. Bristol LS, ibid. 67.

for all interests and separate registers for mortgages and encumbrances. He followed the Commission in allowing two sorts of registration, the one for possessory titles, the other for guaranteed. The latter would be insured on the Consolidated Fund, in return for a small premium paid into it. The Registrar would investigate title, using Examiners of Titles if needed, but could refer difficult cases to Chancery, which could appoint a conveyancer to do the work if necessary. There would be just a central registry at first, and the Lord Chancellor would have power to prescribe solicitors' fees, on the *ad valorem* principle.

Critics likened Westbury's plan to registration of deeds.[84] If interests created by trusts and settlements were to have substantive registration, then all the necessary deeds would have to be lodged with the Registrar, to be investigated by him at length. Westbury claimed that what would be registered would be the title created by the deeds, that this would not involve copying the contents of deeds on to the register, and that after title had been registered the deeds themselves would be of no legal interest. His opponents doubted that the contents of deeds could be so simply erased. They preferred the Commission's simpler scheme, for all that it changed the book law.[85] Further there was a cumbrousness to the reliance on Chancery evident in both Westbury's and Cranworth's bills. Chancery was not expert in conveyancing, hence the Conservatives' preference for a Landed Estates Court, which would have a conveyancer at its head. But if registration were to be of the mirror variety, then much of the Registrar's work would involve trusts, which very much was Chancery business—hence the complicated provisions in Westbury's bill. Finally, there was the question of cost. Here at least Westbury was on reasonably firm ground, since he proposed creating only one new institution, whereas the Conservatives wanted two. But there was to be considerable argument about staffing and salary levels, and in the event Westbury had to jettison the insurance scheme because of

---

[84] St Leonards, (1862) 165 PD (3rd ser.) 366; Chelmsford, ibid. 903; Cairns, (1862) 167 PD (3rd ser.) 245; and cf. (1861) 37 *LT* 224, 241.

[85] (1862) 13 *Law Mag. & Law Rev.* 357; M&PLA and Bristol LS, (1861) 37 *LT* 298; ILS, (1861–2) 6 *Sol. Jo.* 635; Liverpool, ibid. 669. There was general criticism of Westbury for excluding the profession from the drafting and then forcing the measure through by party strength.

Treasury objections. In consequence the procedure for establishing a guaranteed title had to be very painstaking, thus slow and costly, and the standard to be reached, Chancery's 'marketable' title, one that many reformers had already warned was unattainably high.

Cranworth's and Westbury's bills went down to the Commons, where in thin Houses the lawyers retrod the ground.[86] Most of the problems that were to become so familiar over the next fifty years were canvassed. There would be difficulty in settling boundaries—Westbury, of course, had had to accept that no national map was available, and even if it were someone would have to adjudicate upon disputes. Registration might seem optional for a landowner, but it would become a matter of compulsory defence for his neighbours, for adverse claimants, and for holders of subordinate interests when the application for a registered title was made. It would cost too much. The stipulated qualifications and status of the registry officials were overdone. A bureaucratic registry should not have judicial powers, nor quite so many rule-making powers. It might be better to make a long bill even longer by including the detailed rules in it. All these were questions that did not go away. So too out of Parliament, where Cassandra Malins would have felt less isolated than in the chamber. Barristers wrote pamphlets favouring this scheme or that. Law societies' subcommittees reported that they preferred the Commission's scheme, but that if Westbury's it must be, then amendments should be urged.[87] There was virtually none of the opposition aroused by Cairns's bills in 1859. The law journals and law societies saw Westbury as offering Rolls-Royce registration—a wonderfully complete thing, but so far beyond the reach of ordinary clients that it could scarcely be opposed.[88] In the event Westbury's bill was pushed through by use of government influence, Cranworth got his Declaration of Title Act but lost its companion, the Security of Purchasers bill that would have allowed a skeleton certificate of title to develop into a private register of trans-

---

[86] (1862) 167 PD (3rd ser.) 238, 637, 1106.

[87] See n. 85 above.

[88] (1861) 37 *LT* 349, 456; and cf. 557—contrast (1861–2) 6 *Sol. Jo.* 519, which was, however, passive. In the end the *Solicitors' Journal* preferred Cranworth's dual scheme of certification and endorsed deeds, ibid. 576.

actions for each particular estate. Westbury thought that incompatible with the trend towards state registration.

5. 1871: Bethell Dethroned

Cassandra was right. Westbury's path was a dead end. The inquest was established in 1868, owing something to Cairns's brief return to office as Lord Chancellor and something also to loud complaints from solicitors about the inefficiencies and high charges of the Middlesex Deeds Registry.[89] These origins explain why the Commission of Inquiry was mostly a narrowly based committee of legal experts; mostly, but not entirely— there was a Treasury interest too.[90] From October 1862 to January 1868 there had been only 507 applications for first registration, of which about half had by then been granted.[91] The fees received totalled about £4,800, of which £500 had been paid directly to the Treasury by the Land Securities Company for use of Registry services under the Mortgage Debentures Act.[92] On the assumption that these are net fees, not subject to deductions for fees payable to examiners of title or for expenses incurred in mapping, the Registry had recovered in five years just about its bill for one year's salaries: £650 for two clerks, £2,500 for Registrar Follett, and £1,500 for Assistant Registrar Holt. Colonel Leach, who did the mapping, came free. His salary fell on the Tithe Commissioners' payroll.[93] The Liberal barrister Osborne Morgan's gibe that the weeds in the Registry courtyard grew as high as a man, making it as desolate a

[89] (1863–4) 8 *Sol. Jo.* 667; (1866–7) 11 *Sol. Jo.* 458, 702, 1022; (1867) 186 PD (3rd ser.) 1872; (1867) 188 PD (3rd ser.) 80; (1868) 191 PD (3rd ser.) 1146.

[90] Noted by the M&PLA, (1870–1) 15 *Sol. Jo.* 9.

[91] (1867–8) HLP xxi. 207.

[92] Mortgage Debentures Act 1865, 28 & 29 Vict., c. 78; (1865) 177 PD (3rd ser.) 262; 179 PD 719. The Act was not based on Scully's principles, see 177 PD 272, and for earlier discussion and debate: (1863–4) 8 *Sol. Jo.* 149, 184; (1864–5) 9 *Sol. Jo.* 408, 974; (1864) 174 PD (3rd ser.) 1594; 175 PD 1048, 1053, 1706. For the first meeting of the Land Securities Co. see (1864–5) 9 *Sol. Jo.* 912.

[93] Figures: (*a*) fees: (1864) HLP xxiii. 389; (1865) HLP xvii. 323; (1866) HLP xii. 641, (1867–8) HLP xxi. 207; (*b*) salaries: (1863) HCP xlviii. 309; Leach, in Royal Commission on the Operation of the Land Transfer Act and . . . the Registry of Deeds for the County of Middlesex Report, (1870) HCP xviii. 595 (hereinafter referred to as 1870 *Report*), qq. 62–7.

property as any that had ever fallen into the clutches of Chancery,[94] was tolerably accurate. Indeed, in the long run, and entirely unintentionally, Holt's appointment may have been Westbury's greatest contribution to the history of title registration, not because of the man, but because the Treasury never forgot how Westbury had insisted upon his untrammelled right to appoint an assistant before the need was shown.[95] As a symbol of Treasury determination to block this hole in the public purse the Chancellor of the Exchequer himself was added to the membership of the Royal Commission of 1868–70, which was charged with investigating the failure of Westbury's Act and with making recommendations for the future of registration generally.[96]

The Commission's first task was easily accomplished. Contrary to Westbury's own defensive posturing the solicitors were not to blame for landowners' virtual boycott of the registry; instead, as had always been predicted by everyone except Westbury, the fault lay in the Act's very construction. In offering indefeasible titles without an insurance fund, Westbury had been driven to stipulate that Chancery's 'marketable title' standard be proved in each case. This requirement of a 60-year root of title and the absence of even hypothetical blemishes was fanciful, since 40- or even 20-year titles were commonly regarded as being wholly safe. And special conditions of sale habitually prevented purchasers from raising the sort of arcane doubts that were meat and drink to Lincoln's Inn practice. Further, Westbury's stipulation that indefeasible titles were to come with defined boundaries had been a disaster. The notice-giving procedure was cumbersome, and many landowners shied away from it simply because they feared that their neighbours would be bound to react by raising objections, quite likely resulting in litigation. The Commission concluded that the supposed benefits of the Act could be bought only with a delay, trouble, and expense far in excess of the normal experience of an ordinary sale. Finally, while admitting that the Act had been operative for too short a period for there to be much

[94] (1874) 220 PD (3rd ser.) 1246.
[95] Second Report of the Select Committee on Civil Service Expenditure, (1873) HCP xvii, qq. 2334 ff., esp. 2341.
[96] 1870 *Report.*

evidence on the question, the Commission pronounced emphatically against the very idea of a mirror of title register:

> Some again feel that there is little use in obtaining a clear title at great expense, when it is not to be kept clear, but is to be loaded with the record of every subsequent transaction. . . . Our opinion is, that whatever may be the case with respect to transfers effected immediately after registration, the burden of entering on the register all subsequent transactions will be found to be very great, and that titles will thereby become as much involved as before.[97]

The solution? A return to the principles of the 1857 Commission, using the Cairns bills of 1859 as a model—or, at least, the registration part of them, since by a majority the Commission recommended against a Landed Estates Court.

The perception this committee of lawyers had of the value of registration dictated both the rejection of Westbury's Act and the adoption of the 1857 Report. It was that registration is a private law boon to those owners of land who see their land as an item of commerce: no more. The question then became one of identifying their needs:

> If people want cheapness and speed [which was the Commission's article of faith], and we offer them expense and delay, they will reject the offer, though it be accompanied with the most ample security. If men are content with good title, why should we force them to take and pay for indefeasible ones? If they are content with parcels imperfectly described or defined, why should we compel them to take perfection at a cost of money, time and trouble? To these questions we find no satisfactory answer.[98]

This perspective indicated a relatively modest job for registration:

> The problem is, not to find a perfect system of land transfer, recording with mathematical accuracy the nature and extent of the land and every interest in it, so that the record shall absolutely dispose with the necessity of ordinary examination and inquiries, but to find a system, which not impairing the present security of owners or purchasers, and not exonerating a purchaser from the easy and obvious task of looking at the outward and visible state of the property, and making inquiry of the persons in outward and visible possession of it, shall enable the

---

[97] 1870 *Report*, paras. 35, 57.   [98] Ibid., para. 63.

legal ownership to be readily passed from hand to hand, and dispense with the necessity of inquiring after invisible equities and interests whose only evidence is contained in private documents.[99]

Perhaps this is less modest than it looks. The use of the word 'present' indicates the Commission's acceptance of contemporary devices immunizing purchasers from beneficial interests, and its rejection of Westbury's condemnation of the 1857 recommendations as a scheme of 'fictitious' ownership. So,

> when we speak of 'absolute ownership' or 'fee simple', we do not mean that the Act of Registration is to transfer what is technically called the legal estate; but that the registered owner shall, for all purposes of transfer to purchasers, represent and have power to deal with all legal and beneficial interests[100]

subject only to the entry of cautions and 'stops' on the register.

Since indefeasible titles were neither wanted nor desirable, the Commission concluded that title registration 'is to be no more than the name imports, *viz.*, a public record of the ownership as it exists'.[101] So an owner could register whatever root of title he had, be it sixty years or six. Then it would be up to a purchaser to make of it what he would. But since the act of registration would render future purchasers free from subsequent dealings that had not been protected on the register (unless they concerned interests falling within the category rather unhelpfully designated 'not encumbrances'), as time passed purchasers would become more and more likely simply to accept whatever the register provided, without further investigation. In this way 'practical indefeasibility' would be attained. In essence this was the Cookson scheme adopted by the 1857 Commission. It became the orthodoxy in the subsequent debates, being accepted into the Hatherley bill of 1870, Lord Selborne's of 1873, and both Lord Cairns's bills of 1874 and 1875.[102] It would take time, of course, but these grandees agreed also that a general reduction in limitation periods should accom-

---

[99] Ibid., para. 64.
[100] Ibid., para. 66.
[101] Ibid., para. 60.
[102] Hatherley: Transfer of Land Bill, (1870) HLP xvii; Selborne: Land Titles and Transfer Bill, (1873) HLP iv. 183, see (1873) 215 PD (3rd ser.) 116, 216 PD 341; Cairns: Transfer and Title of Land Bill, (1874) HLP v. 7, see (1874) 218 PD (3rd ser.) 318, 1667; 219 PD 727; (1874) 220 PD 1226.

pany these reforms, an aim accomplished without difficulty by Lord Cairns in 1874.[103]

The Commission was divided on the fate of Westbury's Act. Some members wanted it repealed, others wanted it frozen, henceforward applying only to those estates already registered under it. The Report settled for its rather uncomfortable coexistence with a new Act to give effect to the Commission's own recommendations—with provisions for one-way transfer out of the 1862 Act. The Registrar himself thought that Act wholly unsatisfactory, and proposed its replacement with a scheme updated from Lord Cairns's of 1859, with a Landed Estate Court to declare indefeasible titles and a powerful Registry to give effect to registration and subsequent dispositions.[104] This view continued to attract some adherents, but they were a minority.[105] On the other hand the reasoning that led the Registrar to his conclusion, though rejected by the Commission, attracted many outside it.[106] Starting from the accepted premiss that the principle of title registration was beyond challenge, the question was simply how to make it work. He accepted that delay and expense had been the concomitant of Westbury's scheme, but carrying this further than the Commission he asserted that

It is vain to hope to obtain any system of registration of title, as distinguished from registration of deeds, which will not be accompanied by more or less of delay and expense to the party registering, and require more or less of constant judicial inquiry, interference and supervision.[107]

So, as 'every system of registration of title [also] in some degree interferes with the freedom of action of the landowner and his legal advisers',[108] there had to be either inducement or compulsion for the system to take effect. If inducement were chosen, then it must be an immediate benefit to the present landowner

[103] Vendor and Purchaser Act 1874, 37 & 38 Vict., c. 78, s. 1.

[104] 1870 *Report*, appendices 3, 4, 5.

[105] It attracted Giffard, Walpole, and Waley from the Commission; and see Waley's paper to the Social Science Association, (1871–2) 16 *Sol. Jo.* 235.

[106] Including Birmingham LS, (1874–5) 18 *Sol. Jo.* 535, in favour of indefeasibility; certification schemes necessarily implied indefeasibility, see e.g. (1875–6) 19 *Sol. Jo.* 33 for their continuing attraction. Liverpool LS tended towards favouring compulsion, (1873–4) 17 *Sol. Jo.* 824; cf. letter, (1874–5) 18 *Sol. Jo.* 528.

[107] 1870 *Report*, appendix 5, para. 11.

[108] Ibid., para. 16.

that was offered, not a future benefit to his successors. Only indefeasible title would suit. Alternatively, if non-indefeasible titles were to be the norm, compulsion was the only answer. The Commission simply asserted its disbelief and, in line with its assumption that registration was a boon offered to landowners, decided against compulsion, as its predecessor had also done, so too Lord Cairns's bills.

Having got so far with reasonable consensus the Commission then fragmented on what seemed to be mere details.[109] One could understand similar divisions in the 1857 Commission, whose members though part of the brotherhood advocating registration were also individual progenitors of rival schemes that had brought the Commission itself into existence. But this was not true of their successors, who were lawyers chosen simply for their general professional expertise. Yet the question of whether leases and, particularly, mortgages should be eligible for substantive registration independently of the fee simple from which they derived, or whether, by contrast, they should merely be protected by entry on the register against that fee simple, produced such division that two members included it as one reason for their dissent from the whole Report, and three more added notes to the Report, qualifying their signature of it. At root lay the nature of land-ownership in contemporary society, and the relation between legal analysis and the operation of the market. The Report itself recommended mere noting on the register for mortgages, but substantive registration for some classes of lease.[110] Mortgages, it said, created mere 'pecuniary interests' in the land, not intrinsically different from beneficial interests under trusts, whereas for at least some classes of lease the possessory element took them out of this category. This could be countered from two directions. First, if land is leased so as to be sublet, the lessee is merely an income receiver in very much the same way that a beneficiary is; therefore if a beneficiary's 'ownership' is not sufficient to merit substantive registration, nor should a tenant's be. On the other hand, to deny substantive registration to a mortgagee is to

---

[109] Sometimes an excuse for inactivity, e.g. Jessel, S.-G., (1872) 209 PD (3rd ser.) 562.

[110] 1870 *Report*, para. 70.

deprive him of a registration certificate, and hence of the chance of easy trading of his security interest. Since an important impulse for title registration was the increased facility it gave for secured borrowing, nothing should be done to deter lenders. The Report and the subsequent bills grappled with these problems as best they could. Unanimity was unobtainable; in the end voting power would decide.

In contrast the Commission skipped lightly past questions of administrative structure as though there could be no problem. Its members were mostly lawyers after all, except for the Chancellor of the Exchequer, who could bide his time. It endorsed its predecessor's recommendation that there be provincial registries, on the grounds that much of the delay and expense under Westbury's Act was attributable to centralization in London. These registries could start in a humble way, it thought, say as adjuncts to county courts, or perhaps in the offices of a local solicitor. It concluded with a plea that Chancery be given extended powers to sanction sales of settled land in the interests of commerce, and finally, as its predecessor had done, it recorded that it had detected considerable depth of feeling among solicitors that something really ought to be done to modernize their mode of payment for land transactions. Oh, yes—there was a unanimous recommendation for the abolition of the Middlesex Deeds Registry.

6. 1875: The Final Synthesis, the Land Transfer Act

From 1870 to 1875 a text for a registration statute was worked up by agreement between the Conservatives' and Liberals' leading lawyers, with participation of law societies. Lord Hatherley began the process in 1870, with a bill accepting the Commission's basic thrust, but which on points of detail tended to adopt the positions held by the semi-dissenters, going back to the 1857 Report.[111] This became the new orthodoxy, so that, for example, substantive registration for mortgages and for long leases became the norm. In 1873 Hatherley's successor, Lord

---

[111] See n. 102 above.

Selborne, produced an amended version,[112] which on Lord Cairns's advice he then handed over to a leading conveyancer, Sir Charles Hall, for expert revision. The Hall was rewarded with promotion to the bench,[113] and his version of the bill was duly inherited by Cairns, who became Lord Chancellor when the Conservatives ousted the Liberals. But that 1874 bill had a harder passage than anticipated, ultimately being stood down by Disraeli to make time for extended debate on a bill regulating church discipline. Reintroduced in 1875 it became law after another long session's debate. For all the difficulty in its passage, however, the Land Transfer Act represents in its technical details the culmination of the process begun within the legal profession by Wilson's pamphlet of 1844, reached, in contrast to Cairns's bills of 1859, through co-operation with conveyancers and law societies. Yet its enactment was a hard struggle.

The reason was that the Liberals wanted registration to be compulsory and Cairns, advancing what he at first regarded as an agreed text, was unwilling to dissent. But whereas Lord Selborne might have agreed to the establishment of district registries as the *quid pro quo*, Cairns would not. Hence solicitors faced the greatest possible disruption of their established ways, the greatest possible obstacle to speed and efficiency in conducting their clients' affairs—at least in the view of provincial solicitors—and, if registration was to threaten their earnings, the most acute version of that threat: compulsion plus centralization.

Compulsion had not been much of an issue until now. Its emergence in the early 1870s came as part of a revival of a more general 'land question' among some Liberal politicians, coinciding with the period of the Commission's deliberations. Shocked at the narrow distribution of land in England and Wales,[114] concerned at inefficient agricultural production and low living

---

[112] See n. 102 above.

[113] *DNB* and (1873–4) 56 *LT* 15, 52; (1874) 218 PD (3rd ser.) 318.

[114] See generally, W. R. Cornish and G. de N. Clark, *Law and Society in England, 1750–1950* (1989), 166–72; T. A. Jenkins, *Gladstone, Whiggery and the Liberal Party, 1874–1886* (1988), chs. 1–3; F. M. L. Thompson, *English Landed Society in the Nineteenth Century* (1963), ch. 10; D. Martin, 'Land Reform', in Patricia Hollis, ed., *Pressure from Without in Early Victorian Britain* (1974).

standards of agricultural labourers, jealous too of the continuing political power of the landed élite, they began once again to question the legal institutions that supported landed power. In these years after the second Reform Act they harried and taunted the landed leadership of both parties. Questions of primogeniture, entail, settlement, agricultural leases, tenant right, and so on became an important part of the political agenda. Title registration was peripheral to all this—it was scarcely mentioned by J. S. Mill's Land Tenure League,[115] for example—so when it came into issue it did so in a confused and contradictory way.

Neither Commission had proposed compulsion, nor had Cairns in 1859. It had been pressed as an alternative to indefeasible titles by Registrar Follett, on the grounds that registration would not be effective otherwise, but though he had assumed that effectiveness was essential, he had not said why.[116] For the moderate wing of the Liberal party the answer had little to do with registration as such. As Selborne put it in 1875,

> There was an essential difference between a measure which merely added one more to the methods of conveyancing of which men now had the choice, and one which made registration compulsory and irrevocable. The two systems were wide as the poles asunder. That which made registration compulsory and irrevocable was the proper instrument and machinery for introducing a general reconstruction and reform, gradual and progressive, into the whole system of land titles.[117]

Cairns retained the Commission's perception of the function of registration, and thus at first dissented from Selborne's plan.[118] It was not yet known whether the system would work well, and it might fall hard upon small transactions, he thought, especially if there were to be no local registries. And there were not, the Treasury having learnt its lesson from Westbury's Act now refused to allow their establishment unless a need could be proved for a particular area, which was obviously impossible

---

[115] For coverage of the Land Tenure League by the lawyers' press see (1871) 51 *LT* 96, (1870–1) 15 *Sol. Jo.* 447, 527.

[116] Above, pp. 116–7, and below, 135–6.

[117] (1875) 222 PD (3rd ser.) 744, cf. (1873) 215 PD (3rd ser.) 1116. See also William Harcourt, (1874) 220 PD (3rd ser.) 1261.

[118] (1873) 216 PD (3rd ser.) 341.

for a scheme still embodied in a bill.[119] Yet when he took Selborne's bill over in 1874 Cairns kept the compulsion clause, justifying it on the grounds that it was such a mild compulsion—unregistered transactions would still take effect in equity—that it was scarcely worth the opposition.

Not all Liberals shared Selborne's view. In the Commons, barrister George Osborne Morgan opposed first compulsion, and then registration altogether, as a distraction from the main task of abolishing entail and settlement. Far from being a necessary first step to general reform, registration was for him a dangerous palliative that would leave the more important questions unaddressed. His opposition delayed the bill critically in 1874 and nearly did so again in 1875.[120]

With the Liberals divided on the relation between registration and general reform, the way was open for re-examination of the link between registration and overreaching, since if the attraction of registration lay primarily in the width of the legal powers it conferred upon landed proprietors, perhaps that effect could be achieved directly by general law reform, without need for registration at all. This had been the essence of Cranworth's scheme, though he doomed it by involving Chancery.[121] Ayrton's proposal to the 1857 Commission had claimed that skeleton deeds could do much the same job as title certificates, if allied to overreaching powers.[122] Conveyancer Edward Wolstenholme, later a member of the 1870 Commission, had reached the same conclusion in 1862, seemingly independently.[123] Now that it seemed uncontroversial to propose such powers,

---

[119] Cf. (1873–4) 18 *Sol. Jo.* 527. Cairns's 1874 bill (n. 102 above) provided for the creation of district registries with Treasury consent, cl. 159 (of the original bill). Selborne's bill (n. 102 above) probably also allowed their creation by cl. 159(4), the Treasury being safeguarded by the presence of the Chancellor of the Exchequer on the Registry Board, cl. 146.

[120] (1874) 220 PD (3rd ser.) 1245; (1875) 224 PD (3rd ser.) 1414, 1924.

[121] See above, p. 110–11.

[122] See above, p. 96.

[123] Wolstenholme, 'Simplification of Title to Land'. See also F. Vaughan Hawkins, *Optional Mobilisation of Land: A Scheme for Simplifying Title and Land Transfer* (1869). Hawkins had previously espoused a typically conservative package of reforms: *The Title to Landed Estates Bills and the Solicitor-General's Speech Considered* (1859), with which cf. Joshua Williams, 'On the True Remedies', and correspondence at (1868–9) 13 *Sol. Jo.* 938, 943, (1869–70) 14 *Sol. Jo.* 464, and (1874–5) 58 *LT* 305. See also H. W. B. Mackay, *An Apology for the Present System of Conveyancing* (1870).

G. J. Johnson—Birmingham solicitor, secretary of his local law society, and Professor of Law at Owen College—revived the idea in a series of public papers.[124] Since Ayrton's day there had been changes making it more plausible. Progress was being made in the introduction of scale fees for conveyancing, which would make short-deeds positively desirable to solicitors and bring predictability to their clients' bills, though as yet London and the provinces were in a state of civil war on the question of which scale should be adopted nationally.[125] Moreover, in so far as one of the unpredictabilities in the costs equation was caused by the rich variety of conditions of sale adopted by individual solicitors when drafting contracts or conditions of auction, law societies were intervening to produce greater professional discipline. Liverpool led, stimulated by the need to produce standard conditions for use in their own auction rooms. Birmingham followed, circulating drafts and final copies of standard conditions of sale for voluntary adoption to all solicitors in the city, whether or not they were members of the society.[126] So, Johnson concluded, if the task is simply to find the way in which private dealings in land may best be facilitated, at the very least there should be an experiment. A voluntary registration system should be pitted against a system based upon abbreviated private deeds, both backed by wide overreaching powers, and then the more successful could be adopted generally.[127] It was not that he opposed registration, far from it; just that it seemed to him only one of the possible ways forward.

For the time being this was not a serious option. Registration

---

[124] For his appointment see (1857–8) 30 *LT* 93. His papers were to the M&PLA: (1870–1) 15 *Sol. Jo.* 159, crediting James Anderton, solicitor; (1874) 57 *LT* 436; (1873–4) 18 *Sol. Jo.* 943—circulated to members of Birmingham LS, (1874–5) 19 *Sol. Jo.* 215. See also his paper in 1873: (1873–4) 56 *LT* 9, (1872–3) 17 *Sol. Jo.* 963, (1873–4) 18 *Sol. Jo.* 48; correspondence, ibid. 487, 505. He was memorialized in Birmingham Law Library, (1913–14) 58 *Sol. Jo.* 345. See also W. Wesley Pue, 'Guild Training vs Professional Education', (1989) 33 *Am. Jo. Leg. Hist.* 241, 277–284.

[125] (1869–70) 14 *Sol. Jo.* 30, 349, 457; (1870–1) 15 *Sol. Jo.* 236; (1871–2) 16 *Sol. Jo.* 9, 201, 354; (1873–4) 18 *Sol. Jo.* 1, 10, 24–5, 64, 104, 118, 324,* 515; (1874–5) 19 *Sol. Jo.* 336; (1871–2) 52 *LT* 375; (1874) 57 *LT* 107, 119; (1874–5) 58 *LT* 68, 151,* 153,* 180, 192. (Asterisked refs. esp. informative.)

[126] Liverpool: (1865–6) 10 *Sol. Jo.* 150, and see (1866–7) 11 *Sol. Jo.* 159, 199; (1860–1) 36 *LT* 97, (1861–2) 37 *LT* 84. Birmingham: (1870–1) 15 *Sol. Jo.* 220; (1874–5) 19 *Sol. Jo.* 215 (or (1874–5) 58 *LT* 237).

[127] Cf. Birmingham LS, (1875–6) 20 *Sol. Jo.* 257.

was espoused by both parties and had for too long been identified with progress for law societies now to abandon it. Instead their committees worked diligently on the textual details, while one or two societies even approved compulsion. But most shared a package of views that opposed compulsion,[128] opposed centralization in London, and wanted proprietors to be able to withdraw their land from the register at any time they wanted.[129] This stance was both principled and self-interested. The ideology of registration, at least until very recently, had been that it provided private law benefits for landowners, and it would be unprincipled to deny landowners choice or force benefits upon them, especially untried benefits, especially untried *law-reforming* benefits, which had often promised much but produced only extra costs, extra muddle, and a string of Acts 'to further explain and amend . . .'. And as Johnson had argued, from the hitherto accepted premiss of the need to streamline transactions, several possible schemes were open. So it was perfectly principled to oppose compulsion, especially premature compulsion. But the opposition was also self-interested. Though solicitors had been exonerated by the Commission, not many shared Cookson's enthusiasm for registration. While fees from initial registration would smooth the transition, solicitors divided on the question whether thereafter higher turnover would compensate for lower transaction fees, and

---

[128] Manchester LA, (1874–5) 58 *LT* 330; Liverpool (briefly) (1872–3) 17 *Sol. Jo.* 824, and see the vote at an APLS meeting, (1873–4) 18 *Sol. Jo.* 576 and correspondence, ibid. 528.

[129] For this paragraph and the next, see:

M&PLA: (1870–71) 15 *Sol. Jo.* 309; (1873) 55 *LT* 453.

ILS: (1873–4) 18 *Sol. Jo.* 553; (1874–5) 19 *Sol. Jo.* 54; (1874) 57 *LT* 246.

Liverpool LS: (1870–1) 15 *Sol. Jo.* 42; (1872–3) 17 *Sol. Jo.* 824; (1873–4) 18 *Sol. Jo.* 31; (1870–1) 50 *LT* 30; (1871–2) 52 *LT* 34; (1873) 55 *LT* 286.

Birmingham LS: (1870–1) 15 *Sol. Jo.* 220; (1873–4) 18 *Sol. Jo.* 535; (1874–5) 19 *Sol. Jo.* 357; (1875–6) 20 *Sol. Jo.* 257; (1870–1) 50 *LT* 226; (1874–5) 58 *LT* 347.

Bristol LS: (1873–4) 18 *Sol. Jo.* 575; (1874) 57 *LT* 44.

Other law societies: (1873–4) 18 *Sol. Jo.* 494, 654, 694; (1874) 57 *LT* 68.

APLS: (1873–4) 18 *Sol. Jo.* 515, 545, 565, 576; (1874–5) 19 *Sol. Jo.* 122; (1874) 57 *LT* 52, 87, 108.

Journals: (1873–4) 18 *Sol. Jo.* 425, 448, 464, 525, 527, 528, 663; (1874–5) 19 *Sol. Jo.* 269, 290, 309, 329, 370, 609, 785; (1873–4) 56 *LT* 87; (1874) 57 *LT* 59, 139, 348; (1874–5) 58 *LT* 98.

Correspondence: (1873–4) 18 *Sol. Jo.* 489, 505, 597; (1873) 55 *LT* 50, 107; (1874) 57 *LT* 22.

some doubted whether a satisfactory *ad valorem* scale would ever materialize. More critically, the bills spoke of applications being made to the registry by the proprietor 'or his agent', which implied a dismantling of the conveyancing monopoly and a further loss of work to unqualified, uneducated, untaxed semi-professionals of a sort who plagued solicitors in other avenues of business. Though the ILS was usually successful in getting the offending words removed, apprehension remained. Further, some solicitors doubted whether registered conveyancing could ever match the deeds-based system in speed, flexibility, and confidentiality, and hoped that if the scheme were tried voluntarily, the product of thirty years of professional effort, a broad consensus between law societies, reformers, conveyancing barristers, and all, and if it were to fail, then solicitors would be left as masters in their own house.[130]

Centralization split the law societies. Birmingham thought it justified if registration were voluntary, but the big northern societies thought that even then district registries were necessary to make registration attractive. All provincial societies were adamant that district registries would be essential if registration were compulsory, both because of the delay and inefficiency London registration would introduce into provincial transactions and also because they were unwilling to see provincial solicitors forced to share conveyancing fees with the London solicitors whom they would have to employ as agents if registered transactions had to be completed in the capital. Only a very few provincial solicitors maintained an office in London,[131] and though one might speculate that a centralized compulsory land register might have stimulated such a development, the prevailing view was that its main effect would be to make London solicitors richer and provincial ones poorer. London solicitors, or at least some of them, were not disposed to make self-sacrificing gestures at this prospect, since the probable tendency of the other important law reform pending at that

---

[130] J. M. Clabon, (1874) 57 *LT* 436, details at (1874–5) 58 *LT* 171; cf. ibid. 281. For Clabon's general conservatism see also (1872) 53 *LT* 145, details at (1872–3) 54 *LT* 26, and (1873–4) 18 *Sol. Jo.* 597.

[131] See the *Law List, passim.* The desirability of having a London branch-office was canvassed from time to time, e.g. (1859) 33 *LT* 17; but there were risks, (1861–2) 37 *LT* 13.

time, the Judicature Bill, was exactly the opposite.[132] The Council of the ILS therefore refused to oppose centralization, and was ambivalent about compulsion.[133]

These tensions among solicitors had important effects on professional organization, which in turn influenced the course of land titles legislation. In the 1840s the Council of the ILS had responded to the threat posed by the M&PLA by increasing its own critical participation in the legislative process and by trying to widen the society's provincial base. It had been unsuccessful in the latter, but the erosion of rural and small town support for the M&PLA after 1860[134] forestalled any serious challenge to the ILS in the country, leading to such complacency in the ILS that in 1870 its president even claimed that since all provincial solicitors used London agents, the latters' prominence on the ILS council in fact amounted to representation for country members.[135] In the northern cities, however, M&PLA membership was widespread and ILS membership a rarity, leaving the M&PLA as virtually the Law Society of the north.[136] But it had always tended to run its affairs from London, the seat of the legislature, which strained its finances and led to difficulties in obtaining day-to-day involvement of the leaders of the local law societies of Liverpool, Manchester, and Leeds. These men, however, led societies increasingly influential in their own areas, increasingly successful in the direct lobbying of ministers and Members of Parliament, and even in sponsoring their own bills—the more so since the bigger societies had started to obtain corporate status to perpetuate their existence.[137] Now in the early 1870s they began to find that title registration and judicature reform where splitting the management committee of the M&PLA along regional/metropolitan lines. The fear grew

---

[132] e.g. (1873) 55 *LT* 56, 65, 176; (1875) 59 *LT* 208, 309.

[133] (1873–4) 18 *Sol. Jo.* 553; (1874) 57 *LT* 79, 246.

[134] See above, n. 60 and accompanying text.

[135] N. T. Lawrence, ILS President, (1870) 49 *LT* 235.

[136] See above, n. 60. For what follows see T. Marshall's paper to the M&PLA, (1873) 57 *LT* 71, 95; (1873–4) 18 *Sol. Jo.* 67, cf. C. Saunders, ibid. 122. Marshall was from Leeds, whose hostility to London was to recur: see below, pp. 206–7, 213, 217.

[137] Corporate status: Liverpool, (1868–9) 13 *Sol. Jo.* 33; Manchester, (1869–70) 48 *LT* 424, (1873–4) 56 *LT* 296; contrast the M&PLA, (1873) 55 *LT* 453. 'Own bills': Liverpool, (1870–1) 50 *LT* 30, cf. (1868–9) 13 *Sol. Jo.* 827.

that the lack of a single representative body was giving solicitors less political influence than such as the Licensed Victuallers Association or the Trades Unions Congress.

One response of the leaders of the biggest provincial law societies was to seek greater influence within the ILS. In 1873/4 they negotiated an amalgamation between the M&PLA and the ILS,[138] gaining the symbolic concessions that the ILS would continue to hold the annual provincial meetings pioneered by the M&PLA and that former M&PLA members could transfer to the ILS without paying the entry fee. But they failed to get the ILS Council to increase beyond ten the number of 'extra-ordinary' seats on the council reserved since 1872 for chairmen of provincial societies without direct election. However, by urging their members to join the ILS, and then by organizing votes in council elections, provincial societies were able to maintain their elected representation even in the face of increasing competition for seats, Jevons of Liverpool and Saunders of Birmingham winning places in 1873.[139] But the day-to-day work of the Council's committees had still to be done in London,[140] so the provincial leaders' impact tended to be more of a negative sort, especially as their positive efforts naturally went into maintaining their own individual law societies' input into the legislative process. At much the same time the ILS Council was coming under attack[141] from a different direction, from some London solicitors who found themselves virtually disenfranchised by its oligarchic ways and who believed that its élitist

[138] As with so much else, Liverpool ILS took the initiative. See (1870–1) 50 *LT* 30; (1871) 51 *LT* 432; (1871–2) 52 *LT* 34; (1872) 53 *LT* 145; (1872–3) 54 *LT* 26; (1873) 55 *LT* 453; (1873–4) 56 *LT* 71, 296, 361, 370, 417, 469; (1874) 57 *LT* 6, 44, 52. There is a colourless account in Kirk, *Portrait*, 39.

[139] (1873) 55 *LT* 258–62, 308, 327; (1873–4) 56 *LT* 277.

[140] (1875) 59 *LT* 321.

[141] For this paragraph see: (*a*) for dual pressure on the ILS from below and from the provinces: (1872–3) 54 *LT* 197, 204, 284, 333, 393, 422, 472, 486; (1873) 55 *LT* 1, 14, 19, 31, 38, 52, 55, 67, 111, 126, 150, 155, 209, 258–62, 265, 291, 308, 327, 346; (1874) 57 *LT* 246, 311, 316, 383; (1874–5) 58 *LT* 240, 358; (1875) 59 *LT* 233, 324.

(*b*) for the Legal Practitioners' Society, which included barristers too: (1873–4) 56 *LT* 43, 79, 88, 178, 186, 352; (1874) 57 *LT* 119, 408; (1874–5) 58 *LT* 52, 68, 174, 436, 456; (1875) 59 *LT* 38, 47, 65, 83, 84, 99, 136, 190.

(*c*) for ILS élitism: Kirk, *Portrait*, 157–8.

(*d*) for comment: (1874) 57 *LT* 227, 383; (1874–5) 58 *LT* 173; (1875) 59 *LT* 207, 244, 284, 324.

concerns left ordinary practitioners unprotected from encroach-ments from accountants, unqualified legal agents, and the lower end of the bar. Unlike provincial solicitors, these men had no law societies other than the ILS, so they founded, and sub-sequently formed the backbone of, a new organization, the Legal Practitioners' Society, which took an aggressive view of solicitors' rights, to the point of drafting and piloting bills through Parliament. The contrast between its concern for ordi-nary practitioners and the élitist concerns of the ILS Council was such that some provincial law societies affiliated to it, seeing it as a prototype for a new national law society that would not be dominated by the City and Lincoln's Inn. The impact of these two movements was to force a sort of democracy upon the ILS Council, so that elections to it began to be seriously contested and information about its workings more openly disseminated. But the London members of the Council, though relatively homogeneous in their economic interest, were divided on the basic question of what sort of society the ILS should be, a progressive party being roughly balanced by a 'rest and be thankful' party. One result of all this was that the Council now found it difficult to maintain strong views on anything.

Meanwhile the provincial leaders began to replace the M&PLA.[142] In 1874, of about 7,000 provincial solicitors the ILS had only 689 on its books and the M&PLA 420, not all of whom did transfer their allegiance on the amalgamation. But there were thirty-five local law societies, whose combined member-ship was estimated in 1875 as approaching 4,000. So provincial leaders began to meet together under the title of the Associated Provincial Law Societies, forming policies and determining tactics that wholly ignored London. Though at first snubbed by Lord Cairns, who would deal only with the ILS, by the follow-ing year they had gained a foothold at Westminster through a meeting with the Attorney-General, as indeed, given their ease of access to local MPs, they were bound to do. During 1874 and

[142] Contrary to the implication in Kirk, *Portrait*, 39, this had been part of their plan from the beginning: (1870–1) 50 *LT* 30; (1871–2) 52 *LT* 34. For the figures in this paragraph see (1873–4) 56 *LT* 71, 95; (1875) 59 *LT* 261. For the APLS generally see: (1874) 57 *LT* 52, 87, 108, 129, 140, 420; (1874–5) 58 *LT* 98; ((1873–4) 18 *Sol. Jo.* 565, 576). For Cairns's snub: (1874) 57 *LT* 98, 139; and for the meeting with the A.-G., (1874–5) 19 *Sol. Jo.* 122.

1875 as Cairns's bills trudged through Parliament, it was the APLS that called the solicitors' tune, to the extent even of imposing some of its views on the Council of the ILS, thus neutralizing the economic interest London agency solicitors had in compulsory centralized registration. So although nearly all provincial societies willingly accepted the principle of registration and worked on improving the technical details of these bills, for as long as Cairns insisted upon compulsion without district registries the APLS campaigned fiercely against him.

Their weapon was their knowledge of their local land markets. Proponents of title registration had probably never realized how much their work was based upon assumptions about the sort of landowner who would use it. Unwittingly they had assumed the sort of transaction they knew best, which was not small house purchase. Now that registration was to be compulsory its effect had to be assessed for all sorts of owner, particularly for the newly enfranchised urban working class, who could expect to share the benefits compulsion was supposed to bring. Law societies then proceeded to rediscover the basic truth that in practice any scheme of registration made small transactions more expensive. Preston was the first,[143] followed by Johnson's Birmingham Law Society, which conducted a large-scale survey of house and land transactions in its area, the first time such a thing had been done.[144] It showed that there were very many small sales and mortgages, with consideration prices of £300 or less, costing little in lawyers' fees and taking virtually no time to complete. It would scarcely be possible for an official registration system to do the job cheaper or quicker. Other solicitors and other localities told the same story. Preston Law Society mobilized its local building societies, which petitioned against compulsion, followed by those in Lancaster.[145] Cairns was surprised. The need for title registration was premissed upon purchasers' supposed concern for title; but these surveys demonstrated that at the bottom end of

---

[143] (1874) 57 *LT* 6, 68.

[144] (1873–4) 18 *Sol. Jo.* 505.

[145] (1874) 57 *LT* 150, 164, 197. It was often said that building societies would appoint a solicitor to do their conveyancing only if he agreed to use their own low scale of fees. Many solicitors advertised their office-holding with building societies in the *Law List*, and cf. (1873–4) 18 *Sol. Jo.* 104.

the market, a vigorous market at that, purchasers and their advisers scarcely bothered with a title at all. Compulsion would bring them cost, not benefit. Further, if the Conservatives had an ulterior reason for title registration it was that it might help small capitalists invest more easily in land, which they regarded on the whole as being the preserve of the relatively wealthy. But these new figures showed that such investment already happened, and that registration might deter it. Consequently Cairns amended his bill so that compulsion applied only to transactions worth more than £300.[146] Shortly afterwards Disraeli held the bill over for a session. When it returned Cairns announced that there would be no compulsion for anyone: he was persuaded by this flow of information from law societies, he did not want to draw an arbitrary line, and he did not think compulsion viable unless district registries were to be instituted.[147]

Why were they not? Though Cairns and the Liberal opposition did now link district registries and compulsion as two sides of the same issue, most law societies also demanded district registries for their own sake, claiming that this new-style conveyancing would only prove attractive to the market if it could be done quickly and if registers were open to easy inspection. Like the Royal Commission they urged that district registries could be humble affairs and their staff ministerial rather than judicial. The difficult job of inspection of title could be done in London by the Registrar and his Assistants, who would have judicial rank and would be paid by salary.[148] District staff could be paid by fees, thus meeting Treasury objections. Further, if a local solicitor were to become District Registrar he would have an interest in demonstrating to his colleagues the advantages of registration, thus helping overcome the *vis inertiae* that everyone acknowledged to be an obstacle to acceptance of a voluntary scheme. Lord Cairns's postbag was already bulging with applications from provincial solicitors, for posts whose

---

[146] (1874) 219 PD (3rd ser.) 727; Lawrence was surprised too: Royal Commission on Agriculture, (1882) HCP xiv, q. 54747.

[147] (1875) 222 PD (3rd ser.) 155; see also ibid. 1041, 1776.

[148] For a good statement of the argument see (1873–4) 18 *Sol. Jo.* 425; ibid. 528.

existence he denied![149] If the Liberals had been in office Lord
Selborne might have persuaded the Treasury of this case,[150] but
Lord Cairns balked at having local solicitors as registrars. He
did not agree that their duties would be ministerial, so since
they would have to use a judicial discretion when making
registration decisions they could not be paid simply by fee—the
difficulty of the decision would not necessarily be related to the
value of the land. He hinted that solicitors were not up to that
job, and saw difficulties in allowing a solicitor-registrar to
continue private practice in his own locality, for fear of abuse of
the information thereby gained.[151] District registries would have
to be scaled-down versions of the one in London, hence the
Treasury objections stood. The result was that although the text
of the Land Transfer Act represented the consensual culmination of more than a generation's professional thought, political
bargaining had located it in an institutional setting least conducive to its success: voluntary registration at a London registry.

7. Retrospect, 1844–1875

It is striking how strongly rooted in the intellect title registration
was. Based upon relatively abstract reasoning, it had much
more in common with James Humphreys's *Code* than with the
incrementalism of Brougham[152] or Duckworth. And yet, as their
piecemeal law reforms[153] one by one knocked away the problems to which title registration might have been the solution,
still the idea persisted. In 1846 it was being offered by James

---

[149] (1875) 222 PD (3rd ser.) 1795; this speech is illuminating on Treasury
influence.
[150] Ibid. 747; cf. (1873–4) 18 *Sol. Jo.* 48, 527.
[151] (1875) 222 PD (3rd ser.) 155. See solicitors' campaigns to have their
eligibility for posts at least left open: (1873–4) 18 *Sol. Jo.* 452, 515, 585; (1874–5)
19 *Sol. Jo.* 309; (1874) 57 *LT* 51, 52, 60, 87.
[152] See his preference for 'practical Benthamism', (1860) 35 *LT* 226.
[153] The latest was Lord Cairns's Vendor and Purchaser Act 1874, initially
greeted warmly. As so often the case with such piecemeal reforms, its defects
quickly became visible: (1874–5) 58 *LT* 58, 237, 281; (1874–5) 19 *Sol. Jo.* 215, 785;
(1875–6) 20 *Sol. Jo.* 169. Its curious s. 7, abolishing priority of mortgages gained
by 'tacking', was thought to have been included in anticipation of compulsory
title registration. It was repealed retrospectively by Lord Cairns's Conveyancing
and Law of Property Act 1881, s. 73.

Stewart to the landed interest as a boon; in the 1870s it was being offered by Selborne to his back-benchers as a step towards reform of that very same landed interest. Its genesis had certainly been intellectual, in the sense that it was conceived as a system based upon general propositions rather than as a solution to an identifiable problem. The basic premiss was that land was just property, that it was not special; hence Wilson's painstaking set of analogies and contrasts. Of the most important advocates of title registration, Cookson was a solicitor with some conveyancing experience, Field's was more commercial.[154] Wilson's own unfamiliarity with landed interests may be inferred from his heroic assumption that parochial visitations would achieve registration of nearly all land in the area, with just a few recalcitrants to be whipped into line by compulsion. It had become commonplace by 1875 to see title registration's value in its facilitating transactions for those property-owners who saw land simply as an item of commerce[155]—indeed, it was such a perception that opened the way for such descendants of Ayrton as Wolstenholme and Johnson.

This proto-assimilation of real and personal property determined many features of the narrative. Deeds registration need have no philosophy. It left the ordering and reconciliation of conflicting interests to the traditional law as mediated through conveyancers. But it was the essence of title registration that it incorporated an ordering into its own structure, hence, for example, the inability of the 1870 Commissioners to agree whether mortgagees were property-owners or rentiers. Indeed, it was precisely his rejection of the value of assimilation that led Bethell down the blind alley of mirror of title registration; just as, from a different point on the land/politics spectrum, Osborne Morgan rejected registration because he thought its underlying basis in assimilation of landed and personal property might make real inroads into the power of the landed interest more difficult. Thus as the land question re-emerged onto the political

---

[154] Field: (1859–60) 4 *Sol. Jo.* 263. Cookson: see his evidence to the House of Commons Select Committee on the Registration of Assurances Bill, (1852–3) HCP xxxvi. 397, qq. 1 ff.

[155] See above, sect. 5, for the 1870 Commissioners. The numerical significance of such owners was sometimes denied: G. J. Johnson, (1870–1) 15 *Sol. Jo.* 159; editorial, (1873–4) 18 *Sol. Jo.* 448; and cf. J. M. Clabon, (1873–4) 18 *Sol. Jo.* 597.

agenda of the 1870s and 1880s, registration could attract the middle ground, overlapping both political parties. But it had not been devised for their purposes; indeed, it is hard to see that it had been devised for any particular purpose. Like a patent medicine, it could be advertised as a cure for whatever illness was fashionable.

So the advocacy shifted direction. In the 1840s James Stewart directed his appeal to the big landowners, who would regain through registration what they had lost by the repeal of the Corn Laws. This assumption runs through most of the early papers on the subject, and is consistent with the experience of the men who were advocating it—they were lawyers to the wealthy. There was no sign at all that the wealthy thought that there was a problem, though if their lawyers said that there was and were offering to put it right they would no doubt go along with them. But somewhere along the line, at about the time of the second Reform Act, the emphasis shifted, and title registration came to be seen as a boon for all landowners, however humble.

Consider the number of occasions on which the point was made that in practice the ordinary operation of the market already made small transactions quick and cheap. Solicitor Robert Baxter from Doncaster told the Select Committee on Burdens on Land so, and was ignored.[156] Solicitor John Greene produced evidence of it for St Leonards; he was treated disdainfully by Bellenden Ker, but in the end Cranworth acknowledged the truth of the claim by tapering the fees payable under his deeds registration proposal.[157] Yet building societies had been saying the same thing. Then the 1857 Commission heard evidence from a Mr Pyne, clerk to the Board of Copyhold and Tithe Commissioners—the sort of functionary who would have to operate any scheme the lawyers invented.[158] He urged the Commission to pay heed to the rate of change in land dealings: there had been two million houses in England and Wales in 1830, he thought; in 1851 there were more than three and a quarter million. The Commission should assume a similar rate

---

[156] Above, p. 62.
[157] Above, pp. 78, 81.
[158] (1857, 2nd session) HCP xxi. 245, 595–604.

for the future, and plan for that. They should see that much of this new construction resulted from the activities of small speculative builders, whose costs would be increased by deeds registration, and who, he thought, were disfavoured enough by the law as it was.[159] Similarly, there were the building societies, whose special statutory regime for mortgages reduced their legal costs to a trifling level; they too would suffer from the proposal. Finally, there were the railway companies, who habitually engaged in hundreds of small transactions to acquire land for their new lines; the problems of deeds registration, be it nationally or locally based, would add immensely to their difficulties. Painstakingly he demonstrated how impossible it would be to run a system for this number of small transactions. But he need not have bothered. The Commission had dismissed deeds registration, and, with that, did not feel that they had anything to learn from Mr Pyne. When they wanted facts they would ask lawyers. So the first question on their questionnaire asked for views about transaction costs. Most barristers and solicitors receiving it declined to answer, saying the matter was beyond their experience—which itself says a lot about what was going on—but fortunately for the Commission one recipient, Lincoln's Inn conveyancer George Sweet was more diligent. He unearthed nineteen bills from his records, producing their totals to the Commission without any explanation of what they covered.[160] Some of them did seem expensive, so the Commission simply used Sweet's reply as though it were statistically significant and concluded that indeed there were savings to be made. One doubts that George Sweet had handled a simple house purchase in his life, but he was the sort of man to whom the Commissioners listened, whereas Mr Pyne was not. A good idea should not be discarded just because the facts do not fit.

So yet again the point had to be made. But this time it was law societies that made it, Preston first, then Birmingham, and in a way that could not be ignored, since they provided for the first time information that could be called systematic.[161] Law

---

[159] Cf. Harold Perkin, *The Origins of Modern English Society, 1780–1880* (1969), 416.

[160] (1857, 2nd session) HCP xxi. 633 and *Report*, para. 18.

[161] Above, p. 128. Some law societies sometimes asserted the opposite: e.g. Liverpool, (1861–2) 6 *Sol. Jo.* 669.

societies had thrust their way into the law-making process partly in a quest for improved status, partly also because of their local knowledge.[162] But the way in which laws were made inevitably cast law societies as respondents, and their Chadwick-like factual surveys would be perceived as obstructive, however influential they were and however ignorant had been the proponents of the bills in question.

It was much the same with localism. By their very nature originators of title registration schemes based their assumptions on general text-book learning as modified by 'best practice' as it applied to the sort of dealings with which they were familiar. Regional variations could play havoc with the resultant schemes, as could regional variety in patterns of land tenure, if that is a different thing. As we saw, the 1870 Commissioners were divided on the question of whether a lease should be treated as an encumbrance or as an interest meriting separate registration. All, however, assumed that there was an answer to the question. But perhaps there was not. In some places long leases were the dominant tenure, with the landlord's interest amounting to not much more than an annual charge. Indeed, Lord Cairns seems not to have realized that by confining his bills in 1857 and 1859 to registration of the fee simple he would have denied even the middle classes of London the benefit of his schemes: London was leasehold. Oxfordshire solicitors became very agitated about the difficulty of fitting Oxfordshire long leasehold into Bethell's scheme. Manchester and Bristol Law Societies lobbied furiously to have their local chief rents properly accommodated, for if they could not be, wholly new ways of financing house building would have to be found in those areas.[163] Of course these problems could usually be solved by amendments to proposed bills. But once again the pattern cast solicitors as the opponents.

It was not only local tenures which modified text-book practice, so too did the market. It took a long time for the grandees to appreciate that because special conditions in contracts were so common, blots on title were not a problem, but that for that very reason certificated title would be impossible. The certifier

---

[162] For a strong statement of solicitors' place in law reform see the President of Liverpool LS, (1871–2) 52 *LT* 34.
[163] (1859) 33 *LT* 8, 13; (1861–2) 6 *Sol. Jo.* 392, 409.

would never be morally justified in accepting market risks. The implications of the use of special conditions were simply never explored. A similar question arose about the assertion by some of the more cautious reformers that title registration's greatest value would come where land was bought speculatively, to be laid out in lots for house-building. Registration before sub-sale would save sub-purchasers most of their legal costs. But what legal costs? Was it true, as one solicitor thought it was, that in such circumstances sub-purchasers were generally content to assume that the speculator's solicitor had done his job properly, at least if both were well known in the neighbourhood, and simply to accept the title without investigation?[164] Originators of title registration schemes did not have the means for gathering these sorts of information. Law societies did, and pressed the results for all that they were worth. But in doing so they exposed an ambiguity in the role of solicitor. As lawyers they saw law as important and wished to participate fully in its making. As men of business their function was to smooth the passage of other men's business deals, which they did through tailoring the terms on which their local markets worked. These two roles might clash; there would be occasions when law and solicitors were alternative solutions to a problem.

Such a predicament was not visible so long as the Wilsons, Cooksons, and Fields were driving the title registration band-wagon.[165] But Bethell's Act brought a new player into the game, the Registrar. Though dismissed by the 1870 Commissioners, Follett's expansionary ambitions were unmistakable. He was astounded that they could even think of going back on the principle of indefeasibility introduced by Bethell's Act. He thought it beyond their terms of reference even to consider such a thing. For him title registration was a fact whose value was literally beyond question. The only issue was how to make it work. Something like this attitude had been seen in Bellenden Ker and Coulson, when they were content to see an impractic-

---

[164] As an argument for registration: Liverpool LS, (1861–2) 6 *Sol. Jo.* 669, but cf. (1872–3) 17 *Sol. Jo.* 824; ILS, (1868–9) 13 *Sol. Jo.* 799; editorial, (1873–4) 18 *Sol. Jo.* 448. For doubts: (1860–1) 37 *LT* 515, and see Wolstenholme's evidence to the Royal Commission on Agriculture, (1881) HCP xvii, qq. 51, 180–90.

[165] Early threats by Robert Torrens to oust solicitors from the land transfer process were dubbed 'puerile' by the *Sol. Jo.*—(1862–3) 7 *Sol. Jo.* 502.

able deeds registration system established so that, on its failure, the officials in charge could then devise a better one. Since Follett breathtakingly admitted that registration inevitably increased expense and reduced freedom of choice, then if indefeasibility was not practicable his logic propelled him to compulsion. The system demanded no less.[166] Bureaucratic expansionism involved a bid for control of the law-making process which in due course might catch solicitors between the rock of the Registry and the hard place of the Treasury.

The content and timing of the Land Transfer Act were in a sense quite accidental. It could so easily have been Cairns's bills of 1859 that were enacted, or Cranworth's scheme for registration without a registry. As a final footnote, another accident may have been influential too. Readers may recall that private title insurance was mooted as a part of title registration, and wonder what became of the suggestion—its acceptance might have opened the way to a purely private enterprise registration system, why ever not? It was not outlandish, because one insurance company did already offer insurance against some risks encountered in land transactions. Its chairman wrote that at present demand was surprisingly low; and he thought it unlikely that his company would change its habit of basing premiums upon the risk in the individual case—for it to work in conjunction with registration would of course need the premium to be either a flat charge or a fee on the *ad valorem* principle. But this chairman was a man well known for investigating every business possibility that came his way, and his reluctance here was out of character. He was E. W. Cox, to whom Cookson and all his works were anathema.[167]

---

[166] (1870) HCP xviii. 595, appendices 3, 4, and esp. 5, which at paras. 11 and 16 contains the admissions about cost and loss of freedom.
[167] (1859) 33 *LT* 145, 150; (1859–60) 34 *LT* 81.

Interlude

4

Perfecting a Private Market

This chapter bridges the concerns of Part I and those to follow in Part II. For lawyers its focus is the legislation of the early 1880s, the Settled Land Act and the Conveyancing Acts, statutes which contemporary conveyancers saw as a new dawn. After them things were never the same again: the old world derided by Brougham had finally passed. But solicitors who believed that the bright new day would bring peace would be disappointed: the dawn was false. A plateau had been reached, not the summit.

Looking back we can see that until the 1870s politicians had had to be persuaded by the law reformers that their concerns with technical questions of land law were worth taking up. And looking ahead we see that by the mid-1880s the position was reversed: political parties had identified land transfer as an urgent problem, with lawyers and their institutions serving the subsidiary role of promoting and negotiating a solution. The signs were already there. Dispute brewed over settlement of land, the use of entailed estates, and the related question of intestate primogeniture.[1] In the first chapter of Part II the difficult years of the 1880s will be considered, years in which a grand solution was pressed for all these questions and for what was seen as the related issue of title registration. But first there

---

[1] See H. J. Perkin, 'Land Reform and Class Conflict in Victorian Britain', in J. Butt and I. F. Clark, eds., *The Victorians and Social Protest* (1973); W. R. Cornish and G. de N. Clark, *Law and Society in England, 1750–1950* (1989), 166–72; Eileen Spring, 'Landowners, Lawyers and Land Law Reform in Nineteenth Century England', (1977) *American Journal of Legal History*, 40.

Tracts included Joseph Kay, *Free Trade in Land* (1879); Arthur Arnold, *Free Land* (1880); Sir George Osborne Morgan, *Land Law Reform in England* (1880); G. C. Brodrick, *English Land and English Landlords* (1881); Sir George Shaw-Lefevre, *English and Irish Land Questions* (1881).

is the interlude, beginning with a committee that even at the time looked stranded in no man's land.

1. Osborne Morgan's Committee, 1878–1879

Lord Cairns's remodelled Land Registry was a failure. It did less work even than under Westbury's Act,[2] to the consternation of economically minded MPs.[3] Sir Robert Torrens, originator of the rival scheme of land registration popular in the colonies and latterly a Liberal MP, blamed the solicitors and the Act's text in about equal measure.[4]

In July 1879 a House of Commons Select Committee chaired by George Osborne Morgan published a report on land transfer.[5] It is sometimes treated by lawyers as being especially significant, since by a small majority it recommended 'simplification' of the law in preference to title registration, and is thus seen as a harbinger of the 1925 legislation. Dr Offer sees it as a victory for evil—'Conservatives and solicitors' led by the turncoat Osborne Morgan.[6] In fact party alignment counted for nothing, and there was only one solicitor on the Committee. Though he this time voted against title registration, he had previously sponsored a bill in its favour.[7]

The Committee's immediate cause had been serious panic at the unearthing of a conspiracy to borrow money on forged leases. This had been going on since 1863, had netted about £300,000, and culminated in early 1878 with the life imprisonment of its perpetrator, one Dimsdale.[8] Shortly afterwards an accountant named Downs was convicted of obtaining £40,000 from conveyances on which he had forged the seal of the British Land Company.[9] When it was observed that Dimsdale had operated

---

[2] Select Committee on Land Titles and Transfer, Report, (1878–9) HCP xi, p. iv; (1877) 235 PD 1359 ff.

[3] (1878) 240 PD 980; (1879) 246 PD 708; (1880) 255 PD 708; cf. (1883) 282 PD 1765 ff., esp. 1770–1.

[4] Royal Commission on Agriculture, Evidence, (1882) HCP xiv, qq. 65453 ff.

[5] (1878–9) HCP xi.

[6] Avner Offer, *Property and Politics, 1870–1914* (1981), 36.

[7] George Burrow Gregory; (1871–2) 16 *Sol. Jo.* 662; his bill was drafted by Assistant Registrar Holt, (1878–9) HCP xi, Evidence, qq. 511, 658.

[8] (1877–8) 64 LT 202; (1877–8) 22 *Sol. Jo.* 218, 220, 237, 241.

[9] (1877–8) 22 *Sol. Jo.* 416, 498.

in Surrey, and that Middlesex, though blighted in its conveyancing by the expense and cumbrousness of its deed registry, did at least seem the safer for it, even otherwise stolidly conservative solicitors joined the clamour for an extension of that hitherto maligned system.[10] Joshua Williams and George Sweet, doyens of the conveyancing barristers, dusted off their old schemes for revitalizing the Middlesex registry, each quite different of course. Osborne Morgan raised questions in the House, correspondence in *The Times* continued interminably, and a delegation from the Building Societies Protection Association urged national registration of deeds upon the Home Secretary.[11]

Though the upshot was the appointment of Osborne Morgan's Committee, at his own urging, his reasons are opaque. His antipathy to title registration had been apparent for some years, but he never spoke enthusiastically for deeds registration. He was one of the Liberals critical of primogeniture, entail, and settlement, so he may have seen his committee as contributing to the conveyancing aspects of that question—his suggestion that trustees' powers be extended is consistent with that.[12] The initial terms of reference for his committee made no mention of deeds registration.[13]

Several of the Committee's members were identifiable with one form of land transfer system or another from the start. There was a Scottish and an Irish barrister, who duly voted for the sort of deeds registration familiar to them at home.[14] Alderman Sir Sydney Waterlow had led the deputation from the Building Societies Protection Association which had urged deeds registration upon the Home Secretary in the aftermath of the Dimsdale affair.[15] On the other side there were two quite senior politicians, Conservative Spencer Walpole, seemingly an

[10] e.g. John Clabon, who later blamed panic over the Dimsdale frauds for his uncharacteristic advocacy of deeds registration, (1879–80) 24 *Sol. Jo.* 897; his evidence to the Osborne Morgan Committee is at (1878–9) HCP xi. 1, see. qq. 270 ff.

[11] Williams and Sweet: (1877–8) 22 *Sol. Jo.* 177, 183, 201–2, 217, 241. *The Times*: ibid. 265, 579, 587. Osborne Morgan: ibid. 237, (1878) 239 PD 1885. Building societies: (1878–9) 22 *Sol. Jo.* 498, 569.

[12] (1878) 239 PD 1885; cf. (1876) 230 PD 594.

[13] (1877–8) 22 *Sol. Jo.* 559.

[14] Patrick Martin, William Watson.

[15] (1877–8) 22 *Sol. Jo.* 498, 569.

ever-present member of any committee considering title registration, which he strongly favoured, and Robert Lowe, a Liberal
whose record on title registration was the same as Walpole's.[16]
They were joined by G. R. Ryder, a barrister who was chairman
of the Lands Improvement Company and the Land Securities
Company, whose origins were linked to title registration, as
explained above.[17]

The real significance of Osborne Morgan's Committee lies in
how its members reacted to the evidence presented to it. It was
told by Sir Henry Thring, first Parliamentary Counsel to the
Treasury (nominally official draftsman, but more influential
than that), that a new title registration Act would make no
difference. 'It is not a question for an Act of Parliament,' he
said, 'it is a question for Treasury administration: it is a question
of money.'[18] District registries were not on the Treasury agenda.
Lord Cairns agreed with Thring that the question was one of
'less urgency and less demand now'.[19] He thought that there
was no need to extend the Act, because 'great competition'
among solicitors had already shortened deeds and reduced fees,
especially for small transactions in the provinces, where costs
were now very low.[20] If registration had contained a state
interest, public subsidy of its fees might be justified, in which
case registration might spread quickly, he thought.[21] But it was
perfectly clear that he regarded it instead as 'vendor and
purchaser' business, for which the real cost should be charged.
Indeed, for all his defence of his Act, Cairns disclosed that he
had not wanted it in the first place. His own preference was for
a Landed Estates Court to simplify title: but in 1875, 'finding
the State in the possession of the office of Registry, which could
not be displaced, and must be utilised', he had had to make do
with a revised registration system.[22]

---

[16] Walpole and Lowe sat on the 1853 Select Committee, the 1857 Royal
Commission, and the 1870 Royal Commission, voting with the majority each
time.

[17] Above, Ch. 3 n. 92 and accompanying text; *Dod's Parliamentary Companion
1879*.

[18] (1878–9) HCP xi, qq. 95–101, 109–13.

[19] Ibid., q. 2863.

[20] Ibid., qq. 2863, 2890.

[21] Ibid., q. 2919.

[22] Ibid., qq. 2863, 2924; cf. q. 3057.

Liberals in general were the party of economy, and it had been Robert Lowe's own 'acute and frugal mind' as Chancellor of the Exchequer in 1869 which had established a Treasury stranglehold over government law reform by the establishment of the Parliamentary Draftsman's office.[23] Further, in the late 1870s a major tenet of Liberal radicalism was that the land monopoly should be broken up by exposure to market forces. Ideological inconsistency would be obvious if title registration served merely to replace traditional conveyancing with a state monopoly. Cairns's claims that there was no state interest in title registration and that competition between solicitors was doing the Liberals' job for them were nicely calculated.

So the minority report[24] prepared by George Shaw-Lefevre, a Liberal champion of 'free trade in land', had to demonstrate that title registration was compatible with free market values. This he did by placing much of the blame for its failure to date upon the passivity of the Registry. It was not enough to draft a good Act, appoint a good barrister to head the Registry, and then sit back. A registry seen as an instrument in a private market should be run on active business principles. Government should *push* the Act. The system should then be given a proper trial in one locality. Middlesex was the obvious choice, since its deeds registry was expensive and a disgrace. That registry should be transformed into a title registry, where the additional costs of selling the 1875 Act to the public would be met by savings from abolishing the sinecure offices still extant in the deeds registry. On the crucial question of compulsion he was understandably somewhat ambivalent, settling for a weasel-like 'probably'.

Osborne Morgan hated the thought of turning 'the Government into a huge firm of solicitors'.[25] Where Shaw-Lefevre was unwilling to absolve solicitors entirely from blame, Osborne Morgan did, since there must have been thousands of land purchasers since 1875 well able to judge the merits of title registration for themselves.[26] Without any hint that he disap-

---

[23] Sir Courtenay Ilbert, *Legislative Methods and Forms* (1901), 84.
[24] (1878–9) HCP xi, pp. xxix ff.; cf. Thring's evidence, *passim*.
[25] Ibid., q. 129.
[26] Ibid., p. iv.

proved, Osborne Morgan recorded that one reason for their shunning the Registry was their dislike of officialdom—a verdict damning almost any system of title registration.[27] Further, although his Report did say that the 1875 Act was as good as it could be made, that praise was severely qualified. The Act's system of creating an 'owner pro hac vice'—the 'artificial' or 'fictitious' ownership under which subordinate interests in the land would disappear from it on a sale—was open, he thought, to 'inherent objection [which] has hardly received sufficient consideration in the Report on which the Act of 1875 was founded'.[28] This is an important point, because what Osborne Morgan eventually proposed was a 'simplification' of the underlying law of title, which might easily be taken to mean the sort of general extension of overreaching powers proposed by Ayrton, Johnson, and Wolstenholme in the past[29] and vigorously advanced to the Committee by Wolstenholme once again. But the label of 'fiction' which he attached to the 1875 Act applied equally to Wolstenholme's proposal, so Osborne Morgan's twin espousal of market principles and integrity to 'the law' left him with just a list of incrementalist reforms. Statutory short-forms should be introduced, an *ad valorem* scale for legal fees should be instituted, mortgage by legal charge should be established, and the Statute of Uses—which contributed to the wordiness and general unintelligibility of conveyances—should be repealed. Further—a point on which the minority agreed, and notwithstanding Lord Cairns's discouragement[30]—automatic descent of land to the heir on an intestacy should be abolished, and a system of 'real representatives' parallel to that of personal representatives should be introduced. In addition there should be a general registry of deeds, which Osborne Morgan acknowledged would do nothing to reduce costs but which would increase security. That was inevitable, given the Committee's origin and composition.

The Land Registry's own proposal had been very different from the schemes hitherto discussed, the result without doubt of Treasury misgivings. There were clear divisions within the Registry about its future role. Registrar Follett conceded a

---

[27] (1878–9) HCP xi, p. v.
[28] Ibid.
[29] Above, pp. 121–22.
[30] (1878–9) HCP xi, q. 2964.

continuing place for solicitors in registered transactions,[31] but not so his deputy, R. H. Holt. Holt's new world would be fully statist. There would be no solicitors, on whose shoulders all blame for the Act's failure lay, a state of affairs that was a 'disgrace to a civilised society'.[32] Fees would be reduced to a few shillings, because 'every person [would do] his own business'.[33] Solicitors, he thought, had no place even on first registration.[34] But the corollary of every man's doing his own business was that 'every person [would be] responsible for his own work'—except apparently the Registry, which he seemed to think ought not to carry the same liability for negligence that solicitors did.[35] However, that question would rarely arise, since

We propose that persons shall register their own titles and be responsible themselves for what they do; that there shall be the least possible trouble given to the office in registering a possessory title, in order that there may be the least possible expense charged to people registering.[36]

He would not even require a declaration by an applicant or his solicitor that the actual occupation or receipt of the rents was in accordance with the paper title, since that would reintroduce solicitors by the back door.[37] Further, if registration were to be compulsory but centralized, leases and mortgages would have to be kept off the register in order not to overwhelm the office, though he agreed that this was bad theory.[38] This was a far cry from the state insurance schemes envisaged by registration's first proponents. Cairns had found 'the State in the possession of the office of Registry'. That office now wanted to cut the law to suit whatever meagre cloth the Treasury would release. Holt won no supporters.[39]

---

[31] Minutes of Evidence, (1878) HCP xv, qq. 133–64, and cf. q. 2477. He was easily led by Osborne Morgan, e.g. q. 86.

[32] Ibid., qq. 977–89.

[33] Ibid., q. 857.

[34] Ibid., q. 881.

[35] Ibid., qq. 857, 955–7; and cf. qq. 882–3.

[36] Ibid., q. 958.

[37] Ibid., q. 959.

[38] Ibid., qq. 961–2; he thought district registries too expensive, q. 833. Cairns thought them essential because of the present low cost of small transactions, (1878–9) HCP xi, q. 2873.

[39] Liberal barrister Sir Henry Jackson, who in 1881 was appointed to the

2. The Conveyancing Acts: The ILS Ascendant

No sooner had Osborne Morgan's Committee reported than a Royal Commission on Agriculture was appointed, whose terms of reference enabled it to investigate whether the law of entail and settlement did stultify production. Shortly afterwards the Incorporated Law Society's annual provincial meeting in October 1879 was held at Cambridge, a suitably rural setting for its president to address the allied question of market economics, 'whether the law in any way aggravates the difficulties of agriculture by impeding the free dealing with land', and if so what could be done about it.[40] As Osborne Morgan was sourly to note, the president, Nathaniel Tertius Lawrence took an optimistic view.[41] He had also done some work to quantify market turnover, and he was thoroughly familiar with conveyancing techniques, at least so far as large estates were concerned. His conclusion was that 'well-drawn modern settlements do not impede the dealing with land, except in the way of mortgage, and that the obstacles and difficulties, which are now experienced in the letting and selling of land are due far more to mortgages than to settlements.' Not much need be done to the law of settlements. Apart from a few technical bits and pieces it would suffice for all powers of leasing, mortgaging, and selling habitually included in well-drawn settlements to be incorporated henceforward into all settlements by statute. Lawrence thought that the usual power of sale required concurrence of the life tenant and the trustees of the settlement, so to facilitate sales he proposed that alternatively a life tenant might apply to a court for permission.

But mortgage law needed extensive overhaul. Mortgaged property should be made much easier to sell, and while property was under mortgage both mortgagor and mortgagee should

---

bench but died before taking his seat, proposed immediate compulsory registration on the 1875 model, with district registries. He was absent from the meeting at which the report was finalized, and his proposal was not put to the vote. See also (1878) 239 PD 1900.

[40] The account that follows is from (1878–9) 23 *Sol. Jo.* 931 ff.

[41] Morgan, *Land Law Reform in England*, 23.

have the powers needed to ensure its efficient management. Further, second mortgages should be made safer. Two obstacles needed attention, the twin doctrines of consolidation and tacking. By the first, 'where a man mortgages different lands at different times for separate loans to the same person, the mortgagee is placed in the same position as if all the land had been mortgaged to him for the sum total of all the loans, so that [in effect] a second mortgage may be defeated if the mortgagor should have mortgaged some other estate to some other person for more than its value.' Lawrence proposed it be abolished. Tacking was more difficult. By this doctrine a mortgagee could refuse to surrender his security unless he were repaid not only his original loan but also any subsequent advances he may have made secured on the same land, notwithstanding that there had been intervening mortgages to other lenders in the meantime. Those lenders would thus be squeezed out, provided only that the first lender had not known about them when he made the further advances. In this situation fraud by mortgagors was said to be common and tacking was thought to be unfair. It had been abolished by the Vendors and Purchasers Act 1874, only to be retrospectively reinstated by the Land Transfer Act 1875.[42] As Lawrence explained, without it 'the system of continuous loans to builders, in proportion to the progress of their works, and other similar transactions' would be impossible. Though Lawrence rejected both title registration and deeds registration, here he made an exception. A simple register of mortgages could be added to the duties of the Inclosure Commissioners[43] at minimal expense; it would enable any lender to know whether land proferred as security was already subject to mortgage. Tacking would then wither away. If a statutory shortform were introduced for mortgages, then the whole mortgage document could be registered, making the Inclosure Commissioners' job simply that of bookkeeper. This had been the thinking in 1874, Cairns then anticipating that title registration would become compulsory in the following year. When it did not, tacking had had to be restored.

[42] Vendors and Purchasers Act 1874, s. 7, repealed by Land Transfer Act 1875, s. 129.

[43] For the function of the Inclosure Commissioners in private land-ownership see David Spring, *The English Landed Estate* (1963), ch. 5.

Adding powers by statute to settlements and mortgages would shrink their length considerably. Yet 'the trouble and responsibility of the solicitor would be the same as now, except that he would be relieved from superintending a certain amount of copying'. An *ad valorem* scale for conveyancing charges was therefore the third major item in Lawrence's prescription.

It was a performance well calculated to appeal to land market theorists in both parties. Land settled or mortgaged would have someone somewhere with approximately the powers of an owner, and once a decision to sell had been taken, legal impediments to a smooth transfer would be removed. Further, and in Lawrence's eyes more importantly, facilities for using land as security for loans would be improved from both borrowers' and lenders' points of view. To Osborne Morgan all this was merely a palliative,[44] but he would hardly greet enthusiastically an analysis demonstrating the unreality of his own claims that settlements caused serious practical problems.

Lawrence's address was published as a pamphlet and then worked up into a full-scale legislative proposition by an ILS committee.[45] To Lawrence's basic structure the committee added a battery of technical proposals designed to simplify conveyancing while retaining its essential form. The resulting 30-point plan was sent to the Lord Chancellor, Lord Cairns, in January 1879. When Cairns summoned E. P. Wolstenholme, then the most junior but the most adventurous of the Conveyancing Counsel to the Court, they agreed that both a bill to enable limited owners to deal with land as a prudent owner in fee simple would, and a bill to reduce the length of deeds should be prepared.[46] Without fee, and giving his time freely to attend committees, Wolstenholme superintended the drafting of what were to become the Settled Land Act 1882 and the Conveyancing Acts 1881 and 1882.[47] That government draftsmen were not used is a sign of the essentially private nature of

[44] Morgan, *Land Law Reform in England*, 23.
[45] N. T. Lawrence, *Facts and Suggestions as to the Law of Real Property* (1880); (1879–80) 24 *Sol. Jo.* 591–3. Lawrence also gave evidence to the Royal Commission on Agriculture, (1881) HCP xvii, qq. 54689 ff.
[46] (1907–8) 52 *Sol. Jo.* 494. For ILS co-operation see (1895–6) 40 *Sol. Jo.* 243 (Lawrence).
[47] He received £52. 10s. expenses: Select Committee on Conveyancing Bill, (1882) HCP viii. 259, 323.

the exercise. Royalties from Wolstenholme's published annotations may in due course have paid him for what the public purse did not.[48]

Before turning to these Acts a word should be said about Wolstenholme.[49] From Lord Westbury's day he had been advocating a radical revision of real property law involving the abolition of most legal estates and their replacement by a regime of trusts, intellectually the most complete of the 'assimilation' schemes on offer. For him it was no more than a simple rationalization of the legal position in fact achieved by the sum total of powers and duties commonly found in settlements of land, save that he thought it preferable to vest the fee simple in the life tenant rather than in the trustees of the settlement. He had argued his case strongly to Osborne Morgan's Committee, as also to the Royal Commission on Agriculture. But he made no headway. Indeed, at this time there appears to have been more interest in a rival proposition said to have originated long ago with Nassau Senior. This was that if the intricacies of real property law caused conveyancing problems, the easiest solution was simply to abolish the concept of realty. Since leases were, anomalously perhaps, merely personalty, one could just enact that henceforward all land should be treated as though it were held on a million-year lease.[50] Entails and life estates, contingent remainders and the like, cannot be created in personalty, so the problem of fragmented ownership would disappear. The only permissible subsidiary legal estate would be the sublease. Automatic descent to the 'heir at law' applied only to

[48] E. P. Wolstenholme and R. O. Turner, *The Conveyancing Acts 1881 and 1874* (1882), and *The Settled Land Act 1882* (1883).

[49] For this paragraph see E. P. Wolstenholme, 'Simplification of Title to Land: An Outline of a Plan' (1862), in *Papers read before the Juridical Society*, ii (1862). Evidence to the Select Committee on Land Titles and Transfer, (1878) HCP xv, qq. 2449 ff.; Evidence to the Royal Commission on Agriculture, (1881) HCP xvii, qq. 55117 ff.

[50] Select Committee on Land Titles and Transfer, *Report*, (1878–9) HCP xi, q. 2938 (Lowe). For discussion see Evidence to the Royal Committee on Agriculture, (1882) HCP xiv, qq. 64163–8 (Shaw-Lefevre), (1881) HCP xvii, q. 55153 (Wolstenholme). For a scheme whereby an owner could voluntarily convert his realty to personalty see Francis Vaughan Hawkins, *Optional Mobilization of Land: A Scheme for Simplifying Title and Land Transfer* (1869). For subsequent variants on the same theme see below, pp. 173–74 (Stephen) and Ch. 8, sect. 2 (Underhill).

realty, so it and its accompanying conveyancing problem of the retrospective checking of pedigrees would be instantly abolished. How simple.

Neither bill adopted Wolstenholme's own preferred scheme. The Settled Land Bill was a regime of powers, leaving the law of estates untouched. Some parts of the Conveyancing Bill were probably introduced by Wolstenholme, but most of it came from the ILS. At a deeper level Wolstenholme and Lawrence were agreed. Each advanced his own scheme as an alternative to title registration, which Wolstenholme had always disliked.[51] It lacked the creative flexibility of the traditional system, he thought, and exposed landowners to quite unnecessary officialism. So his willingness to assist Cairns can be explained in at least three ways: as responding to an intellectual challenge testing his skill and appealing to his vanity—much in evidence when dealing with critics later; as following the tradition that in the absence of a Ministry of Justice the senior conveyancers did give their law-reforming services to Lord Chancellors; and as helping render title registration unnecessary. We must not assume too close an identification between Wolstenholme and solicitors, however. When he learned that they, but not barristers, would have representatives on the Remuneration Committee he reacted with an anguished call to arms. If an *ad valorem* scale were introduced, requiring solicitors to pay for barristers' advice out of their own pockets in all but the rarest cases, not only would the conveyancing bar practically cease to exist but yet one more step would have been taken towards the 'practical amalgamation' of the two professions, a dreadful prospect.[52]

The politics of the bills' progress have not been investigated, but are unimportant to this analysis. The chronology was that Cairns presented a Conveyancing Bill and a Settled Land Bill in 1880, but the Conservatives lost office before they could pass.[53] Though Cairns relaunched them later that year, both were

---

[51] See n. 49 above, esp. (1878) HCP xv, q. 2463; and cf. his qualified adherence to the report of the Royal Commission on the Operation of the Land Transfer Act etc., of which he was a member: (1870) HCP xviii. 595.

[52] Wolstenholme and Turner, *The Conveyancing Acts 1881 and 1874* (1st edn. 1882), preface, pp. ix–x.

[53] Conveyancing and Law of Property Bill, (1880) HLP iii. 187; Settled Land Bill, (1880) HLP v. 273, 337; (1880) 250 PD 1164 ff.; 251 PD 278 ff.

blocked by the new Liberal administration.[54] In the following year Liberal politician and solicitor Henry Fowler persuaded his government that the Conveyancing Bill stood independent of the entail and settlement question, and could be passed without prejudice to it.[55] So in 1881 it went into committee, but with too little time for all its controversies to be resolved. Accordingly a reduced version of the bill was passed: Conveyancing and Law of Property Act 1881.[56] A Solicitors Remuneration Act was also passed, without difficulty. It did not establish an *ad valorem* scale, but instead provided for the appointment of a remuneration committee empowered to establish remuneration rules which might include the *ad valorem* principle. Though it also allowed for free contract between solicitors and clients, subject[57] only to disallowance for unfairness or unreasonableness, it is clear that the establishment of the *ad valorem* principle was the real prize.

In 1882 the Liberal block on the Settled Land Bill was lifted, Cairns piloting into law a slightly expanded version of his original bill. He also secured a further Conveyancing Act which restored some of the material omitted in 1881[58] and corrected a few mistakes in the previous year's Act. In their later stages the bills were supported by the Liberals' Lord Chancellor, Lord Selborne, who has been identified with the Goschen wing of his party, that restricted its approval of land reform to the traditional Liberal aim of liberating land-ownership from all fetters on free contractual dealing.[59] This had not quite been Lawrence's scheme in the first place. But during the bills' passage Cairns made two substantive changes. One conferred the power of sale directly upon limited owners without need for court approval, the other made the new regime applicable

[54] (1880) 252 PD 884, 1586 ff.

[55] (1881) 260 PD 686: Wolstenholme and Turner. *The Conveyancing Acts 1881 and 1874* (1st edn. 1882), preface, p. vi.

[56] Conveyancing and Law of Property Bill, (1881) HLP iii. 259; HCP i. 495; in committee (1881) HCP viii. 795; Cairns, (1881) 264 PD 1641.

[57] Contracting out was an ILS initiative, (1879–80) 24 *Sol. Jo.* 692.

[58] Notably s. 2, instituting official searches at the Central Office of the Supreme Court of Judicature, and s. 3, restricting constructive notice. But Cairns's attempt to use the bill to reduce protection for married women remained blocked: see (1882) HCP viii. 259, cls. 7 and 8.

[59] John Roach, 'Liberalism and the Victorian Intelligentsia', (1957) 13 *Cambridge Historical Journal*, 58.

to existing settlements as well as to future ones.[60] These amendments are consistent with the view that the Act resulted from a coalition of conservatives, representing the minimum legal change capable of presentation as freeing land from the supposed shackles of settlement.[61] 1882 was the year in which the Royal Commission on Agriculture reported, concluding in passing that the shape of the land laws was not at all to blame for the agricultural depression.[62] Apart from the question of sale, however, the text of the Settled Land Act owed a lot to Lawrence and the ILS.

So too did the Conveyancing Acts 1881–2, which have an importance beyond their dry subject-matter. Their provisions can be broadly divided into two: those which reduced the labour of conveyancing, and those which altered substantive land law. Some of the sections in the first category tackled the processes involved in conveyancing, some the documents thereby produced. To make sales of trust land easier the rules concerning appointment of trustees were improved.[63] So that inability to locate an incumbrancer would no longer prevent a sale altogether, money to cover the value of his share could now be paid into court.[64] To prevent purchasers' solicitors dragging out the transfer process, vendors could limit the documents purchasers were entitled to call for, and the facts of which they could require proof.[65] Opportunities to challenge the operation of powers of attorney were reduced.[66] Trustees were given more extensive powers over infants' land.[67] Other sections reduced the length of conveyancing documents. 'General words' commonly found in conveyances would now be included by statute without need for recitation, as would

[60] For the former change see Eileen Spring, 'Landowners, Lawyers and Land Law Reform'; for the latter see (1882) 266 PD 1076 (Cairns).

[61] Perkin, 'Land Reform and Class Conflict in Victorian Britain'.

[62] Royal Commission on Agriculture, *Report*, (1882) HCP xiv. 29. It approved Cairns's Settled Land Bill and thought it 'highly expedient to facilitate and cheapen the transfer of land', but not if that meant giving 'special facilities' to 'stimulate the artificial growth' of small proprietorship.

[63] Conveyancing and Law of Property Act 1881, ss. 31–8.

[64] Ibid., s. 5.

[65] Ibid., ss. 3, 8, 13.

[66] Ibid., ss. 46–8; Conveyancing Act 1882, ss. 8, 9.

[67] Conveyancing and Law of Property Act 1881, ss. 136–7.

covenants for title.[68] Numerous new rules of construction were enacted, removing the need to include lengthy technical formulas.[69] Most of this originated with Lawrence and the ILS.

There was a complex economic relationship between these parts of the Conveyancing Acts and the Solicitors Remuneration Act. Lawrence saw the latter as the necessary corollary of the former, thinking particularly of their word-saving tendency.[70] But the Acts reduced work as well as words, suggesting that causation ran also in the reverse direction: scale fees caused 'simplification' of the law in solicitors' financial interest. Of course, the Conveyancing Acts' restrictions on inquiry into title were not new, they simply sanctified by law what had hitherto been done by conditions of contract. But this is no answer, since scales were not new either. During the 1870s the principle of *ad valorem* fees was widely accepted, the only intractable problem being the consolidation of the various rival scales into one national code—a matter eventually solved by authority rather than consensus.[71] Contemporaneously the large law societies developed their own standard conditions of sale, sometimes explicitly to speed sales.[72] But the only way in which sales could be speeded—save trivially by sparing solicitors the bother of identifying which proffered conditions of contract were novel—was through reducing permissible inquiry into title. This symbiosis between the remuneration Act and the strictly conveyancing parts of the Conveyancing Acts can be seen again in a novelty introduced by the 1882 Act.[73] Instead of solicitors' having to send a clerk to search the records of the

[68] Ibid., ss. 6, 7. For commentary see (1882–3) 27 *Sol. Jo.* 798. A statutory short-form mortgage was introduced by ss. 26–9, sch. 3, pt. II.

[69] Ibid., ss. 49–64.

[70] (1878–9) 23 *Sol. Jo.* 930, 935–6.

[71] See above, Ch. 3 nn. 69 and 125, and their accompanying texts, and below, sect. 3. In 1877 the *Solicitors' Diary* came into the editorship of Charles Ford, who expanded its reference section to include *inter alia* the ILS recommended *ad valorem* scale. Ford was Honorary Secretary of the Legal Practitioners' Society (above, Ch. 3 n. 141 and accompanying text), and generally had prickly relations with the ILS Council; see Harry Kirk, *Portrait of a Profession* (1976), 34–5 and references, and below Ch. 5 n. 226.

[72] e.g. Bristol (1876–7) 21 *Sol. Jo.* 130; Nottingham, ibid. 261, (1877–8) 22 *Sol. Jo.* 308; Sheffield, (1876–7) 21 *Sol. Jo.* 381; *Dart on the Law of Vendors and Purchasers* encouraged the process ((6th edn. 1888), ed. W. Barber, R. B. Haldane, and W. R. Sheldon, i. 139).

[73] Conveyancing Act 1882, s. 2.

Courts of Justice for judgments and the like that might bind land the subject of a sale, henceforward for a small fee 'official' search certificates could be obtained, the contents of which would be conclusive. Any risk that the search might be much longer than expected would thus shift from the individual solicitor to the public fee fund.

The symbiosis is yet more complex than this. Many of the conveyancing reforms are perhaps best seen as stemming from law societies' experience in formulating standard conditions of contract, and it is true that from the very beginning of that involvement direct economic interests had been present—Liverpool Law Society had aimed to give its own auction room a competitive edge.[74] But once the idea had been accepted, notions of balance and fairness soon underpinned the promulgation and revision of standard terms of contract. Liverpool Law Society, for example, amended its code in 1877–8 to discourage what we would now call gazumping.[75] Gloucester Law Society regarded some of nearby Bristol Law Society's conditions as too onerous for purchasers, initiating a negotiation to settle their difference.[76] It was common for law societies to take up conveyancing questions in their locality as arbiters of fairness, good practice, and legality. Sheffield, for example, worked for three years to persuade the Duke of Norfolk to drop clauses in his leases prohibiting assignment without licence, other local landowners then falling into the new line.[77] Leicester confronted the Inland Revenue on the question of the proper stamp duty payable on transfers of mortgages.[78] Bristol battled long, though unsuccessfully, to get the local sanitary authority to drop onerous conditions of contract in its sales of surplus lands, even taking an opinion from Wolstenholme.[79] This local law-making served to secure law societies in their communities simultaneously with casting the underlying law in the image of

[74] See above, Ch. 3 n. 126 and accompanying text.

[75] (1877–8) 22 *Sol. Jo.* 597, 625; cf. (1881–2) 26 *Sol. Jo.* 641. By 1884 Liverpool LS was running an arbitration system, (1884–5) 29 *Sol. Jo.* 52. See also (1884–5) 29 *Sol. Jo.* 692, and for standardization of trust terms, (1885–6) 30 *Sol. Jo.* 602.

[76] (1881–2) 26 *Sol. Jo.* 640, 647.

[77] (1878–9) 23 *Sol. Jo.* 341, 353, 361.

[78] (1877–8) 22 *Sol. Jo.* 726.

[79] (1880–1) 25 *Sol. Jo.* 133, 877; (1881–2) 26 *Sol. Jo.* 731; for the litigious sequel see (1882–3) 27 *Sol. Jo.* 741; (1885–6) 29 *Sol. Jo.* 343.

the profession that operated it. The Conveyancing Acts continued that process.

So too with the Acts' substantive reforms, much came from the solicitors. Most of Lawrence's prescription for improving mortgage law was enacted, an ILS contribution to the 'land question'. But there was no provision for registration of mortgages. Lawrence's scheme had been dropped by the ILS committee,[80] perhaps for fear that any support for registration might encourage the Land Registrar to try for more. Tacking was to continue as a problem. On the other hand the ILS committee introduced a modernization of landlord and tenant law into the Acts. Leasehold covenants were to be made more effective, but limitations on the equitable power to relieve deserving cases from forfeiture were removed.[81] Taken together these alterations to mortgage and to lease law were a significant achievement for the ILS, a sign of its importance in law-making beyond its narrow self-interest.

MPs' perception of solicitors' importance did not extend quite so far as their own, however. In committee, Conservative MP Edward Whitley, sometime president of Liverpool Law Society, proposed a clause to extend the solicitors' conveyancing monopoly to the drawing of all documents 'referred to in this Act or any Act herein mentioned' plus the doing of all acts 'authorised by this or any such Act as aforesaid and usually done by a solicitor'.[82] It failed. His attempt was not an isolated aberration. At much the same time the ILS was pursuing the law stationers all the way to the House of Lords to prohibit their use as agents by solicitors in obtaining probate from Somerset House, in supposed breach of the proctors' monopoly to which solicitors were heir.[83] That action also failed, and in the *Solicitors' Journal*

---

[80] Its report was simply silent on the question: (1879–80) 24 *Sol. Jo.* 591. What was left became Conveyancing and Law of Property Act 1881, ss. 15–29, sch. 3, pt. II.

[81] Ibid., and Conveyancing and Law of Property Act 1881, ss. 10–14.

[82] For the bill see (1882) HCP i. 522; Whitley's clause (cl. 16) is printed at the committee stage, (1882) HCP viii. 259, 265. For Whitley see (1880–1) 25 *Sol. Jo.* 33 and Frederic Boase, *Modern English Biography*.

[83] *ILS v. Shaw and Blake, ILS v. Waterlow Bros. and Layton* (1881–2) 9 QBD 1 (CA, Mar. 1882); *Law Society v. Skinner, Law Society v. Waterlow* (1882–3) 9 App. Cas. 407 (HL, May 1883). See also (1880–1) 25 *Sol. Jo.* 554, (1881–2) 26 *Sol. Jo.* 512.

drew some criticism for political ineptitude.[84] Nor were these the only examples of solicitors' self-confidence. Cairns and Wolstenholme proposed a clause in the Conveyancing Bills aimed at neutralizing the principal theoretical advantage enjoyed by title registration as a system of land transfer, its avoidance of repetitive re-examination of the same title-documents. A solicitor who partially dispensed with examination of a title 'previously investigated and accepted' by another solicitor would not be liable for negligence if there were a defect.[85] Solicitors had previously claimed that this dispensation was common practice in small purchases anyway, but now they rejected the proposal.[86] How would the later solicitor know whether the earlier had investigated the title? How, without seeing the earlier contract for sale, would he know whether the title had been 'accepted' as a result of the investigation or as a result of stipulations in the contract? To investigate the contract would be to treat it as a document of title for the first time. All this was true, and as Cairns had to admit, the introduction of scale fees diminished the attraction of his clause.[87] Even so the solicitors may have been missing the political point.

3. 1882: The ILS Complacent

As the eighties opened, solicitors' labours seemed to have brought their rewards. Late in 1882 the new law courts on the Strand in London were finally opened, and in deference to the years of work put into the project by the solicitors, the then president of the Incorporated Law Society was knighted.[88] The solicitors were cock-a-hoop. It was the first occasion, said Sir

---

[84] (1882–3) 27 *Sol. Jo.* 481.

[85] Conveyancing and Law of Property Bill 1880, cl. 4: (1880) HLP iii. 187; Conveyancing and Law of Property Bill 1881, cl. 5: (1881) HCP i. 495; Conveyancing Bill 1882, cl. 2: (1882) HCP i. 521.

[86] (1879–80) 24 *Sol. Jo.* 340; (1880–1) 25 *Sol. Jo.* 312, 768, 771; (1881–2) 26 *Sol. Jo.* 274, 379, 625.

[87] Memorandum accompanying Conveyancing Bill 1882, (1882) HLP iii. 323; (1882) HCP i. 521.

[88] For this account see (1882–3) 27 *Sol. Jo.* 91, 216. Kirk, *Portrait*, 156, rather misses the significance of the event, though he does record the erection of the statue to E. W. Field.

Thomas Paine himself, on which their social status had been recognized as equal to that of the bar. The ILS elders voted to commission a portrait of Sir Thomas, despite protests from the groundlings that a society £32,000 in debt should not spend money on self-congratulation. Sir Thomas gave credit where it was due, to the founders of the ILS and to his predecessors as president. The physical monument on the Strand, the land legislation in the statute book, Sir Thomas claimed proud ILS paternity for both.[89]

But just as not everyone thought Street's architecture the best that could have been done, so there was one detraction from ILS pleasure in their legislative creation. It concerned the implementation of the Solicitors Remuneration Act. Against initial resistance the president of the ILS had elbowed his way on to the all-important rule-making committee established by the Act.[90] But on hearing this news provincial societies had lobbied successfully for parity with London, and Paine had been joined on the committee by one Enoch Harvey, president of the Liverpool Law Society.[91] Far worse, when the definitive Remuneration Order emerged from the committee it was obvious that Liverpool had outsmarted the ILS at the last. The statutory, national, *ad valorem* scale, almost as long in its gestation as the Strand courts themselves, mirrored exactly the division of professional labour negotiated by Liverpool solicitors within their city, quite different from that current in London. On many detailed points it had been the provincial scale that had been copied rather than that promulgated by the ILS. The Order bore Harvey's signature, but not that of the president of the ILS, who sulked in defeat.[92] Even in solicitors' triumph, the old divisions remained.

---

[89] (1881–2) 26 *Sol. Jo.* 752 ff.

[90] (1879–80) 24 *Sol. Jo.* 339, 591–3, 692, 887; (1880–1) 25 *Sol. Jo.* 231, 699.

[91] (1881–2) 26 *Sol. Jo.* 77. Then followed a period of attempts to agree a scale: ibid. 1, 7, 78, 191, 207, 212, 213, 222, 230, 505, 566, 571, 590.

[92] *Statutory Rules and Orders Revised* (1890), vi. 399. For links with Liverpool see: (1881–2) 26 *Sol. Jo.* 712, 718, 724; (1882–3) 27 *Sol. Jo.* 3. For concurrence of Manchester LA see (1882–3) 27 *Sol. Jo.* 258. For ILS sulking see (1881–2) 26 *Sol. Jo.* 666, 741 (at length), 753. Commentary and reaction continued for years; for starters see (1881–2) 26 *Sol. Jo.* 666, 696, 699, 704, 707, 727, 730, 738; (1882–3) 27 *Sol. Jo.* 1–2, 7, 23, 25, 36, 46, 53, 62, 67, 90, 143, 191, 201, 206, 212, 216, 219, 254, 299, 335, 530, 545, 565, 741; (1883–4) 28 *Sol. Jo.* 30, 113, 145, 150, 219, 259, 292. The most difficult question concerned division of labour with auctioneers.

But a triumph it was. As an anonymous reviewer in a law journal wrote late in 1881, 'by the general public the last session of Parliament is almost entirely identified with the passing of the great "Message of Peace" to Ireland, but by the legal profession it will not improbably hereafter be looked back upon as the date of a new and important departure in the science and art of Conveyancing.'[93] Sir Thomas Paine thought the Acts would 'mitigate, if not stop, for some time to come the cry for a general registry, which has, in fact greatly diminished in the past few years'.[94] The Acts owed much to the solicitors, and took for granted a model of land transfer based upon free market principles and minimal government intervention. They owed little or nothing to the political themes which were shortly to become so important—which is why they would fail to achieve what Paine hoped.

[93] (1881) 7 *Law Rev. & Law Mag.* n.s. 106.   [94] (1881–2) 26 *Sol. Jo.* 753.

Part II

1875–1940

5

Professionalism, Officialism: Solicitors and the State

1. Land Reform: Ideology and Politics

Within the broad fold of the Liberal party, radicals had long identified a land question, which in true individualist fashion they equated with the issue of ownership. From the 1860s one prescription focused upon the legal institutions of the landed aristocracy—primogeniture, entail, settlement—which should be abolished. For men who believed in the superiority of market forces to solve social problems it was imperative to remove 'artificial' impediments to a system of private property based upon individual initiative and responsibility. The onset of agricultural depression in the late 1870s heightened these claims; 'land in fetters' was land unable to adapt to straitened circumstances. As a result of the settlement system, it was said, farmers were mere leaseholders, unable and unwilling to invest the fixed capital the land needed. Poor housing conditions for both urban and rural poor could be traced to the same source: settlement prevented sale, reduced land supply, and drove rents up. Alternatively, settlement encouraged the urban leasehold system, whereby any increased capital value of the land accrued to the landlord, together with any buildings on it at the end of the lease, depriving the house-owner of incentive to improve the property.[1]

Concern with ownership had been shared with radicals who

[1] Joseph Kay, *Free Trade in Land* (1879); Arthur Arnold, *Free Land* (1880); Sir George Osborne Morgan, *Land Law Reform in England* (1880); G. C. Brodrick, *English Land and English Landlords* (1881); Sir George Shaw-Lefevre, *English and Irish Land Questions* (1881). And see T. A. Jenkins, *Gladstone, Whiggery and the Liberal Party, 1874–1886* (1988), 85, 90.

rejected the tenets of Liberalism: socialists whose solution was state ownership of land—nationalization. In the late 1860s some Liberals and some socialists formed a tentative liaison, possible only through abandoning ownership as the central issue and substituting for it the question of value. J. S. Mill himself argued that when land's value increased through proximity to a land market caused by social development, the landowner's profit was an 'unearned increment' not arising from his own efforts and hence fairly taxable, even if unrealized.[2] Land taxation offered an alternative solution from either stance. At one extreme it substituted for land nationalization by expropriating the entire value of land, leaving the formal shell of ownership intact but irrelevant. Such was the aim of the American, Henry George, who calculated that such a land tax would raise enough revenue for all other taxes to be abolished. His book[3] went into an English edition in 1881, and shortly afterwards George visited England on lecture tours. Milder versions were of course possible, compatible with the ideology of private property. If land brought its owners benefits not available from other forms of private wealth, taxation could simply remove them. Forms of ownership deviant from the norm of individual proprietorship could be penalized. Aristocratic owners who accumulated land could be driven by taxation into releasing it to the market. Here was the basis of a new Liberal radicalism.

A tax on land values became part of Liberal policy and a major focus of their efforts. As Michael Daunton has written,

> It linked with opposition to the leasehold system and the demand for leasehold enfranchisement; it offered a solution to the housing problem and to the mounting pressure on local taxation; it united rural and urban interests in support of Liberalism on the land question.[4]

But though land taxation offered a unified solution to problems of poverty, employment, and poor housing, so too in its day had the prescription of the 'land in fetters' group. Even within the Liberal party the latter retained adherents among those

---

[2] J. S. Mill, *Principles of Political Economy* (1848), D. Winch, ed. (1970), 169; Michael Freeden, *The New Liberalism* (1978), 42 ff. See especially E. Eldon Barry, *Nationalisation in British Politics* (1965), chs. 1, 2.

[3] *Progress and Poverty* (1879).

[4] M. J. Daunton, *House and Home in the Victorian City* (1983), 227.

hostile to the extension of state power inherent in the new Liberal radicalism. And on all other points the ideologies were very similar.

What was 'artificial' about entail and settlement of land was that they differed from the forms of settlement permissible for personal property, and differed in a way damaging to society by splitting ownership into relatively impotent fractions. A similar argument could be made about intestate primogeniture: it served only to maintain the ideological separateness of realty, penalizing relatively humble people who forgot to make a will and whose property then devolved in a way they would have thought inappropriate. What was needed was 'assimilation' of realty to personalty. Land was simply one species of property, not something special justifying privileges because of some, largely notional, burden of responsibility that landowners had to bear.

Thus 'assimilation', by stressing the unity of all forms of property, originally served to justify the removal of tax privileges from land. So in 1879 Lord Cairns resisted the seemingly innocuous proposal that land, on the death of its owner, should cease to devolve automatically on the heir but should instead descend through a 'real representative' as personalty descended through a personal representative. This, declared Lord Cairns, inevitably raised the question whether land should become subject to probate duty.[5] To admit the creation of real representatives would be to throw a sop to the Cerebus of socialism, fumed an outraged Conservative peer just eight years later.[6] But whereas Cairns had seemed merely temporizing, this peer sounded antediluvian. The proposal he was denouncing was contained in a Conservative bill. Times had changed. From being an aggressive claim against landed privilege, 'assimilation' became a defensive rampart against socialist plunder of property in general. If land is just wealth, then a Georgist attack on my land is no different from a socialist attack on your money. You must defend me or you too will perish.

Title registration went the same way, albeit as a very minor

[5] Cairns: Evidence to Select Committee on Land Titles and Transfer, (1878–1879) HCP xi, q. 2964.
[6] Lord Arundell of Wardour, 313 PD (3rd ser.) 1758.

issue.[7] Some Liberal proponents of free trade in land had long coupled title registration with abolition of entail as twin planks in the opening of land to market forces—Arthur Arnold, in particular. But the catalyst that brought political importance to the land transfer question was the expansion of the Parliamentary franchise in 1884, and the accompanying redistribution of seats which increased membership of the House of Commons from 416 to 643. In preparation for the next general election, each party had to find an appeal to an electorate doubled in size and containing for the first time significant numbers of agricultural labourers. The Liberal establishment adopted 'free trade in land' as its orthodoxy.

Under these conditions Joseph Chamberlain bid to secure the Liberal Party for the Radical cause. The Radical Programme, developed in a series of articles throughout 1885 and then supported in speeches during the election campaign, put heavy emphasis on land issues, especially rural land issues.[8] Chamberlain took it for granted that all Liberals supported free trade in land, which he took to include 'the registration of title, the cheapening of transfer, the abolition of settlements and entails and of the custom of primogeniture in cases of intestacy'.[9] But the predominant effect of this recipe from old radicalism would be that land became a better investment for the rich, so the new Radical Programme stressed instead the need for democratically elected local government units to be established, and for them to have powers of compulsory acquisition to provide cottages, allotments, and even small farms for ordinary rural people. Purchase should be at a fair price, not at the inflated values landowners customarily demanded for sales for public purposes. To pay for the programme there should be local rating of urban land, that is, on the property interest of the ground

[7] See e.g. T. A. Jenkins, *Gladstone, Whiggery and the Liberal Party, 1874–1886* (1988), 214 (Hartington).

[8] Joseph Chamberlain *et al.*, *The Radical Programme* (1885), ed. D. A. Hamer (1971); Richard Jay, *Joseph Chamberlain: A Political Study* (1981), ch. 5; D. A. Hamer, *Liberal Politics in the Age of Gladstone and Rosebery* (1972), ch. 5; T. A. Jenkins, *Gladstone, Whiggery and the Liberal Party, 1874–1886* (1988), 202–9. And see J. L. Garvin, *The Life of Joseph Chamberlain* (1935), i. 384–407, for the influence of Henry George on Chamberlain.

[9] Joseph Chamberlain, *Speeches*, ed. Charles W. Boyd (1914), i. 175; and cf. p. 147.

landlords; and to pay for other desirable social improvements there should be increased death duties payable upon land, and a tax on unoccupied or sporting land, at its full value. Tenant right should be recognized, and a system of 'fair rents' instituted. Landowners must expect to pay ransom for the continued existence of their private rights, hitherto enjoyed at community expense.[10]

This not only alarmed Conservatives, but drew hostile reaction from the Whigs still in the Liberal Party. For Chamberlain this was immaterial; his aim was both to purge the Liberals of Whiggishness and to provide a programme of social reform for the new electorate, not communist and hence not based upon an analysis of class. Only landowners were to blame for the nation's evils, not capitalists.

Lord Salisbury's strategy for the Conservatives was essentially defensive, especially for the interests of property.[11] But, much though he would have liked to, he could not plan for victory simply as a party of resistance. He had to adopt at least some part of the Disraelian tactic of offering mildly progressive measures of social improvement, especially to attract propertied voters in suburban and borough seats, who were being frightened by Chamberlain's radicalism. His election speech at Newport in October 1885 accordingly

> presented a package of domestic reforms designed to meet the concerns of advanced Conservatives but carefully limited to minimize the offence to loyal vested interests. . . . He advocated cheaper legal costs for transferring land titles, a reform advocated by Radical assailants of the landed interest; but Salisbury reassured landowners by reminding them how oppressive they too had found these costs.[12]

It was only three months since he had publicly expressed 'very great scepticism' that legal costs or legal practice deterred small purchasers in rural areas, and his doubts that title registration

---

[10] See particularly his speeches at Hull (5 Aug. 1885) and Birmingham (20 Oct. 1885) in *Speeches*, ed. Boyd; and those at Warrington, Glasgow, and Inverness in Joseph Chamberlain, *The Radical Platform: Speeches* (1885).

[11] Peter Marsh, *The Discipline of Popular Government: Lord Salisbury's Domestic Statecraft, 1881–1902* (1978), chs. 2, 3.

[12] Ibid., p. 80; cf. Robert Blake, *The Conservative Party from Peel to Churchill* (1970), 160.

would make any difference.[13] But if enlightened suburbanites thought that it was progressive to institute title registration, so be it—it was harmless. The abolition of entail was a trickier matter. Though Salisbury privately professed himself indifferent to its fate, he declined to offend his right-wingers by officially adopting this plank of old radicalism as Conservative policy.[14] Let it wait until the Liberal moderates had changed sides and become irrevocably absorbed into the Conservatives.

It follows from this analysis that title registration certainly, and abolition of entail probably, were more important to the Conservatives as earnests of their reforming credentials than they were to Liberals bent on real social change. Further, though what had once been radical proposals now held central ground common to both parties, title registration connoted a degree of state involvement in private affairs that fitted uneasily with an older Liberal tradition of small government—as one Radical Liberal candidate gleefully pointed out by mocking Goschen's late adherence to the cause.[15] Chamberlain himself quickly noted that if even Conservatives now espoused title registration and could be expected soon to adopt reform of entail, something much more would be needed to achieve desirable aims like the restoration of the agricultural labourer to possession of the land.[16]

2. 1884–1886: A Period of Uncertainty

Political enthusiasms can wane, especially when elections are over. That title registration would turn out to be the political answer to the land transfer question was not as obvious as Dr Offer makes out. The objective was to cheapen land transfer so as to be seen to be promoting the wider ownership of land. Evidence that conveyancing was expensive was scanty, and

---

[13] (1885) 299 PD (3rd ser.), 108.
[14] W. S. Churchill, *Lord Randolph Churchill* (2nd edn. 1907), 437–8, cited by Avner Offer, *Property and Politics, 1870–1914* (1981), 43. For the context see R. F. Foster, *Lord Randolph Churchill* (1981), 241.
[15] C. A. Fyffe, 'The Coming Land Bill', *Fortnightly Review*, 43 (Mar. 1885), 285; reply by Lord Stanley at ibid. 297, and rejoinder by Fyffe, ibid. 557.
[16] See nn. 9 and 10 above.

remains so today, and there was an embarrassingly wide range of solutions to the supposed problem. For example, one reason for expensive conveyancing might be that entail and settlement complicated land titles. Abolish or simplify them, and there would be no need for title registration.[17] Alternatively, perhaps title registration had failed *because* entail and settlement so complicated title that it was too expensive to register (another stick with which to beat the aristocracy). In that case the abolition of entail would be a necessary prelude to a new registration system, not a substitute for it.

In addition, there was the renewed alternative of deeds registration, brought back into play by the Osborne Morgan committee's response to the Dimsdale frauds. Armed with the new discovery that deeds registration worked well in Scotland, and that Irish experience might solve the index problem, some lawyers convinced themselves that it might become an acceptable substitute for title registration.[18] It would assure solicitors' place in the land transfer process, provide safeguards against fraud, and perhaps not cost too much extra to the client now that scale fees were in place.

For the Conservatives, Sir Hardinge Giffard, later Lord Halsbury, floated a scheme in 1884 to reform the Middlesex Deeds Registry as a first instalment towards adopting the Osborne Morgan committee report.[19] He had some rather distant support from G. B. Gregory, the solicitor-MP on Osborne Morgan's committee, but the Liberals blocked his bill on the grounds that it either went too far, in putting life into an office nearly uniformly condemned, or not far enough, in confining the reform to Middlesex.[20] Their own positive response was a doomed bill to transfer the deeds registry business to the title registry,[21] discussed further below.

---

[17] This is the most satisfying explanation of Osborne Morgan; cf. (1884) 285 PD (3rd ser.), 1304.

[18] G. B. Gregory, (1884) 284 PD (3rd ser.), 783, and cf. (1885–6) 30 *Sol. Jo.* 804; cf. W. Fowler, (1884) 291 PD (3rd ser.), 386. Select Committee on Land Titles and Transfer, (1878–9) HCP xi. 1, evidence of T. A. Dillon, esp. qq. 2540–51. This technological advance was reported in the press—see (1878–9) 23 *Sol. Jo.* 506. See also Dix (1885–6) 30 *Sol. Jo.* 231, 234, 284.

[19] Middlesex Land Registry Bill, (1884) HCP v. 331.

[20] (1884) 284 PD (3rd ser.) 778, 1672.

[21] Middlesex Registry of Deeds Bill, (1884) HCP v. 339.

According to local users, deeds registration had always been a success in Yorkshire, so debate in 1884 over proposals to reform the registries in the three ridings attracted an audience from those contemplating a national scheme. One bill originated from the Yorkshire Justices, who had statutory responsibility for the three registries, and who believed that arrangements for election of registrars were no longer acceptable. The posts were sinecures, deputies doing the work. Elections had become expensive, and the recently enacted Corrupt Practices Act, which reduced the cost of Parliamentary elections, did not apply. Every male freeholder had a vote; but no list was kept. Henceforward the offices should be salaried, election simply by Quarter Sessions.[22] Very soon a rival bill emerged, sponsored by a different group of Yorkshire MPs who proposed instead to vest the patronage in the Lord Chancellor.[23] Led fittingly by a solicitor, their aim was to secure these professional posts for professional men, solicitors of course, but at the cost of a centralization that cut across the Yorkshire grain. Those issues dominated the debates, with the Justices' bill prevailing.[24] But it was common ground that the opportunity should be taken to reform the substantive law. In particular, priorities of competing interests were to be settled by registration date, so that judicial decisions applying the equitable doctrine of notice were no longer to prevail. Registration of deeds in Yorkshire would in practice become compulsory. In the Commons this aspect of the bills won enthusiastic support from Osborne Morgan and from Gregory,[25] who was now promoting deeds registration as the most acceptable solution to the conveyancing question. The revised Yorkshire scheme combined with administrative devices such as the 'search sheets' used in the Scottish registry would in effect amount to a title registration system, he argued,

[22] Yorkshire Registries Bill, (1884) HCP vii. 725. For an election of a registrar see (1863) 7 *Sol. Jo.* 483, 570.

[23] Yorkshire Land Registries Bill, (1884) HCP vii. 703; clause 31 reserved the Registrars' posts to solicitors. For its fate see Select Committee on Yorkshire Land Registries Bill and Yorkshire Registries Bill (Osborne Morgan, Chairman), (1884) HCP xvi. 593. Yorkshire Registries Act, 1884, s. 37 settled for barristers or solicitors of seven years' standing.

[24] 285 PD (3rd ser.) 1290 ff.; 290 PD (3rd ser.) 1716 ff.

[25] Ibid. For Gregory see also 282 PD (3rd ser.) 1769; 289 PD (3rd ser.) 1740; (1885–6) 30 *Sol. Jo.* 804.

because after a few years' operation the search sheet would usually be accepted as evidence of a marketable title. Efficiency would be achieved by use of professional searchers familiar with the registers, as happened in Scotland.

The sequel to the Yorkshire Registries Act was salutary and unhappy. A fatal error had been made, necessitating a corrective Act that very same year.[26] Then the Yorkshire bankers rose in arms, because the clauses fixing priority by registration date abolished tacking, depriving them of their additional security when making further advances on a loan or when allowing further credit on an overdraft secured by a general mortgage.[27] Some local law societies also complained that the bill had upset previously approved practice and that their attempts to give evidence to this effect in 1884 had been blocked.[28] A compromise was found and duly enacted,[29] but it had taken three Acts to do the job of one, and even then there were doubts whether the new clause worked.[30]

More serious was the lack of positive support for deeds registration from senior lawyers in either political party. Even Halsbury had been tentative; Cairns, Selborne, and the Liberals' Attorney-General, Henry James, had been hostile.[31] Yorkshire had been let go its own way largely because it already had deeds registries. The city of York fell outside the registry area, and its local law society wished it to stay that way.[32] The ILS Council was carefully non-committal; deeds registration might deter fraud, and the system did work in Scotland, but it did not reduce the investigation of title, and the old objection of added expense remained.[33]

Yet the office that did reduce investigation of title was a sickly thing, expensive and virtually idle. The situation united propo-

---

[26] Yorkshire Registries Act (1884) Amendment Act 1884.

[27] (1884–5) 29 *Sol. Jo.* 103.

[28] Leeds ILS: (1884–5) 29 *Sol. Jo.* 135; Sheffield ILS: ibid. 307. See also ibid. 297, and (1885–6) 30 *Sol. Jo.* 203.

[29] Yorkshire Registries Amendment Act 1885. For strong criticism of the episode see (1885) 79 *LT* 327.

[30] Bar Committee, *Land Transfer* (1886), 25; *Dart on Vendors and Purchasers*, (7th edn. 1905), ii. 870.

[31] See nn. 20 and 24 above.

[32] (1885–6) 30 *Sol. Jo.* 807.

[33] (1885–6) 80 *LT* 250.

nents of 'economy', advocates of an effective title registration system, and those who simply wished to see it abolished. Parliamentary Supply debates in 1883 and 1884 were particularly bloody.[34] The Liberal government made no attempt in defence, but pointed out the difficulty in closing down the Land Registry. Follett and Holt had been appointed in 1862 under Westbury's grand design: they had judicial tenure. The government's proposed solution was to annex the Middlesex Deeds Registry. It ran at a big profit, payable to the sinecure office-holder Lord Truro. He could be paid off and the profit appropriated to the Land Registry, which would now get some work to fill its day. True, there would be no necessary saving to the public purse. But at least fees in the deeds registry could be officially regulated. Some solicitors had been agitating about excessive or illegal fees for several years,[35] so there would be an indirect public benefit from the scheme. When the Liberals finally plucked up courage to schedule this bill for debate it was greeted with ridicule and outrage by their own radicals, shunted off into a Select Committee, and abandoned.[36]

The Land Registry's failure also reopened the question of what substantive form title registration should take. In 1884 Sir Robert Torrens, who had patiently been promoting his own system of title registration for many years,[37] gained his only significant success in England. The Social Science Association decided that a Torrens bill would solve the land transfer question without need for any further simplification of the law,

[34] 282 PD (3rd ser.) 1764; 291 PD (3rd ser.) 381. And see (1889) 333 PD (3rd ser.) 1231 for a further instalment.

[35] Accounts of overcharging were common: e.g. (1884–5) 29 *Sol. Jo.* 97. Prime mover was Francis Munton, whose litigation culminated in *Munton* v. *Lord Truro*, (1886) 17 QBD 783. Its early stages were: (1882–3) 27 *Sol. Jo.* 636; (1884–5) 29 *Sol. Jo.* 114; (1885–6) 30 *Sol. Jo.* 249, 587. It would have started again: (1890–1) 35 *Sol. Jo.* 387.

[36] Middlesex Registry of Deeds Bill, 1884; 288 PD (3rd ser.) 787, 994, 1313; 289 PD (3rd ser.) 1740. And cf. (1882) 283 PD (3rd ser.) 865.

[37] He gave papers to the Social Science Association in 1863, 1872, 1878, 1880, and 1881 ((1885–6) 30 *Sol. Jo.* 271); Evidence to the Royal Commission on Agriculture, (1882) HCP xiv, qq. 65, 453 ff. Registrar Follett opposed the introduction of a Torrens scheme in England: Evidence to the Select Committee on Land Titles and Transfer, (1878) HCP xv, q. 78. For extensive evidence on the practical operation of Torrens systems see *Registration of Title (Australian Colonies)*, (1872) HCP xlii. 499.

and sent a delegation to the Attorney-General to tell him so.[38] But James was unenamoured of any form of registration, certainly opposed to compulsion, and rather inclined towards 'simplification' of either the Osborne Morgan or the Wolstenholme variety.[39] His Lord Chancellor, Lord Selborne, did approve title registration: but only if compulsory and only if the Treasury could be won round to funding district registries.[40] A year later the Duke of Marlborough sponsored a Torrens bill in the Lords,[41] the only one ever introduced in England. But by then the Liberals were out of office, the Conservatives were in as caretakers, and their Chancellor, Lord Halsbury, was circumspect.[42] Unlike Marlborough, whose promotional article in the *Fortnightly Review* and letters to the press were rabidly hostile to solicitors,[43] Halsbury stressed the need to co-operate with the legal profession, a sentiment with which Selborne agreed. Until the profession made its choice between title and deeds registration, Halsbury thought Marlborough's proposal premature.

It was the politicians who made the choice, as the much-heralded election approached.[44] Title registration it was to be. Under this stimulus an indigenous scheme emerged. It came in September 1885 from Horace Davey, eminent barrister and radical Liberal, and was largely a reversion to the Cookson scheme of long ago.[45] On the first devolution of a piece of land after a stated day, whether on death or by *inter vivos* transfer,

---

[38] (1883–4) 28 *Sol. Jo.* 501.

[39] 284 PD (3rd ser.) 785; and see (1888–9) 33 *Sol. Jo.* 536, 539 for his further opposition to compulsory title registration. One reason why the Liberals may have been less persistent than the Conservatives in pursuing compulsory registration is that they had more lawyers of ability and independent mind.

[40] 299 PD (3rd ser.) 106.

[41] Real Property Registration Bill, (1884–5) HLP vi. 1.

[42] 299 PD (3rd ser.) 104; it was during this debate that Lord Salisbury doubted that title registration would affect costs, ibid. 108–9.

[43] *Fortnightly Review*, 43 (Mar. 1885), 544; (1885) 79 *LT* 355, (1884–5) 29 *Sol. Jo.* 755. Cl. 113 of his bill allowed for 'land brokers' to replace solicitors in registered conveyancing, following Australasian precedents, on which, however, for New Zealand, see (1885) 79 *LT* 332, (1904–5) 49 *Sol. Jo.* 765, and, generally, 'Registration of Title (Australian Colonies)', (1872) HCP xlii. 499, answers to circular q. 4.

[44] See above, sect. 1.

[45] It was outlined in letters to *The Times*, (1884–5) 29 *Sol. Jo.* 742, 749; they are collated and analysed at (1885–6) 30 *Sol. Jo.* 252. For Davey see *DNB Second Supplement*, and (1907–8) *Proc. Brit. Acad.* 371.

its title would become compulsorily registrable. The title thereby gained would be subject to the rights of anyone in possession at the time of registration, including anyone in receipt of the rents and profits. Purchasers would thus have to make what the *Solicitors' Journal* considered to be the usual and prudent inquiries on site,[46] but this would enable the Registry to dispense with a long judicial investigation. Davey proposed that the limitation period be reduced to twenty years, so that after a title had been registered for that long the register would be conclusive. There should also be an additional register of encumbrances. His scheme was worked over by a conveyancing barrister, Howard Elphinstone, who suggested a further register containing information of adverse rights paramount to title, and one or two other refinements.[47] Both men wanted a registered owner to have statutory power to convey for all purposes. Deputy Registrar Holt declared that the scheme would work, and the *Solicitors' Journal*, after an exhaustive investigation in 1886 of all current proposals, gave it its vote, if afforced with an insurance scheme to guarantee good title and with a few administrative additions to deter fraud.[48]

There were now the makings of both a politicians' and a lawyers' consensus, but with a limit. In January 1886 Registrar Follett died,[49] just as the Conservatives surrendered office to the Liberals, victorious in the election. Deputy Registrar Holt was snubbed: both parties agreed that for financial reasons he must forgo promotion and should continue to run the Registry as Deputy, as he had in fact been doing hitherto. A statute was rushed through enabling him to exercise the few powers reserved personally to the Registrar.[50] Expansion of registration may have been a cross-party aspiration; but that was no reason for throwing good money after bad.

One month later, and before it became clear whether title registration would be pressed, came a splendid irony. The

---

[46] (1885–6) 30 *Sol. Jo.* 252.

[47] (1886) 2 *LQR* 12. Elphinstone, a career conveyancing barrister, became a Conveyancing Counsel to the Court in 1895. Provision for his suggested additional registers was made in the Land Transfer Bill, 1888, cl. 27.

[48] (1885–6) 30 *Sol. Jo.* 213, 233, 252, 257, 267–9 (verdict to Davey), 283, 299–301.

[49] (1885–6) 30 *Sol. Jo.* 252, 225 (obituary).

[50] Land Registry Act, 1886; 302 PD (3rd ser.) 996.

system so easy to regard as thoroughly Benthamite was attacked root and branch by the man sometimes considered the last of the Benthamites.[51] In the Conservative *National Review* Sir James Fitzjames Stephen, a judge, proposed instead the abolition of real property law.[52] Legally by far the most radical proposal, it was offered as politically conservative.

It is worth the detour. His first move was to dismiss lawyers' incremental reform as obfuscation:

what can we say of arbitrary rules providing that the difficulties arising from the logical interpretation of statutory substitutes for technical evasions of statutory attempts to prevent the evasion by legal fictions of the practical application of a false principle, shall be set aside? This, however, is an accurate description of Lord Cairns' most useful legislation on this subject.

Only a new start would do:

1. From the   day of   , all property whatever shall be, and shall be deemed to be, personal property. Estates in land shall cease to exist. All property shall descend, on the death of its owner, according to the law now relating to the distribution of personal property. Gavelkind, Borough English, and all other customs as to the inheritance of land, of whatever tenure, shall be abolished.
2. All property may be effectively transferred, bequeathed, and otherwise dealt with by any instrument which is now effectual for the conveyance of personal property, and by the use of any language which expresses sufficiently the meaning of the person who uses it; provided that no transaction for which a written instrument is now required shall be carried out without writing.
3. All owners of property shall have the same power of settling and dealing with property, either by will or by deed, as they now have with respect to personal property, and no other.

Clause 3 was Stephen's solution to the 'bitter controversy' of entail. Whereas Osborne Morgan and Shaw-Lefevre had proposed its abolition, and the introduction of complex limitations on future estates in land, Stephen allowed full rein to successive

[51] A. W. B. Simpson (ed.), *Biographical Dictionary of the Common Law* (1984), 489 (Steve Uglow).
[52] 'The Laws Relating to Land', *National Review*, 6 (Feb. 1886). For his politics at this time see James A. Colaiaco, *James Fitzjames Stephen and the Crisis of Victorian Thought* (1983), 191 ff.; Robert Rhodes James, *Lord Randolph Churchill* (1959), 303–4.

interests, but only behind trusts. This he recommended 'not only on its own merits, but because a consistent Liberal can hardly object to it without going a great deal further than Liberals in general go; whilst a reasonable Conservative ought to acknowledge that it would give him all to which he can justify a claim on reasonable grounds'.

So too with his main proposal. Only Radicals thought land was special. But they were wrong; the danger in one man's owning Yorkshire was the same as in his owning the Great Western Railway. It was untrue now that settlement made land unsaleable, but this change would make it so obviously untrue that the argument could not be made in good faith at all. It would 'exhibit in the strongest light that the real objections to the existing land laws are not properly objections to the law at all, but to the existing distribution of property, and to the social differences which depend upon it'.

Conservatives need feel no alarm; 'little or no practical change would be made', for all the fundamental principles of real property had long since been evaded by use of techniques superimposed from the law of personalty. Solicitors need have no fears. It would be absurd to suppose that this change would abolish conveyancing itself; an ordinary person would no more be able to draft a lease or any but the simplest will than he would be to cook his own dinner or build his own house. Stephen's experience in drafting a registration scheme in India convinced him that it was both 'artificial' and expensive. Land and houses would never be 'sold like stock till land becomes, so to speak, a mere right, an abstract idea, like stock or shares'. To round it all off there should be a codification (true to character), which would also deal with some of the necessary differences between land and chattels—concerning servitudes, leases, and mortgages, for example. His details were weak here, especially on mortgages; like Humphreys,[53] what he provided was an outline of a code.

Stephen owed something to Wolstenholme and to Senior's 'leasehold' proposal, though he did not acknowledge it. A more conventional development of the Wolstenholme theme had been propounded in October 1885 by John Hunter, a member

---

[53] See above, p. 3 (Humphreys).

of the ILS Council.[54] He had added a new proposal for the registration of deeds to its more familiar features of the abolition of all freehold estates save the fee simple and the curtaining of successive interests behind trusts in which trustees had wide overreaching powers. As usual, initial reaction from other senior solicitors was discouraging, and when the Council itself published a review of all current proposals it was ambivalent.[55]

With this great wealth of material before them the elders of the legal establishment asserted their professional importance by sitting in judgment, as though politicians did not exist. The ILS Council issued a 'Statement'[56] on current proposals, as judiciously weighed as could be managed given the subject-matter, and it was for the first time joined by a body aspiring to general representation of the bar. This was the Bar Committee, established in 1884 to give voice to junior barristers' professional concerns, but anxious also to claim a wider role. The *Law Times* was unimpressed; in 1887 it begged barristers to 'realise that they are being simply walked over by the "lower" branch; that while the Incorporated Law Society is going hand in hand with the Lord Chancellor in the only law reforms contemplated, the Bar is doing nothing . . .'.[57] Doing nothing maybe, but it had said something, in the form of a subcommittee report on 'Land Transfer' published in March 1886.[58]

These two reports—ILS and Bar Committee—projected very similar values. In particular they united against outsiders. Both analysed the Torrens system so as to show its inapplicability to England.[59] The Bar Committee's report, ignorant probably of Stephen's article but referring to the earlier 'long leasehold' proposal, dismissed that sort of root and branch reform as 'as dangerous and complex a device as could be adopted'[60]—very

---

[54] (1884–5) 29 *Sol. Jo.* 782.

[55] Ibid. 784; (1887–8) 32 *Sol. Jo.* (799), 803.

[56] *Statement on the Land Laws*; repr. (1885–6) 80 *LT* 228, 249, 271, 290, 307.

[57] (1887) 83 *LT* 91.

[58] Bar Committee, *Land Transfer* (1886). The chairmen were Horace Davey, succeeded by John Rigby, radical Liberals both. But E. W. Byrne was a Conservative, and H. W. Challis, a conveyancer assisting the committee, became strongly opposed to title registration: (1890) 6 *LQR* 157.

[59] Bar Committee, *Land Transfer*, 84 ff.; *Statement*, 271, 290; and cf. Registrar Follett, n. 37 above.

[60] Bar Committee, *Land Transfer*, 94.

like their predecessors' treatment of Humphrey. Of the various proposals from politicians for restricting future estates, the ones taken seriously were those from lawyer-politicians: Arthur Arnold's was simply brushed aside.[61] The Bar Committee report castigated Cairns's Act for sacrificing legal principles for political expediency.[62] Similarly, both reports stressed that it is the neutral professional who has the knowledge needed for a wise solution, be it legal or factual. The Bar Committee report especially rebuked Torrens for irresponsible advocacy involving selective and distorted evidence.[63] It criticized even Howard Elphinstone for assuming the facts necessary for his argument to work.[64] The Bar Committee report found it impossible to believe that solicitors should be ousted from the land transfer process.[65] The ILS continually asserted its good faith and its achievements in the law reform process and pleaded to be incorporated within it.[66] The shared commitment to professionalism could scarcely be clearer. As the solicitors were themselves wont to argue, the Bar Committee report now asserted that the army of district registrars and their assistants, necessary if title registration were to be compulsory, would lack the expertise needed to examine and certify title.[67] Law is difficult; that is how lawyers constitute a profession.

Neither report was enthusiastic about title registration or believed it much needed; both thought it could be made to work. The Bar Committee report found the 1875 Act bad, and that to make it compulsory would raise an outcry sufficient to cause its repeal; the ILS thought it the least unacceptable scheme on offer.[68] Beneath this apparent disagreement, however, there was agreement that the best strategy for compulsory registration would be to adopt something like the Davey scheme: register title without official examination ('possessory title'), have subsequent dealings done by registered transaction only, allow this title to harden into an 'absolute title' by lapse of time, and

[61] Ibid. 91; *Statement*, 308 ff., and cf. (1885–6) 30 *Sol. Jo.* 299 ff.
[62] Bar Committee, *Land Transfer*, 61–4.
[63] Ibid. 73, 97.
[64] Ibid. 97.
[65] Ibid. 45.
[66] *Statement*, 229, 249, 309.
[67] Bar Committee, *Land Transfer*, 71.
[68] Ibid. 82; *Statement*, 290–1.

insure all register entries against fraud or error, in which case the 'true' owner would be restored to the land and compensation paid to the person who had been misled by the false entry in the register. Since the Settled Land Act gave full power of sale to the limited owner in possession there was no pressing need for further reform. Settlements could be integrated into the registration system simply by registering as proprietor the person with the statutory powers—as the Land Registry was in fact already doing, albeit in defiance of the 1875 Act.[69] Introduction of a real representative would help title registration, though not much according to the Bar Committee report.[70] To aid that it would be sensible to abolish entails[71]—a step that both reports thought politically uncontroversial, given that entails could be barred anyway. Finally the Bar Committee report, echoing again a common cry, criticized the Crown's insistence on securing debts owed to it against land, and the analogous procedure of charging succession duty on the land itself, for making investigation of title more tedious and expensive than need be.[72] These detailed points were more or less common currency among lawyers, and formed the basis of a lasting consensus.

3. 1887–1889: Halsbury Frustrated

Before any progress was announced the Liberal party split over home rule for Ireland. The Conservatives were returned to office in July 1886. In October the radical speech at Dartford from Lord Randolph Churchill,[73] their leader in the Commons, renewed the commitment to title registration, announcing to the world that Halsbury had a scheme in preparation. In April 1887 Halsbury unveiled his first Land Transfer Bill; and in 1888 his second; and in 1889 his third.[74] Politically these bills were very ambitious. Not only did they combine compulsory title

---

[69] Bar Committee, *Land Transfer*, 93.
[70] Ibid. 92–3; *Statement*, 308.
[71] Bar Committee, *Land Transfer*, 51; (1888–9) 86 *LT* 423. Cf. Land Transfer Act 1875, s. 68.
[72] Bar Committee, *Land Transfer*, 94.
[73] For analysis see R. F. Foster, *Lord Randolph Churchill* (1981), 90–7; Peter Marsh, *The Discipline of Popular Government* (1978),98, 102.
[74] Land Transfer Bills, (1887) HLP vi; (1888) HLP v; (1889) HLP iv.

registration with the abolition of entail and intestate primogeniture, but, at the outset at least, Halsbury had chosen a most far-
reaching system of registration. Horace Davey's scheme had
moved title registration away from its earlier association with
sale by proposing that it be compulsory on every transfer of
land, whether on sale, settlement, death, or whatever. Halsbury
followed suit. Then he proposed that the duty to register fall
not on the transferee, but on the transferor—to induce anyone
selling just part of an estate to register title to the whole. Anti-
evasion clauses were draconian: the 1888 bill provided that until
a transferee's title were registered he would have no power to
create any legal or equitable interest in the land. It was arguable,
therefore, that if he died leaving a will before registration it
would be void and his devisees disinherited![75] Under the 1889
bill it was not compulsory to register a transfer by death; but
the registration fee would be charged whether or not registration actually took place, and would be collected with whatever
succession duty was payable.

Apart from that, the bills tended towards the lawyers' consensus,[76] increasingly so as Halsbury gave way to them and to
Liberals. The 1889 bill, for example, put the duty to register
back on to the transferee. Similarly, after initial doubts, Halsbury accepted that if there had been a mistake on the register
the true owner should be restored to his land, and the insurance
fund compensation should go to the duped transferee.[77] Indeed,
Halsbury was anxious to involve the legal profession in improving his bill. He sent it out to consultation with ILS and Bar
Committee,[78] he accepted multitudinous amendments, and he
even persuaded the Treasury to reduce the period for which

[75] (1887–8) 32 *Sol. Jo.* 318, 331; (1888) 323 PD (3rd ser.) 1757 ff.; 327 PD (3rd
ser.) 648 ff. Cf. the impact on public authorities: (1886–7) 31 *Sol. Jo.* 460; meeting
of ILS and provincial societies: (1887–8) 32 *Sol. Jo.* 318.

[76] But only after great pressure from Herschell: (1887) 317 PD (3rd ser.) 15;
and see (1888) 323 PD (3rd ser.) 1765, 325 PD (3rd ser.) 140; (1886–7) 31 *Sol. Jo.*
563, 619. See too the letter from William Williams, solicitor and veteran
proponent of title registration, (1886–7) 31 *Sol. Jo.* 630. The *Solicitors' Journal*
credited the scheme of the bills to Davey, and the drafting of the clauses
concerning real representatives to Elphinstone, ibid. 359, 373.

[77] Land Transfer Bill 1888, cl. 53; and see Selborne's successful amendment,
(1889) 337 PD (3rd ser.) 1558.

[78] (1886–7) 31 *Sol. Jo.* 440; *Fourth Annual Statement of the Bar Committee*, May
1887; *Sixth Annual Statement of the Bar Committee*, Mar. 1889.

land remained charged for succession duty.[79] None the less, there were serious funding difficulties. The central theme was that registration with possessory title should be easy, that registered transactions thereafter should be covered by an insurance fund, and that after five years unchallenged registration a title could be upgraded into an 'absolute title' by a simple process of 'confirmation'. But the insurance fund was not being provided by the Treasury: it would have to be raised by *ad valorem* fees on landowners, albeit very modest ones.[80] Yet compulsory registration extended beyond sales, and was geared to encourage owners to register whole estates on transferring just a part, so there was reluctance to impose the whole charge on these unwilling users of the registry. Some fees were therefore waived, but with it was lost some of the insurance coverage.[81] Difficulties were compounded by the legal structure of the 1887 bill, which was not a code in itself but simply a long set of amendments to the 1875 Act, with which it would have to be read. Further, many of the crucial details were left to rules, which were not yet available.

Halsbury failed, for all his persistence. Four possible reasons can be identified. First, he did not get all the support he might have expected. The Free Land League withheld its blessing— the bill delayed compulsory registration too long, and its inclusion of leaseholds, which they disliked anyway, tended to unnecessary complication.[82] The Building Societies Association disliked reliance on unpublished rules, and felt that the scheme was geared too much towards large proprietors at the expense of small.[83] Secondly, and ultimately decisively, there was resistance from landed peers to the real burdens to be imposed upon them by the form of registration adopted and, after that was modified, to the 'assimilation' provisions in the bill. Thirdly, there was lawyerly concern that Halsbury's initial plans deviated too far from the consensus.[84] These were taken up

[79] Following a letter from G. B. Gregory to *The Times*: (1886–7) 31 *Sol. Jo.* 471.
[80] A farthing in the pound; Selborne in particular could not understand anyone objecting to that: (1889) 337 PD (3rd ser.) 664.
[81] For commentary see (1886–7) 31 *Sol. Jo.* 424.
[82] (1887) 83 *LT* 84; (1887–8) 32 *Sol. Jo.* 332.
[83] (1887–8) 32 *Sol. Jo.* 113.
[84] (1886–7) 31 *Sol. Jo.* 421, 424, 439, 471, 490, 521 (ILS Council), 532 (John Hunter), 589, 655 (Gloucs. and Wilts. LS); (1887–8) 84 *LT* 355, 408, 423, 446, 466;

particularly by Lord Herschell for the Liberals, and though that ultimately led to an alliance between him and Halsbury over the final text, crucial time was lost.[85] Finally, there was opposition from solicitors, to which we shall return.

Initial lawyerly response was favourable. The *Law Times* approved both the bill and the principle of compulsion.[86] The *Solicitors' Journal*, by now regarding itself as the solicitors' semi-official spokesman, warned against the inappropriateness of opposition and hoped at last for a workable system.[87] The weakness of the 1875 Act in its eyes had been that indefeasibility of title (which included, of course, the indefeasibility of every successive dealing with land having an absolute title) necessarily required Registry staff to proceed with great caution, hence slowly and expensively. Now that the insurance principle was to be introduced the Registry would be justified in taking only the usual care that any businesslike solicitor would take:

what appears to have been forgotten [in 1875] was that *in ordinary business people do not proceed cautiously*; they proceed indolently, confidingly, eagerly, recklessly; they prefer risk to trouble, suspicion, restraint, delay. A system that proposes to conduct ordinary business without ever running a risk will never fulfil the requirements of the case.[88]

The 1887 bill was withdrawn so that it could be reintroduced in consolidated form. Even at this stage the *Solicitors' Journal* strongly urged solicitors to make registration a success, and there was no sign from the ILS of the storm to come.[89]

---

and see Benjamin Lake, (1887–8) 32 *Sol. Jo.* 799. For barristers see Sargant, (1887) 3 *LQR* 272; Humphrey, (1889) 5 *LQR* 275; Challis, (1890) 6 *LQR* 157. Halsbury was resistant to all except technical changes until eventually they were forced upon him: (1887–8) 32 *Sol. Jo.* 415; (1888–9) 33 *Sol. Jo.* 186 (Leeds ILS).

[85] (1886–7) 31 *Sol. Jo.* 571. For Herschell see (1887) 313 PD (3rd ser.) 33; (1888) 323 PD (3rd ser.) 1765, 1774; (1888) 325 PD (3rd ser.) 140; (1889) 337 PD (3rd ser.) 681. For criticism of his alliance with Halsbury see (1888–9) 33 *Sol. Jo.* 555.

[86] (1887) 83 *LT* 3.

[87] (1886–7) 31 *Sol. Jo.* 374, 390, 437.

[88] Ibid. 424 (emphasis original).

[89] Ibid. 520–1, 529 (Vice-President Henry Markby), 541 (ILS Council), and editorials at 603, 671, 780, 793, and 809. John Hunter's attempt to side-step title registration by substituting an assimilation bill got little support, ibid. 532–7; and cf. (1885–6) 30 *Sol. Jo.* 796.

The senior men on the ILS Council were, however, worried that Halsbury's bills might diminish their profession's status.[90] They lobbied for solicitors to be accorded places on the Land Transfer Board which would administer the scheme, and for Registry posts to be open to them. They were anxious also that the rule-making power should not be vested in the Lord Chancellor as Halsbury proposed, since that in practice would vest it in the Registrar. He thereupon conceded a share of the power to the Board itself. Local law societies were far more worried about compulsion.[91] Of the big societies only Liverpool approved; three-quarters opposed it.[92] The ILS Council fought shy, but was none the less pushed steadily into opposition as provincial solicitors, aided by the *Solicitors' Journal*, became convinced that Halsbury's aim was to exclude them from the land transfer process altogether—for which they blamed Registry expansionism and Treasury parsimony in equal measure.

That realization came slowly, from two sources. First were the bills themselves. Despite all ILS efforts, they continued to say that fees might be set for 'agents' using the Registry, without repeating the 1875 Act's formula that reserved paid agency to solicitors.[93] Given Treasury restrictions, perhaps that was how registered conveyancing was to be made even cheaper than the existing streamlined system under the Conveyancing Act and the Remuneration Order? The result according to solicitors would be the most undesirable touting for business on the steps of the Registry, and unqualified estate agents and auctioneers might move into a business where the public needed the protection that only a profession could provide.[94]

[90] 'Report', (1886–7) 31 *Sol. Jo.* 541; see too the terms of its questionnaire to local law societies, (1887–8) 32 *Sol. Jo.* 3; cf. ibid. 276 (Worc. and Worcs. ILS), 795 (editorial commenting on Benjamin Lake's paper at ibid. 799); see also Lake's earlier paper on professional themes, (1886–7) 31 *Sol. Jo.* 537.

[91] (1886–7) 31 *Sol. Jo.* 541; (1887–8) 32 *Sol. Jo.* 129.

[92] (1887–8) 32 *Sol. Jo.* 46 (Liverpool). There were occasional letters in like vein: (1887–8) 32 *Sol. Jo.* 21.

[93] The culprit was Land Transfer Bill 1888, Schedule, para. C, which was rather a flimsy foundation for such a mega-fear. It was buttressed, however, by cls. 45(2) and 81(5), which contrasted sharply with Land Transfer Act 1875, s. 111(4) and with Land Registration General Rules 1875, Rule 38 (*Statutory Rules and Orders Revised*, iv).

[94] (1886–7) 31 *Sol. Jo.* 421, 425, 505, 521. C. F. Brickdale's letter to *The Times*, ibid. 563, wrote of dispensing with solicitors, but not of replacing them with lesser beings. No doubt he saw officials as all that was needed.

The second source of anxiety came from Registry behaviour. It was still losing money, still had to make do with the 1875 Act, and was still vulnerable to periodic outbursts of Parliamentary scorn and outrage.[95] Under these pressures it began to do as Shaw-Lefevre had urged—it began to market itself. It had to raise its fees, but it managed to do so in a way that made registration easier, much as Holt had proposed to Osborne Morgan's committee.[96] Its public notices began to say that registration was easy enough to be done without professional help.[97] And finally, with Halsbury's 1889 bill imminent, it advertised itself aggressively in *The Times*. In print so large that the *Solicitors' Journal* was unable to reproduce it, it declared that vendors would hardly ever require a solicitor, and that 'most purchasers of average business capacity will be able to do their own work also'.[98] Uproar.[99] The *Solicitors' Journal* condemned the Registry for acting as a tradesman; one correspondent gravely determined that the Notice 'lacked legal savour'. Beyond that, if the Registry ousted solicitors from the skilled work of land transfer it was predictable that the unskilled 'touts' would intervene as intermediaries between officials and laypersons. In protest nearly 200 firms of solicitors in the Strand area of London petitioned their MP, reminding him of their business franchise. He was W. H. Smith, now the Conservatives' leader in the Commons. Halsbury had the Notice withdrawn.[100]

Whether law societies' determined lobbying of MPs[101] would have won the day in the Commons was never tested. It had taken two years for Halsbury's bill to be remoulded in the shape of the lawyers' consensus, and now that he had Herschell's approval Halsbury hoped to bypass the Lords,[102] where die-hard resistance to 'assimilation' was incorrigible. He tried procedural means to muzzle opposition, but failed.[103] In 1889 his

---

[95] See n. 34 above.

[96] Land Registry Rules, 1889 (*Statutory Rules and Orders Revised*, iv); (1888–9) 33 *Sol. Jo.* 164, 181.

[97] (1888–9) 33 *Sol. Jo.* 164, 181.

[98] Ibid. 193, 198.

[99] For what follows see (1888–9) 33 *Sol. Jo.* 250, 264, 266, 279, 283.

[100] Ibid. 343, 347.

[101] Ibid. 433, 435, 447, 461, 501, 517, 539, 569, 585, 615; (1889–90) 34 *Sol. Jo.* 98.

[102] Avner Offer, *Property and Politics, 1870–1914* (1981) 44.

[103] (1888–9) 33 *Sol. Jo.* 555.

bill fell when the Lords rejected clauses introducing real representatives—an amendment carefully chosen to indicate to the
Conservative leadership that it was the impact of this particular
registration scheme on traditional property interests that was
the problem, not registration itself.[104] Lord Beauchamp forced
the point home:

> The primary object of the land laws . . . is not that land should be
> bought and sold, but that a person should enjoy peaceably the land
> which belongs to him. . . . The interests of the land of this country are
> of far more importance than satisfying the theories of the pedants and
> fanatics with regard to the transfer of land.[105]

The debates suggest an easy analysis. The Conservative
leadership wanted title registration and offered a measure of
'assimilation' to Liberals as a bait. Gladstonian Liberals would
have liked the reform of entail, but were ambivalent about title
registration. Conservative backwoodsmen may not have cared
much about title registration in principle, but did if it hurt their
pockets; and they disliked 'assimilation'. So in straining to
maximize political gains from land law reform Halsbury had
united both old property in the Lords and new property in the
professions against him, and because it was technically difficult
to produce a satisfying bill quickly he had allowed time for his
opponents to cohere. The Conservatives abandoned the abolition of entails and dithered over reintroducing the title registration scheme.[106] The ILS and the provincial law societies
prepared a vigorous campaign against it,[107] but the bill was
abandoned without need for its operation. The first great
struggle was over.

Landed peers had no doubt opposed Halsbury because their
interests were threatened, whether or not it had taken organized effort by solicitors to bring the point home. But in the
debates solicitors' own interests were acknowledged and
approved, and whether or not the speakers believed the argu-

---

[104] e.g. Earl of Milltown, (1889) 337 PD (3rd ser.) 679. The crucial vote is
recorded at ibid. 1566.

[105] Ibid. 671.

[106] (1889–90) 34 *Sol. Jo.* 1 (Lord Derby), 55 (Halsbury), 243, 559.

[107] (1889–90) 34 *Sol. Jo.* 236, 311, 341. The ILS expenditure which Dr Offer
finds so sinister (*Property and Politics*, 44) was on lunches for its committee
members: (1888–9) 33 *Sol. Jo.* 611.

ments they clearly thought them plausible. It is pertinent then to look at the case that the ILS Council made for solicitors. Though propelled by provincial law societies into a more vigorous opposition than it would have chosen,[108] the Council's published criticisms were judiciously worded.[109] They do of course contain much detailed analysis of the bills and some political argument against compulsion, but the unmistakable major theme is the defence of professionalism. This is important because in his analysis of solicitors' resistance to title registration Dr Offer advances as an explanation for their success, which he magnifies, the view that their 'property' was threatened with confiscation.[110] By this he means their monopoly rights over conveyancing that enabled them to extract a 'rent' from the service they provided, above what might otherwise be earned.[111] Expanded versions of this analysis of professions, which build upon sociologists' notions of 'personal capital', have since become commonplace,[112] and they emphasize all the features that are so well illustrated by the solicitors: their control of the market for services by high entry barriers of education and premium, the reduced competition among themselves, their powers of discipline internally, and their enforceable monopoly powers. But this novelty of the 1980s would have come as no surprise to solicitors of the 1880s. It was exactly what they were shouting from the rooftops.[113] They made no secret of their wish to defend monopoly power. It was in the public interest. It resulted from a bargain with the State, for which they paid in high education costs and an annual licence fee. They accepted onerous standards of behaviour and forfeited

---

[108] (1886–7) 31 *Sol. Jo.* 448, 520, 538; (1887–8) 32 *Sol. Jo.* 129, 189, 259, 318, 415, 632; (1888–9) 33 *Sol. Jo.* 367; ((1888–9) 86 *LT* 428). For London solicitors see (1888–9) 33 *Sol. Jo.* 483, 569.

[109] (1886–7) 31 *Sol. Jo.* 521, 541; (1888–9) 33 *Sol. Jo.* 319, 375, 393; and cf. (1886–7) 31 *Sol. Jo.* 519 (Markby), 532 (Hunter), (1887–8) 32 *Sol. Jo.* 351 (Lake), 799 (Lake); cf. also (1887–8) 32 *Sol. Jo.* 208 (Halifax LS), 276 (Worc. and Worcs. LS).

[110] Offer, *Property and Politics*, esp. 51, 82–7.

[111] Harold Perkin, 'Professionalism, Property and English Society since 1880' (Stanton Lecture, University of Reading, 1981).

[112] Harold Perkin, *The Rise of Professional Society* (1989, 1990), ch. 1.

[113] (1886–7) 31 *Sol. Jo.* 425; (1888–9) 33 *Sol. Jo.* 250, 279, 391, 393, 409, 413, 423, 569, 583; (1889–90) 34 *Sol. Jo.* 91, 121; and cf. the Marquis of Bath, (1889) 337 PD (3rd ser.) 658.

the freedom of contract accorded to non-professionals. The ILS had kept its side of the bargain by devising the Conveyancing Act; it should now be given a fair trial. Title registration should be an adjunct to the professional structure rather than a replacement of it. The ILS Council's comments on Halsbury's bill said all this in so many words.[114] It was all of a piece with their insistence on membership of the Land Transfer Board, their resistance to administrative rule-making to the extent that it excluded them from the legislative process, and their abhorrence of official discretion. In its most aggressive form title registration was the antithesis of legal professionalism because it threatened both the top and the bottom of what Harold Perkin has identified as professionalism's hallmark, the 'vertical professional hierarchy':[115] the bottom through loss of relatively low-level work, the top through loss of its privileged place in law-making.

4. 1890–1892: The Pains of Professionalism

The solicitors' set-to with Halsbury had come suddenly. As recently as 1887 the *Law Times* had seen the ILS co-operating with him to the exclusion of the bar.[116] In that same year the ILS had obtained its due share of the Queen's jubilee bounty when its president had been knighted.[117] At ILS meetings in 1887 and 1888 land transfer issues had shared the platform about equally with broad questions of whether ILS membership should be compulsory for solicitors, to mark a perceived rise in honour and status.[118] President Benjamin Lake's address[119] in 1888 stressed too the great legislative achievements of that year: the Solicitors Act which extended ILS control of the profession by a

---

[114] (1885–6) 30 *Sol. Jo.* 213 ((1885–6) 80 *LT* 307); (1886–7) 31 *Sol. Jo.* 521, 533 (Hunter), 541; (1887–8) 32 *Sol. Jo.* 795 (Lake); (1888–9) 33 *Sol. Jo.* 393; and cf. ibid. 578 on public trustees. See too the 'fusion' debate, (1888) 85 *LT* 12; Brian Abel-Smith and Robert Stevens, *Lawyers and the Courts* (1967), 227–30.

[115] Perkin, *Rise of Professional Society*, ch. 1.

[116] See n. 57 above.

[117] (1886–7) 31 *Sol. Jo.* 571. The *Solicitors' Journal* had hoped that solicitors' services to law reform would bring a suitable reward, ibid. 487.

[118] (1886–7) 31 *Sol. Jo.* 529 (Vice-President Henry Markby), 531 (President H. W. Parker), 536; (1887–8) 32 *Sol. Jo.* 799 (President B. Lake), 803.

[119] (1887–8) 32 *Sol. Jo.* 799.

further stage or two, thereby increasing its professional authority; the Trustee Act, a monument to altruistic law reform; and
the Land Charges Registration and Searches Act. This last,
wholly an initiative from within Council, had united into one
all the various registers in which statutory charges against land
had to be recorded, an important step in streamlining conveyancing.[120] Though the ILS preference had been to lodge the
register in the Central Office of the courts, it had not complained
when an amendment had switched it to the Land Registry
instead, nor even when the memorandum accompanying the
bill had said that it would facilitate title registration.[121] And such
participation in government was to continue. In the next couple
of years Council busied itself in negotiating a compromise with
the Municipal Corporations Association to secure the registration of charges under the Public Health Act,[122] pressed the
Board of Trade to institute a register of bankruptcies,[123] and
staked their place in the governance of legal education in the
proposed University of London.[124] There is no sense here of a
profession at general odds with government.

Meanwhile the Land Registry had good fortune at last. The
ILS gift of the Land Charges Registration and Searches Act
swung it into modest profit in 1890, the first in its twenty-eight
year existence (see Appendix). Then Lord Truro died. Almost
before he was decently buried his powers as Registrar of the
Middlesex Deeds Registry were transferred to the Land Registry.[125] In the following year the two registries were amalgam-
ated; Holt was finally promoted to Registrar, a post vacant since
Follett's death.[126] The ILS Council did not oppose the transfer

[120] Land Charges Registration and Searches Act, 1888. The stimulus was *re
Pope* (1886) 17 QBD 743. See (1886–7) 31 *Sol. Jo.* 361, 532 (Hunter), 639; (1887–8)
32 *Sol. Jo.* 348, 467, 640. (1888–9) 33 *Sol. Jo.* 85 credits the Act to William Godden
of the ILS Council.
[121] (1888) HLP v. 255. See too Land Transfer Bill, 1888, cl. 89, foreshadowing
the transfer of responsibility from the SCJ to the Registry.
[122] (1890–1) 35 *Sol. Jo.* 684; (1891–2) 36 *Sol. Jo.* 668.
[123] (1891–2) 36 *Sol. Jo.* 668.
[124] (1890–1) 35 *Sol. Jo.* 601, 658; Abel-Smith and Stevens, *Lawyers and the
Courts*, 172–3.
[125] Middlesex Registry Act 1891; 352 PD (3rd ser.) 216, 782.
[126] Land Registry (Middlesex Deeds) Act 1891; 355 PD (3rd ser.) 641, 865;
(1890–1) 35 *Sol. Jo.* 476, 603, 637–8; (1891–2) 36 *Sol. Jo.* 565. Until 1894, when he
became Assistant Registrar, c.f. Brickdale was usually styled 'barrister assisting
at the Registry'.

of Truro's powers to Holt, despite urgings from the *Solicitors' Journal*, and when they did intervene at the second stage of the marriage it was on public interest grounds. They succeeded in strengthening the accompanying rules so as to avoid a reduction in the Registry's liability, but not in their argument that now that the private profit element had been eliminated from Middlesex deeds registration, office fees should fall to match those of the Yorkshire registries.[127] Profits soared,[128] proselytizing continued,[129] and the Registry's newly secure place in government was signalled when county councils compulsorily buying land for smallholdings were required to have it registered with absolute title.[130] ILS protests were rebuffed.[131]

The ILS Council might be enjoying the participation in government that their status as professional leaders brought, regarding the spat with Halsbury as a cloud in an otherwise clear sky, but country practitioners were less sanguine. They had already linked probable loss of business from title registration with its actual loss through nationalization of bankruptcy administration.[132] Then in 1891 came two proposals for reform of trusteeship. The first, for institution of corporate trustees, was worrying, but not greatly so since solicitors might control the companies and since the companies might well depend upon solicitors for business. But the second mooted the introduction of a Public Trustee, an innovation pioneered in New Zealand.[133] It was this threefold conjunction of bureaucratic involvement in bankruptcy, land transfer, and trusteeship, with its concomitant expansion of rule-making, that moved the ILS

---

[127] (1891–2) 92 *LT* 244; (1890–1) 35 *Sol. Jo.* 717; (1891–2) 36 *Sol. Jo.* 235, 668; and see (1885–6) 30 *Sol. Jo.* 203 for earlier pressure from Yorkshire solicitors to keep Yorkshire deeds registry fees down.

[128] See Appendix.

[129] (1880–90) 34 *Sol. Jo.* 55; (1890–1) 35 *Sol. Jo.* 64, 399; (1891–2) 36 *Sol. Jo.* 183; (1892–3) 37 *Sol. Jo.* 417.

[130] Small Holdings Act 1892, s. 10.

[131] (1891–2) 36 *Sol. Jo.* 495, 516, 533, 749–50.

[132] e.g. (1888–9) 33 *Sol. Jo.* 423; W. R. Cornish and G. de N. Clark, *Law and Society in England, 1750–1950* (1989), 230–7.

[133] (1887–8) 32 *Sol. Jo.* 445; (1888–9) 33 *Sol. Jo.* 518, 583; (1889–90) 34 *Sol. Jo.* 81; and see the response of Manchester ILA, ibid. 373, 382, urging payment for private trustees; (1890–1) 35 *Sol. Jo.* 717; (1891–2) 36 *Sol. Jo.* 95, 391, 408; Abel-Smith and Stevens, *Lawyers and the Courts*, 206–7.

to publish its first tract against an 'officialism' which threatened its autonomous professionalism.[134]

Halsbury's reaction was astute. Accepting the ILS Council's much-advertised claim that solicitors should be involved in legislation he invited it to prepare its own Public Trustee Bill.[135] And it did, until forced to abandon its draft by disapproval from the provincial societies.[136] Its own move was astute too, if defensive. It promoted a bill requiring rule-making authorities to give forty days' notice of their intentions, coupled with a duty to consider representations made by 'public bodies', a term specifically including the ILS.[137] Though the bill passed the Commons twice in this form, it reached the statute book in 1893 shorn of the definition clause conferring public status on the ILS—Lord Chancellor Herschell had seen to that.[138]

The contradictions always latent in the Council's version of professionalism finally broke into the open as the general election of 1892 neared. At a speech to a dinner party given in his honour, Thomas Marshall, retiring Secretary of Leeds ILS, urged solicitors to defend their privileged status.[139] They existed only by their privileges, he said, and now that their influence over the newer sort of MP was likely to wane it was time to adopt the tactics of a trade union. He won enthusiastic support from the *Solicitors' Journal*, which urged its readers to confront Parliamentary candidates with their views and to cast their votes according to the responses received.[140] Benjamin Lake replied in 'astonishment and dismay'.[141] He was an important figure on the ILS Council, especially in its disciplinary functions, and he was the chief negotiator on the title registration question.[142] Later the *Solicitors' Journal* credited him above other Council members for making Council responsive to ordinary

[134] (1891–2) 36 *Sol. Jo.* 245, 258, 276; Offer, *Property and Politics*, 45; and see (1891–2) 36 *Sol. Jo.* 668, (1892–3) 37 *Sol. Jo.* 383, 390.
[135] (1891–2) 36 *Sol. Jo.* 295, 298.
[136] Ibid. 301, 630–1.
[137] Statutory Rules Procedure Bill, (1890–1) HCP x. 239, 243; (1893–4) HCP viii. 297; (1893) 13 PD (4th ser.) 603; (1891–2) 36 *Sol. Jo.* 801.
[138] Rules Publication Act 1893; for Herschell's amendments see (1893–4) HLP viii. 437 ff.
[139] (1891–2) 36 *Sol. Jo.* 490.
[140] Ibid. 517.
[141] Ibid. 538.
[142] See above, n. 119; below, sects. 5 and 6; (1888–9) 33 *Sol. Jo.* 512.

practitioners.[143] But in his eyes solicitors gained their influence through facilitating and suggesting new measures, not as a trade union using privilege for personal gain.

Lawyers exist for the service of the public, not the public for the profit of lawyers. Solicitors are entitled, and often bound, to point out the evils which, in their judgement as skilled men of business, will be the result of a contemplated change in the law, but if, notwithstanding their remonstrances, the change is made, it is their duty to carry the law into effect, and, so far as in them lies, to avert or minimize the apprehended evil.[144]

That would not prevent their opposing compulsion, which was contrary to principle, nor defending their privileges like any other class. But it limited them to persuasion, and to co-operation.

The *Solicitors' Journal* replied in kind.[145] A provincial practitioner wrote that Lake was the one solicitor in a hundred who could afford to belong to 'a learned and respected profession simply for the honour and glory thereof'.[146] Marshall circulated a pamphlet to all provincial law societies advising them how to question Parliamentary candidates.[147] The *Solicitors' Journal* reported the process to be under way.[148] Lake stuck to his guns;[149] compulsory title registration should be opposed by argument, but when it came, as it would, solicitors would be better placed to bargain over the manner of its introduction if they stood aloof now. In his view, compulsory land transfer would anyway permanently increase their personal gains. But the ILS Council could not withstand the tide; it too issued a circular on the questioning of candidates.[150] At ILS meetings stalwarts of Council such as William Godden, who had been responsible for the Land Charges Registration and Searches bill, and that year's president, Richard Pennington, urged members to argue on behalf of the public only, and to remember solicitors'

---

[143] (1888–9) 33 *Sol. Jo.* 604.
[144] (1891–2) 36 *Sol. Jo.* 538.
[145] Ibid. 535, 549, 570.
[146] Ibid. 571; a range of letters was published at ibid. 590–1, but cf. ibid. 586.
[147] Ibid. 585.
[148] Ibid. 619.
[149] Ibid. 607, but cf. ibid. 604.
[150] Ibid. 603.

place in the wider scheme of law and government.[151] But votes by acclamation went to the aggressive trade unionists.[152]

The Liberals won the election, to muted cheers from the *Solicitors' Journal*, which had feared Halsbury's revenge. Herschell might not be a 'figure head (ornamental or otherwise) for the schemes of departmental-faddists'.[153] To the Journal's disappointment[154] he continued where the Conservatives had left off, splitting Halsbury's bill into a title registration part and a part assimilating intestate succession to realty with that of personalty, introducing both in three successive years.[155] The Lords rejected the latter each time, but passed the former without demur in 1893 and 1895. The alliance between old and new property had been severed, particularly by Herschell's reversion to the vision of title registration that made it compulsory only on sale. Solicitors would have to choose.

For Avner Offer,[156] 'Gladstone's last ministry of 1892 was even more firmly committed than its predecessors to land-law reform with the result that the solicitors were increasingly isolated.' Taking his cue from Assistant-Registrar C. F. Brickdale, he relates that 'increasingly blatant tactics of harrassment and delay both within the House and without . . . succeeded in blocking the bill in 1893, 1894 and 1895'. But though one might expect that solicitors' increasing politicization would generate a battle, and that they would win cross-bench support for their hostility to officialism, yet the confrontation was much less than Dr Offer supposes.

He exaggerates Liberals' commitment. Gladstone's ministry was occupied above all with Ireland, secondarily with local government.[157] His party was concerned with the succession to

---

[151] Ibid. 648, 801.

[152] (1891–2) 36 *Sol. Jo.* 639, 650, 797 (810, 811).

[153] (1891–2) 36 *Sol. Jo.* 725.

[154] (1892–3) 37 *Sol. Jo.* 242.

[155] Land Transfer Bills: (1893–4) HLP vi. 5; (1894) HLP v. 217; (1895) HLP v. 327, (1895) HCP iii. 569.

Law of Inheritance Amendment Bills: (1893–4) HLP vi. 51; (1894) HLP v. 255; (1895) HLP iv. 355.

[156] Offer, *Property and Politics*, 45–6.

[157] D. A. Hamer, *Liberal Politics in the Age of Gladstone and Rosebery* (1972), 174–207. Rosebery succeeded Gladstone as Prime Minister in March 1894. If one theme held the Liberals together during this period it was antagonism to the obstructive powers of the House of Lords. Herschell's Land Transfer bills

the leadership and its own future direction. In none of its other policies was it noted for discipline or resolve. Nor is it clear how strong the practical party commitment to title registration was. Solicitors claimed that there was no public demand, though this ignored intermittent building society enthusiasm.[158] But it was their self-justification for taking an overtly political stance, that proposals for 'officialism' stemmed either from individual politicians seeking personal political capital or from officials desirous of extending their functions and magnifying their office.[159] They did not criticize the sort of social welfare legislation to which advanced Liberals were moving, claiming only that where professionals could do the job, they should. This is why Herschell had continually to claim that title registration was a new function, beyond the abilities of private professionals.[160] But though he indignantly rejected the ILS's accusation that he was merely fronting for the Registrar, he conspicuously did not attempt to relate title registration to any other Liberal cause. Instead he repeated his own personal commitment to it, presenting his bills as though they were apolitical departmental legislation, not the stuff of great political principle.[161] Dr Offer's account of solicitors' obstruction is also overstated. There was a lot of noise; but the bills fell for other reasons. The first bill came down from the Lords only in August; it took just a signal of opposition for the timetabling problems of the Government of Ireland Bill to do the rest.[162] In 1894 the second bill was fatally

---

started in the Lords, demonstrating their remoteness from the centre of politics. And see Michael Freeden, *The New Liberalism* (1978), 118 f., for an account of radical Liberal thought.

[158] Herschell, (1893) 11 PD (4th ser.) 741. But the Building Societies Association tended to oppose particular title registration schemes, and individual societies shunned voluntary registration, to Herschell's puzzlement: (1895) HCP xi. 1, qq. 321–4; cf. ibid., q. 975 (Hunter). See further, below, Ch. 6 n. 145 and accompanying text.

[159] (1891–2) 36 *Sol. Jo.* 603 (ILS Council); (1892–3) 37 *Sol. Jo.* 226; (1893–4) 38 *Sol. Jo.* 187 (Leeds), cf. ibid. 166 (Newcastle-upon-Tyne); (1895) HCP xi. 1, q. 3224 (Lake).

[160] Offer, *Property and Politics*, 46–7; (1893) 11 PD (4th ser.) 739; (1892–3) 37 *Sol. Jo.* 434.

[161] (1895) 32 PD (4th ser.) 1121. His major speeches are at (1893) 11 PD (4th ser.) 735; (1894) 23 PD (4th ser.) 1207, 24 PD (4th ser.) 1; (1895) 31 PD (4th ser.) 857, 1121.

[162] (1893) 16 PD (4th ser.) 747, 974. Dr Offer is content to label as 'blatant

side-tracked in the Lords by Lord Salisbury's mischief-making over the 1894 Finance Bill.[163] Only in 1895 did solicitors in the Commons make a stand. What they achieved was reference to a Select Committee, with a tight timetable that might have brought the bill back in time for its final stages that session.[164] If the issue was essentially departmental, albeit with continuing overtones of old radicalism, a Select Committee would be a proper means of investigating a policy that had not been discussed in any detail in the Commons for twenty years. It was nothing to do with the ILS that the government collapsed in mid-hearing.

5. Denouement: The Liberals' Select Committee

ILS strategy towards the inquiry for which they had been lobbying[165] was fivefold. First they organized law societies into collecting and presenting empirical evidence about actual costs in small transactions—the same strategy that had persuaded Cairns to drop compulsion in the 1870s.[166] This time it would probably not have worked. Barristers of course are fierce in cross-examination, whatever verdict they themselves favour. But R. B. Haldane, with R. T. Reid, A.-G. one of the two prominent Liberal barristers on the Select Committee, was particularly so. In so far as one can tell from his examination of law society witnesses, he thought that if traditional conveyanc-

---

tactics of harassment and delay' the question asked by H. D. Greene in Sept. 1893. This was whether it was proper for the Land Registry to spend public money advertising the benefits of registration in what he claimed was a one-sided way, and while the question was contentious: 17 PD (4th ser.) 938. That the Land Registry was also an advocate in its own self-interest escaped Dr Offer, and with it, interesting questions about the nature of law-making and government. H. D. Greene was a QC, not a solicitor.

[163] (1895) 31 PD (4th ser.) 857; (1893–4) 38 *Sol. Jo.* 462.

[164] (1895) 33 PD (4th ser.) 383.

[165] (1893–4) 38 *Sol. Jo.* 422, 449, 551, 584, 753, 779. See also (1892–3) 37 *Sol. Jo.* 158 (Leeds), 745; (1893–4) 38 *Sol. Jo.* 166 (Newcastle-upon-Tyne), 275 (Wakefield); (1894–5) 39 *Sol. Jo.* 467.

[166] See e.g. (1892–3) 37 *Sol. Jo.* 504; (1893–4) 38 *Sol. Jo.* 293. It was presented to the Select Committee: (1895) HCP xi. 1, app. 1 and 5, and *passim*. See too the link with the theory of land transfer at (1893–4) 38 *Sol. Jo.* 4, 5; cf. (1894–5) 39 *Sol. Jo.* 537.

ing was cheap in small transactions it was because risks were taken that would be obviated by registration, and that even if not, registration would not add significantly to the bill.[167]

Secondly, the ILS Council looked for an alternative to registration. By coincidence John Hunter, he who had presented an assimilation paper in 1885,[168] was ILS President in 1894. He used the opportunity to urge again the adoption of a Wolstenholme-type scheme, arguing that simple opposition to registration would be insufficient.[169] But though he won some support from Benjamin Lake, it soon became clear that solicitors both on and off Council were hopelessly divided. The essence of the scheme was that by abolition of all freehold legal estates except the fee simple, and by putting behind a curtain all the resultant trusts necessary to cope with successive interests, conveyancing could be restricted to basic dealings with the legal ownership, subject only to leases and mortgages. The critical question was how best to protect owners of equitable interests from the default of their trustees, particularly whether there should be a register in which beneficiaries could lodge caveats against dealings, entitling them to a short period of notice if a transaction was mooted. There was such a thing in the register of consols, to which Wolstenholme's scheme was kin. In 1862 Wolstenholme had not thought a caveat system necessary, but it had been part of Hunter's recent paper and Wolstenholme now believed that without some deference to the principle of registration his scheme stood no chance of Parliamentary acceptance.[170] On this issue Council fragmented.[171] Some members thought him wrong, and, going further, some thought it preferable to amend his scheme so as to reduce protection for beneficiaries even more. There were those who agreed that caveats were necessary but who feared that to vest the register in the Land Registry would give it just one more prop to survival. And there were those who felt that any system of

---

[167] Select Committee on the Land Transfer Bill, (1895) HCP xi. 1, qq. 125, 308–9, 1871–87, 1941–2; it was probably true also of Reid, ibid. qq. 3744–53.
[168] See n. 54 above.
[169] (1893–4) 38 *Sol. Jo.* 779, 782; (1894–5) 39 *Sol. Jo.* 304.
[170] (1894–5) 39 *Sol. Jo.* 24 (Elphinstone), 56; (1896–7) 41 *Sol. Jo.* 161, 798.
[171] (1894–5) 39 *Sol. Jo.* 805, 824, 830, 843; (1895–6) 40 *Sol. Jo.* 78, 320; and see letter from F. H. Bartlett worrying at the register's bulk, ibid. 77. Liverpool ILS was favourable, (1895–6) 40 *Sol. Jo.* 100.

caveats would add to the cost and trouble of conveyancing, quite unnecessarily so in country areas where solicitors knew their titles well enough not to have to make any inquiries at all.[172] This last reason linked with opposition from some York-shire solicitors opposed to the possible supersession of their deeds registries and hostile to centralization in London.[173] Hunter and Council candidly told the Select Committee that there was no agreement, in full detail.[174] Wolstenholme pre-sented his scheme to the Select Committee, but Haldane manœuvred him into agreeing that in all its essentials it was just a scheme for registration without a registrar—designed for the political purpose of avoiding officialism.[175]

The crux of ILS strategy was a reasoned argument against compulsion. Its leading spokesman was Benjamin Lake, who probably had more experience of title registration than anyone on or appearing before the Committee, and who firmly adhered to its values, methods, and objectives.[176] Compulsion was his only objection on principle; the rest of his evidence was geared towards improving the scheme. As things turned out, with the Committee's inquiry aborted by the government's fall, the centre-piece of its inquisition was a long tussle between Lake and Haldane, at the end of which Reid, the Attorney-General and Committee chairman, virtually offered Lake a place in the governance of the new system.[177] Lake's political argument was that competition was best. It had stimulated the conveyancing reforms of the 1880s; it was stimulating the Hunter/Wolsten-holme proposal now.[178] Monopoly was bad. When Haldane chided him with solicitors' restrictive practices, Lake retorted that all the evidence showed that where supply of solicitors outstripped demand there was strong price competition. Hal-dane replied that this was a 'large question' and moved on.[179] Lake's fear was that a registry with monopoly powers would be

[172] (1894–5) 39 *Sol. Jo.* 56, 77; (1895–6) 40 *Sol. Jo.* 623.
[173] (1894–5) 39 *Sol. Jo.* 299 (Sheffield); (1895–6) 40 *Sol. Jo.* 358 (Wakefield).
[174] (1895) HCP xi.1, app. 4 and q. 1081 (Hunter).
[175] Ibid., qq. 608–13, 652–8; and cf. qq. 1102–13, 1157, 1161 (all Haldane to Hunter).
[176] Ibid., qq. 2497, 2513, 2914–15, 2931, 2948–9, 2952, 3266.
[177] Ibid., q. 3336.
[178] Ibid., qq. 2970, 2973, 3062, 3605.
[179] Ibid., qq. 3221, 3243.

complacent, authoritarian, and unresponsive. He stressed how ignorant the Registry's officials were of the great wealth of variety in land transactions, how they wholly lacked experience of dealing with business men, how they always thought they knew best and would never listen to practical men who really did know.[180] The only way registration would succeed would be for it to operate in competition with the best that the traditional system could offer, and let the better scheme win.[181] Since no Report was forthcoming we do not know how the Committee would have responded. Haldane pressed Lake and other solicitors to say whether they thought the Solicitors Remuneration Order scale too high.[182] It is possible, though a little unlikely, that he had in mind the crude point that solicitors were charging too much.[183] But he may have been probing to see whether a Wolstenholme Act could be accompanied by a scale reduction, which would be the only way in which it could match registration's claim to progress. If so, Lake met him well. The scale was justified, he thought, because it reflected the responsibility carried, though he did not always charge it himself. But where responsibility had already been explicitly reduced, for example under the brewery companies' scale which contained provisions for further streamlining traditional conveyancing, then lower fees were universally accepted.[184]

Some of the other solicitor witnesses presented the argument against compulsion in 'property' terms, along Dr Offer's lines.[185] But John Hunter, with Lake the ILS representative, seems to have been genuinely shocked when it was suggested to him that solicitors as a class were claiming compensation from the government for loss of office. He disclaimed any such intention, saying that their case was quite unlike that of the proctors, who

---

[180] Ibid., qq. 2894 ff., 2971; and cf. q. 2606.

[181] Ibid., q. 2970.

[182] Ibid., qq. 1871–87, 1995 ff., 2763 ff., 3221 ff.

[183] This would have been an unwise argument for an active proponent of title registration to make, cf. ibid., q. 308. See ibid., qq. 1995–6, 3224 ff.

[184] Ibid., qq. 3161 ff.

[185] Lake himself, ibid., q. 2936. The 'property' question was kept alive in the *Solicitors' Journal* through the remembrance of a speech by Lord Halsbury at the Mansion House in Nov. 1886 decrying socialist confiscation. Where was the difference, it asked? See generally (1888–9) 33 *Sol. Jo.* 574; (1889–90) 34 *Sol. Jo.* 577; (1895–6) 40 *Sol. Jo.* 124.

had been compensated when the ecclesiastical courts had been abolished.[186] It is a sign of distrust of the ILS that the question should have been put.

On the other hand, Reid's offer to Lake, and the general tone of the very long and detailed argument between Haldane and Lake over the workings of the 1875 Act, the Australian experience, and the operation of registration systems in continental Europe, served to reinforce the fourth element in ILS strategy, that a registration scheme in which solicitors were wholeheartedly involved would be incomparably better than one relying on ignorant and office-bound bureaucratic barristers. But for that to be achieved Lake stressed two conditions. The first would clearly have been accepted by the Committee—that solicitors must be involved in the rule-making process, which ought not to rest in the Registrar's own hands.[187] The second was more difficult. It was that solicitors must keep a place in the land transfer process. Again, without a Report and without the cross-examination of Holt and Brickdale, we cannot be sure. But though Haldane and Lord Chancellor Herschell probably thought that in simple cases a landowner could manage on his own, they seem not to have disputed that many would choose not to and that a great deal of work 'off the register' would remain in solicitors' hands.[188] There was no enthusiasm for replacing solicitors with unqualified semi-professionals.

Lake took strongly against what he saw as Registry hostility to solicitors.[189] He contrasted it with the Probate Registries, which were allowed to do work previously done by solicitors if asked by the public, but not to advertise. He reminded the Committee of the Rule change in 1889, which had repealed the previous Rules requiring certain registration documents to be attested by solicitors. Even the Bank of England register, so often used as a model for registration, had not gone that far. He stressed how solicitors were subject to the highest standards of professional discipline in the country, and how their nationwide network serviced a national land market. Pressed by Haldane

---

[186] (1895) HCP xi. 1, qq. 1297–8; cf. a letter published at (1888–9) 33 *Sol. Jo.* 423.

[187] Cf. (1895) HCP xi. 1, app. 3, 'Report of the Institute of Conveyancers'.

[188] Ibid., qq. 138–9, 1153 ff.

[189] Ibid., qq. 2894–901, 2918, 2932–5, 2971, 3334 ff.

he admitted that the *ad valorem* scale for solicitors' fees at the Registry was actually more generous than his own accustomed charges, but unlike John Hunter he would not see this as a sign of conciliation from the Registry.[190]

Finally the ILS argued that the bill was technically bad.[191] Like all Herschell's bills it was brief and incremental in character. It was misleading for Herschell to present them as fragments of Halsbury's. Those had been compendious, had departed extensively from the 1875 model, and were expressed in as clear and rational terms as could be hoped. Herschell adopted instead Holt's original strategy of making the 1875 Act compulsory, relying on an expanded rule-making power to devise the substantive changes made necessary by passage of time. He added an insurance fund to the 1875 Act, taking some of the wording from Halsbury's efforts—his bills and his Local Registration of Title (Ireland) Act 1891, which had followed much the same pattern when introducing uncontroversially a limited measure of compulsory registration into Ireland. Similarly, the procedure for descent of land through real representatives adopted Halsbury's model, though omitting from the registration bills the abolition of intestate primogeniture that had accompanied it in Halsbury's bills. But essentially the proposal was for the 1875 Act to be made compulsory.

The Committee analysed this issue in minute detail, and its lawyer-members were obviously intent on making very substantial amendments.[192] They did not dispute that Halsbury's experience in 1887 and 1888 showed the difficulty of using the 1875 Act as a model. Nor did they seriously dispute that barristers, solicitors, and bankers were the right people to demonstrate its weaknesses and suggest alternatives. The ILS, incidentally, marshalled evidence from bankers against the bill, principally on the ground that the 1875 Act interfered with their commercial practices.[193] It is worth dwelling on this, since it

---

[190] Ibid., q. 3171 (Lake), 1190 (Hunter).

[191] So much of the cross-examination concerned this that precise reference is impossible. App. 3 and 8 give barristers' criticisms. Note particularly q. 1098 (Hunter). See also (1892–3) 37 *Sol. Jo.* 350, 382, 745, 758–9, 774. *The Times* agreed: leader, 19 Mar. 1893, quoted at (1892–3) 37 *Sol. Jo.* 766.

[192] e.g. (1895) HCP xi. 1, qq. 625, 1102.

[193] Ibid., evidence of W. J. Bonser, F. Seebohm, and S. O. Ward; see too qq. 3193–5 concerning building societies.

demonstrates both Herschell's reliance on the Registry staff[194]—
a point repeatedly hammered home by Lake[195]—and that staff's
ignorance of commercial dealings. Bankers' mortgages, the
point of contention, were virtually the only substantive question
of registration tackled in the bills. They were usually effected by
depositing title-deeds without formality as security for a short-
term loan, what a lawyer would see as an equitable mortgage if
accompanied with a written statement to that effect or perhaps
just an equitable lien if not. Bankers had raised doubts that such
a thing would be possible under a system of registration, for
there would be no deeds to deposit.[196] When introducing the
bill in 1893 Herschell followed the Brickdale line that there was
no technical difficulty, simply one in fixing an appropriate fee.
This was a simplification. If the land certificate issued to a
registered owner was a document of title, then land transactions
could be effected off the register by contract, custody of the
certificate providing the purchaser or mortgagee with sufficient
practical security. But because of the fear that 'off the register'
transactions would be used to outflank registration, the 1875
Act had been constructed so that the land certificate was not a
document of title. Thus a mortgagee by deposit of the land
certificate had no safety, since the registered proprietor could
deal with the land notwithstanding the deposit of the certificate
with the mortgagee. However, a caution could be registered to
protect the deposit of the certificate. But cautions were not
regarded by the Registrar as proper entries, because in themselves they were merely warnings, and it was feared that if
used in preference to the formal mechanisms of transfer and
charges they would subvert the register. So fees for cautions
were set on the same pro rata scale as formal transactions. This
made them much more expensive than their unregistered equivalent, especially given banks' use of standard forms and
retained solicitors. Hence Herschell's view that the issue was
only cost. It took some effort to get Brickdale to see even this,
his first reaction being to deny the problem, and his second to
say that inhibitions, which were cheap, would do the job. It

[194] He sometimes used it to avoid detailed questions: ibid., qq. 334, 358.
[195] e.g. ibid., qq. 3334 ff.; cf. qq. 3488–9.
[196] For this account see: (1893–4) 38 *Sol. Jo.* 35, 44, 53, 410; (1893) 11 PD (4th ser.) 742; (1894) 23 PD (4th ser.) 1210; (1895) HCP xi. 1, evidence of F. Seebohm.

then had to be pointed out to him that his own book on registry practice said that since inhibitions were in the nature of injunctions they would rarely be issued. And even now he missed the point, which was that bankers' mortgages were essentially informal and short-term, so that *any* additional formality would hinder ordinary dealings.

So when introducing the 1894 bill, Lord Herschell announced that a new scheme involving deposit certificates had been devised to reconcile bankers' practice with the logic of registration. As the *Solicitors' Journal* tartly remarked, the old system *had* been wrong. To anticipate,[197] there were technical problems with the 1894 solution (notwithstanding Herschell's confidence in it), so that a different one was hurriedly slipped into the 1897 bill when the bankers rebelled. And bankers complained loudly to the Royal Commission on Land Transfer, which was an inquisition on the working of the 1897 Act, about deficiencies in *that* solution. Yet each time, Brickdale denied that there was a problem, then announced a solution to it, then denied that there was a problem . . . and so on.

6. Land Transfer Act 1897

Benjamin Lake worried that the Liberals' fall might bring the Registry undeserved good fortune.[198] The Select Committee wound itself up just as it had completed the evidence against any extension of registration, all subjected to searching cross-examination from its members sympathetic to Herschell's bill. But now Brickdale could put the contrary case in private, and to the new Lord Chancellor, Lord Halsbury, whose colours were

---

[197] See below, n. 219 and, on mortgages generally, Ch. 6 n. 138 and accompanying text.

[198] (1894–5) 39 *Sol. Jo.* 827, cf. 805. Council pressed ahead with an assimilation bill: Conveyancing Bill, (1897) HLP iii. 99. Its memorandum claimed an immediate effect much more extensive than that of the Registration of Title Bill 1895. However, a conveyancers' committee of the Bar Council (the successor to the Bar Committee) pronounced against its basic principle: General Council of the Bar, *Annual Statement, 1897–8*, 5; (1897–8) 42 *Sol. Jo.* 400. Solicitors had been very divided: (1894–5) 39 *Sol. Jo.* 830, 843; (1895–6) 40 *Sol. Jo.* 78, 166, 172, 233, 242, 281, 358, 420, 623; (1896–7) 41 *Sol. Jo.* 161, 484, 689.

well known.[199] Brickdale was an inventive, persuasive, charming, polite, meticulous zealot; in his own words, something of a 'visionary reformer'.[200] When he finally got his way and a new system was enacted it was he who ran it, and ran it so well that it was commonly said that without him it would have collapsed. He was convinced of his rightness, and was assiduous in investigating every detail of every complaint brought against the Registry, both general and particular; nearly always he found them to be wrong. Yet as has been seen from his series of pronouncements about bankers' mortgages, and as the Royal Commission on Land Transfer was later to confirm, his readiness to conclude that only 'ignorance of the register' underlay complaints often blinded him to faults visible to ordinary commercial men.[201]

Lake's fear was only partly justified. On every point bar one the ILS Council had persuaded the Select Committee.[202] But that one was their most cherished wish, and from the Registry's perspective too: compulsion. Halsbury took up where Herschell had left off, employing a small committee to draft a bill meeting all the defects in the 1875 Act as they had emerged during the Committee hearing, but with registration to be compulsory upon sale, compulsion to extend gradually area by area as Herschell had also planned. Haldane was on this drafting committee, and Lake himself had some influence.[203] The government was thus able to present the bill as one with which the ILS concurred.[204] On that footing it passed into law, as the Land Transfer Act 1897.

---

[199] Just as Holt, while deputy to Follett, had been regarded as the Registry's guiding spirit, so now Brickdale had succeeded to his role as well as to his position. For his career see *Who Was Who, 1941–1950*, sub nom. Fortescue-Brickdale.

[200] (1909) HCP xxvii, q. 1350, and cf. q. 1007. For examples of his style see (1885–6) 30 *Sol. Jo.* 316; (1888–9) 33 *Sol. Jo.* 462; Land (Registration of Title) (Germany and Austro-Hungary), C. 8139, (1896) HCP lxxxiv. 85; *Report on Observations of the Law Society on the Land Transfer Bill*, (1894) HLP xi. 453, app. 2.

[201] See below, Ch. 6, sect. 2. 4.

[202] Memorandum to the Land Transfer Bill, (1897) HLP vi. 1; Halsbury, (1897) 46 PD 1566; cf. Lake, (1899–1900) 41 *Sol. Jo.* 255, 270; Ellett, ibid. 269; ILS Council, ibid. 369 ff.

[203] Haldane: (1897) 50 PD (4th ser.) 939; Lake, ibid. 941, (1896–7) 41 *Sol. Jo.* 793, 797, 802.

[204] (1897) 50 PD (4th ser.) 941 (Balfour, Haldane).

For Dr Offer ILS participation in this process, which he tends rather to minimize, dated from late 1896 and was caused by public opinion:

> . . . in spite of remonstrances from provincial solicitors the Law Society was forced by the unanimity of public opinion to enter negotiations with Lord Salisbury's new government. (See the press welcome to the blue book on registration in Germany.) In 1897 a compromise was reached whereby compulsory registration of title would be introduced as an 'experiment' into the Administrative County of London. . . . Representatives of the provincial solicitors staged a revolt and were only appeased by one further concession, the so-called 'County Veto'— a provision that County Councils would have to approve any extension of registration into their areas. . . . A sharp reaction from discontented London solicitors soon threw the Council of the Law Society, the affluent group of solicitors who had made the 'compromise', on the defensive . . . Greater militancy had been building up since the early 1890s. It erupted in the Commons 'rebellion' of 3 August 1897, and it threw up an alternative leadership and an alternative style of conflict.[205]

Much of that analysis is contentious. The chronology is wrong: Brickdale's blue book was published at the end of 1896,[206] but ILS Council members had announced publicly almost a year earlier that their powers of direct opposition had ended.[207] This was a necessary corollary of their successful agitation for an inquiry, their participation in it, and the way they had presented their case. There were of course some provincial solicitors who remonstrated,[208] unsurprisingly since there were 15,000 practising solicitors at the time, half of them outside London. But at this stage there was no opposition from provincial law societies, indeed they seem to have sympathized with the Council's conclusion.[209] There was later a fierce accusation from the

---

[205] Offer, *Property and Politics*, 68, 69.

[206] Land (Registration of title) (Germany and Austro-Hungary) C. 8139, (1896) HCP lxxiv. 85. It was answered, too late, by a solicitor: Edmund Kell Blyth, *The German and Austrian Systems of Land Transfer and their Application to England* (1897).

[207] (1895–6) 40 *Sol. Jo.* 243 (Lawrence); cf. (1894–5) 39 *Sol. Jo.* 827 (esp. Lake), (1896–7) 41 *Sol. Jo.* 807 (Hunter). The tenor of all three meetings was that direct opposition would be futile, but that an assimilation bill might perhaps work. But opinions on the wisdom of such a bill were very divided: (1894–5) 39 *Sol. Jo.* 805, 827 f.; (1895–6) 40 *Sol. Jo.* 78, 233, 807 f.; (1896–7) 41 *Sol. Jo.* 807.

[208] e.g. (1896–7) 41 *Sol. Jo.* 265, 288, 710.

[209] Ibid. 644 (Gloucs. and Wilts. ILS); (1897–8) 42 *Sol. Jo.* 16 (Sussex); cf. letter, ibid. 230, 268.

president of Leeds ILS that the thinly attended meeting in February 1897 of the Associated Provincial Law Societies, which approved the Council's stance, had been manipulated by Council members.[210] But he got little support from outside Yorkshire.

The 'rebellion' of 3 August 1897 was also from Yorkshire. It originated with Yorkshire solicitors, who were interested only in Yorkshire matters and were in no sense 'representatives of the provincial solicitors'.[211] Their concern was only that if Middlesex turned out not to be the trial area for compulsory registration, Yorkshire as the other deeds registration county almost certainly would be.[212] That this was not a matter confined to solicitors is clear from the speeches of the Yorkshire members, who were barristers, not solicitors.[213] One of them had introduced the 1884 reform of Yorkshire deeds registries.[214] The clause they wrung from the government in response immunized Yorkshire county councils from loss caused by transfer of business from their deeds registries to the title registry in London.[215] Similarly, the final strengthening of the county council veto that was achieved by the Yorkshire members at this time was clearly designed to assuage Yorkshire regionalism,[216] though it was one for which solicitors had been unsuccessfully pressing and which they greeted warmly.[217] As Arthur Balfour acknowledged, it effectively made the experimental nature of the bill perpetual,[218] now that the power of extension had been removed from Lord Chancellor and Land Registrar.

The ILS had achieved more than Dr Offer says. First, it had been accepted that the bills prepared for Herschell by Registry staff between 1893 and 1895 would not have been suitable.

---

[210] (1897–8) 42 *Sol. Jo.* 235, 287. For the APLS meeting see (1896–7) 41 *Sol. Jo.* 344, 357, 369; and for an earlier shot from Leeds see ibid. 725.

[211] (1896–7) 41 *Sol. Jo.* 682, 691.

[212] (1897–8) 42 *Sol. Jo.* 16 (Leeds ILS).

[213] (1897) 52 PD (4th ser.) 294; and see the support for the bill from Alfred Billson, 50 PD (4th ser.) 942.

[214] John Stuart Wortley, see above, p. 168.

[215] Land Transfer Act 1897, s. 23. Henry Fowler, who in other respects spoke for the ILS on this occasion, demurred at the part of this section which would have compensated for loss of future fees, forcing its removal: (1897) 52 PD (4th ser.) 206, 331.

[216] Land Transfer Act 1897, s. 20(8); (1897) 52 PD (4th ser.) 301 ff.

[217] (1896–7) 41 *Sol. Jo.* 691.

[218] (1897) 52 PD (4th ser.) 303; also Webster, A.-G., ibid. 318.

Solicitors' claims to expertise were vindicated. The Registrar's (and Haldane's perhaps) took a further blow when bankers threatened to resist the bill unless yet a further variant on the 'bankers' mortgage' clause were substituted for the one proposed.[219] It was. Secondly, a place on the Rules Committee for an ILS nominee was firmly entrenched by statute.[220] Thirdly, the statutory monopoly of conveyancing for reward was extended into the Registry itself: solicitors alone could be paid agents there.[221] At an ILS meeting in 1896 a Bristol solicitor had suggested this as a tolerable compromise if compulsion were unavoidable.[222] Its acceptance meant that solicitors need now fight on only one front. Fourthly, the county veto, combined with the clause forbidding any extension for three years, combined with the rhetoric of government spokesmen in introducing the bill, combined with various promises about where would or would not be the area for first introduction, made much more likely the need for a second inquiry before any significant extension would occur. Both the ILS Council and the Yorkshire law societies knew that they could have defeated the bill.[223] But they chose not to because they knew that they would not get terms so good again, and they would have 'for ever alienated the good feeling of the Lord Chancellor'.[224]

It is unclear whether Dr Offer means that the Council took a defensive attitude against title registration or against revolt from within the solicitors' ranks. His evidence, that it laid plans to collect instances of the Act's failings even before it came into force, suggests the former, but the context suggests the latter. But there was nothing new in the former,[225] and I can find no evidence for the latter.[226] There was some apologizing for the

---

[219] (1897) 50 PD (4th ser.) 939; (1896–7) 41 *Sol. Jo.* 544, 633.

[220] Land Transfer Act 1897, s. 8(4).

[221] Land Transfer Act 1897, s. 10. This was one element in the ILS/APLS conditions of acceptance: (1896–7) 41 *Sol. Jo.* 344.

[222] J. Sinnott, (1895–6) 40 *Sol. Jo.* 242.

[223] ILS: (1897–8) 42 *Sol. Jo.* 237 ff.; Yorkshire: ibid. 16; and see the closely reasoned account by Benjamin Lake, (1896–7) 41 *Sol. Jo.* 802.

[224] (1897–8) 42 *Sol. Jo.* 238 (Cornelius Saunders).

[225] Cf. (1887–8) 32 *Sol. Jo.* 303.

[226] A subjective judgement, of course. I am influenced by the intermittent rebellions faced by the ILS Council from time to time, which seem absent in 1897. One reason was that rebellions from the lower orders had to emanate from London solicitors in order to qualify in Dr Offer's terms. But

defeat, but it was met with sympathy. A determined warrior did emerge from the ranks: Mr J. S. Rubinstein. But his zeal was directed outwards against the Registry, not inwards against the Council,[227] and was anyway very little different from what had gone before. Rubinstein himself was known in ILS circles as a legal commentator and crusader in professional and legal causes. He was not the outraged newcomer Dr Offer implies him to have been.[228] There was a spirited contest on registration

---

J. S. Rubinstein, for example, seems to have thought that the Council behaved honourably as a London society in its dispute with Yorkshire (see (1897–8) 42 *Sol. Jo.* 238). Further, by coincidence, the most noted habitual thorn in the Council's side, Charles Ford, was a member of the LCC who approved of title registration (ibid. 237–8). He was a leader in the sense that he was a well-known antagonist of the Council, he edited the *Solicitors' Diary*, and had some link or other with the *Law Times*. He might have attracted a following, though he usually found himself heavily outnumbered. Rubinstein, though equally clearly falling outside the inner circle, very conspicuously identified with the values and aspirations of the Council, working for many years within the ILS structure. See n. 228 below for an outline of his career. For Ford see Ch. 4 n. 71; Harry Kirk, *Portrait of a Profession* (1976), 34, 43; and, for later examples, (1902–3) 47 *Sol. Jo.* 472, 656, 712; (1903–4) 48 *Sol. Jo.* 440.

[227] Of course, he urged vigour on the Council, see e.g. Kirk, *Portrait*, 44; but that scarcely makes him an alternative style of leader. Only rarely was his criticism of the ILS Council biting: (1906–7) 51 *Sol. Jo.* 232. His paper 'How to Set our House in Order', (1899–1900) 44 *Sol. Jo.* 801, was taken personally by W. Melmoth Walters, an ILS grandee, but not by President Ellett or ex-President Manisty, who recognized that it was not hostile. More usually he spoke well of it, e.g. (1901–2) 46 *Sol. Jo.* 669, and the president would speak well of him: (1900–01) 45 *Sol. Jo.* 674. Perhaps Dr Offer means only that Rubinstein worked energetically outside usual law society circles?

[228] He first appears as a publicist for the United Law Students Society ((1875) 59 *LT* 391, (1874–5) 19 *Sol. Jo.* 359) and then as its secretary ((1876–7) 21 *Sol. Jo.* 182), writing *The Articled Clerk's Handbook* in 1877 (with Samuel Ward). When newly qualified he gave a paper on the Conveyancing Act to an ILS meeting, drawing attention for doing so: (1880–1) 25 *Sol. Jo.* 887, 904, 927. His annotated version of *The Conveyancing Acts 1881, 1882, and the Solicitors Remuneration Act* (1882) reached its fifth and final edition in 1884. His *Conveyancing Costs under the Solicitors' Remuneration Act* (1882) was again preceded by a paper to an ILS meeting: (1881–2) 26 *Sol. Jo.* 761. It reached its final (12th) edition in 1924. Also in 1882 he published an annotation of the *Married Women's Property Act*, but there was no further edition. He attended further annual provincial meetings in 1884 and 1885, giving a paper on 'How to Recruit the Society's Ranks' at the latter ((1883–4) 28 *Sol. Jo.* 826 ff., (1884–5) 29 *Sol. Jo.* 785–6, 801). He was also active at ILS annual general meetings, in 1883 urging that solicitors lobby for a statue of George Jessel to be erected in the law courts, and in 1885 asking the ILS council to initiate evening meetings so that ordinary practitioners could attend more easily: (1882–3) 27 *Sol. Jo.* 636; (1884–5) 29 *Sol. Jo.* 628, 651. His paper to the London jubilee meeting in 1887, on the law of husband and wife,

between him and Lake, but understandably so: the setting was a debate in front of a law students' society, at which they were guest speakers.[229] Lake won, incidentally. The only truly virulent criticism of the Council came from Sydney Gedge, a solicitor and Member of Parliament, who had tried to block the bill in the Commons and blamed the Council for surrendering.[230] So far as I can discover he won no supporters. I can see only continuity where Dr Offer sees change. It seems to me that Council conceded compulsion in a manner that left as many of their options open as possible, while preserving intact, indeed extending, their vision of professionalism through reasserting their monopoly of conveyancing for reward, through establishing themselves on the Rules Committee, and through maintain-

---

was his last until general issues of professionalism brought him back into law society work nearly a decade later ((1886–7) 31 *Sol. Jo.* 540). This started, however, not with title registration but with concern over court procedure. An article in the *Fortnightly Review* (vol. 65, Jan. 1896), 'The Law's Delay', argued that rule-making power should be transferred to the ILS, a theme which he repeated in a paper to its annual provincial meeting that year ((1895–6) 40 *Sol. Jo.* 832, published also as a pamphlet with the same title). His motion to that effect was watered down by the Council. (It was characteristic of Rubinstein to propose an extreme measure, but willingly to compromise.) Even after becoming embroiled in title registration business he remembered this general theme, using it as an introduction to his analysis of title registration in *How to Set a House in Disorder* (1904). Before the Land Transfer Act made registration compulsory in his own area, his only contribution to the question at law society meetings seems to have been in 1885: (1884–5) 29 *Sol. Jo.* 784. Apart from his papers on title registration, he gave one on 'Law Reform' to the 1899 provincial meeting and one on 'Setting our House in Order' in 1900: (1898–9) 43 *Sol. Jo.* 796, (1899–1900) 44 *Sol. Jo.* 801. His 'Blight of Officialdom', given to the 1903 annual provincial meeting, and greeted by loud cheering ((1902–3) 47 *Sol. Jo.* 829), ended with a rousing list of frustrated professional causes: why has England no school of law? why no codification? why such poor judicial appointments? why such cumbersome procedure? why does sensible law reform [which he detailed] take so long? why do the courts close for three months in the summer? An excitable man, given to oratory certainly, but in my view he was well within ILS traditions and values: an exemplar rather than a leader, and in no sense 'alternative'.

Two footnotes: (i) he became an advocate for the admission of women, (1913) 135 *LT* 276.

(ii) he became solicitor for the landlord Arlidge, as in *Local Government Board* v. *Arlidge*. For the full range of reported litigation see [1909] 2 KB 127, [1915] 3 KB 325, [1915] AC 120, [1916] 1 Ch 59, [1917] WN 346, [1918] 2 KB 298. Anti-officialism in several of these cases meant freedom for the landlord to do as he would.

[229] (1897–8) 42 *Sol. Jo.* 48.

[230] (1897–8) 42 *Sol. Jo.* 235 ff.; and see ibid. 164, 719.

ing the good will of the Chancellor and his likely successors. This seems to have been the predominant opinion among the big law societies, at least.[231]

There was however a strong adverse reaction from Yorkshire, with talk of dwindling ILS membership and even of secession. It is not altogether clear what caused it, since Yorkshire solicitors' ostensible fear, that their county rather than London would be the trial area, seemed groundless given the strength of the assurances they had won in August 1897. The argument arose when the ILS Council was consulted by the London County Council on the desirability of a London area being the testbed for registration, and replied that it should not.[232] Among the other bodies giving the same reply were fourteen vestries (marshalled by Rubinstein, according to Dr Offer), seven district boards, the Institute of Bankers, the Auctioneers' Institute, the Ecclesiastical Commissioners, and the Building Societies Association—notwithstanding Dr Offer's view that it had been among the most persistent advocates of registration. In addition there had been unsolicited opposition from several building societies, various land companies, and the Union of House and Land Investors. It all made no difference, since government had made it clear that London it would be, and since the politics of the LCC were favourably inclined to registration anyway. However, there was a twin impact on internal law society politics. First, the extent of opposition from non-lawyers awakened some doubts that Council had tried hard enough. Secondly, Yorkshire law societies became very angry.[233]

The anger was obviously in part caused by the fear that the Council, having colluded in the Act's passage, might now be conniving in a Great Escape for London. But there was another complaint: that the Council had reached its decision without consultation with provincial societies (who would have told it to lie in the bed it had made, so the Yorkshire solicitors

---

[231] There may have been some unarticulated hostility from some small law societies; see Augustus Helder MP's list of telegrams, (1897) 52 PD (4th ser.) 304.

[232] For this and the next paragraph see (1897–8) 42 *Sol. Jo.* 112, 157, 164, 210, 216, 226, 235, 271, 287.

[233] Yorkshire societies had inordinate pride in 'their' deeds registries; see e.g. (1886–7) 31 *Sol. Jo.* 538, (1887–8) 32 *Sol. Jo.* 190—and any other ILS occasion on which title registration was discussed.

thought). The fierce debate that followed focused then upon what sort of body the ILS Council was, and what was the nature of its professional mandate. Again, however, most of the other big provincial societies rallied round the Council, supporting its view that there were indeed times when it had to act as the London local law society. None the less, this was the second time recently that Council had laid itself open to charges of being cavalier towards provincial societies, and if there is one change that might be apparent in the years immediately after 1897 it is that Council did become more careful in its relations with them.

Although I can find very little evidence of dissatisfaction outside Yorkshire with the ILS Council's behaviour, there is one exception. The *Solicitors' Journal* itself tended to doubt that compulsion was as irresistible as the Council made out.[234] Perhaps if it had sought help from all those bodies which later told the LCC that registration was unwelcome. . . ? And look how easily the bankers got their way by threatening to sink the bill. Yorkshire too—just a fortnight's work and they achieved a tougher county veto than the ILS had managed in a year. It did not blame Benjamin Lake. His attendances at ILS meetings and at its committees singled him out as one of its most active governors.[235] He was chairman of the disciplinary committee; he had been featured in *The World*.[236] He supported the principle of registration and made no secret of it. It was wholly unsurprising that it should be he who filled the ILS place on the new Rules Committee.[237] He had voluntarily registered the title of his own estate at Orpington,[238] and he prepared a pamphlet for his office on how to register titles, offering it for sale at 6*d*. a copy to any solicitor who would like it.[239] But perhaps some others had followed him too weakly? This line of criticism, muted perhaps, but certainly visible,[240] received a most unex-

---

[234] For this and the next three sentences see (1896–7) 41 *Sol. Jo.* 251, 265, 377, 633, 691, 793; (1897–8) 42 *Sol. Jo.* 92, 157.

[235] See e.g. the tables of attendances at (1888–9) 33 *Sol. Jo.* 541 and (1890–1) 35 *Sol. Jo.* 576 (chosen at random).

[236] Reprinted, (1888–9) 33 *Sol. Jo.* 512 (June 1889).

[237] (1897–8) 42 *Sol. Jo.* 263; Howard Elphinstone (see n. 47 above) was also a member. The *Solicitors' Journal* praised the Rules, (1897–8) 42 *Sol. Jo.* 178, 461.

[238] But the experience of registering part of his Devon estate deterred him from trying again; (1895) HCP xi. 1, qq. 2685–7.

[239] (1898–9) 43 *Sol. Jo.* 166.

[240] e.g. (1899–1900) 44 *Sol. Jo.* 221.

pected boost in 1901 enabling the *Solicitors' Journal* to take a vigorous and critical line in the difficult early years of registration in London: Benjamin Lake was sent to prison.[241]

During his years of professional service his practice had been managed by his cousin, his only equity partner. But in 1899 he died. Lake mentioned casually to his managing clerk that he would shortly take his own son as partner, but was greatly alarmed with the reply that he should perhaps look at the accounts first. His alarm turned to horror when he realized that the firm had been insolvent since 1888, and that his cousin had been misappropriating clients' money to meet other debts as they became due. By his own account he panicked, and did the same; he found similar dealings in 1897 rather harder to explain away. The popular press revelled in his fall, carrying every detail of his insolvency hearings. At his trial, taunted with his record as chairman of the disciplinary committee, he was humiliated by Sir Edward Carson, the new Solicitor-General, handling his first official prosecution in characteristic style. In the week that Queen Victoria died, the *Solicitors' Journal* appeared with its front page edged in black, mourning for Her Majesty, and that Benjamin Lake had been sentenced to twelve years penal servitude for fraudulent misappropriation of trust funds.

In his fall he performed one last unwitting service to The Law Society. He became their scapegoat. Collective responsibility need no longer be maintained. It could be pretended that nobody else had been actively responsible for the deal.[242] Their only fault had been feebleness in not standing up to him. But It Must Never Be Allowed To Happen Again. And it never was. The next time Council's tactics looked too dilatory to block an ambitious Lord Chancellor, the *Solicitors' Journal*'s stern reminder of their duty included the words, 'we need not recall the course of events since Mr Benjamin Lake threw up the sponge after a successful resistance of something like ten years . . .'. That was in 1911; a decade after his conviction, and two years after his death.[243]

---

[241] For the account that follows see (1897–8) 42 *Sol. Jo.* 701; (1899–1900) 44 *Sol. Jo.* 565, 613, 678, 762; (1900–1) 45 *Sol. Jo.* 15, 48, 64, 85.

[242] This began at once: (1899–1900) 44 *Sol. Jo.* 565; (1902–3) 47 *Sol. Jo.* 444.

[243] (1910–11) 55 *Sol. Jo.* 801; obituaries at (1909) 127 *LT* 208, (1908–9) 53 *Sol. Jo.* 610.

6

1897–1912: The Old Order Resurgent

For solicitors these were the tensest years. They culminated in a Royal Commission which from 1909 to 1911 investigated the workings of the 1897 Act, reported, and laid the foundation for what ultimately became the property legislation of 1922–5. Before then, for the first decade or so of the new regime, there was a fierce institutional struggle between Registrar and law societies for control of the future of land transfer. Both lost; but that was not foreseen.

1. 1897–1908: Mastery Contested

1.1. In their struggle the solicitors were nearly always on the defensive. Registrar Brickdale could choose when to propose geographical extensions, or new codes of rules, or amendments to the Acts, be they concerned with substantive law or removal of the county veto. Only when an election was near could the ILS reiterate its creed of private professional enterprise against the discretionary powers of hydra-headed officialism.[1] It was not a good time for the ILS Council. The Lake scandal and some other spectacular crashes[2] called for urgent action.[3] But anything needing legislation seemed out of the question. Even the

---

[1] Council of The Law Society, Memorandum on Officialism, July 1905, reported in (1904–5) 49 *Sol. Jo.* 607. For lobbying of candidates see e.g. (1904–5) 49 *Sol. Jo.* 115; (1905–6) 50 *Sol. Jo.* 242, 293; (1906–7) 51 *Sol. Jo.* 115.

[2] e.g. Ingram, Harrison, & Lyon for £527,000 (1899–1900) 44 *Sol. Jo.* 178; Keighley, Sismey, & Arnold for £364,000, mostly secured, ibid 222.

[3] Ibid. 424, 431, 446, 453, 462, 470, 472, 489–90, 505, 511, 518, 546; Harry Kirk, *Portrait of a Profession* (1976), 98–103.

Council's innocuous little bill making it more difficult for bank-
rupt solicitors to renew their practising certificate was blocked
year after year in the Commons,[4] as were its incrementalist bills
to tidy up some remaining corners of conveyancing and to make
some amendments to the Married Women's Property Acts.[5] It
was more the frustration at failure to get their Solicitors Bill
passed that caused a demoralization that Dr Offer notes,[6] not
Lake's conviction itself; just as it was inability to get even
uncontroversial law reform measures passed that caused some
spokesmen to doubt the utility of Parliament as a law-making
forum.[7] Further, the 1888 Solicitors Act had led to expectations
of the ILS that it could not satisfy. The Act had created a
disciplinary committee to investigate malpractice and report to
the courts,[8] and the ILS received payment from public funds for
doing this job.[9] But the Council itself had no public regulatory
function. It could suggest rules, even lay them down, it could
not enforce them.[10] So though, with some effort, it was generally agreed that all solicitors should keep their clients' money in
a bank account separate from their own, and though there were
some council members who favoured introducing some sort of
insurance scheme to protect against fraud, the ILS Council
could rely only on moral and professional force. Perhaps, then,
all solicitors should have to become ILS members—so that
expulsion would mean loss of professional standing?[11] A long
round of consultation began, including questions about the

[4] Kirk, *Portrait*, 100; (1904) 1 *Law Society's Gazette*, 304–5; (1900–1) 45 *Sol. Jo.*
715; (1901–2) 46 *Sol. Jo.* 275, 657.

[5] (1904) 1 *Law Society's Gazette*, 304–5; (1901–2) 46 *Sol. Jo.* 670, 732; (1902–3)
47 *Sol. Jo.* 674; (1903–4) 48 *Sol. Jo.* 290.

[6] See n. 4 above; Avner Offer, *Property and Politics, 1870–1914* (1981), 57 n. 20
(the full BLL reference to his source is x Cw.UK.670 L415p.).

[7] (1905–6) 50 *Sol. Jo.* 78; cf. (1901–2) 46 *Sol. Jo.* 33, 732; and see (1900–1) 45
Sol. Jo. 808 at 811 for suggested reform of Parliamentary procedure, continued
at (1901–2) 46 *Sol. Jo.* 26, 239.

[8] Solicitors Act 1888, ss. 12–15; John Hunter (1899–1900) 44 *Sol. Jo.* 789.

[9] Kirk, *Portrait*, 78–80. The ILS claimed poverty: (1895–6) 40 *Sol. Jo.* 244, 489.
The ambiguity of its position exposed it to attack from within and without:
(1897–8) 42 *Sol. Jo.* 92; (1900) 82 PD (4th ser.) 31.

[10] Kirk, *Portrait*, 78–80; (1903–4) 48 *Sol. Jo.* 98; The Law Society, *Report of the
Special Committee on Solicitors' Practice*, 1907.

[11] Kirk, *Portrait*, 40–2; (1900–1) 45 *Sol. Jo.* 469 at 472, 725, 817, 818; (1901–2) 46
Sol. Jo. 88, 618; (1902–3) 47 *Sol. Jo.* 246, 259, 595. And cf. The Law Society, *Report
of the Special Committee on Malpractice*, 1900 (BLL ref. in n. 6 above).

composition and tenure of the Council itself and the relation of the ILS with provincial societies. But the resulting new Charter of 1903 achieved little beyond a small measure of further representation for provincial societies, and is significant mainly because thereafter the society's name became simply The Law Society. Tensions were scarcely suppressed. When the proceeds of sale of New Inn were earmarked for legal education a fierce North/South argument developed, as the Council proposed to divert the windfall to London.[12] But, pace Dr Offer, there was no complementary pressure from below. The leading opposition candidate at council elections was falling further behind, and Council and Mr J. S. Rubinstein continually declared themselves to be agreed about the iniquity of title registration.[13]

1.2. Law societies did not see themselves as opposing 'the state', or even the government, far less the popular will.[14] Title registration never again had the political popularity briefly enjoyed in the 1880s. Solicitors' conviction was that the public was indifferent to the issue, and that that lack of enthusiasm extended to institutions qualified to judge—banks, building societies, and the like. Rather, they saw their opponents as being 'advocates of registration', or 'officials', with whom they competed for the government's ear. They expected government perhaps, and Parliament certainly, to adjudicate fairly between the rival claims of different sorts of institution to mediate the conflicting interests inherent in any property transfer system. On the one hand there was law, with its ancient hierarchies of learning and its imposition of responsibility to courts; there was private enterprise, hence responsiveness to the client; there was professional self-discipline, the liability to account to one's peers; there was value to society in the existence of independent

---

[12] (1902–3) 47 *Sol. Jo.* 684, 751, 826; for the background, Kirk, *Portrait*, 62.

[13] (1900–1) 45 *Sol. Jo.* 699 (Harvey Clifton); for Rubinstein, ibid. 469, 674; (1902–3) 47 *Sol. Jo.* 842; (1903–4) 48 *Sol. Jo.* 783 ff. When an inquiry was finally won Rubinstein was publicly thanked by the then President of The Law Society, (1907–8) 52 *Sol. Jo.* 430.

[14] This paragraph is extrapolated from the various ILS papers on 'officialism' already cited, plus (1900–1) 45 *Sol. Jo.* 469; (1901–2) 46 *Sol. Jo.* 362, 533, 732 (Manchester ILA); (1902–3) 47 *Sol. Jo.* 112 (W. H. Thomas). The emphasis was on calling for an inquiry, e.g. (1901–2) 46 *Sol. Jo.* 657; (1902–3) 47 *Sol. Jo.* 15; (1903) 122 PD (4th ser.) 1382 ff.

professions, necessitating a firm economic base. On the other hand there was official discretion, secret, unpredictable, and unstable; there was public enterprise, hence responsiveness to the Treasury; there was only such accountability as the Registry volunteered; citizens must rely on the goodwill of officials, without assistance from an expert intermediary.

Congruently with this perception, law societies saw the 1897 Act as a reluctant bargain made between them and government; and if the parties were not exactly equal, they were at least parties of the same nature, fit to enter an agreement that obligated both. But in the first few years of compulsory registration one episode after another convinced solicitors that they had been deceived. 'No steps whatever can be taken towards putting the Act into force before 1st January 1898', the Attorney-General had said in the Commons.[15] But the proposed Order imposing the Act on parts of London was issued before that, triggering the consultation period ahead of time.[16] True, the Act said only that no further Order extending compulsion to other counties would be made within three years, not that there would be a legislative embargo for that time; but it none the less seemed a clear breach of faith when Chamberlain's Small Houses Bill required local authorities to register title to houses which they had compulsorily acquired. After a sharp row, Chamberlain acknowledged that a pledge had been given and withdrew the clause, to considerable criticism of solicitors in the Commons.[17] Then there was the City of London.[18] Anxious to avoid compulsion, it had secured for itself a clause in the 1897 bill declaring it to be excluded from the administrative county of London, thereby gaining the power of veto if an extension were proposed. But on the strength of Halsbury's undertaking that no extension would be made without considering its

[15] (1897) 52 PD (4th ser.) 327, Webster, A.-G.

[16] (1897–8) 42 *Sol. Jo.* 58, 75; cf. suspicion of the Registry at ibid. 105, 112, 145 (Rubinstein).

[17] (1898–9) 43 *Sol. Jo.* 450, 471, 503, 597, 665, 779; (1899) 73 PD (4th ser.) 901; 75 PD (4th ser.) 199; the outcome was the innocuous s. 8 of the Small Dwellings Acquisition Act, 1899.

[18] See Kimber, (1903–4) 48 *Sol. Jo.* 787; (1897–8) 42 *Sol. Jo.* 58; (1901–2) 46 *Sol. Jo.* 72, 129, 134, 329, 362, 555; (1902–3) 47 *Sol. Jo.* 112. Halsbury's pledge is at (1897) 52 PD (4th ser.) 323, on the removal of cl. 20(11) of the bill, and cf. ibid. 329.

wishes, its Common Council had dropped its clause. None the less, the City was included in the 1898 designation order and, despite protests resulting in postponement until 1902, it became an area of compulsory registration notwithstanding that the Common Council did not agree. Halsbury's opinion was made plain when he reviewed in *The Times*[19] the 'law' entries in a new edition of *Enclyclopedia Britannica*. He praised Brickdale's land registration section, and criticized Lord Davey's for not blaming solicitors enough.

Then there was the question whether the Act was an 'experiment'. Solicitors argued that that is what had been said—that that was the purpose of the three-year lapse. So when in 1900 the Land Registry was voted £265,000 for a new building it seemed as though another undertaking had been broken.[20] The Act could hardly be experimental if such sums were being sunk into it. The fears were confirmed when initial lobbying from City interests and solicitors for an inquiry into the operation of the compulsion clause was rejected on the twin grounds that an internal inquiry had already investigated the management and working of the office, and that the principle having been settled in 1897 no inquiry into compulsion would be held.[21] The 'bargain' was beginning to look rather one-sided. Strained relations resulted between the ILS and provincial law societies, Leeds in particular. Requests from the ILS Council for provincial help in pressing for an inquiry were brushed off; the ILS had acted as a London society in 1897, it could do so now.[22]

1.3.   The Registry itself faced three major difficulties. First, the overwhelming majority of transactions resulted in the registra-

[19] *The Times*, 24 Oct. 1902.

[20] Land Registry (New Buildings) Act 1900, s. 3; (1900) 82 PD (4th ser.) 864; petitions against, ibid. 264, 409, 1360; 83 PD (4th ser.) 228; 84 PD (4th ser.) 770; solicitors' reaction, (1899–1900) 44 *Sol. Jo.* 73, 214, 326, 355, 406, 594.

[21] (1902) 102 PD (4th ser.) 534; (1901–2) 46 *Sol. Jo.* 257, 475. The internal inquiry revealed some over-staffing: Committee on Organization and Working of the Land Registry, PRO LCO2/181, July 1901. Brickdale was anxious to develop a career structure for well-educated men, ibid., 'Observations on the Report', 25 Nov. 1901.

[22] (1901–2) 46 *Sol. Jo.* 26, 670 (Gloucs. & Wilts.), cf. ibid. 733; (1902–3) 47 *Sol. Jo.* 15, 130.

tion only of possessory titles,[23] so that on subsequent dealings a blend of registered and traditional conveyancing was needed. — Costs to the landowner were increasing rather than decreasing. Secondly, the Registry's administration was structured in such a way that some transactions which were very simple in traditional conveyancing became more difficult—the purchase and contemporaneous mortgage was the most spectacular example.[24] Thirdly, the conceptual basis of registration was that registered proprietors possessed a set of legal *powers*, which was different from the traditional basis of conveyancing based upon possession of a legal *estate*.[25] The 1897 Act had to be read with the 1875 Act, fleshed out by the accompanying Rules. But there were still gaps, which were difficult to fill by reference to traditional practices based upon different assumptions. Embarrassingly for the Registrar, the major deficiency concerned one of the most common transactions, the simple legal mortgage.[26] The solution that became orthodox involved the mortgagee in taking *both* a registered charge and a conveyance of the fee simple by deed, with consequent costs.[27] In addition to these major problems were two minor ones. First there were numerous teething troubles. In addition to the two statutes the Rules numbered 280 clauses and 67 forms in 1898, increasing to 345

[23] *Report of the Registrar of the Land Registry on the First Three Years*, etc., Cd. 111, (1902) HCP lxxxiii. 595; *Land Registry Return of Work*, (1906) HCP xcix. 271; *Report of the Registrar of the Land Registry for the Years 1902–1905*, Cd. 3132, ibid. 279. For early comment see (1900–1) 45 *Sol. Jo.* 1.

[24] (1900–1) 45 *Sol. Jo.* 636; (1903–4) 48 *Sol. Jo.* 309.

[25] (1902–3) 47 *Sol. Jo.* 330, 400; *Capital and Counties Bank* v. *Rhodes* [1903] 1 Ch. 631. Evidence of T. C. Williams and H. W. Elphinstone to the Royal Commission on the Land Transfer Acts, (1911) HCP xxx. 1, qq. 10545 ff., 4428.

[26] (1900–1) 45 *Sol. Jo.* 338, 689; (1902–3) 47 *Sol. Jo.* 143. T. Cyprian Williams believed that the property boom after the Crimean War misled the draftsmen of the 1875 Act into thinking that sale would always be an adequate remedy; the 'old remedy' of entry and holding possession until the mortgagor was time barred was preferable in a falling market, but the mortgagee first needed the legal estate: (1911) HCP xxx. 1, q. 10577. For problems with mortgages of leases see (1897–8) 42 *Sol. Jo.* 616; (1899–1900) 44 *Sol. Jo.* 590, 600; (1900–1) 45 *Sol. Jo.* 357; (1901–2) 46 *Sol. Jo.* 315.

[27] (1900–1) 45 *Sol. Jo.* 338 (T. C. Williams); (1903–4) 48 *Sol. Jo.* 451; (1905–6) 50 *Sol. Jo.* 353 (H. W. Elphinstone). Registrar Brickdale said that only about half of mortgages of registered land used double documents, Evidence to the Royal Commission on the Land Transfer Acts, (1911) HCP xxx. 1, p. 538 (on qq. 3618–19).

clauses and 72 forms in 1903.[28] Inevitably some well-meaning solicitors got things wrong, and when they did the Registry officials did not always help them out.[29] There were also times when the Registry seemed to be shuffling responsibilities rightfully theirs on to solicitors.[30] Secondly, the political fanfares necessary to get the Act on to the books in the first place had raised expectations that the text of the Acts could never warrant. In particular, close scrutiny of the insurance provisions revealed that in many instances a claimant would be barred from an indemnity by his own unknowing participation in a mistake. This view was quickly taken by Registry officials and confirmed in litigation in 1905, reducing one of the system's most vaunted advantages.[31] As the *Solicitors' Journal* remarked, the Treasury was less friendly to the Registry than it could have been.[32] With some justification it reminded its readers in 1901 that the preamble to the 1875 Act had been repealed by a statute law revision Act in 1893, and with it the claim that registration facilitated conveyancing.[33]

That it did not was certainly the view of many of the London institutions—local government units, building societies, banks—whose pressure on government for a public inquiry built up steadily.[34] In particular it was the opinion of Edward Wood,[35] secretary of the largest building society in southern England and President of the Building Societies Association. He had opposed compulsion from the beginning and now regarded himself as vindicated. It was not just, as Dr Offer relates, that he told Registrar Brickdale this privately; he proclaimed it

[28] Land Transfer Rules, 1898 SR&O, no. 575; 1903 SR&O, no. 1081, postponed by 1903–4 SR&O 48/137 to allow time for familiarization.

[29] (1901–2) 46 *Sol. Jo.* 96, 101, 548; (1902–3) 47 *Sol. Jo.* 600.

[30] (1901–2) 46 *Sol. Jo.* 42, 47, 290, 313–14. Boundaries were the major problem.

[31] (1900–1) 45 *Sol. Jo.* 480; *A.-G. v. Odell* [1906] 2 Ch. 47, cf. *Gibbs v. Messer* [1891] AC 248. See the evidence of the Permanent Secretary to the Treasury to the 1908–11 Royal Commission, (1911) HCP xxx. 1, qq. 4296–310.

[32] (1905–6) 50 *Sol. Jo.* 388; also (1904–5) 49 *Sol. Jo.* 494, 620, and n. 108 below.

[33] (1900–1) 45 *Sol. Jo.* 636 on Statute Law Revision (no. 2) Act, 1893. It was a debating point; preambles were always repealed.

[34] (1900–1) 46 *Sol. Jo.* 362, 533, 657, 668; (1902–3) 47 *Sol. Jo.* 61, 62, 104, 112 ff., 605 658; (1903–4) 48 *Sol. Jo.* 655; (1903) 122 PD (4th ser.) 1382 ff.; Offer, *Property and Politics*, 72 n. 22. And see the extraordinary speech by the Recorder of Tewkesbury, (1903–4) 48 *Sol. Jo.* 607.

[35] (1901–2) 46 *Sol. Jo.* 362: (1902–3) 47 *Sol. Jo.* 114–15; Offer, *Property and Politics*, 74.

publicly to anyone who would listen. It is difficult to fault the
ILS Council's verdict in 1902, that 'the system does not appear
to have commended itself to many of the large building and
land societies and other bodies competent to form an opinion,
and derives what vitality it possesses from official efforts.'[36]

Some of these efforts were geared towards an extension of
the system as it stood. In October 1902 it became known that
Northamptonshire County Council was considering asking for
extension of compulsion to its area.[37] Rubinstein and Wood
both wrote advising against; Brickdale was interviewed. At the
crucial council meeting there was opposition from local bankers,
solicitors, and a land developer. The proposal was dropped as
being premature. There were rumours from time to time that
Brickdale was proposing some other extension, or agitating for
the abolition of the County veto.[38] Mostly, however, Brickdale
recognized that he would not achieve a widespread compulsory
system until he had managed to switch the emphasis from
possessory to absolute titles. Only then would registration be
unencumbered by concepts from the past and conveyancing
freed from the clutches of lawyers. One step, for once recognized by solicitors as being entirely within his jurisdiction, was
to rearrange the fee structure.[39] From 1903 applicants for absolute title need pay only a small part of the fee immediately, the
remainder being added to the (low) transfer fee on the first
subsequent transaction. Landowners or their solicitors stead-
fastly refused to see the benefits involved, and the initiative had
little effect.[40]

A much more radical proposal stemmed from Edward Wood.
At a meeting of building societies in Cheltenham, also
addressed by Brickdale and Rubinstein, Wood suggested that
possessory titles should be capable of upgrading after having
been on the register for two years or more without challenge—

[36] (1901–2) 46 *Sol. Jo.* 618.

[37] First Report of the Royal Commission on the Land Transfer Acts, Cd. 4510,
(1909) HCP xxvii. 733, evidence of S. G. Stopford Sackville, qq. 2136–56;
(1902–3) 47 *Sol. Jo.* 21, 114–15; Offer, *Property and Politics*, 72.

[38] Yorkshire: (1901–2) 46 *Sol. Jo.* 533, 669; (1902–3) 47 *Sol. Jo.* 15; (1904–5) 49
Sol. Jo. 45, 115, 211; 'New Domesday', (1903–4) 48 *Sol. Jo.* 747, 757.

[39] Land Transfer Fee Order, 1903 SR&O 1080, rule 7; (1902–3) 47 *Sol. Jo.* 166.

[40] *Report of the Registrar of the Land Registry for the Years 1902–1905*, Cd. 3132,
(1906) HCP xcix. 279.

a reversion in fact to Halsbury's initial 'confirmation' plan.[41] Brickdale agreed only cautiously, probably because Wood argued that the insurance fund should cover the risks. Wood was much taken with his suggestion, and became an enthusiastic proponent of registration conditionally upon its acceptance. But for as long as registration were predominantly of possessory title he urged resistance to the Act's extension.[42] Brickdale tried. The difficulty was that either a change in the Act was needed, or a change somewhere in the Rules. The latter was attempted, Brickdale proposing that his duty to inquire into a title upon an application for upgrading should be relaxed after a possessory title had been on the register for two years.[43] It was on the strength of this proposal that the government rejected a further plea for an inquiry.[44] But Brickdale was disappointed.[45] The lawyers on the Rules Committee refused to countenance what they saw as a substantive change of limitation law. An angry Lord Chancellor required them to think again, but they returned the same answer. Halsbury then made his own Rule notwithstanding the Rules Committee's recommendation, but settled for a six-year period rather than Brickdale's two. But even after the Registry took to mailing pamphlets advertising the facility to holders of possessory title, it came to very little. Perhaps its only major result was to fix in solicitors' minds the view that Halsbury was dictatorial, and to occasion yet another London/Leeds row when Arthur Middleton, sometime President of the Leeds ILS, demanded that The Law Society remove its representative from the Rules Committee in protest at Halsbury's treatment of it. He had to be talked down by representatives of other northern societies.

The new Rules of 1903 tried to deal with many of the problems

---

[41] (1902–3) 47 *Sol. Jo.* 104, 114–15.

[42] (1903–4) 48 *Sol. Jo.* 547.

[43] *Report of the Registrar of the Land Registry on the First Three Years*, Cd. 111, (1902) HCP lxxxiii. 595, paras. 146–56.

[44] (1903) 119 PD (4th ser.) 85; (1902–3) 47 *Sol. Jo.* 172; and see (1903) 122 PD (4th ser.) 1382 ff.

[45] For this account see (1902–3) 47 *Sol. Jo.* 665, 684, 701; (1902–3) 48 *Sol. Jo.* 137, 152, 221, 321, 363, 389, 427, 438. For the mailing see (1904–5) 49 *Sol. Jo.* 695, 699, 707, 711, 781; (1905–6) 50 *Sol. Jo.* 190. There is a copy of the circular at PRO LAR1/3.

that had been identified in their precursors' operation.[46] But in length and complexity they were tantamount to a new system, and it was becoming clear to everyone that a further inquiry would be needed. Among the barristers, three representatives of the next generation of experts had concluded that a complete rethinking of property law concepts was needed, going beyond even Wolstenholme's extensive use of conveyancing devices to ease land transfer.[47] Even Howard Elphinstone, for so long a supporter of registration, and a member of the Rules Committee, concluded that there were too many basic problems for extension without an inquiry to be warranted.[48] These barristers were not agreed whether title registration would be an integral part of a new property code, or whether it would be rendered superfluous, but Brickdale adopted their gist, that basic concepts needed rethinking to suit a registered system.[49] And thus the long build-up to an inquiry began. All three interest groups— solicitors, specialist barristers, Registrar—jockeyed for public platforms, issued position papers, lobbied for allies, and tried to influence the terms of reference of the inquiry that was now likely, especially after the Conservatives lost office in 1906.[50]

---

[46] 1903 SR&O, 1081; discussion at (1903–4) 48 *Sol. Jo.* 256, 273, 293, 309, 325, 347, 366; and of the attempt to solve the 'contemporaneous mortgage' problem at ibid. 309, 367, 345, 349.

[47] T. Cyprian Williams (ed.), *[Joshua] Williams on Real Property* (19th edn., 1901), 651–7; Charles Sweet, (1901) 13 *Juridical Review* 285; J. E. Hogg, (1904) 20 *LQR* 74, 292; (1905) 21 *LQR* 29.

[48] (1906) 22 *LQR* 27; and see (1905–6) 50 *Sol. Jo.* 91; for early commitment to title registration see Report of the Select Committee on Land Titles and Transfer, (1878–9) HCP xi. 1, qq. 358–84.

[49] *Report of the Registrar of the Land Registry on the Years 1902–1905*, Cd. 3132, (1906) HCP xcix, para. 54.

[50] The *Solicitors' Journal* called it a 'pamphlet war', (1908–9) 53 *Sol. Jo.* 353: *Solicitors*: Council of The Law Society, *Some Reasons against Registering Land at the Land Registry* (1906); reply to Brickdale's 1906 *Report*, (1906–7) 51 *Sol. Jo.* 286; *Remarks on the Present Situation in Regard to Compulsory Land Registration* (1907); note the use of Benjamin Cherry as an emissary (and the openness of the disclosure), (1907–8) 52 *Sol. Jo.* 242. J. S. Rubinstein, *The Land Registry Fiasco: The Reign of King Stork* (1907).
Registrar: 1906 *Report*, see n. 49 above; evidence to the Select Committee on the Housing of the Working Classes Act, (1906) HCP ix. 1, 328–45—Rubinstein was snubbed, (1906–7) 51 *Sol. Jo.* 168.
Barristers: Sweet, (1908) 24 *LQR* 26; Hogg, ibid. 290, and see the dispute between them at (1907–8) 52 *Sol. Jo.* 217, 297; Williams, (1907–8) 52 *Sol. Jo.* 527. Hogg's *Treatise on the Law Relating to the Ownership and Incumbrance of Registered Land* was published in 1906.

Dr Offer recounts Brickdale's eagerness for the battle, his opinion of The Law Society as 'desperadoes', of their tactics as 'abominable in the sight of all men', of his wish to take his 'revenge'.[51] This is the language of an obsession which coloured his perception of the problems and his fidelity to fact. Take, for example his 1906 *Report* on the years 1902–5.[52] It made light of the difficulties, blamed solicitors' obstruction for whatever defects could not otherwise be explained away, and declared that the time had come for extension of the scheme. In a bold rewriting of history he announced that the County Council veto in the 1897 Act had been enacted only to prevent premature extension swamping the Registry and causing delays. Since the executive could be trusted to proceed piecemeal anyway, the hurdle should be removed by repeal of that section, leaving the way open to extension by executive discretion. He had no aversion to an inquiry first, but it should be on the right subject; what had happened in the Registry in the past was irrelevant to the future, partly because it had been corrupted by solicitors' obstructionism, partly because changes in the Rules had been made to correct previous errors; therefore the subject of the inquiry should simply be to establish the benefits bound to arise if the improved system could be run in the proper way.

Brickdale always had been an advocate, and in the run-up to an inquiry rhetoric such as this was to be expected. None the less it seems to have been getting in the way of dispassionate analysis. Let one example suffice. There had been great difficulties caused by mortgagees insisting on retaining possession of mortgagors' land certificates, notwithstanding that they were issued with their own charge certificates. The consequent expense and complication was indeed unfortunate, and the practice was contrary to the spirit of the Act. But Brickdale was wrong to lay the blame on 'the conservatism of the solicitors',[53] operating through their hold over lenders, who in turn could dictate terms to borrowers. The reason lay nearer home, in Rule 164, which provided that after a foreclosure action, title would

---

[51] Offer, *Property and Politics*, 75.

[52] See n. 49 above; para. 58 has the false explanation for the veto, and there is a good example of advocacy in para. 82.

[53] Ibid., paras. 80–1; (1907–8) 52 *Sol. Jo.* 333, and cf. *Weymouth* v. *Davies* [1908] 2 Ch. 169, and Hogg, (1906–7) 51 *Sol. Jo.* 304.

be transferred to a mortgagee only on production of the land certificate. This did not bother Brickdale, because the Registry did not insist upon observance of its Rule. In practice a new title certificate was issued if the former mortgagor was uncooperative. But even if solicitors knew this, they would obviously feel unsafe advising their clients to ignore the Rules in reliance upon a mere administrative practice that might change at any time. It was clearly sensible to take the Rule seriously and get possession of the Certificate from the start. Yet then solicitors were blamed as fiercely for following the Rules as they were when acting in ignorance of them.

At the heart of episodes such as this lay fundamental disagreement about the role of executive discretion in property transactions. For solicitors, rules had a permanence to them, they were relatively fixed points around which transactions could be structured. For Brickdale they were means to an end, to be waived or adapted at the wisdom of the judge/legislator.[54] None the less, Brickdale did think in terms of rules and concepts—fashioning the former as he went along, calling for the modernization of the latter so as to fit his administrative machine. His perception was part-way between the barrister's and the bureaucrat's. Solicitors, I think, thought more in terms of the transactions concerned, rather than the rules through which they must be fashioned. These transactions could be simple, like a mortgage, or compound, like a purchase and contemporaneous mortgage, or a sale reserving a rentcharge. The underlying law might be complex, but it had become well known over time, and thus the necessary documentation had become easily manageable. Further, the paperwork required for any particular sort of transaction could be modified for the occasion without increasing the time taken, the cost, or, beyond marginally, the length of the documents needed (where, anyway, the cost of prolixity now fell on the solicitor). The underlying law had, as it were, resulted in an intelligent formulary system. Solicitors' perception lay somewhere between the barrister's and the businessman's—they were, as

---

[54] First Report of the Royal Commission on the Land Transfer Acts, (1909) HCP xxvii. 733, q. 1007: 'But it would not paralyze the Registry? *Brickdale*: I never believe in paralyzing anything.'

they liked to say, men of business themselves; law was only part of their trade. As a result there was a considerable difference between their vision of an efficient system and the Registrar's, and a mutual lack of understanding conducing to distrust. Because it had always been lawyers with whom businessmen worked, the sort of transactions they wanted were the ones the solicitors knew how to do, and vice versa. But the Registrar, office-bound and thinking in rules and concepts, was having to learn the ways of the world from scratch. It would have taken mutual trust for a synthesis to be reached, but that was beyond hope.

1.4.   Dr Offer's description of this period differs from mine.[55] He sees the solicitors' profession as being isolated and in a deep malaise. His explanation for their opposition to the Registrar is one-dimensional: it was simply a question of economic interest, of economic survival even. He asserts unquestioningly the absolute value of title registration: its defeat in 1925 (for such it was) was accomplished only 'to satisfy the vested interest of a determined group in a lucrative *and largely superfluous function*'.[56] That the profession should have been in malaise is unnecessary to such an analysis, but is none the less stressed by Dr Offer. Probably he sees their supposed economic weakness as lending desperation to the solicitors' resistance, hence their tenacity, their willingness to use any tactics, however base.

In Dr Offer's view the solicitors' profession in 1903 had sunk so low that it had only a 'tenuous hold on gentility'.[57] It 'required a catastrophic war to restore the fortunes of the profession'.[58] But though he cites some gloomy papers by solicitors,[59] he ignores a source that seems to prove their falsity. Writing in 1965, Guy Routh discussed an internal Whitehall analysis of professional earnings.[60] Commissioned in 1913 to determine appropriate salaries for professionals in the public

---

[55] *Property and Politics*, 52–8, 60–5, 69–75.
[56] Ibid. 84, emphasis added.
[57] Ibid. 55.
[58] Ibid. 63.
[59] See n. 67 below.
[60] Guy Routh, *Occupation and Pay in Great Britain* (1st edn., 1965), esp. 62–7. The second edition (1980) is less useful since it aggregates barristers and solicitors into 'lawyers'.

service, it was based upon income tax returns and thus reflected actual earnings (or, at least, declared earnings, which are unlikely to have been higher). It showed that at all points in the hierarchy bar two, solicitors were the most prosperous profession of all. The exceptions were that their top decile earned significantly less than the top 10 per cent of barristers, though more than any other profession's top decile; and their bottom quartile was marginally worse off than the equivalent doctors, though again relatively better off than the bottom slice of any other profession, barristers included. What better way is there of testing the wealth and 'gentility' of one profession than by comparison with others?

It is possible of course that there had been a radical transformation from a dismal period in the early years of the century. Such an argument, however, is not open to Dr Offer, whose analysis of the property market cycle correlated with the number of solicitors in practice concludes that 1913 was one of the worst years, far worse than 1903.[61] When considering the salaries sought by newly qualified men in 1912–13, and also the prices asked by solicitors selling their practices, Dr Offer is puzzled to find that they were not following the decline in the property market,[62] suggestive of a kind of false consciousness, a clinging to high expectations in bad times. Surely however this evidence tends rather to support Dr Routh's conclusion that even in hard times solicitors were relatively well-off. Dr Offer's men may have recognized the property cycle for what it was, a cycle that would turn; and compared with their peers in other occupations they were still ahead. It is hard to resist the conclusion that the profession as a whole was prosperous.

The top quartile in Routh's study fell at £790, against £700 for doctors and £680 for barristers, but the median was only £390 as against £370 and £210 respectively.[63] How those solicitors felt about their earnings depends upon their origins and upon

[61] *Property and Politics*, fig. 4.4, p. 54; table 4.2, p. 66. At that late stage there is a little evidence of an association between depression in the property market and resistance to registration, (1911–12) 132 *LT* 144 (Liverpool ILS).

[62] Ibid. 60–1. Even if Dr Offer is right it is hard to believe that the weaklings would have been influential in policy-making, or that law societies so concerned about 'standards' would have mourned their loss.

[63] See n. 60 above. For comparisons see Harold Perkin, *The Rise of Professional Society* (pb. edn., 1990), 91–4.

whom they compared themselves with, raising again the diffi-culty of finding a convincing comparator other then their rival professions. To judge by letters to the professional press, and by papers given to professional meetings, there was nothing untoward about this period.[64] Senior solicitors did sometimes wring their hands about poverty in the lower reaches of their profession, but the context was usually the same—a meeting of one of the solicitors' benevolent societies.[65] It was natural that men dispensing bounty should have the unfortunate on their minds at that time, and that they should appeal for greater generosity. But the need was no greater than with any other occupational group; indeed, a barrister present at one such meeting thought that it was less for solicitors than for his own profession.[66] And the poor are always with us, even poor solicitors; nobody was arguing that they were getting poorer or more numerous.

Dr Offer cites a series of papers by solicitors which he says portray anxiety about the state of their profession in general and about overstocking in particular.[67] Their dates cover very nearly one whole turn of Dr Offer's property-market cycle: 1893, 1900, 1903, and 1908.[68] But Harry Kirk adds virtually the whole of the period 1841–71 as a time when 'the profession became acutely conscious or at any rate completely convinced that it was overcrowded', with further angst in 1882, 1893, 1899, and 1906.[69] As an earlier historian of the solicitors wrote wryly in 1896, 'the profession is and always has been overstocked.'[70] This is neurosis, not reality. Further, Dr Offer overstates the effect of the four papers cited. Two were general rambles by the same man, much given to pontificating about the state of the profession in general, one of which drew sharp criticism from a

[64] In the nature of things a judgment incapable of documentation.
[65] Notably Henry Atlee, ILS President, (1899–1900) 44 *Sol. Jo.* 556. Immediate reaction was sceptical, ibid. 545, and the following year's president disagreed: (1900–1) 45 *Sol. Jo.* 599 ff.; for earlier optimism see (1898–9) 43 *Sol. Jo.* 796.
[66] (1902–3) 47 *Sol. Jo.* 621.
[67] W. P. Fullager, (1892–3) 37 *Sol. Jo.* 806, (1899–1900) 44 *Sol. Jo.* 791; R. G. Lawson, (1902–3) 47 *Sol. Jo.* 857; J. W. Reid, (1907–8) 52 *Sol. Jo.* 823.
[68] *Property and Politics*, Table 4.2, p. 66; 1899 was the peak, 1911 the trough.
[69] *Portrait*, 109, 114–16.
[70] Edmund B. V. Christian, *A Short History of the Solicitors*, quoted by Kird, *Portrait*, 109. For Perkin too insecurity was an endemic if paradoxical feature of the *fin de siècle* middle-class psyche: *The Rise of Professional Society*, 95 ff.

member of the audience (unreported by Dr Offer).[71] Another was a general 'status raising' paper, which drew a little discussion but none of it showing serious concern.[72] The fourth was scheduled for an annual provincial meeting, but was crowded out by other papers and was not actually read, though it was printed in the meeting's papers.[73] It was evidently regarded as unimportant, and was anyway using assertions that solicitors were only modestly well-off not in any anxious sense but so as to argue that they gave jolly good value for money, and were public-spirited law-reformers to boot.

Finally, Dr Offer's interpretation of the profession's lack of growth[74] must be questioned, tentatively perhaps, since it is not clear just what he is arguing. He sees a dramatic 'Malthusian population crisis' about to hit the solicitors just before the First War. Somewhat inconsistently he says that 'mortality had overtaken natality', but that the result was only that the profession's growth was halted. The last point is certainly true; aggregating the years 1910 to 1913 the number of practising certificates issued was virtually static.[75] Dr Offer records that entrance examinations were tightened in 1904, but it is most unclear where he includes this in his conclusion, 'it appears that the reduction in intake . . . was not caused by positive intervention but came rather as a market response, through a contraction of the number of openings combined, perhaps, with a diminished attractiveness of solicitors' prospects.' Richard Abel prefers the more straightforward explanation that the stiffening of the exam was responsible.[76] The detailed figures show that the only year of serious decline was 1911, a 0.6 per cent fall. This came five years after a sharp fall in the number of new articles of clerkship, five years being the normal length of articles, correlating quite well with the toughening of examina-

---

[71] Fullager, n. 67 above; and see his paper, 'Why Every Solicitor Should Join The Law Society', (1902–3) 47 *Sol. Jo.* 844; he was contradicted by Harvey Clifton (see n. 13 above), (1899–1900) 44 *Sol. Jo.* 791 at 794.

[72] Reid, n. 67 above; the discussion was whether employing qualified solicitors as clerks was healthy for the profession or not.

[73] Lawson, n. 67 above; Dr Offer makes a lot of this paper.

[74] *Property and Politics*, 60–5.

[75] Richard Abel, *The Legal Profession in England and Wales* (1988), table 2.14. Cf. discussion at an AGM of The Law Society, (1912) 133 *LT* 264.

[76] Ibid. 165.

tion standards. By Dr Offer's calculations 1906 was an indifferent year in the property-market cycle, making economic reasons plausible but not compelling. They would be more likely if an absolute decline in articles of clerkship had followed, shadowing the continued downward trend of the property market. But after the initial fall they fell no further, even though the property market continued to decline, until a further significant drop in 1912 and 1913 when the property cycle hit a trough.[77] These final falls probably can be explained on economic grounds, as Dr Offer does explain them, but they came too late to influence opposition to registration, which had been continuous since 1900. If Abel is right, then the reduction in articled clerks from 1905/6 was planned. Dr Offer *also* says this, but still manages to conclude that what resulted was a crisis from which the profession was rescued only by war, on the grounds that 'a reduction in admissions could prevent the decline in incomes, but a "positive check" in the form of war was needed to redress the balance of population and resources'.[78]

I cannot find anything in this to support the conclusion that the profession was in serious trouble. By external indicators it was doing relatively well. Contemporary papers to the contrary are less alarmist than Dr Offer makes them, drew mixed responses at best, are few relative to the numbers of conference papers given at that time, and little different in content from papers found regularly throughout the nineteenth century. The zero growth-rate seems explicable as a planned raising of standards, save at the very end—after which war so changed the circumstances that nobody can say what would have happened next. Taking a broad view, Abel regards the size of the profession as virtually static from 1890 until 1948;[79] there is no need to get excited about small fluctuations. Bankruptcies among solicitors averaged nearly 45 a year in the decade

---

[77] President C. L. Samson, whose gloomy analysis of the state of the profession in 1912 is partially cited by Offer, *Property and Politics*, 61, was a litigator not a conveyancer and attributed the difficulties to the delays in litigation, their high costs caused by barristers' excessive fees, and uncertain law, with officialism as a very secondary cause. His solution was freedom of contract for solicitors in litigation, enabling the introduction of contingency fees: (1911–12) 56 *Sol. Jo.* 807. No discussion is reported in the professional press.

[78] *Property and Politics*, 63.

[79] Abel, *Legal Profession*, 167.

1894–1903, but only 34 for 1904–13, which must say something for the profession's financial health.[80] It does not look like a profession on the rocks.

One weakness of Dr Offer's reliance on economic analysis is that it cannot explain opposition to the Registrar from non-solicitors. This poses a serious problem, since if they had reasons other than economic self-interest it is possible that solicitors might have shared them, and hence that the one-dimensional explanation offered must fall. Dr Offer's answer is to resort to melodrama. In a later period, when it is barristers whom he must explain, he treats them either as covert hirelings or as irretrievably tainted by prior 'association' with The Law Society, sometimes at second-hand.[81] In this earlier period he does not investigate whether the local authorities, building societies, bankers, and property-owners' associations voicing dissatisfaction with the 1897 Act had independent springs of action. Instead he asserts simply that they were permeated and suborned by solicitors; by one in particular, J. S. Rubinstein, whose only weapons apart from 'political experience' were 'innuendo' and 'muckraking'.[82] Dr Offer even understates Rubinstein's efforts, for though he relates his 'audacious capture' of the Land Law Reform Association in 1901, he overlooks a precisely similar episode in 1906, which, if the *coup* were as Dr

[80]

1894: 39	1901: 55	1908: 38
1895: 47	1902: 43	1909: 32
1896: 51	1903: 52	1910: 23
1897: 50	1904: 42	1911: 33
1898: 38	1905: 31	1912: 42
1899: 39	1906: 29	1913: 36
1900: 32	1907: 34	

Source: Board of Trade Annual Reports, HCP.

[81] *Property and Politics*, 76: Haldane contaminated by association with Davey, who was associated with The Law Society. For Davey see above, Ch. 5 n. 45 and accompanying text; the Chairman of the Royal Commission on the Land Transfer Acts regarded him as a supporter of title registration: (1911) HCP xxx. 1, q. 4968. Similarly *Property and Politics*, 44, where Underhill's early experience characterizes him as a member of a 'group', for whose existence there is no evidence. For Underhill as a supporter of title registration see (1899–1900) 44 *Sol. Jo.* 410. Dr Offer's adherence to conspiracy theory is noticed by John Gooch, *Times Higher Education Supplement*, 12 Jan. 1990, p. 23. Benjamin Cherry was once used by The Law Society as an emissary: (1907–8) 52 *Sol. Jo.* 242, though this was openly acknowledged. Whether one acknowledged event (missed by Dr Offer) proves a conspiracy is for readers of both works to judge.

[82] Offer, *Property and Politics*, 70, 72.

Offer asserts it to be, was a trifle careless of the Association.[83] The one exception Dr Offer allows is that he records Edward Wood's private letter to Registrar Brickdale complaining of the Act's inadequacies. Wood's opposition, however, went much further than that, as shown.

There is no need for such flights of fancy. Building societies, local authorities, and the rest could distinguish three related but different issues: cheap and quick conveyancing, which is where their interest lay, the principle of title registration, and the operation of the 1897 Act. Some solicitors argued that no scheme of title registration would ever achieve cheaper or quicker conveyancing than the traditional system as modified in 1880–2. Be that as it may, it was perfectly clear that the 1897 Act was not doing so. Therefore an inquiry should be held to determine the reasons. It was as simple as that; and that was the motion that Rubinstein had twice carried at the Land Law Reform Association. It was perfectly understandable that anybody concerned with the land market and anxious about the direction of land transfer practice should hold an open meeting, inviting the champions from each side to address it. Rubinstein was no more permeating these bodies from his side than was Brickdale; both were advocates to willing audiences. Nor does it alter that analysis that both men should have sought out opportunities; nor that different people should have anticipated different outcomes from the inquiry.

This casts doubt upon Dr Offer's main thesis. Once admit that the people supposed to benefit from a title registration scheme turned against it, then solicitors' opposition would at least in part have an altruistic side to it, akin to their law societies' efforts to persuade authority to take a less rigorous approach to the stamp duty imposts levied on written instruments, or to mitigate the incidence of estate duty.[84] Put crudely, but in a way Dr Offer never faces, there is no incompatibility between being self-interested and being right. And as I have been arguing, professional self-interest has many facets.

I do not share the view that we are witnessing a weak

---

[83] Ibid. 72; (1900–1) 45 *Sol. Jo.* 609; (1905–6) 50 *Sol. Jo.* 367.

[84] For stamps, see e.g. (1901–2) 46 *Sol. Jo.* 657; (1902–3) 47 *Sol. Jo.* 130; for estate duty, (1899–1900) 44 *Sol. Jo.* 343.

profession, clinging to a position which had already been eroded by contradictions in the economic forces on which it was based. Rather, I see a strong, well-organized profession, albeit one still in the process of consolidation. It is impossible to say how many of its members, how many of its significant members, believed that compulsory title registration would permanently undermine its economic foundations. Some no doubt. But others did not; Haldane and Herschell had probably thought not;[85] the Royal Commission would regard the idea as ridiculous—there were simply too many aspects to a land transaction other than the act of transfer for solicitors to be ousted. We can account for some opposition to the Registrar this way, but not much. But even solicitors who regarded the foundations as safe might fear for the superstructure. The solicitors' professional ideal encompassed the entire law enterprise; wherever decisions were made the law societies should be there, be it in the making of law, its administration, or its application. That way came power, prestige, and perhaps even some advances on to the territory of the barristers. The conjunction of a Land Registrar with sovereignty over land transfer and a Public Trustee offering an alternative administration for family finances threatened that ideal, even if both new institutions generated so much new work that no solicitor lost a penny.[86] And finally, as a third strand in their opposition, to oppose this particular statute would itself bring credit to the profession if, as many believed, the Registry was making simple transactions complicated and cheap ones dear. Such opposition was itself part of the professional ideal.

Finally, Dr Offer's analysis is not only one-dimensional, it is one-sided. Accept that economic factors are dominant, then what economic factors were driving Brickdale? Was it *really* the case that it was in the public interest for solicitors to be ousted from land transfer (and not replaced by para-professionals), or was this claim simply the product of forces operating on the Land Registry, whose interest was to maintain its own life?

---

[85] See above, Ch. 5 n. 188 and accompanying text.

[86] They also feared that public officers tended to support each other on bad points of law; for the best-known example see (1904–5) 49 *Sol. Jo.* 178, 183 (esp.), 544, 549. For solicitors and the Public Trustee see Patrick Polden, 'The Public Trustee in England, 1906–1986', (1989) 10 *Jo. Leg. Hist.* 228.

Treasury recalcitrance, Parliamentary anxiety, and a declining property market combined to threaten its survival. Unlike solicitors, the Land Registry had a very limited ability to diversify—though, as Dr Offer records without analysing, Brickdale tried hard enough to persuade politicians that it was an embryonic Land Office, home of a cadaster, facilitator of taxation, source of information, keeper of the New Domesday.[87] If he had succeeded, would he still have thought it worth pursuing the solicitors? In 1915 J. S. Stewart-Wallace, barrister, Vinerian Scholar, and spokesman for the seven First Class Clerks who adjudicated upon applications for absolute title, made a sustained and bitter complaint to the Royal Commission on the Civil Service.[88] The principle insisted upon by the Treasury that the Registry must be self-financing had reduced to an unacceptable level the salaries paid to men of the liberal education, professional qualification, and ability necessary for this difficult work. Failure to extend compulsory registration combined with the Registry's isolation from the regular Civil Service deprived them of career prospects. Morale had been low 'for years'; complaints about conditions of service were made daily at all levels. His evidence spoke longingly of extension, as did that of Brickdale, who renewed his plea for a gradual merger of the Registry with the Cadaster Office and the Land Valuation Department. The crisis had accentuated since 1911; by 1915 the Registry was near to breaking. Expansion clearly seemed the only answer. If the Registry was to replace a profession it must itself offer the benefits of a profession, as Stewart-Wallace's plaint so eloquently demonstrated. Yet the Treasury applied shopkeepers' principles.

2. 1908–1911: Verdict of the Technocrats

2.1. Politically the early century had been difficult for law societies. But rumoured threats to remove the county council veto, opening the way to extension of compulsory title registra-

---

[87] *Property and Politics*, 76. For an earlier attempt see (1903–4) 48 *Sol. Jo.* 747, 757.

[88] Sixth Report of the Royal Commission on the Civil Service, (1914–16) HCP xii. 1, qq. 54651 ff.; for Brickdale see qq. 50994 ff., esp. 51258–61 and 51295.

tion to the provinces without prior inquiry, brought the northern provincial societies back on to speaking terms with The Law Society.[89] With the return of the Liberals in 1906 its Council could hope that the corner had been turned. Bills once blocked began to work their way on to the statute book.[90] The Public Trustee Act was worded to encourage its use where need was greatest, for small estates.[91] It emphasized too a role for the Public Trustee as a mere custodian of funds, which would not necessarily oust solicitors and others from day to day management or control of discretionary decisions. Threats from the Board of Trade to impose departmental auditing of solicitors' accounts came to nothing beyond pushing The Law Society into recommending the keeping of separate accounts for clients' money.[92] The Royal Commission was part of this new climate, if begrudgingly so.

It was announced in August 1908. Almost immediately the Rules Committee published drafts of an entirely new code designed to substitute absolute for possessory title.[93] The new drafts compelled transferees to submit their full title to the Registrar even if seeking only possessory title; he would then offer absolute title if he saw fit; fees for the two sorts of title were to be the same, a major innovation to be financed by abolishing the former ceiling on charges and extending the pro rata scale upwards indefinitely. As the Leeds ILS put it, 'the new rules amount practically to a new Act of Parliament with respect to compulsory registration on a system differing very materially from the Act of 1897.'[94] They would almost certainly have been *ultra vires* for that reason, and maybe also for the unreasonableness entailed in compelling an owner to submit his deeds to a scrutiny suitable for a title he was not seeking. In

[89] (1904–5) 49 *Sol. Jo.* 45, 55, 109, 115, 240 ff. (on the 'Derby meeting'), 307, 316. But see Charles Ford, ibid. 653, 655.

[90] Solicitors Act 1906; Married Women's Property Act 1907; but the Conveyancing Bill and the Settled Land Bill remained blocked, (1905–6) 50 *Sol. Jo.* 370, 393, 588; (1906–7) 51 *Sol. Jo.* 292, 510, 635, 777, 782; (1907–8) 52 *Sol. Jo.* 310, 795; (1908–9) 53 *Sol. Jo.* 102.

[91] Public Trustee Act 1906, ss. 4 and 5; and see s. 11(2), Polden, n. 86 above; (1905–6) 50 *Sol. Jo.* 354.

[92] (1905–6) 50 *Sol. Jo.* 745; (1906–7) 51 *Sol. Jo.* 103, 139, 151, 157; Kirk, *Portrait*, 102.

[93] (1907–8) 52 *Sol. Jo.* 721 ff., 756, 779; (1908–9) 53 *Sol. Jo.* 7, 72, 77, 127, 130.

[94] (1908–9) 53 *Sol. Jo.* 64.

the event the draft was modified sufficiently to escape this charge, though the Rules eventually issued[95] were still a major departure from the spirit and possibly the letter of the supposedly governing Acts.

Once again the timing looks like a direct challenge to the solicitors; the Rules were bound to be taken as an attempt to bypass Parliament. Further, and in the spirit of Brickdale's 1906 *Report*, they look designed to insure against the effect of any adverse findings the Commission might make—for how could that any longer matter if the situation had been remedied by a Rule change? So it turned out to be; time and again Brickdale would parry questions from Commissioners with the reply that all had changed since the episode complained of.[96] It was even possible to make a virtue of it, as shown in a passage from the 1906 *Report*:

one of the advantages of the extensive application given to the Land Transfer Acts during the last seven years is that experience has been gained of their application to a great variety of unforeseen circumstances, and a large amount of professional talent has been expended on a scrutiny of some of their less obvious features and characteristics.[97]

Heads I win, tails you lose.

2.2. With one exception, solicitors and Registry officials were kept off the Royal Commission. The Attorney-General said that the Commission was to be without preconceptions.[98] The exception was Richard Pennington, there by virtue of his position on the Rules Committee, and not as an advocate for solicitors.[99] Of the remaining eleven good men and true, six were barristers, one being the bar's current representative on the Rules Committee. A couple of bankers, a couple of landowners, and Edward Wood for the building societies made up the lay element. The Chairman was Viscount St Aldwyn, the former Michael Hicks

---

[95] Land Transfer Rules, 1908, 1908 SR&O 944; Fee Order, ibid. 945.

[96] Second Report of the Royal Commission on the Land Transfer Acts, (1911) HCP xxx. 1, at pp. 578 (answer to Syrett) and 563 (answer to Beale), and qq. 11069 ff.

[97] *Report of the Registrar of the Land Registry for the Years 1902–1905*, Cd. 3132, (1906) HCP xcix. 279, para. 53.

[98] (1908) 194 PD (4th ser.) 1580, Robson, A.–G.

[99] (1908) 125 *LT* 546.

Beach, who had had an outstanding political career, managed his own 4,000 acres without help from an agent, had a history of interest in moderate land reform, and kept in touch with local affairs by retaining a place on Gloucestershire County Council.[100]

The Commission's composition and terms of reference pre-determined the nature of the inquiry and its outcome. 'To consider and report upon the working of the Land Transfer Acts, and whether any amendments are desirable' excluded the twin questions of repeal and of replacement by a simplification or assimilation scheme. That did not stop barristers and law societies from urging them, of course, but it firmly located the inquiry on Brickdale's territory. The Commission adopted a broadly adversarial stance. It first heard Brickdale and his supporters, whom it cross-examined intensively. It published this evidence verbatim in 1909,[101] giving time for the opposition to consider it. It then heard the opponents; cross-examined them; showed the draft of evidence to Brickdale and allowed him a final reply to their detailed points, subject again to cross-examination. It reported in 1911.[102] The shape of the Report was predictable from the outset: the Commission would come up with a list of defects that should be corrected before further extension, with suggestions as to how that should be done. In that the list turned out to be longer and the suggestions much less optimistic than Brickdale obviously expected, the Report was a defeat for him. His wildly exaggerated claims were not supported, nor were his simple schemes for extension thought an adequate response to the serious difficulties which the commissioners found to exist. But in that the Report stopped well short of the outright condemnation that many solicitors expected, and in that it gave only lukewarm approval for the assimilation schemes presented to it, they too were left unsatisfied.[103]

---

[100] *DNB 1912–21.*

[101] First Report of the Royal Commission on the Land Transfer Acts, Cd. 4510, (1909) HCP xxvii. 733 (hereinafter 'First Report').

[102] Second and Final Report of Royal Commission on the Land Transfer Acts, Cd. 5483, (1911) HCP xxx. 1 (hereinafter 'Second Report').

[103] (1910–11) 55 *Sol. Jo.* 263, 357. Brickdale's disappointment is clear in his evidence to the Royal Commission on the Civil Service, (1914–16) HCP xii. 1, q. 51066.

This is hardly surprising given the contortions solicitors had to perform in opposing the Registry. In the political arena they had to make contradictory claims: on the one hand that they would be ousted from conveyancing, which would be unprincipled confiscation of their livelihood incompatible with liberal principles, but on the other hand that they would *not* be ousted from conveyancing, because only then would registered conveyancing be more expensive than the traditional variety. Their task before the Commission was no easier: they had to argue that contemporary conveyancing was well adapted to both simple and complex business dealings, and just as quick and cheap as anything registration could provide, at the same time as claiming that the only solution to present difficulties was major reform of the underlying tangle of real property law.[104] Brickdale's problem was very similar: he wanted to show that his system was so simple that it could be operated by ordinary people without professional assistance, yet also that the vast majority of individual complaints garnered by the solicitors stemmed from their failure to study and apply the Land Registration Rules which, properly understood, provided an answer to every problem (or could be made to do so by prompt amendment).

2.3. The two major battle-grounds were cost and ability to deal with complexity. On the first, solicitors marshalled a great deal of evidence to show how actual conveyancing costs under the traditional system as modified by the 1881 legislation were not high, to which Brickdale responded by showing that Registry charges were even less.[105] The solicitors replied that these charges represented only a part of the actual bill, to which Brickdale answered that any additional bills tendered by solicitors were superfluous because the users of the Registry could manage perfectly without them. It quickly emerged that nobody knew how to interpret the figures. Mr F. Marshall, representing the Newcastle solicitors, built a two-pronged argument that

---

[104] e.g. Council of The Law Society, 'Some Remarks on the Present Situation in Regard to Compulsory Land Registration', (1907–8) 52 *Sol. Jo.* 128, 134.

[105] Second Report, qq. 6103 ff. (Leeds), 6243 ff. (Bradford), 6575 ff. (Lincs.), 6682 ff. (Huddersfield), 6723 ff. (Newcastle), 7106 ff. (Bristol), 7556 ff. (Birmingham); for Brickdale's response see p. 548 and qq. 12232 ff., 12268, 12276–7.

Brickdale's evidence seriously underestimated the real costs of dealings with registered title.[106] First, he said, it wrongly excluded the cost of pre-contract requisitions and inquiries. The ensuing argument disclosed that nobody could say with confidence whether the fee included in the scale of legal fees allowed for registry business was even intended to cover preparation of the contract. If it was not, then Brickdale's figures did not compare like with like. Equally serious was Marshall's argument that any annual losses incurred by the Registry on its Land Transfer Act business should be included. The Registry was required to balance its books, but on the basis that it must within forty years recover the cost of its building and the freehold land on which it had been erected.[107] Its annual figures looked sound, but only because of a cross-subsidy from profits on its Middlesex Deeds Registry business.[108] Brickdale replied feebly that Marshall's was an ingenious argument;[109] he never did shake off the Treasury incubus.

Nowhere was the limited nature of the inquiry better demonstrated, or its clear adversarial nature. What the evidence showed was that faced either with superior bargaining power, or with price competition between themselves, solicitors' conveyancing charges already fell significantly below the Remuneration Order's scale.[110] Further, even if Brickdale were right that a solicitor was unnecessary for dealing with the document of transfer, it was also clear from the evidence that there was much more to even a simple sale than that. Pre-transfer contracts were treated as the norm, with their accompanying requisitions.[111] Though the anarchy of local government charges

---

[106] Second Report, qq. 6723 ff., esp. 6759–63; 11789 ff., 12323–51.

[107] First Report, qq. 933–5.

[108] See the evidence of Sir George Murray, Permanent Secretary to the Treasury, Second Report, qq. 4202 ff.; for the cross-subsidy see qq. 4262–8. Note too his insistence that the benefits of title registration were private not public, qq. 4237–43.

[109] Second Report, p. 550 (reply to Marshall).

[110] Materials in n. 105 above; Second Report, qq. 2824 (banks), 2862 (property dealer), 3323 (builder), 6081 (Leeds building societies), 8807 (breweries); and see 3690 and 5269 for the provision of free or nearly-free conveyancing by some institutions. Representatives of building societies were generally hostile to the Registry; for a good example see John Rogers, qq. 6388 ff., and Brickdale's blustering reply at p. 549.

[111] Second Report, q. 10136 (Beale, for The Law Society.)

secured on land had been reduced by the requirement that they be registered under the Land Charges Act 1888, those registers still needed to be searched on a purchase, and local inquiries still had to be made to discover local improvement charges immune from registration.[112] So in practice solicitors would remain necessary.[113] And it should be remembered that their proposed ouster may have originated not as an ideological good in itself, but as a by-product of Treasury unwillingness to subsidize the Land Registry's charges. So perhaps in order to cut conveyancing costs the Remuneration Order's scale fees should simply be reduced? Alternatively perhaps the scale itself should be abolished, leaving solicitors to compete among themselves? This latter course would no doubt need supplementing by prohibitions on anti-competitive rate-fixing by law societies. But it suited neither side to pursue such possibilities; neither solicitors nor the Registrar would seriously consider a link between costs and the market.[114] When it was put to Brickdale that some such solution might be what was needed he was at first unable to provide *any* answer, and had to be prompted by Edward Wood to say that registration would be a superior solution because it offered greater security of title.[115] It is evident, however, that he did not learn this lesson, because not long afterwards he again committed himself to the view that the 'whole object' of registration was the saving of costs, for which he was upbraided by S. O. Buckmaster, KC.[116] Brickdale's obsession with beating the solicitors at the figures game then enabled Buckmaster to score another major point, by asserting that since the Commission's inquiry was only into the extension of the existing system, with its emphasis on possessory title, the Registrar's claims that future dealings in absolute titles would be very cheap were merely 'hypothetical'.[117] The significance of that argument was

[112] T. Cyprian Williams, *The Law of Vendor and Purchaser* (2nd edn., 1910), 588–93, 597–600; Second Report, para. 41.

[113] First Report, qq. 1553–1613; Second Report, qq. 12300 ff.; and cf. Marshall, ibid., qq. 6759 ff. See Second Report, para. 41, on local land charges.

[114] Second Report, qq. 6437, 7838, 10813.

[115] Ibid., qq. 11798 ff.; cf. 1552.

[116] Ibid., q. 11927; in a final outburst to the Commission Brickdale attacked the solicitors' monopoly (qq. 12678 ff.), but in terms that contradicted his argument that his trust of solicitors justified his award of absolute title upon their certifying that a title was sound, as St Aldwyn quickly noted (qq. 12690–5).

[117] Ibid., qq. 12254 ff.

underlined in acid by Philip Gregory, the barrister on the Rules Committee:

Some time or other you will explain where you get from the Act of 1875 this ultimate aspiration of absolute title everywhere?
Brickdale: With submission, I should have thought it was to be found in every line.
Gregory: I have looked for it in vain.[118]

The second major argument was whether the 1897 Act could cope with complexity, and, if so, whether it could do it well enough to make solicitors otiose.[119] Here too Brickdale ran into serious trouble. First the 'simple' forms in his book were demonstrated to be replete with technical language. He replied that these were not the *really* simple forms, but versions of them meant for solicitors. So he produced the forms meant for laypersons, which indeed omitted the technical language. But it was then demonstrated that the omissions made a substantive difference to purchasers, particularly in depriving them of the protection offered by the general law through covenants for title, which Brickdale had to concede.[120] Further, there were intractable problems in providing simple forms for transactions whose essence depended upon precise documentary terms. Mortgages, for example, were just as long and complicated in their registered form as in ordinary deeds.[121] So were leases. Brickdale's claim that laypersons could none the less conduct such transactions without professional help was just ridiculed by members of the Commission.[122] Brickdale would no doubt like to have replied that his officials would help where they could, but this too raised problems. When it was pointed out

[118] Ibid., qq. 12263–4.
[119] Second Report, *passim*?: Marshall on mineral rights (qq. 6723 ff.), Inskip generally (qq. 7079 ff.—and note how much of his evidence was used by the Commissioners in their final examination of Brickdale), Carslake on underground railways (qq. 7856 ff.) and Bevir on commercial mortgages (qq. 8387 ff.) are the most interesting. Problems with boundaries, easements, positive and restrictive covenants, and with building schemes, were raised several times: n. 139 below.
[120] First Report, qq. 736 ff. The passage from q. 611 to about q. 850 demonstrates the Commissioners' difficulties with Brickdale's grand claims; note his concession at q. 783 that he was out of touch with contemporary unregistered conveyancing, and compare ibid., q. 1180 and Second Report, q. 10550.
[121] First Report, q. 1090; Second Report, qq. 8387 ff. (Bevir).
[122] e.g. ibid., q. 12300 (St Aldwyn), and see generally qq. 12300–51.

that the complexity of the system was such that the Registry had been so bombarded with requests for assistance that a fee of 5s. had been introduced for approving draft transfers, Brickdale's reply was to deny that the Registry 'ever gives advice'.[123] However, 'you would be surprised . . . how much of [my] time is spent in getting people out of difficulties, or in deciding not to raise difficulties where technical rules have been violated.'[124] No doubt; but to extend the scheme would necessitate delegating the discretion, which raised problems of constitutional law.[125] And even if it were delegated, could junior officials be trusted to exercise it well?[126] In one case where a complicated settlement gave rise to problems, the landowner had resorted to counsel, who succeeded in changing the Registry's collective mind. Brickdale's response was to blame the landowner for dealing with his junior officials, rather than taking the problem to him personally in the first place. After all, it was the first time that that legal point had arisen and juniors could hardly be expected to have seen its subtleties.[127] He did not say how the landowner could have known this, or why he should have to.

The picture was complicated by evidence of a localism apparently unexpected.[128] Preferences for particular legal forms still varied markedly from place to place. They often concerned such important business transactions as financing and completing new building developments, and could reach extraordinary complexity yet remain largely unknown outside their particular locality. One example was so difficult for the Commission to understand that Viscount St Aldwyn was moved to complain that perhaps such complexity should simply not be allowed.[129] But this was to miss the point, which was that in all these examples local lawyers and local businessmen were locked together in symbiotic relationships; it was not a question of

[123] Ibid., p. 579 in reply to qq. 10912–13.
[124] Ibid., q. 12485 (Lord Faber, 'I am glad to find that there is something, after all, more powerful than the rule').
[125] e.g. Buckmaster, First Report, qq. 1290 ff.
[126] e.g. First Report, qq. 1900–5. Note Brickdale's emphasis on executive discretion (Second Report, q. 12475) and Cherry's on rule-making discretion (ibid., q. 7221).
[127] Second Report, p. 528, in reply to q. 10926 ff.
[128] e.g. Second Report, qq. 6607 ff. (Sunderland), 7455 ff. (Manchester).
[129] Ibid., q. 8996.

lawyers dictating forms to businessmen, more that, in the way things had developed in that area, all participants had come to accept a particular way of doing things which all regarded as well suited to their needs. Local pride in local methods frequently led participants to suggest their national adoption, complexity notwithstanding. Yet land registration schemes, or simplification schemes for that matter, were inevitably based upon generalized notions of typical transactions, London based. Part of the opposition they aroused was thus opposition to standardization and to London. Part of the continuing need for solicitors was as intermediaries between different parts of the country, their professional organization providing a system for mediating between regions.

In dealing with this sort of problem the Commission was handicapped by lack of an accepted set of political responses to commercial complexity. Its parallel, the complexity of family settlements, was easy enough: the Commission was against it. Indeed, its moments of most confident exasperation all came in that context, particularly when they could be combined with fulminating against some such symbol as the Statute of Uses.[130] It was not just that commercial complexity left it rather nonplussed, it was also that solutions acceptable to family wealth seemed less so when applied to commercial wealth, even when they were analytically identical situations. The limitations of Brickdale's utilitarian rationalism were vividly illustrated when he compared the problems of commercial companies with those of settlements.[131] Where a settlement existed, a purchaser under the traditional system of conveyancing had to satisfy himself that the limited owner purporting to deal with the land had legal power to do so, whether conferred by statute or by the settlement deed. The registration system, however, could shift the risk from the purchaser to the other persons interested under the settlement, making the distribution of powers a matter of only internal interest. This was done by making the register conclusive, protecting those others by whatever cautions and restrictions they or the registered proprietor chose to enter. Could not the same be done for companies, asked

---

[130] e.g. ibid., pp. 49, 53.   [131] Ibid., qq. 11613 ff.

Brickdale? At the moment he had to check the directors' powers on each transaction, a tedious and time-consuming task which he would like to shed. Why not draw the analogy with trusts, regard the distribution of powers as an internal matter only, and encourage shareholders to protect themselves with the 'regular' devices available for beneficiaries? Lord Faber, a banker, was immediately hostile—such a suggestion he thought clearly contrary to the interests of shareholders. Viscount St Aldwyn could not accept the analogy at all—'you cannot surely consider a company in this matter on the same footing as a private person?', he asked Brickdale, who withdrew as gracefully as he could.

There were three sorts of answer to the conundrum of complexity, each with disadvantages. First, forms could be kept simple, but proliferated so that in combination they could be used for any dealing, no matter how complex. Brickdale sometimes suggested this, but was met by two criticisms: that multiple forms meant multiple expenses, and that everything could be got into a single deed in the unregistered system. Secondly, where legal consequences turned on precise words in consensual transactions, the actual text should become part of the register, for example, in the cases of restrictive covenants, leases, mortgages, and settlements. But nobody then could dispense with a solicitor. Thirdly, the actual texts should remain behind the register, the interests created by them to be protected by entries prohibiting dealings save with the Registrar's approval (i.e. restrictions), thus enabling the Registrar to combine the function of solicitor and judge. Brickdale was obviously attracted by this, but the Commission was unconvinced. The constitutional problems worried them, as did the difficulties of reconciling such a broad discretion with the problems of bureaucratic hierarchy inherent in any large organization.[132] All this undermined Brickdale's major claim, that the Registry could provide a cheaper alternative to solicitors in all forms of land transactions, thereby eliminating the legal middlemen to the greater good of everyone else.

[132] See nn. 125, 126 above, and Second Report, para. 53, p. 28.

2.4.   There was no doubt that several of the solicitors' complaints were based upon ignorance, misunderstanding, and sometimes sheer perversity.[133] The Commission itself saw Rubinstein in action, having to treat him very roughly to get him to stick to the point.[134] More damagingly for his credit, evidence was also received from the Birkbeck Building Society, whose solicitor he was, which though adduced to show how expensive registered transactions were, in fact showed Rubinstein to be overcharging on a grand scale.[135] Perversity was not confined to solicitors. A complaint by the Lincoln's Inn conveyancer Charles Sweet was shown to result from his overlooking a most obvious clerical error in his client's transcription of a Registry precedent.[136] Brickdale's comment that 'the trouble seems therefore to have been mainly due to the witness's unfortunate readiness to impute want of common sense to the department' is a suitable epitaph for many more than Sweet. Poor Sweet: not only was he so easily flattened on that example, but many of his suggestions for reform turned out to be embodied in the Rules already. And his credit took a severe jolt when, following his obvious inability to see that the fact that very few simple titles came his way in Lincoln's Inn might predispose him to a pessimistic view of registered conveyancing, he answered 'yes' to the question, 'do you mean to suggest that an owner not having a professional qualification should be prevented from doing his own business for himself?' Unlike his peers, Cherry and Underhill, who also had their sticky moments on their first examination by the Commission, Sweet was not invited back to redeem himself, having to make do with elaborating his suggestions through the pages of the *Law Quarterly Review*.[137]

---

[133] e.g. J. A. Burrell (Second Report, qq. 4704 ff.) and T. C. McKenzie (ibid., qq. 6607 ff.) clearly did not know the Rules; and see Brickdale's reply in Appendix 1. There was badly muddled evidence from C. F. J. Jennings, solicitor and member of the City of London's Common Council, ibid., qq. 7284 ff. Brickdale's comment that many solicitors thought of the register last when they should have thought of it first (p. 565) was apt.

[134] Second Report, qq. 4925 ff., 5561 ff. His complaint of unfair treatment to the *Solicitors' Journal* was brushed aside, (1910–11) 55 *Sol. Jo.* 418. The essence of his evidence was an unwillingness to get to grips with a new system.

[135] Second Report, qq. 5759 ff. and p. 547; and see evidence of George Bishop, Secretary of the Woolwich Equitable Building Society, ibid., qq. 4537 ff.

[136] Ibid., qq. 3873 ff.; Brickdale at p. 540.

[137] (1912) 28 *LQR* 6.

This could be prolonged by many further examples. But equally many were the complaints which the Commission thought fully justified. Moreover, disturbingly many of them went to the very essence of registration and, alarmingly, in several cases Brickdale seemed utterly unable to appreciate this. The Commission agreed with the barristers that mortgages were a problem.[138] Boundaries were a major difficulty, so were collateral rights possessed by registered proprietors, easements, for example, or the benefit of restrictive covenants.[139] Unless they could be guaranteed, the register would be incomplete, even positively misleading. But how could they be guaranteed unless the Registrar somehow had jurisdiction over the neighbouring land? Even then, was it right that an executive figure should have such a judicial power? Even Brickdale had to admit that the Rule carrying the benefit of easements to transferees of registered land was 'a gloss on the Act'.[140]

It must have been very damaging to Brickdale's credit that he seemed unable to appreciate so many of the subtle and complicated difficulties unearthed by solicitors. Just because some solicitors made foolish complaints or were ignorant of the Rules, it did not follow that all the problems could be attributed to professional ineptitude. Yet Brickdale certainly gave the impression that he did. Of ninety-one complaints presented on behalf of The Law Society with enough detail to allow identification in the Registry's records, forty-nine he claimed 'really show no defect in the system at all, but a good deal to be desired in some of those who do business with the Registry'.[141] He selected a few of these by way of illustration in his final oral evidence to the Commission. The barristers, Buckmaster and Gregory in

---

[138] Second Report, pp. 14, 38; cf. Elphinstone, ibid., q. 4458; Williams, qq. 10430 ff., *passim*.

[139] Boundaries: First Report, qq. 337–63, 1926 ff.; Second Report, qq. 11280 ff., 11520. Rights generally: Second Report, qq. 11869–70 (Buckmaster). Easements: Second Report, pp. 16, 39; First Report, qq. 1953 ff.; Second Report, qq. 10545 ff. (Williams), 12062–71. Covenants: First Report, qq. 611–29; Second Report, q. 4475 (Elphinstone, and see Brickdale's acceptance in Appendix 1), 10545 ff. (Williams), 11597.

[140] Second Report, qq. 1953–4; his Rule was belatedly legitimized in *Celsteel* v. *Alton House* [1985] 2 All ER 562. See too his extra-legal registration of limited owners as proprietors: First Report, qq. 393, 2092a ff.

[141] Second Report, pp. 563 ff.

particular, went through them slowly, making him explain
every detail so that they understood. Then they turned and
looked at them from the complainants' point of view, saw that
there were in fact points of substance, and tried to get Brickdale
to do the same. Eventually they succeeded, with the result that
at least four of his own selected best cases were indeed found
to show defects in the system.[142] Further, Brickdale's assertion
that complaints based upon unfamiliarity with the system were
inadmissible met with little favour from the barrister members.
Things would improve, he thought, as people learnt what they
had to do.[143] 'That may be,' replied Gregory, 'but the point is
that you are trying to make out that this is an improved system
of conveyancing. On the unregistered system no difficulty could
have arisen . . .'. 'You cannot work a system if people will not
exercise reasonable diligence,' said Brickdale. 'It is an extraordinarily difficult and subtle point, and I am not surprised at
any solicitor or counsel missing it . . .', returned Gregory, with
whom Buckmaster agreed.[144]

Bankers and building societies were at best equivocal and
more often hostile to extension of the system.[145] One of London's best-known builders gave evidence against the Registry.[146] The *coup de grâce* came when the Commission realized
that it had had rather little evidence in favour of extension from
landowners or land-dealers, the 'shrewd businessmen' who so
impressed Buckmaster.[147] So the Commission advertised for
them to come forward; but only one person did. Similarly with
County Councils, where was their evidence in favour of extension? Again an advertisement, and Lord St Aldwyn attended
his own County Council when they discussed whether to
reply.[148] The Commission, he said, would regard failure to
respond as a sign that extension was not wanted. There was no
response, from that or any other council.

---

[142] Ibid., qq. 11171–320.

[143] Ibid., qq. 11346–7.

[144] Ibid., qq. 11309–10.

[145] Of the bankers, only Knowles (First Report, qq. 2745 ff.) was in favour.
Brickdale acknowledged lack of building society support, ibid., q. 912.

[146] Willett, Second Report, qq. 8570 ff.

[147] (1908–9) 53 *Sol. Jo.* 687, (1909) 8 PD (5th ser.) 268; Buckmaster, Second
Report, q. 12042, and cf. qq. 12012 ff.

[148] (1909–10) 54 *Sol. Jo.* 23.

In this way Brickdale lost his contest with the Commission. But so too did the law societies, whose arguments proved too much. If, suspending doubts that the whole story had been told, conveyancing really was as cheap as all that, should not the official scale be reduced, and reduced substantially? Asked this question directly, solicitors either parried it or said 'no', except for the representative from Bristol, who did his standing with the Commission good by agreeing that a reduction would be justified—but only at the bottom end of the scale.[149] Brickdale's dismissive comment on their assimilation scheme, 'it does not enable an ordinary man to do his own work in any case, and I cannot see that it would perceptibly reduce costs or delays',[150] was never answered, nor was there any response to his challenge to the solicitors to produce figures to prove him wrong. Further, if simplification worked for traditional conveyancing, so would it work for registered conveyancing, and Brickdale's parting shot to the Commission invited them to adopt such a scheme expressly for the purpose of easing the extension of his system.[151]

2.5. Though the Commissioners' bark in cross-examination was worse than the bite of their Report, which was aptly described as the work of 'Mr Facing Both Ways',[152] their disregard for Brickdale's expansionist claims and the law societies' exaggerated reactions is apparent on every page. It was duly noted that some lay witnesses had spoken well of the Registry, but they 'were mostly landowners desirous of selling or leasing their land for building, and therefore represented by no means a large proportion of land owners in the country'.[153] Since 'comparatively few purchasers of land contemplate dealing with their property in the early future',[154] the present high cost of registering possessory title was not outweighed by possible savings on future dealings after the possessory title

---

[149] See n. 114 above; Bristol: Inskip, Second Report, qq. 7104 ff. (obit., (1909–10) 54 *Sol. Jo.* 15).

[150] First Report, q. 1367; cf. Second Report, pp. 553–4 (Brickdale on Cherry).

[151] Second Report, qq. 12394 ff., 12719a; cf. First Report, q. 1369.

[152] (1910–11) 55 *Sol. Jo.* 263.

[153] Second Report, p. 2.

[154] Ibid., p. 29.

had matured into absolute title. Given the improvements in traditional conveyancing since 1882, 'it is not too much to say that up to the present time the effect of Compulsory Registration with Possessory Title in London has been to place a purchaser there at a disadvantage as compared with a purchaser elsewhere'.[155] 'But the principle of transferring the ownership of land through the medium of a Registry of title has been so long accepted by Parliament that those who opposed it devoted themselves mainly to criticisms of the mode in which it is applied by the existing system.'[156] And since the Commission also approved of the theory of registration, they were not going to recommend repeal. So there should be an expansion of absolute title, even though 'the evidence taken by us teems with proof of what may be an unreasonable, but is a thoroughly English, dislike of the control by a public department of the procedure to be followed in transfers or other dealings with land, which is denounced as "officialism"'.[157]

Note two things about their approach. First, a reduced formulation of registration is used—it is only about 'the transfer of ownership'. Secondly, the mass of opinion from country solicitors in favour of repeal is ignored; they are simply excluded from 'those who opposed it'. This was quite deliberate; they had produced a lot of evidence, 'but as very few of them had any experience of the Acts, it does not throw much light on the working of the system'. [158] The early pages of the Report are also notable for the descriptions of those who appeared before the Commission: typically they are 'witnesses', whom 'we examined'. The barristers fared quite differently: 'we were fortunate in obtaining the assistance of eminent counsel who both criticised the existing system of Land Registry and gave evidence as to various schemes now current for amending the Law of Real Property . . .'.[159] Two, Cherry and Cyprian Williams, appeared on behalf of The Law Society; five others were invited by the Commission itself. Clearly they were regarded as neutral experts, with no axes to grind, whose views were to be

---

[155] Ibid., p. 30.
[156] Ibid., p. 26; a disingenuous comment in light of the terms of reference.
[157] Ibid., p. 26.
[158] Ibid., p. 3.
[159] Ibid., p. 3.

taken seriously. In contrast to the country solicitors whose lack of direct experience was held against them, the opinions of Arthur Underhill, Benjamin Cherry, Cyprian Williams, and the others on purely hypothetical problems were accepted almost without demur.

All these counsel accepted the theory of registration, all thought the present system inadequate, all thought that it could be made to work, but they differed greatly as to how. Of them all, it was Underhill's 'exceedingly valuable suggestions' about settlements and mortgages that made most impression.[160] But there is a problem here, for though everyone was agreed that mortgages had already created serious difficulties, those supposed to be attributable to settlements were simply theoretical— very little settled land had yet come on the register, and there had been no problems with that which had. On the other hand the Settled Land Act had caused serious difficulties in the general law, particularly where several settlements operated together in respect of the same land, so that in addition to the statutory powers vested in the appropriate person there could be extended powers vested in several others: the notorious 'compound settlement'. Brickdale protested that such problems should not yet be treated as real, and that when it came to the point he would be able to use his discretion sensibly to reach acceptable answers as he had always done with settlements in the past.[161] But though the Commission paid high tribute to Brickdale's ability and dedication it was not inclined to rely on the Registrar's discretion. Lesser men than he might run the system in future.[162]

Even so, such a policy choice does not explain the readiness with which the barristers' hypothetical cases were transmuted into present problems. Not only was it true, we are told, that 'in fact the registration of the tenant for life [as registered proprietor] interferes with the due operation of the Settlement',[163] but also that 'the cheap and easy working of the existing system of Registry of Title is gravely impeded by causes

---

[160] Ibid., p. 35.
[161] Ibid., p. 538, q. 1164 and cf. qq. 12382 ff., 12992*a* ff.
[162] Ibid., p. 28.
[163] Ibid., p. 36.

arising from [the differences between real and personal prop-
erty], especially through complicated settlements by way of
uses . . .'.[164] There was no evidence whatsoever for either of
these statements of fact, both are based simply upon predictions
by the barristers, and by Underhill in particular. His solution
was to register the trustees of a settlement as proprietors, but
only if they had the fee simple; if nobody had the fee simple
the land should have no registered proprietor, instead simply
being recorded as subject to a settlement.[165] As Brickdale noted,
this was a reversion to the 1862 scheme, being essentially a
hybrid of title and deeds registration.[166] Underhill's similar
suggestion for mortgages was also accepted, that they be done
off the register, merely taking priority from date of registration.[167] And so with easements, they 'do not appear to be fit
subjects for registration at all', and thus should bind and be
created just as under the traditional system.[168] Finally, there
seemed no point to the Commission in noting on the land
register 'land charges', statutory charges on land to recoup
money spent or loaned by public authorities for various purposes, since they bound transferees anyway.[169] Prospective
purchasers should search the particular statutory registers for
them. What all this amounted to was a register that would often
operate just to transfer title. Registration was to be an adjunct
to existing professional structure.

The Report's final chapter concerned reform of real property
law, which really meant doing something about settlements.
For many years The Law Society's modest Settled Land Bill had
been blocked in Parliament, notwithstanding that it sought only
to remedy obvious anomalies. While the Commission regretted
such lack of progress, it noted that

(1) The *status quo* is described as intolerable to those who deal with
settled estates. [Something of an exaggeration of the evidence received]

(2) The whole difficulty is the product of legislation for facilitating
sales of Settled Land.

(3) Fresh legislation is required to sweep it away. That an enabling
statute can give rise to such trouble points to something radically

---

[164] Ibid., p. 52.
[166] Ibid., pp. 539, 545.
[168] Ibid., pp. 39–40.

[165] Ibid., qq. 5364 ff.
[167] Ibid., p. 38.
[169] Ibid., p. 41.

wrong in the law concerning settled land and raises the question whether such remedial legislation is all that is needed.[170]

The alternative views, that perhaps the Settled Land Act was not a very good piece of legislation, or that Halsbury's amendments in 1888 would have met the point, were not even raised. The Commission clearly sympathized with Williams and those like him who believed that the time had come for a major rethink. Was it to start with a clean sheet as Williams wanted?[171] Or should instead a more modest assimilation scheme like Wolstenholme's be tried? The Commission would not say. Wolstenholme's bill for The Law Society, drafted in 1896 and re-presented now by Cherry, tackled the settlements problem by vesting the fee simple in the appropriate limited owner.[172] But though the Commission noted Brickdale's opinion that this was insignificant and inappropriate as an *alternative* to registration, it concluded that 'thus Mr Underhill expressed the view that without some such scheme registration of title could never be made simple, cheap, speedy and satisfactory'.[173] Once again we see the transformation of prediction into fact, and also we see the Commission glossing over the barristers' divisions, for Underhill would have vested the fee in the trustees of the settlement.

Thence the Commission turned to the more ambitious schemes propounded severally by Cyprian Williams and J. W. Hills, MP, a solicitor who had once favoured registration but now believed that structural reform must precede it.[174] But they did little more than describe them, saving that a far more complete inquiry would be needed before such extensive changes were made. They ended vigorously, but obscurely to anyone outside the charmed circle:

---

[170] Ibid., p. 49.

[171] Ibid., qq. 10430 ff., esp. 10570–6.

[172] Conveyancing Bill 1897, (1897) HLP iii. 99, discussed at Second Report, q. 6784 and index entries under 'Wolstenholme'. His preference for vesting the fee simple in the limited owner rather than in trustees was discussed at qq. 7228–66. Note especially Cherry's dissent from Williams's fresh-start assimilation proposal.

[173] Ibid., p. 52

[174] For Williams see n. 171 above. John Waller Hills was elected to The Law Society Council as a reformist in 1907 ((1906–7) 51 *Sol. Jo.* 665, 675). He had a long political career.

we may observe that land held for a term of 999 years at a peppercorn rent is, as the law stands, Personal Property: and the mere extension of this principle to land held in fee would by itself abolish nearly the whole of the artificial distinctions between Real Estate and Personal Estate which have been created by Act of Parliament and ancient custom with regard to methods of transfer and descent.[175]

Mr Justice Stephen would have recognized that.[176]

2.6.   What are we to make of all this? On the major issue the Commission was unambiguous: there was no lay demand for registration, its advantages had not yet been demonstrated, the existing system needed amendment and a further period of trial before it stood 'a reasonable chance of obtaining that public appreciation and support without which it could not be made compulsory in other parts of the country'.[177] The solicitors could breathe again. The Commission's subtext was also clear. Registration is here to stay, but cannot, and probably should not, be made so simple that solicitors can be eliminated—so they should stop making such a song and dance about it all. By the same token Brickdale's simple nostrums for the extension of the system are unacceptable, both because they are based upon the false premiss that everyone can act for himself and because of his excessive reliance on official discretion. Further incremental changes should be tried and tested before the system is extended. Yet there are real systemic difficulties at present, as demonstrated by the neutral and learned barristers' evidence. They should be encouraged to produce schemes to irradicate these structural faults, which should then be tested themselves. In due course we may get it right, but we cannot expect to do so quickly, and we certainly will not do so for as long as Registrar and Law Society remain locked into their present territorial dispute.

Thus the Commission passed the initiative from the major protagonists of recent years, the Registrar and the law societies, and towards the conveyancing barristers. It was their analysis of the Land Transfer Acts, their conception of what amounted

[175] Second Report, p. 53.
[176] See above, pp. 173–4.
[177] Second Report, p. 30.

to a 'problem', their schemes for reform that captured the Commission. Avner Offer is inclined to view them simply as mercenaries for The Law Society, paid advocates against the Registrar in the battle for economic survival. This is a misreading. It is impossible to read their detailed evidence and believe this. They all thought that registration could be made to work, they were all anxious that it should be their own suggestions that should prove it. Several of them presented bills to that end, and showed alacrity in modifying them to meet the Commissioners' initial criticisms. That that might first involve structural reform of real property law was so much the better—Cherry and Sweet each proffered his own version of Wolstenholme's bill. Williams, Underhill, and some of the others each came clutching his own, sometimes in the alternative. Each bill reflected a different conception of what was required: Underhill and Sweet produced bills descending to minute detail on small points, casting the shape of the law around difficult and rare problems; Williams the academic started from basics with a grand scheme for assimilation. Of course Cherry and Williams were retained by The Law Society to say all this in the solicitors' economic interest. Sweet's bill had been drafted at the instance of The Law Society. But that was because they had already written papers to that effect:[178] they were used by The Law Society because those were their views; they did not hold their views because it suited The Law Society. If they had merely been acting on a brief they would not have disagreed so strongly on what type of reform bill was needed—it would not have been in their clients' interests to put forward such divided counsel. No, the major effect of the Royal Commission on Land Transfer was that control over real property law returned to Lincoln's Inn.

3. Aftermath

Lord Chancellor Loreburn showed no sign of recognizing these features of the Commission's deliberations, indeed, he showed little sign of having read its report and none at all of having

---

[178] See above, nn. 47, 50.

even glanced at its published evidence. In a brief debate initiated by Halsbury in the Lords,[179] Loreburn once again blamed solicitors' self-interest entirely for all the difficulties the Registry had faced, saying that their 'criticisms, misleading to the ignorant public, were so rife that it was thought desirable to appoint a Royal Commission . . .'. Now that that was over, the main job of extending the system could be continued. Lord Halsbury agreed whole-heartedly with both his diagnosis and his prescription. Viscount Haldane did not. While conceding that self-interest had caused some opposition to change, 'there are many eminent legal practitioners who have given the matter careful consideration, and while most desirous to do the best in the public interest are greatly impressed by the difficulties surrounding the subject . . . there has been a good deal of legitimate criticism about the first fruits of the new system.' Dr Offer sees this as evidence of Haldane's impending betrayal of the cause: he 'alone stood up to defend the solicitors against an all-party attack'.[180] Even if he had stood alone this would be an exaggeration—repetition of old canards from Halsbury and Loreburn scarcely constitutes an 'all-party' anything. But he was *not* alone. He was joined by Viscount St Aldwyn himself, who supported everything Haldane had said. Moreover, St Aldwyn conceded the costs argument by saying that there should be a public subsidy to the Registry, a subsidy that might be made palatable to the government by linking the Registry to the Land Valuation Department, which evaluated tax liabilities under the Finance Act 1910, enabling some of the Registry's costs to be charged to the latter department. St Aldwyn also accepted that the Commission had become a lawyers' inquiry. 'If the Commission has had any success,' he said, 'it is really due to the never-failing attention which was paid to the subject by the five legal gentlemen, four barristers and one solicitor— gentlemen of the highest experience and standing in their profession—who sat on the Commission . . .'.

But St Aldwyn's 'if' was significant, and seemingly unsatis- fied. During the Commission's deliberations Brickdale had approached Loreburn and Lloyd George directly to urge the

---

[179] (1911) 9 HLD 535–66.
[180] *Property and Politics, 1870–1914*, 77; (1977) 40 *MLR* 505, 509.

creation of a grand Domesday Office, and he had been accepted.[181] The political link, though it is not easy to assess its strength, was that land taxation played a central role in Lloyd George's budgetary plans at that time, that that necessitated systematic land valuation, and that a title register, a valuation, and a cadaster seemed to merge into one another as instruments of the proposed new central control over land.[182] Lloyd George's public explanations of the relation were bafflingly obscure,[183] and politically it was the valuation element that was paramount, not the registration of titles.

Even though by 1911 the land taxation element in Lloyd George's plans had been reduced, enough of it remained for law societies to busy themselves producing alternative plans for minimalist registries to do the political job without impinging upon the skilled work of mediating land transfers; even deeds registries might suffice.[184] But to no avail. The Law Society failed to persuade Loreburn that there should be no extension of registration until an amended system had had a further trial, or that there should be a parallel trial of traditional conveyancing under a statute simplifying the substantive law.[185] Senior posts in the Land Registry were increased from two to seven in anticipation of the expansion.[186] Then Loreburn resigned, ill and out of sorts with most of his Cabinet colleagues.[187] He was succeeded by Haldane, fresh from reforming the Army, who

[181] Ibid. 76 and 508 respectively.

[182] For the politics of the land question 1909–14 I have relied on Bruce K. Murray, *The People's Budget, 1909–10* (1980), Bentley B. Gilbert, 'David Lloyd George: The Reform of British Land-Holding and the Budget of 1914', (1978) 21 *Hist. Jo.* 117 and *David Lloyd George: A Political Life* (1987), H. V. Emy, *Liberals, Radicals and Social Politics, 1892–1914* (1973), and Peter Rowland, *The Last Liberal Governments* (1971).

[183] e.g. (1909) 8 PD (5th ser.) 21, 1016, 2049, 2068, 2084, 2150.

[184] (1910–11) 55 *Sol. Jo.* 357, 763, 783, 787; (1911–12) 56 *Sol. Jo.* 25, 48, 67, 101, 807, 817, 831, 840; (1912–13) 57 *Sol. Jo.* 393 (Birmingham and Sheffield), 628. Of the assimilation schemes, T. C. Williams's fresh start was the clear favourite.

[185] Avner Offer, (1977) 40 *MLR* 505, 510; (1911–12) 56 *Sol. Jo.* 255, 475, 625, 636; (1912–13) 57 *Sol. Jo.* 393 (Sheffield ILS). Brickdale's aggressive advocacy was renewed, ibid. 545, 567, 569, drawing the usual pained Law Society response, ibid. 654.

[186] Sixth Report of the Royal Commission on the Civil Service, (1914–16) HCP xii. 1, q. 54669.

[187] Stephen Koss, *Lord Haldane: Scapegoat for Liberalism* (1969), 95–6; R. F. V. Heuston, *Lives of the Lord Chancellors, 1885–1940* (1964), 165–8.

dropped Loreburn's plans and did instead what the Royal Commission had recommended. Brickdale would get all his amendments, some of them as the Commission had suggested but others showing more sympathy for the spirit of the registered system. But he would get no extension until after a further trial. Meanwhile there would be a general measure of simplification and assimilation, as The Law Society had tepidly wanted and as Lincoln's Inn had prescribed, to be followed by a thorough review and consolidation of existing law.

For Dr Offer,

the evidence which explains this *volte face* is circumstantial and cumulative, but is nevertheless quite clear. The policy can be explained in terms of a personal and political rivalry with Loreburn and Halsbury and of loyalty to his professional circle. He let these loyalties overcome his normal admiration for German efficiency.[188]

Since the basis of the Domesday plan would have been the 1897 Act with its manifold defects rather than any German registration scheme, that last remark is well off target. Further, there is no evidence whatsoever that Haldane and Loreburn's mutual dislike was causative.[189] We are left with 'professional loyalties'. I suspect that Dr Offer is thinking of the professions' financial good health, though he does not elaborate. I doubt that, but I agree with the general point. Alone, however, it would not have been enough. Haldane was far closer to central Liberal policy-making than Loreburn had ever been, but for him to be able to force through a change of direction on this point argues either a considerable power or, in my view far more likely, that the issue was politically unimportant. Its only coherent link with Lloyd George's plan had been through his land taxes, but by 1913 even he accepted that these were counter-productive and mistaken. The Liberal land reforms projected in 1913 and

---

[188] (1977) 40 *MLR* 505, 511. The undated 'Domesday Office' file at PRO LAR1/107 covers this period, 1910–11.

[189] The hope expressed in (1977) 40 *MLR* 505 n. 39 was not fulfilled in *Property and Politics*. There is no evidence that Haldane's rivalry with Reid was 'exacerbated' by Reid's promotion to the woolsack ahead of Haldane in 1905—for which Haldane had only himself and perhaps Asquith to blame—or that Haldane thought Loreburn responsible for it. Dr Offer's reference to Heuston, n. 187 above, cannot carry his point. For 1905 see Heuston, *Lives*, 141–4. 197–200; Koss, *Lord Haldane*, 37, and also his *Asquith* (1976), 73.

1914, a synthesis of rival proposals from Haldane and Lloyd George, were directed at ownership and management, not at the market. They concerned compulsory purchase, fixity of tenure, town planning, and, above all, improving housing quality and raising agricultural wages in a war on working-class poverty. Brickdale's concerns look desperately old-fashioned in that company.

There is another element in the analysis, 'law'. Haldane was not just a property lawyer by training but he also believed in law as an entity and law reform as an important activity. In 1903 he had been enlisted into the Webbs' intellectual club, the Co-efficients, the nucleus they hoped of a new political party. Notwithstanding his writing on social policy and Liberal theory, his allotted area was law.[190] In 1918 he chaired a committee on the Machinery of Government whose report, in a chapter reputedly written by himself, advocated a Ministry of Justice, primarily so that expert lawyers could be employed to promote law reform and to study 'the development of the subject at home and abroad'.[191] The proposal was enthusiastically endorsed by The Law Society, who had advocated it on that very ground, but sunk by the Whitehall establishment, which did not want to see the lawyers encamped in their territory. If I am right that the registration question had once again lost its political importance, becoming one of law, then for Haldane to turn it over to the profession was absolutely consistent. He had a professional loyalty of a wider kind than Dr Offer recognizes; 'professional perception' might capture it better. The issue was land law; and land lawyers were to control it.

[190] L. S. Amery, *My Political Life*, i (1953), 223–4.
[191] *Report of the Machinery of Government Committee*, Cd. 9230, (1918) HCP xii. 1, esp. 64, 74. Beatrice Webb was a member. See Gavin Drewry, 'Lord Haldane's Ministry of Justice', (1983) 61 *Public Administration* 396.

7

Lawyers' Law: The Conveyancing Bills of 1913/14

1. 'A Cautious and Somewhat Conservative Spirit'[1]

1.1. The choice for Haldane lay between Stephen and Wolstenholme. Stephen represented a step towards a unified property-law code, a true assimilation.[2] It could be done directly, by spelling out principles as Cyprian Williams would have liked; or indirectly by deeming realty to be personalty, and leaving the general learning of the profession to draw the right conclusions. Sweet and Underhill had inclined towards this sort of step, the Royal Commission had hinted its approval, and it was Williams's bill that won what favour there was from law societies in the pessimistic days of 1911.[3] Wolstenholme had never supported systematic assimilation,[4] and Benjamin Cherry continued to oppose it after his mentor's death in 1908.[5] But the law of realty, while remaining separate, could be cut back; successive estates could be abolished. Then settlements would have to be created behind trusts. Successive interests would be assimilated to personalty in that sense, the law of trusts forming a buckle between the two major divisions of property law.

'Trusts of personalty' themselves fell into two types. Trusts

---

[1] Haldane, (1913) 14 HLD 1672.

[2] See above, pp. 173–4.

[3] See above, Ch. 6 n. 184; *Memorandum of the Land Transfer Committee of The Law Society on the Lord Chancellor's Conveyancing Bills*, Feb. 1914, 11 *Law Society Gazette* 70.

[4] Wolstenholme was consistent in his advocacy of his own scheme, dismissing the 'leasehold' method of assimilation as politically difficult: Evidence to the Royal Commission on Agriculture, (1881) HCP xvii, q. 55153.

[5] Second Report of the Royal Commission on the Land Transfer Acts, (1911) HCP xxxi, qq. 6782 ff.

of stocks had a mechanism whereby beneficiaries could block dealings with the trust assets by lodging a *distringas* in a company register, whereas with trusts of money they could not. In 1870 Wolstenholme's judgment was against protection through registration:

by common consent of conveyancers, trusts affecting mortage money are not, in properly arranged transactions, allowed to encumber the title to land. Again, in the case of mortgages or debentures issued by railway and other companies, the owner of a partial interest is not registered. To leave the owner of the partial interest unprotected as against the persons in whose name the money is secured, and who is generally chosen by the owners of the partial interests, has become a habit, no inconvenience is felt, and there is no necessity to encumber the register for the purpose of affording a protection which is now waived in many cases where it is available.[6]

He maintained this view before Osborne Morgan's Committee in 1878, fearing the expense of the search. Potential liability would thus be shifted from purchasers to trustees, as was already the case for personalty settlements. Would this not deter prudent men from becoming trustees? 'It is a duty that you have to undertake for your relations; nobody would undertake it if he could avoid it,' replied Wolstenholme bleakly. Perhaps, too, the new system would be less secure than the old, but 'if you want to do away with the expense, you must give up some security'.[7]

By 1894, when he re-presented his plans,[8] there had been two changes. First, his Settled Land Act had vested expanded powers of management in limited owners, including the power of sale; trustees played only a secondary role. So Wolstenholme now proposed that where the Act applied, which was whenever successive interests existed, the fee simple should be vested in the limited owner. Secondly, political expediency had won him round to a *distringas* registry for those trusts of land falling outside the Settled Land Act. But at a time when fear of trustees' default was fuelling the push for a Public Trustee, the gesture

---

[6] Royal Commission on Land Transfer, (1870) HCP xviii, Note of Dissent, p. xlv.

[7] Select Committee on Land Titles and Transfer, (1878) HCP xv. 467, qq. 2449 ff. (quotations from q. 2715).

[8] (1894–5) 39 *Sol. Jo.* 4, 56; and see above p. 199 n.

was not enough. It was only by a whisker that the ILS adopted his bill, several law societies disagreed, and a conveyancing committee of the Bar Council rejected it out of hand.[9] Of the barristers advising the Royal Commission only Cherry supported it, and even then he was equivocal.[10]

Yet Haldane's vote went to Wolstenholme.[11] His White Paper accepted that settlements were a general problem, but rejected the expanded role for trustees that was the inevitable consequence of the out-and-out assimilation schemes.[12] To vest the fee simple in the limited owner would be the 'logical outcome' of the Settled Land Acts.[13] Once this conservative view was accepted the whole of Wolstenholme's package could be, and his 1897 bill could be used as the starting-point for new legislation.[14] Its obvious attraction was that it made quite clear how ordinary conveyancers should in future conduct typical transactions, which was the main purpose of the exercise. Furthermore and as Brickdale had always said, Wolstenholme's bill was registration without a register.[15] By enacting as the conveyancing code for unregistered land a set of principles mirroring so accurately the theory of real property law encoded in the Land Transfer Acts a degree of unity was achieved and, as Haldane argued, the exercise would make lawyers familiar with the concepts in a way that would facilitate the ultimate

[9] See above, Ch. 5 nn. 171 and 172 and accompanying text; General Council of the Bar, *Annual Statement, 1897–98*—on which see Cherry's riposte: B. L. Cherry and H. W. Marigold, *The Land Transfer Acts* (1899), p. vii.

[10] Underhill saw his own scheme for settlements as an alternative to Wolstenholme's (1911 HCP xxxi, q. 5414 ff.), and Cherry seems to have supported it, for registered land at least (ibid., qq. 7228, 7234). Both seem to have preferred a regime of *powers* for settlements, vesting them in the limited owner rather than the trustees. T. C. Williams thought Wolstenholme's scheme an acceptable second-best to his own, ibid. 10570 ff.

[11] His rejection of true assimilation was deliberate—see (1913) 14 HLD 858 ff., 1650 ff. He was strongly criticized for it by St Aldwyn (but not, let it be noted, for not pressing on with compulsory registration), ibid.

[12] *Memorandum on the Real Property and Conveyancing Bills*, (1913) HLP ix. 45 (hereinafter '*Memorandum*'); see too *Explanatory Statement as to the Lord Chancellor's Bills*, pub. 18 July 1913, repr. in (1913) HLP vii. 439 (hereinafter '*Statement*'). The second version of the 1913 Conveyancing Bill has useful annotations: (1913) HLP iii 547 (hereinafter '*Annotations*').

[13] *Statement*, p. xxvi.

[14] Prototype: (1895–6) 40 *Sol. Jo* 172; final version: (1897) HLP iii. 99, reprinted in an improved form as appendix to Cherry and Marigold, *Land Transfer Acts*.

[15] Cherry and Marigold, *Land Transfer Acts*, p. vii, thought this a virtue.

acceptance of registration.[16] The Stephen/Williams preference would have been out of harmony with both the Settled Land Act and the Land Transfer Act.

Haldane's version of the Wolstenholme plan was arranged in an appealingly rational way.[17] The central concept was to be the 'proprietary estate'. It was defined, and the ways it could be 'disposed of' were stipulated. A proprietary estate with priority over another became a 'paramount interest', a category into which a stipulated list of other property rights also fell. All rights or interests that were neither proprietary estates nor paramount interests were 'subordinate interests', and if a proprietor attempted to dispose of his proprietary estate in a manner not permitted he would succeed only in creating a subordinate interest, to take effect behind whatever trust mechanism was appropriate in the circumstances. Subordinate interests would normally bind only the trustee constituted to give effect to them, but they could also be protected by entry of a caution or an inhibition on a register to be kept at the Land Registry. These would postpone or prevent dealings with the land. The bill said explicitly that a purchaser for value of a proprietary estate would take it subject to paramount interests and to any subordinate interests protected by cautions and inhibitions which the purchaser was ignoring, but otherwise free from competing interests even with notice.[18] Thus was the Land Transfer Act translated. As Haldane emphasized, the concepts were the same: Wolstenholme's paramount interests and the Registry's overriding interests, Wolstenholme's subordinate interests and the Registry's minor interests, they had the same structure and very nearly the same content. Only at the margin did they differ, because through 'the existence of a Registrar, and of an indemnity fund, it is possible to make "overriding interests" less extensive than "paramount interests"'.[19]

The list of proprietary estates was exclusive. In 1913 they were the legal fee simple, equitable fee simple, the term of years absolute, and, at first only by inference, the equity of redemp-

[16] *Memorandum*, 31.
[17] Conveyancing Bill 1913 (1913) HLP iii. 477, 547.
[18] Ibid., cl. 7.
[19] *Memorandum*, 31, and *Annotations*, cl. 62.

tion. Incidentally, legal estates were limited to the fee simple and the term of years absolute, not that that mattered given the primacy of 'proprietary estates'. Paramount interests also came in an exclusive list, though it was altered and expanded in successive revisions. Proprietary estates with priority to that being transferred were one sort. Easements and such-like things were another, provided that they would have bound a purchaser without notice under the old law. Local land charges registered under the Land Charges Act were also included; and restrictive covenants of which the purchaser had notice; and, explicitly so as to accord with the existing law,[20] 'the estate or right, if any, in respect of occupation of every actual occupier of the land'.

The Conveyancing Bill's robust and rational structure enabled gaps to be spotted and filled with ease, gaps particularly in the protection afforded to purchasers. For example:

in favour of a purchaser, every conveyance of a proprietary estate . . . to a person of full age . . . shall be deemed a proper and valid conveyance, whether appearing to be rightfully made or not, or the purchaser has or has not notice of any irregularity.[21]

On considering a chain of title, therefore, a purchaser need only check the age of each transferee. A similar protection was added for purchasers of settled land. The Settled Land Act condition was retained, that for a sale by a limited owner to overreach subordinate interests the capital money must be paid to trustees and not to the limited owner himself. But how was the purchaser to know to do this? Easy: in favour of a purchaser, land would be treated as settled only if Settled Land Act trustees were appointed or nominated in the conveyance to the vendor or their later appointment or nomination was recorded in a memorandum endorsed on that conveyance.[22] This complemented the basic policy that 'a purchaser of a proprietary estate shall only be concerned with the conveyance or other instrument operating as a disposition of the proprietary estate, and not with the trusts created by that or any other instrument.'[23]

---

[20] *Annotations*, cl. 2(3); and see below, sect. 2.2.
[21] Cl. 16(1).
[22] Cl. 16(2).
[23] Cl. 16(3).

To make assurance doubly sure for purchasers the bill also listed some things excluded from being paramount interests: deeds of arrangement, for example, pending legal actions, various rights in bankruptcy—things that at one time and another *had* bound purchasers, so about which there could have been doubt and argument. Finally, there was a list of things intended not to be affected by the structural changes introduced: mortgages by deposit of documents; rights acquired by limitation or prescription; the courts' jurisdiction to rectify documents, or to set aside transactions for fraud.

Much of the Conveyancing Bill is land law recast in the image of registered conveyancing, which is unsuprising when one remembers that the latter descended from Robert Wilson's scheme of so long ago, which had set out to create a registered system that would incorporate a rational and modern land law.[24] But the process was not altogether one way. Haldane accepted that techniques of mortgaging registered land had been woeful. He rejected the idea gained from a probable misreading of the Royal Commission report that they be done in future entirely 'off the register', but he still aimed 'to enable mortgages to be made in *any form*, and to contain *any* provisions desired by the parties, and in fact to render registered land, so far as is possible, subject to the ordinary law of mortgage in force with regard to registered land . . .'.[25] No fewer than four means of mortgaging were provided, including an improved version of the 'mortgage by registered charge' that had been savaged by the Royal Commission. But that form aside, the only function of the register would be to secure priority. The Royal Commission's view that easements were largely an 'off the register' matter was also accepted. But as will have been appreciated, Brickdale won the argument over settlements. Haldane's extension of the Settled Land Act's logic legitimized his device of registering the limited owner as proprietor and rejected Underhill's 'off the register' analysis. However, in a second move to make registered conveyancing fit better with existing theories of land law, Haldane adopted the relatively narrow view that 'the register is only intended to take the place of the documentary title and not to supersede the usual inquir-

---

[24] See above, Ch. 2, sect. 8.   [25] *Statement*, p. vii (original emphasis).

ies as to possession . . . .'.[26] Accordingly it should become
possible to gain title by adverse possession against registered
proprietors just as against unregistered. Similarly, the rights of
persons in actual occupation should be added to the list of
overriding interests,[27] just as they were to be a paramount
interest in the unregistered system. Finally, not only the law
was synthesized, so too was professional involvement: jurisdiction over solicitors' fees moved from the Registry committee to
the Solicitors Remuneration Act committee, albeit afforced for
the occasion by the Registrar.[28]

Interwoven with the rationalism was conservatism and timidity. The Royal Commission's doubts that mortgage by charge
was flexible enough to deal with changing conditions led to the
retention of the traditional mortgage by out-and-out transfer for
unregistered land without even the option of a new form. The
equity of redemption had therefore to be retained as a proprietary estate potentially paramount. It was authentic Lincoln's
Inn reasoning that led to the retention of the equitable fee
simple as a proprietary estate. 'Dispositions' of proprietary
estates were to be limited to those listed in the bill—a disposition could be by transfer, for example, or by carving out a lesser
proprietary estate. The draftsmen feared that irritated landowners might try to evade these limits by conveying the legal fee to
a corporation and then dealing with the resulting equitable
estate as though the old law continued unchanged.[29] There is a
memory here of those conveyancers who had searched for
devices to avoid compulsory registered conveyancing in London
after 1897. It is the voice of the poacher who has spent his life
finding loopholes, now cast as gamekeeper. There was conservatism too in the survival of the Statute of Uses, the bête noire of
the true reformers. Haldane was quite clear about it: the abuse
of the statute that had led to springing and shifting legal estates
would be met by direct prohibition, leaving intact all the useful

---

[26] *Memorandum*, 13.

[27] Real Property Bill 1913, (1913) HLP vii, schedule 5, cl. 7(3) (i); its accompanying note repeats the argument in *Memorandum*, 13. The expression 'overriding interest' dates from this time, the 1875 Act having used the clumsier 'not
encumbrance'.

[28] Ibid., cl. 81.

[29] *Memorandum*, 27 n.

things it could still do.[30] Thus the form of a conveyance by an existing owner to himself and another would still use the Statute—'to the use of [self and another] in fee simple'—as would some reservations—'to the use that X shall have a rentcharge/easement/term of years, and subject thereto to Y in fee simple'. One might cynically suppose that the real reason was to maintain the unintelligibility of conveyances, were it not that Haldane proposed also to abolish words of limitation.[31] Still, it is clear enough that rational though it mostly was, the bill was geared entirely to its main purpose of cutting down abstracts so as to streamline traditional conveyancing. It said nothing directly about cutting down scale fees, and neither did the Lord Chancellor.

Other structural changes were proposed in this major over-haul of real property law, particularly the virtual abolition of the law of tenure. Copyhold was to go, which the Royal Commission (among others) had wanted, and so were all other special tenures, as The Law Society had tried to achieve in one of its law-reforming bills. Only common socage would survive. Then there was a mass of incrementalist changes, some again stemming from The Law Society's frustrated efforts. They covered settled land, the inheritance provisions of the Land Transfer Act, and a great miscellany of individual rules that had got into a tangle. To indicate their different nature these relatively uncontroversial proposals were kept apart from Haldane's adaptation of the Wolstenholme scheme, which had a bill to itself.[32]

1.2. As Halsbury had done a generation before, Haldane consulted widely.[33] His bills were accompanied by various explanatory statements, which were printed commercially, along with copies of the bills themselves, to achieve wide distribution. And as with Halsbury's scheme, the criticisms,

---

[30] *Annotations*, cl. 3(3); (1913) 14 HLD 1657.

[31] Real Property Bill 1913, cl. 43.

[32] Wolstenholme's scheme is in the Conveyancing Bill, the rest in the Real Property Bill. For examples of Law Society precursors of the latter see n. 35 below.

[33] For this paragraph see (1913) 14 HLD 863; (1913–14) 58 *Sol. Jo.* 23, 42, 227, 437; (1914) 11 *Law Society Gazette* 70.

refinements, and suggestions flooded into the Lord Chancellor's office. A committee was established to work on the bills, chaired by the same Mr Gregory who had made Brickdale uncomfortable at the Royal Commision's hearings. Now Sir Phillip Gregory, Conveyancing Counsel to the Court, former member of the Rules Committee under the Land Transfer Act, his was the guiding intellectual spirit of the Committee's work.[34] Its other members were Benjamin Cherry, J. W. Hills, MP—the Law Society council member who had presented his own assimilation bill to the Commission[35]—F. F. Liddell, who was the government's senior draftsman, and Sir Charles Fortescue Brickdale.

Those of the priesthood not within Haldane's inner sanctum did not care much for his Conveyancing Bill. A Bar Council committee pronounced wholly against it,[36] and one of its co-opted members took its offensive on to the pages of the *Law Quarterly Review*.[37] This was Arthur Underhill, whose views had impressed the Royal Commission. The committee had two major criticisms: the bill was doing the wrong thing, and doing it in the wrong way. To start with conveyancing was to start at the end; far better to start at the beginning, with a major reform of the principles of real property law. For Underhill that meant its abolition and replacement by the law of chattels real. Without that it was merely a 'bill to shorten abstracts, simplify searches and inquiries, relieve purchasers from all difficulty as to questions of pedigree, and render the registration of title to settled

[34] Obit., (1918–19) 63 *Sol. Jo* 36; PRO LCO2/443, Cherry to Muir Mackenzie, 23 Feb. 1920. For Muir Mackenzie's fidelity to Gregory's memory see also LCO2/447, Cherry to Muir Mackenzie, 29 Mar. 1921.

[35] He also presented Law Society bills, e.g. Special Tenure Land Bill ((1911) HCP v. 649), Married Women's Property Bill ((1911) HCP iii. 689), Trustees Bill ((1911) HCP v. 841). He was also active in trying to open his profession to women (see (1913–14) 58 *Sol. Jo.* 418), introducing bills to that effect in 1912 and 1913 ((1912) HCP iii. 159, (1913) HCP iii. 757).

[36] General Council of the Bar, *Annual Statement, 1914*, repr. (1914–15) 138 *LT* 172. The conveyancers' 'Institute' said much the same (and more in sorrow . . .) in their *Report on Part I of the Conveyancing Report and Supplementary Report . . .*, 1914, PRO LCO2/451. (The 'Institute' was a club of élite conveyancers, primarily social, which occasionally produced an opinion on matters of professional interest. See Offer, *Property and Politics*, 33–4.)

[37] 'Lord Haldane's Real Property and Conveyancing Bills', (1914) 30 *LQR* 35, Jan. 1914.

land less onerous and difficult than it is now'. Secondly, they attacked the 'complication' introduced by this supposed simplification. If new principles were to be introduced, with a view to their being operated by conveyancers covering a wide range of intelligence [read: solicitors], it was imperative that the bill should be 'clear, simple and intelligible'.[38] In private Gregory was half-way to agreeing; he told Cherry that even after a year's publicity the two of them were the only members of Lincoln's Inn to understand it.[39] Cherry would probably not have cared. To an identical criticism in 1920 he retorted that it was childish to suppose that clauses stating new principles could be grasped with the same facility as those relating to isolated points.[40]

In its painstaking analysis of Haldane's bill the *Solicitors' Journal* had started at about the point where the barristers finished—that it was all too complicated. But as it worked steadily through the bill, showing solicitors how their transactions would henceforth have to be conducted, discussing the changes, drawing analogies with current practice, it became a convert to Haldane's side.[41] Eventually it commended the bill; in its essentials it was 'simple and practical', 'a successful attempt to reconstruct conveyancing on scientific lines'.[42] Now it came to Gregory's aid—and he appreciated the help, so the journal said later.[43] It condemned Underhill's article as superficial,[44] arguing that though the text was complicated it created a system of law that was easily managed, and therefore simple. Underhill and the Bar Council's committee disagreed: Haldane's insistence on leaving mortgages unreformed, which led to the classification of equities of redemption and bare trusts as proprietary estates, which in turn led to complicated problems of the priorities of competing estates, was anything but simple.

The conveyancers disliked the novel language and concepts

[38] See n. 36 above.
[39] PRO LCO2/443, Cherry to Muir Mackenzie, 23 Feb. 1920.
[40] PRO LCO2/445, Cherry to Schuster, 9 Aug. 1920.
[41] These comprehensive articles are the easiest introduction to the bills: on the Conveyancing Bill—(1912–13) 57 *Sol. Jo.* 682, 695, 713, 726, 737, 750, 761, 770, 781, 791, 797, 799, 807, 818, 832; on the Land Transfer Acts section of the Real Property Bill—(1913–14) 58 *Sol. Jo.* 42, 79, 94, 115, 135, 151, 184.
[42] (1912–13) 57 *Sol. Jo.* 829 and 834.
[43] (1918–19) 63 *Sol. Jo.* 36.
[44] (1913–14) 58 *Sol. Jo.* 244.

introduced, 'the strange, weird, and unfamiliar nomenclature',[45] and it is true that paramount and subordinate estates
coexisted uneasily with the traditional concepts of 'legal' and
'equitable'. To keep the old concepts, to divide all interests into
'legal estates' or 'equitable interests', that was what the Bar
Council's committee wanted. They recognized, however, that
that could not be done consistently with making the legal fee
simple the basis of conveyancing, since if the land was mortgaged the mortgagee would be the legal owner, but the 'real'
owner would be the mortgagor. They could see no solution
save scrapping the bill and seeking a different road to the goal
of assimilation. Underhill was tentatively inclined to abolish the
equity of redemption as an estate binding upon third parties in
any circumstance. 'It must however be admitted that there are
two sides to the question, and no doubt the authors of the bill
have been so deeply impressed with the fact that a fee simple
owner is none the less the real owner because he has executed
a legal mortgage, . . .'[46] that they felt obliged to include equities
of redemption among proprietary estates. Quite so; there is a
warning here that Underhill may not be a man to let realities
stand in the way of neat legal devices.

Benjamin Cherry claimed later that failure to solve the mortgage problem was the *only* reason for the complex calculus in
Haldane's bills.[47] Perhaps; he was there. But Brickdale had long
argued that in the world of registration the distinction between
the legal and the equitable had no place. It is possible that the
new concepts would in time have replaced the old, especially
given the triple provision in Haldane's bills, that only paramount interests and 'protected' subordinate interests could bind
purchasers, that paramount interests were defined exclusively,
and that subordinate interests could be created only where an
equivalent legal or equitable interest could have been created
before. Though Haldane was not working towards a general
synthesis of all property law, his bill did contain the seeds from
which a modern code of land law could have grown. It would

[45] Underhill, 'Lord Haldane's Real Property and Conveyancing Bills'.
[46] Ibid.
[47] PRO LCO2/443, Cherry to Muir Mackenzie, 23 Feb. 1920; cf. his Draft Reply
to Report of the Institute's Sub-Committee, para. 9, PRO LCO2/444, 27 July
1920; and his separate memo on Mortgages by Demise, ibid. 27 July 1920.

only have needed the conveyancers to swallow their dislike of the mortgage by way of legal charge.

Law societies were also unimpressed to start with. The Yorkshire law societies, of course, were particularly anxious that the bills should do absolutely nothing to alter their system of deeds registration, and even began to draft a rival bill to institute it nationally.[48] Rubinstein and others told a Law Society meeting[49] that since the Royal Commission had found against the Land Registry, all that was needed was repeal of the Land Transfer Acts; the Society should oppose Haldane. Hills spoke at length against him; the Society had pressed for a Royal Commission, now it must support its conclusions. Rubinstein withdrew. The Law Society, the Associated Provincial Law Societies, and a host of local societies gave their grudging support, on condition that the bills were consolidated into one and amendments made.[50] And so they were. The result was a monster, the Real Property and Conveyancing Bill 1914.[51] It had 146 clauses spread across nine separate parts, followed by ten schedules: part I—amendments to the Settled Land Act; part II – amendments to the Trustee Act; part III – abolition of copyhold and special tenures; part IV – extinguishment of manorial incidents; part V—amendments to the general law; part VI, and the fifth schedule—'provisions for amending the law as to settlements and for simplifying the title to and transfer of land'; part VII—repeal and re-enactment of the succession and inheritance provisions of the Land Transfer Act 1897; part VIII, and the tenth schedule—amendments to the land registration system; part IX—miscellaneous.

The structural changes that had merited their own bill now appeared as part VI of the new. Their philosophy and nomenclature was intact, but some changes of classification had been made, and there had been so much further elaboration that Wolstenholme's simple scheme was but barely visible beneath a welter of provisos.[52] The solicitors' strong desire to have all

---

[48] (1913–14) 58 *Sol. Jo.* 15 (Wakefield ILS).
[49] Ibid. 437.
[50] Ibid. 227.
[51] (1914) HLP viii. 5.
[52] Paramount interests were split into 'paramount estates' (which, confusingly, contained easements) and 'paramount rights'. The successor to cl. 7, cl. 92, describes exactly what does and does not bind a purchaser, a counterpart to Land Registration Act 1925, s. 20. It also contains the various presumptions of regularity. There is nothing like it in the Law of Property Act 1925.

the relevant law in one statute, plus the inevitably nit-picking amendments that resulted from consultation with virtually the whole of the legal profession, created a mass of detail that all —but swamped the basic provisions. None the less the bill clearly went a very long way towards easing the purchaser's lot: -overreaching where there was a settlement remained conditional,[53] but purchasers were immune from hidden settlements; presumptions of regularity combined with explicit abolition of documentary notice made most other overreaching virtually unconditional. The 1925 legislation does less and, as will be seen, it was meant to do less. And the 1914 bill bore its theory and its objectives on its face; quite unlike the 1925 Act.

The opposition's determination was not tried. Haldane's final version was printed in August 1914. The next four years tested instead his reforms of military administration.

2. Haldane, Notice, and the Rights of Occupiers

2.1. One of the evils afflicting traditional conveyancing, according to Registrar Brickdale, was the ever-present possibility that a purchaser might find himself 'fixed with notice'— a process which he seems to have thought rather like pig-sticking in its gleeful brutality to the innocent and vulnerable.[54] Haldane likewise: 'the greatest difficulty now experienced by conveyancers is on account of the length to which courts have in the past extended the doctrine of notice.'[55] On a casual reading of the bill one might think that he meant to legislate it out of existence:

a conveyance to a purchaser shall have the same effect whether he has or has not notice of the existence of any subordinate estates or interests,

---

[53] The Memorandum to Wolstenholme's 1897 bill ((1897) HLP iii. 99) stressed that all estate owners had full powers (given to them by cl. 6), hence the need for cautions and inhibitions to protect beneficiaries. But although Haldane adopted that clause in both his bills (1913, cl. 6; 1914, cl. 78—oddly punctuated), he subtracted from it in 1914 by cl. 84, which made void transactions by limited owners in excess of their settlement or Settled Land Act powers.

[54] (1909) HCP xxvii. 733, qq. 1984a–2004.

[55] *Annotations*, cl. 7(2); *Memorandum*, 25; (1913) 14 HLD 1654.

or of any other liabilities, rights or claims which the proprietor has power to overreach . . .[56]

But this applied only to subordinate and overreachable interests, not to paramount estates or rights. Into *those* categories fell explicitly the estate or right of actual occupiers and, where the purchaser had notice, the benefit of a restrictive covenant. Estate contracts were not treated as a category as such, and would probably have caused litigation, though they could always have been protected by caution or inhibition. But it is possible to regard them as creating equitable estates, and, if so, some at least might have been treated as paramount estates or rights, depending upon some other rather difficult points of interpretation.[57]

No, the target was neither equitable interests generally nor notice generally. Haldane's explanatory memorandum shows the limits of his concern. After describing in a somewhat exaggerated way how mention or necessary implication of a trust upon the title to a piece of land gave a purchaser notice of the whole contents of the document creating it, it concluded that 'it is the effect of this "notice" and of these equitable rights which is the most troublesome matter in investigating title.'[58] So it was trusts, and documentary notice of both the express and constructive varieties, that were the problem. What problems, precisely? Contemporary practice supplies the answer. Trustees' decisions about how much of a trust needed to be disclosed on a sale of trust land were not easy, and neither were purchasers always sure what further requisitions on title they

[56] Conveyancing Bill 1913, cl. 7(2).

[57] S. Gardner, 'Equity, estate contracts and the Judicature Acts', (1987) 7 *Oxford Journal of Legal Studies* 60. The 1914 bill's Fifth Schedule, pt. 1, included: '(ii) the proprietary estate, legal or equitable, acquired under a lease or a term of years' not exceeding 21 years, at a rack rent. By cl. 144 a 'term of years' could be equitable. But if that made contracts for leases equitable 'estates' and therefore proprietary estates under (ii), so it would under (i): 'the proprietary estate, legal or equitable, in respect of occupation of every actual occupier of the land'. But that would negate the careful definitional limitations in (ii).

[58] See n. 55 above. For a more careful account of documentary notice see T. C. Williams, *The Law of Vendor and Purchaser* (2nd edn., 1910), 170, 245–6; cf. *Dart on Vendor and Purchaser* (7th edn. 1905, by B. L. Cherry, G. E. Tyrell, A. Dickson, and I. Marshall), 877 ff., esp. 882–3.

should require.[59] The resulting uncertainties could lead to delay and expense, as all parties, erring on the side of safety, might find it best to disclose the whole of a trust, the abstract of title becoming long and cumbersome as a result. As one judge put it, 'purchasers will not lay out their money in acquiring property the security of their title to which may depend upon an exhaustive investigation into the execution of trusts, which can rarely be complete and must always seem burdensome.'[60] Of course, underlying this was the rule that a purchaser might be liable to equitable owners if there were irregularities in this transaction or one earlier in the chain; but it was the cost of the procedure for satisfying him that there were no irregularities that was the issue, not the consequences if there were. In the vast majority of transactions, where everything was regularly done, beneficiaries too were disadvantaged by 'notice', since they had no need for its protection but had to bear some of the cost it added to ordinary dealings.

Trustees were only limited owners. They had limited powers under the general law, and though those might be extended in a particular case, such extension needed proving to a purchaser. That proof would necessarily disclose the whole of the contents of that document, which might then cause a purchaser to worry about other matters that would otherwise not have affected him—whether the proper procedure for appointing a new trustee had been followed, for example. Limited powers could often be extended in practice, simply by having the beneficiaries all join in the transaction with the trustees. But for that to work they had all to join, and a purchaser would therefore need proof of the entire equitable title. If an abstract of title disclosed an event such as this a purchaser who might be liable to make good any loss that had occurred was entitled to put in requisitions seeking proof that all had been properly done. Power to requisition, and liability to equitable claimants were in this sense correlatives. So conveyancing by trustees could be expensive, and a trust somewhere in the chain of title might add cost to an otherwise straightforward transaction.

---

[59] The most complete treatment of the problems discussed here are: T. Lewin, *The Law of Trusts* (12th edn., 1911, by C. C. M. Dale and G. A. Streeten), 386 ff.; Williams, *Law of Vendor and Purchaser*, 237–45, 256–88.

[60] *re Soden and Alexander's Contract* [1918] 2 Ch. 258, 264 (Younger J.).

These considerations had led conveyancers to experiment with devices keeping trusts off the title. The best turned out to be the trust for sale, but even that had serious limitations.[61] Though it clearly empowered trustees to sell, it did not authorize them to lease, mortgage, or exchange—save by express power, which needed proving, thereby returning us to our starting-point. But incorporation of Settled Land Act powers by reference would save spelling things out tediously; and if the beneficial interests were declared in a separate document a purchaser could be satisfied of the trustees' powers easily and safely.[62] Even then, however, the trust for sale was no panacea, because the beneficiaries might have elected to terminate the 'for sale' element in the trust and take the land as land. If they had done so the trustees' power to pass good title had lapsed. An oldish trust for sale might therefore lead to just the sort of requisitions that the device as a whole was meant to obviate. And if an abstract disclosed a distribution of the land in kind the trusts would have to be brought on to the title, just to show that it had been properly done.

Another method of keeping trusts off the title was through the use of misleading recitals, conventionally accepted.[63] They appear to have first arisen when trustees of money settlements invested on mortgages. Suppose, for example, that *A* and *B* hold money in trust for *P* and *Q*, and that they lend it to *X*, who mortgages land to them as security. The mortgage will take the usual form of a transfer of the fee simple to *A* and *B*. They now hold the land upon the same trusts as originally attached to the money. Upon repayment they reconvey. In due course *X* contracts to sell to *Y*. If the mortgage described *A* and *B* as the trustees they are, the title now discloses a reconveyance by trustees consequent upon receipt of the money lent. But if there were an irregularity in this, *Y*, having notice of the trust, may be liable to make it good. Suppose, for example, that *B* was not one of the original trustees. Did the power he and *A* exercised extend to successor trustees? Was he properly appointed? If he was not, and if the money had not been properly applied for

[61] Williams, *Law of Vendor and Purchaser*, 266–78.
[62] *Prideaux's Precedents in Conveyancing* (21st edn., 1913, by B. L. Cherry and R. Beddington), i. 481 n., 503.
[63] See n. 59 above.

the beneficiaries, then his receipt would not exonerate X, and possibly not Y. Requisitions are clearly in order . . . just in case. How very tiresome. So A and B would *not* be described as trustees. The mortgage to X would simply say that A and B were owners of the money on a joint account, not actually saying that they were beneficial owners, but implying that they might be. There was no express disclosure of the trust, nor a necessary inference of one. The title thereby stayed simple. Suppose however that before repayment B retired, to be replaced by C. The reconveyance might simply recite that whereas A and B had once been entitled to the money, now A and C were; but Y might have to inquire about that, since there was a danger that this might be a voluntary transfer liable to be set aside in bankruptcy. Futhermore, there was a nasty problem with stamp duty.[64] Voluntary transfers had to carry pro rata stamp duty, whereas transfers between trustees bore only the 10s deed stamp. If the transfer of the land from A and B to A and C had been stamped at 10s., Y would want an explanation— because if he ever had to produce his deeds in court, he might have to make up any deficiency on stamp duty himself. Y might ask X to pay the difference; which would put X to an unnecessary expense; or X might tell Y that no such duty was necessary because the transfer was only between trustees—but that gives Y actual notice of the trust, which is exactly what must be avoided. If these problems could not be overcome, the trusts might as well be put on the title from the start.

The solution suggested by the conveyancers was that the transfer to A and C should recite that they had become entitled in equity to the mortgage money or, what amounted to the same thing, that A and B held on trust for them and were transferring pursuant to a request to do so. That would not be a voluntary transfer, eliminating one of Y's worries. Further, the same stamp duty of 10s. was payable whichever story one believed—whether it was a transfer between trustees or one made consequently upon the prior passing of a beneficial interest. Moreover, if B was retiring, and C had been appointed, then the story was true (or nearly true)—A and B *were* under an

[64] Williams, *Law of Vendor and Purchaser* 170, 245–6; for doubts see John Dixon, (1905) 49 *Sol. Jo.* 317. My text simplifies the problem.

equitable obligation to transfer to *A* and *C*. Judges knew perfectly well that the recitals, though not untrue, were concealing the whole truth. But they also knew why it was being done, and they approved.[65] In one judge's words the courts would always refuse 'to make any inquiry into the trusts, because to do so would defeat a practice which has been introduced for the benefit of Her Majesty's subjects'.[66] Settled practice among conveyancers was part of the common law, at least where judges agreed with it.[67] Purchasers, therefore, were forbidden to raise requisitions into the reasons why *A* and *B* were duty-bound to convey to *A* and *C*. It followed that if, perchance, there had been an irregularity, *Y* was immune from its consequences. This was spelt out at length by another judge:

it can hardly be doubted that the proper and beneficial disposition of trust estates by trustees, who either mediately or immediately have had confidence reposed in them by the author of the trust or the court, should not be hampered by the burden of answering elaborate domestic questions, even if the conventions necessary in the majority of cases to obviate them [i.e. the device outlined above] should destroy, in the comparatively rare instances of abuse, the claim of cestuis que trust to follow the trust property into the hands of the purchaser. It is better this claim should be lost, and the cestuis que trust in these cases be left to their remedy against their trustees personally, than that the value, for the purpose of realization of trust property, should in the mass be generally prejudiced.[68]

Moreover, courts saw no reason why mortgages alone could use this device; purchases by trustees, or transfers to them on trust might take the same form.

Alas, it did not work. There were some minor snags, particularly that the device depended upon each set of trustees appearing to have taken beneficially. So it was valid to imply that *A* and *B* were beneficially entitled, and then became obligated in equity to *A* and *C*, who also might have taken

---

[65] Lewin, *Law of Trusts*, 386 ff.; Williams, *Law of Vendor and Purchaser*, 237–45, 256–88; *re Harman and Uxbridge & Rickmansworth Railway Company* (1883) 24 Ch.D. 720.

[66] *re Harman and Uxbridge & Rickmansworth Railway Company* (1883) 24 Ch.D. 720.

[67] *re Chafer and Randall's Contract* [1916] 2 Ch. 8, 11 (Younger J.)—a case directly in point.

[68] *re Soden and Alexander's Contract* [1918] 2 Ch. 258, 264.

beneficially, and so on. But it was not valid to show A and B or A and C taking initially upon trust. The former showed a trust, but could be treated as a declaration by A and B against their interest; the latter trust could not be explained away like that, and raised obvious questions about the sufficiency of the nominal owners' powers. This was a fine line to draw, one that conveyancers did not always get right.[69] In addition there was always the risk that the solicitors for each side, anxious to do the right thing, would discuss what requisitions could properly be made and answered, and that in doing so enough details of the trusts would be disclosed to give informal notice of the whole lot, thereby creating a need for proper proof.[70] Perhaps in time these problems would have been overcome. It seems probable from the courts' enthusiasm to validate these good conveyancing practices that if it had simply been a conveyancing matter it would eventually have been usual to have kept trusts off the title altogether. But it was not just a matter of conveyancing.

It was also a matter of tax, so serious that it put an end to all hope of extending the device beyond its original habitat, and even cast doubts upon its validity there.[71] The problem was with estate duty. Suppose that we rewrite our original example: S transfers to A and B without disclosing that they are trustees, A and B recite that they have become obligated in equity to A and C, and therefore now convey to them upon their request. So far so good; but now A dies. If he is a beneficial owner, estate duty is payable; if it is not paid it becomes a charge against the land, valid even against a purchaser. Of course, it would not be payable because the Inland Revenue would be satisfied from the collateral deeds executed on each transfer that A was a trustee, on whose death no duty was ever due. But how was a purchaser, from C or further on down the line, to know that? The risk was too great. Co-ownership of land was

---

[69] re Blaiberg and Adams [1899] 2 Ch. 340.

[70] There would be no assistance from the limitation placed on imputed notice in Conveyancing Act, 1882, s. 3(1) (ii)—on which see Williams, Law of Vendor and Purchaser, 247.

[71] Prideaux's Precedents (21st edn.), i. 481 n.; T. Key and H. W. Elphinstone, Precedents in Conveyancing (5th edn., 1897), i. 256, ibid. (9th edn., 1909) i. 574; Dart on Vendor and Purchaser, i. 1230–1.

too common for him to assume without asking that there was a trust here and that the non-payment of duty created no liability upon the land. He could be reassured only by disclosure of the trust.

So the device had to be limited to mortgages taken by trustees of personalty, receiving indirect statutory recognition in the Trustee Act, 1893.[72] A provision to clear up the remaining doubt about inferences to be drawn from the presence of a mere 10s. stamp on transfers of mortgages was included in The Law Society's abortive Conveyancing Bills in the early years of the century, eventually reaching the statute book in 1911.[73] But nothing could be done to get around the estate duty problem, at least, not without Treasury co-operation.[74] So The Law Society's bills adopted a different tactic for sales and purchases. Where trustees of a personalty settlement had power to invest in land, then it should be enacted that the land bought should be held upon trust for sale. Similarly, if they invested upon mortgage and subsequently foreclosed, again a trust for sale should arise. And trusts for sale should, as against a purchaser, be deemed to last until the land was sold, or until conveyed to the beneficiaries or at their order.[75]

'Notice', then, was a problem to the extent that it prevented trusts of land conforming to the model of trusts of personalty, because expense resulted. Left to themselves conveyancers would probably have managed to eradicate trusts from title-deeds, but Haldane's reform was necessary to circumvent the estate duty charge.[76] As a legislator he could also write a more elegant solution than the conveyancers, but like a conveyancer he was tempted to insure his reform against failure. The various presumptions of regularity he introduced were aimed to solve the same problem—again their effect was that purchasers were immunized against deficiencies in trustees' powers.

---

[72] S. 12(3).

[73] e.g. Conveyancing Bill 1907, cl. 14 ((1907) HCP i. 515); Conveyancing Act 1911, s. 13; *re Soden and Alexander's Contract* [1918] 2 Ch. 258.

[74] Haldane's bills aimed to remove the estate duty problem: Real Property and Conveyancing Bill 1914, cls. 66, 96.

[75] Conveyancing Act 1911, s. 10.

[76] This was a common perception; see e.g. (1907–8) 52 *Sol. Jo.* 134 (The Law Society), (1908–9) 53 *Sol. Jo.* 134 (Liverpool ILS).

2.2. The other form of constructive notice, that gained from an equitable owner or encumbrancer's possession of the land, was not regarded as a problem. Far from it, the very first paramount estate listed in the 1914 bill was the 'proprietary estate, if any, legal or equitable, in respect of occupation of every actual occupier of the land'.[77] It was to be one of only two paramount estates capable of trumping a legal proprietary estate in the same land, and for occupiers who had only a 'right' rather than an estate there would be a parallel 'paramount right'. There was one subtraction, that a proprietary estate capable of being overreached under the Settled Land Act could not be a paramount estate.[78] Haldane wrote explicitly that he thereby retained the present law for occupiers.[79] This creates a puzzle, since the formulation used may not have done that. Possession protected all the possessor's equitable rights, collateral ones included, not just those by virtue of which the possession was enjoyed.[80] But the bill's phrase 'in respect of occupation', and the use of the singular 'right' rather than the plural 'rights', suggest a curtailment. The clause was copied almost without alteration from Wolstenholme's prototype,[81] so the change may have been inadvertent, given Haldane's clear statement of intent.

This form of constructive notice seems not to have been regarded as a nuisance by the conveyancing priesthood, probably because the inspection of the land needed to obviate it had a dual purpose.[82] This is how Elphinstone saw it in 1893, when considering whether protection given to beneficiaries of stock settlements by the *distringas* registry would be adequate for land:

the case of land is different. Here some person, either the cestui que trust or his tenant, is in possession; the purchaser, before making his

---

[77] Real Property and Conveyancing Bill 1914, Fifth Schedule.

[78] Ibid.

[79] *Annotations*, cl. 2(3).

[80] *Barnhart* v. *Greenshields* (1853) 9 Moore P. C. 18; *Dart on Vendor and Purchaser*, ii. 884 ff.; Williams *Law of Vendor and Purchaser*, i. 609 ff.

[81] Conveyancing Bill 1897, cl. 3(4) (ii); the policy was acknowledged by Cherry and Marigold, *Land Transfer Acts*, appendix, note to cl. 3(4).

[82] *Dart on Vendor and Purchaser*, ii. 884 ff.; Williams, *Law of Vendor and Purchaser*, i. 400 and 609 ff. Inquiries on site might disclose patent defects for which the vendor would not be liable or might enable timely rescission by the purchaser.

bargain, goes, either personally or by an agent, to inspect the land, and on doing so will probably find that the person who is making the bargain with him is not in possession. He is at once put on inquiry; he will learn from the person in possession whether the intended sale is fraudulent or not.[83]

A little later an anonymous author, from the style and content possibly Elphinstone again, gave this account of current practice:[84]

many practitioners consider that the inquiry as to possession is burdensome. . . . The present writer has discussed the question lately with some leading conveyancers, and finds that there is some discrepancy in their practice. One practitioner said that, in dealing with property in London, he always directed inquiries to be made of the occupiers of the house as to whom they paid their rents, and similar inquiries to be made of the latter, and so on until he reached the head lessee. On the other hand, some conveyancers never direct any such inquiries. The truth seems to be that, in all cases of a purchase, the inquiry is made implicitly before the matter is put into the hands of a solicitor. The intending purchaser or his agent goes to see the land, he states his business, that he is authorized by A.B. to inspect the land; if A.B. is not the landlord, he will be told, and probably will not be allowed to go over the land.

'Notoriety in country and big London' estates was probably a sufficient safeguard; only small properties in towns were really a problem. His conclusion was that 'the Act of 1875 destroys the great safeguard of rendering it necessary to see that title and possession go together.'

Hunt v. *Luck*[85] in 1901 removed the risk that possession by a tenant would be treated as constructive notice of his equitable landlord, but the texts tended to treat the case narrowly, regarding it as authority only that receipt of the rent by an estate agent was not constructive notice of his principal's equitable title.[86] An anonymous note on the case takes us a little further. After saying that most practitioners probably do not

---

[83] (1894–5) 39 *Sol. Jo.* 24; similarly at (1895) 11 *LQR* 357, where he points out that the 1870 Royal Commission on Land Transfer thought that purchasers should still have to inspect the land—(1870) HCP xviii. 595, para. 64 [and, better, 82].

[84] (1894–5) 39 *Sol. Jo.* 537.

[85] [1901] 1 Ch. 45.

[86] e.g. *Dart on Vendor and Purchaser*, ii. 886.

make inquiries, and that mortgagors, being usually anxious to conceal their borrowing from the world at large, do not encourage them, the author continued:

inquiries are more necessary in the case of a mortgage than of a purchase, because in the latter case the vendor on completion will be bound to furnish the purchaser with orders directing the tenants to pay their rents to him, and the purchaser will at once serve these notices on the tenants, and if the vendor has committed any fraud it will be discovered immediately. In case of a mortgage, however, the mortgagee may not require to take possession until after a long interval, so that it is possible to perpetrate a fraud and escape at his [sic] leisure before it is discovered. . . . The inquiries which a purchaser or mortgagee would wish to make would ordinarily be two—namely (1) whether the tenant would recognise the validity of an order signed by the *soi-disant* landlord as entitling the assignee to receive the future rents, and (2) whether the occupier makes any claim in respect of the property beyond his rights as tenant upon the terms stated by the same landlord. It is clearly settled that if a purchaser or mortgagee omits to make the latter inquiry, he takes subject to all the rights of the occupier; and it does not appear to be a very heavy burden to cast upon him to require him to make the former inquiry also.[87]

The treatises on vendor and purchaser added that the first of those inquiries would detect whether the vendor's title had become barred by the Statute of Limitation.[88] Failure to make full inquiry thus entailed accepting three risks: (1) that the vendor had no legal title; (2) that the vendor's equitable title was limited or non-existent; (3) that the person in possession had legal or equitable rights in addition to those already known to the purchaser. Risk (3) can be met by asking the possessor about his own rights, thereby reducing, but not abrogating, risk (2) as well. *Hunt* v. *Luck* removed the other part of risk (2), except in cases of actual notice, and the Haldane/Wolstenholme bills sought to remove it altogether. The difficulty is that inquiries to meet risk (3) were accepted as necessary by everybody, and that the inquiries necessary to meet the remote but serious risk (1) were the same ones that would meet risk (2). So looked at from the point of view of the purchaser or, more likely, of his adviser, there was little to be said in favour of *Hunt*

---

[87] (1900–1) 45 *Sol. Jo.* 199.
[88] Williams, *Law of Vendor and Purchaser*, 399–400.

v. *Luck.* It merely meant that for the saving of an unpredictable amount of work, the purchaser was freed from an unpredictable proportion of an unquantifiable set of risks. So although Haldane's bill undoubtedly did entrench the *Hunt* v. *Luck* principle through requiring 'actual' occupation for a paramount estate or interest, constructive notice in this context had generated nothing like the controversy that documentary notice of trusts had.

Yet the equivalent overriding interest in registered conveyancing was to be wider. The formulation 'The rights of every person in actual occupation of the land or in receipt of the rents and profits thereof'[89] clearly does include collateral rights and equally clearly deprives the purchaser of *Hunt* v. *Luck* protection. Its origin may explain why. The following exchanges are from the Royal Commission's hearings, where the setting is that Registrar Brickdale is contemplating a large extension of absolute titles, which would be guaranteed by the insurance fund. In cases of mistake the fund would compensate a subsequent proprietor who ended up with less than he thought he was buying, unless the deficiency were caused by what is now termed an overriding interest.[90]

Brickdale: Naturally the purchaser knows the land; he looks at it; he is aware, or, at any rate, he should be, that he can make inquiries as to tenants and others; he knows to whom they pay their rent, and so on. But the Registrar . . . has not the same facilities for making inquiries on the ground, and there is to my mind a slightly greater risk of mistakes in title, possibly even owing to intentional and deliberate fraud, which would pass the Registrar but would not pass an ordinary purchaser . . . I think that we might very well save the insurance fund from liabilities under this head by enacting that an absolute title should not include a guarantee against adverse rights which could be discovered by inspection of the ground. It would certainly relieve the responsibility of the Department, and I do not think it would be an unreasonable addition to the responsibility of the purchaser. [For example, sometimes we have registered a title to a house] and then it has turned out some time afterwards that the next-door neighbour, or some other house in the neighbourhood, has come to be registered and has claimed

[89] Real Property and Conveyancing Bill, 1914, Tenth Schedule, cl. 5(3).
[90] First Report of the Royal Commission on the Land Transfer Acts, (1909) HCP xxvii. 733, qq. 1407 ff.

— a cellar running right underneath the house, and has proved his right to it. If we had registered an absolute title . . . it might have resulted in a loss to the insurance fund.

Pennington: But you must stand the racket, must you not, if you are going to give absolute title?—*Brickdale*: That is just what I am rather afraid of.

Pennington: If we [solicitors] did not make proper inquiries as advising on purchase, we should have to pay—*Brickdale*: My feeling about that is that the register was only intended to take the place of the documentary title, and . . . it may fairly leave the people who deal with land in the same position as they are now with respect to the obligation to inquire on the ground to see that there is nobody in — adverse occupation at the time.

Pennington: You are going to water away the insurance fund?— *Brickdale*: That would be my proposition for the consideration of the Royal Commission.

Stewart-Smith: The limits of the exception you suggest are defects which could be discovered by inspection on the ground?—*Brickdale*: . . . that might be rather a narrow definition; because if a cellar runs very deep it would be rather stretching language to say that it could be discovered by inspection on the ground.

Stewart-Smith: Well, inspection on the premises?—*Brickdale*: What I really mean is adverse rights in occupation at the time of the purchaser's acquisition which were also in occupation at the time of first registration of the land—no other . . .

Stewart-Smith: In other words . . . the occupation of some person, whose occupation cannot be accounted for, is notice to the purchaser of the terms of the occupation which may be a defect on the vendor's title?—*Brickdale*: It carries out that principle which we know in conveyancing.

Stewart-Smith: You are going to limit it to that?—*Brickdale*: I should limit it to such of those rights as were in existence at the time of the first registration of the land, so that gradually the risk, such as it is, would disappear.

Stewart-Smith: That I follow; but it must be the possession of some person or persons which puts the purchaser on inquiry?—*Brickdale*: Yes, rights in possession.

Gregory: But there are really two branches of the question that you raise: one is as to what Mr Stewart-Smith has been talking about, the occupation of some person or persons the nature of whose title to occupy the purchaser is bound to find out; and the second is, physical matters . . . arising from the construction of the premises. The one instance that you have given is of cellars. Do you still propose to exclude all cellars that may be connected with some other property?—*Brickdale*: Yes, if in actual occupation at the time of first registration of the land.

Gregory: Supposing that there was a sewer or drain under the land, which was vested in a local authority?—*Brickdale*: You mean not a mere easement?

Gregory: No an actual drain. The ownership of the drain and possibly some small portion of the ground round it is vested in the local authority?—*Brickdale*: Yes.

Gregory: Since that doctrine has been laid down about vesting it has become a considerable trouble to say of a certain property that there may not be such a sewer or drain passing through the property, and, if that is so, the vendor cannot make title to that portion of the ground. You would except that?—*Brickdale*: Yes, it would come within the class I am thinking of.

Gregory: [And flying freeholds?]—*Brickdale*: Yes, I have been particularly thinking of that . . .

Gregory: Then what it really comes to is this, that your registration would be restricted to the surface of the ground level?—*Brickdale*: Even there if it was entirely in the adverse possession of someone else at the time of first registration—*Gregory*: I am speaking of the physical matters, merely the physical part of the difficulty?—*Brickdale*: I should not like to commit myself to a general statement . . . I do not quite accept your test of 'level of the ground' . . . what I am afraid of is that people may take advantage of the Registrar . . . and register properties of which they are not really in possession of any part.

Brickdale: . . . it does not seem to me that it would be really putting upon the purchaser of registered land any burden which he does not now sustain, or a burden which it would be at all difficult to sustain or likely to do him any harm, because he is always there, whereas the Registrar is not always there.

Discuss, as an examiner might say.

It is not very difficult. It was taken as axiomatic that occupiers would maintain their rights, and the question was as to the consequences. The axiom itself went wholly unexamined. But we can see that from Brickdale's point of view,[91] to include in the exception persons 'in receipt of rents and profits' of the adversely occupied land would be necessary to secure maximum immunity for the insurance fund. However, someone like

[91] Cherry supported him: Second Report, (1911) HCP xxxi, q. 7271.

the author of the *Solicitors' Journal*'s note on *Hunt* v. *Luck*[92] might also agree with this wording, since to him the rule in that case lacked rationality. On the other hand, like Stewart-Smith he would want a 'reasonable inquiry' defence. But Brickdale would not, since if the occupation was undiscoverable on reasonable inquiry by a purchaser its absence was hardly the sort of thing that should be guaranteed by the Registry. For Gregory the issues of occupation and (in effect) horizontal boundaries should be kept separate; but for Brickdale one stone would kill both birds.

So just as with traditional conveyancing, the precise formula for protecting occupiers' rights could be made to turn on issues that had very little to do with the rights and wrongs of the occupiers themselves. Moreover, if Brickdale, the guiding spirit of land registration, the arch-expansionist of 'officialism', himself wanted such a limitation which, in the eyes of the Commission, could only serve to make his system less attractive by reducing the scope of the insurance fund, there was hardly likely to be anyone to argue the contrary. Both the Commission and Haldane thought that there would have to be a further trial. If Brickdale wanted to reduce his own chances of ultimate success, that was his business.

[92] (1900–1) 45 *Sol. Jo.* 199.

8

Law Fit for Heroes

1. For the legal profession's first great expositor of modern land law, G. C. Cheshire, the statutory reforms of 1922–5 were explained by a general post-war desire to set the nation's social life in order.[1] It would be easy to agree, since it is a commonplace that the war was a watershed after which nothing was the same again. The bills originated moreover from the Ministry of Reconstruction, and from its Land Acquisition Committee at that, from which much that was novel and radical had first appeared. There were great plans for legal reform. Mirroring the Ministry, the *Solicitors' Journal* opened its pages to projects for 'legal reconstruction' of great ambition. A Ministry of Justice, a united grand school of legal education, admission of women (now a certainty to be welcomed rather than a fear to be joked about), the removal of barriers between the bar and solicitors, the destruction of barristers' privileges, new systems for remuneration (made the more urgent as clerks' wages rose), legal aid schemes for the poor, all these were discussed at length.[2] These were all structural professional matters. Just one old favourite touched our concerns, the spread of state bureaucracy. But even in that context, land law, conveyancing, and registration were but briefly mentioned.

Brickdale was still in post, and as he had persuaded Haldane's predecessor that the Royal Commission's recommendations were trivial, nobody need be surprised that he was ready to try again with his successor. So in 1917, when the Ministry of Reconstruction turned to consider the implementation of post-war land policy, he wrote to the Lord Chancellor's Office: '. . .

---

[1] G. C. Cheshire, *The Modern Law of Real Property* (8th edn., 1958), 5.
[2] (1917–18) 62 *Sol. Jo.* 782, 802, 819; (1918–19) 63 *Sol. Jo.* 4, 36, 64, 95, 111; see also, on the Ministry of Justice, ibid. 188, 196, 217, 226.

it will be advisable to get as tight hold of the Reconstruction
Committee as we can: if the Government are going to buy land
and build a million houses, the purchasers ought not to be left
to the tender mercies of "This Indenture" . . . '.[3] But Brickdale
was peripheral, having to operate at one remove. The priorities
of the Ministry of Reconstruction were far more grandiose than
left room for consideration of relative trivia like modes of land
transfer.[4] Whether it was concerned with acquiring urban land
for housing or rural land for resettlement, or even with strips of
land to build new light railways in rural areas to improve
transport of food to the great cities, its general preference was
to use compulsory powers in the first place and then, where
appropriate, to lease the property thereafter, perhaps on new
forms of secure or semi-secure tenure. Its Acquisition and
Valuation of Land Committee was to devise mechanisms for
achieving these ends, far removed from the subjects of this
analysis so far. Only in connection with the private house-
building programme did the Ministry touch upon Brickdale's
hopes, but its interest was at least as much in the employment
aspect of building as in the subsequent fate of the houses. Its
problems in finding materials at reasonable prices and in ensur-
ing an adequate standard of construction kept it fully occupied.
An internal memorandum accompanying the first draft of the
paper to introduce the Land Acquisition Bill perfectly captures
the Ministry's priorities. The Minister, it assumes, will want to
keep the bill to a manageable size by excluding 'Real Property
and Conveyancing (Lord Haldane's Bill), Land Registration and
the law of Landlord and Tenant'.[5] So, contrary to Dr Offer's
conclusion, I do not think that it was the post-war collapse of
collectivist plans that scuppered Brickdale this time. The collec-
tivists were never very interested in his prescriptions.

2.   The Acquisition and Valuation of Land Committee comprised mainly lawyers whose experience was with the compulsory purchase of land for public projects. So when it turned to

---

[3] Quoted by Avner Offer, (1977) 40 *MLR* 505, 512.
[4] The following is from the Addison Papers, Bodleian Library, boxes 2, 7, 20,
30, and 33. See also Christopher Addison, *Politics from Within* (1924), and K. O.
Morgan, *Portrait of a Progressive* (1980).
[5] Addison Papers, box 33, 2 Aug. 1918.

questions of conveyancing and registration it was reinforced by
the addition of some conveyancing barristers, plus Sir Walter
Trower, President of The Law Society, and Sir Claud Schuster,
Permanent Secretary of the Lord Chancellor's Office. Foremost
of the conveyancers was the senior Conveyancing Counsel to
the Court, Arthur Underhill, who had been Haldane's sternest
public critic. The agenda was set by Leslie Scott, chairman and
Solicitor-General. It was quite simply to consider whether or
not to adopt the Royal Commission's prescription and, if so,
how.[6] The 'if so' was ornamental. From the first meeting to the
last the Committee adhered to the strategy that the conveyancers had outlined and Haldane had tried to implement—minor
reforms of registered conveyancing, major reforms of the underlying land law to enable unregistered conveyancing to compete
on equal terms, then a trial period, then a choice to be made.
Lay witnesses (not that the Committee took much evidence)
and common-law barristers might be predisposed towards registration, but solicitors and conveyancing barristers were not.[7]
Scott and Schuster tried to move the extension of compulsory
registration into a more prominent place, arguing that only an
apparently simple conveyancing system such as that could provide a middle way between Bolshevism and unthinking conservatism.[8] Other committee members thought this outlandish,
Underhill later ridiculed it publicly, Trower indicated The Law
Society's hostility, and Scott gave way.[9] The Committee stood
for continuity, not for post-war change.

The Committee spent about half its time discussing how to
effect the major reform of the underlying law of real property.
Underhill made his bid at the very beginning. He presented a
paper, 'The Line of Least Resistance', which the Committee at
once found attractive.[10] He reiterated his dislike of complica-

---

[6] Records of Proceedings, 1st Meeting, PRO LCO3/41. Meetings 1–9 are in
this file, 10–17 in LCO3/42.

[7] Alfred F. Topham, *The Law of Property Acts 1925: A Series of Lectures* (1926),
3. He was on the Committee as Scott's legal assistant.

[8] 13th meeting, see n. 6 above; also 16th and 17th meetings.

[9] Ibid.; Underhill, 'The Line of Least Resistance', 33 n. (for publication
details, see n. 10 below).

[10] 1st meeting, see n. 6 above. A typed copy is at PRO LCO3/43, and a
rewritten version is appended to the Committee's report: *Fourth Report of the
Acquisition and Valuation of Land Committee*, (1919) HCP xxix. 89.

tion—see Haldane's dreadful new terminology—and of a code—the experts were so disagreed that even to try would be futile. Attempts in that direction by Charles Sweet and T. C. Williams were far too long and complex. Instead the solution was to turn all freeholds into leaseholds. 'That would do away, *uno flatu*, with all the complexities and anomalies of the existing law of freeholds and copyholds; would abolish tenure and seisin . . ., would render obsolete the existing equitable rules as to conversion between heirs and next of kin; would simplify the administration of assets on death; would unify the law of land . . .' He took himself literally; what he would really have liked was on the stroke of midnight to have declared all freeholds to be million-year leaseholds.[11] That was 'too strong meat for the politicians to swallow', but none the less the bill eventually stemming from the committee's deliberations led with an Underhill clause:[12] every fee simple shall

have all the incidents of a chattel real estate held for a term of years certain, save that such estates shall continue in perpetuity and be called freehold estates in fee simple, while the land affected by this section may be referred to as freehold land.

Underhill's sketch of a bill for the Committee contained fewer than twenty clauses working out this basic proposition.[13]

At this stage the Committee took a decisive turn away from its original brief and towards what became the property legislation of 1922 to 1925.[14] Consequent upon Haldane's mega-bill, several smaller bills working over its uncontroversial aspects had been prepared privately by a group of Lincoln's Inn conveyancers which included A. E. Russell, a member of this committee. He and Benjamin Cherry had written two, one on Trustees, one on Settled Land. Cherry and Liddell, the senior Parliamentary Counsel, had prepared one to abolish copyhold and special tenures, the one reform above all others that The Law Society would have liked implemented. Sweet had written an Intestacy Bill; Cherry a bill on perpetually renewable leases.

---

[11] Sir Arthur Underhill, *Change and Decay*, (1938), 113–14.
[12] Law of Property Bill, (1920) HLP v. 323.
[13] PRO LCO3/43.
[14] 3rd meeting, see n. 6 above; authorship of the bills is from 'Statement of Bills', LCO3/44.

Now it was suggested that a subcommittee be established to consider those bills in conjunction with Underhill's. Trower requested that The Law Society might see them, and Scott asked if The Law Society might like to have someone draft a set of bills on the lines of the 'Haldane/Wolstenholme bill . . . as varied by Mr Underhill'. Russell suggested Cherry. And so it came about, with a subcommittee to do the vetting, consisting of Underhill, Russell, Alfred Topham, once a conveyancer but becoming a general Chancery practitioner,[15] and Trower.

Underhill was fond of his 'little bill',[16] but Cherry's first reaction was to try to ditch it, and with it any structural reform of land law until after the various uncontentious incrementalist bills already prepared in Lincoln's Inn had been passed.[17] Underhill's proposal was 'fantastic' and unworkable. It would impose onerous new restrictions on landowners for very little assistance to purchasers. Cherry proved his point with the aid of those abstruse examples involving settled land well beloved in Lincoln's Inn. Nor could he see how the legal estate could be made the basis of conveyancing and the cornerstone of a reformed land law—too much land was in mortgage, and hence at law too many landowners had nothing but an equity of redemption. To treat the lender as the true owner, sweeping the borrower's equity behind a curtain, would deprive the borrower of all management powers. Then the penny dropped, though someone had to tell Cherry: fantasy Underhill's scheme may have been, but it had solved the mortgage problem.

It will be recalled that the cause of the complexity in Haldane's bill was the inclusion of both some legal estates and some equitable interests in the category of proprietary estates, and that the cause of that was the conveyancers' unwillingness to adopt mortgage by charge in place of mortgage by transfer. Underhill had a similar problem with his assimilation scheme, but his Lincoln's Inn friend Charles Sanger found a solution for him:[18] if

[15] Topham, *The Law of Property Acts 1925*, 1.

[16] Ibid. 4–5, 15.

[17] Benjamin Cherry, 'Memorandum on General Principles of Law Reform', LCO3/44; appendix to Record of 9th meeting, see n. 6 above.

[18] Topham, *The Law of Property Acts 1925*, 76; Cherry sourly told Schuster that he had had the same idea long ago, LCO2/443, Cherry to Schuster, 25 July 1919. The logic is explained in 'Mortgages by demise or sub-demise', LCO2/444, 27 July 1920. For Sanger see Underhill, 'The Line of Least Resistance', 32 n.

the only legal estate is to be the term of years, and if the equity of redemption is not to be elevated to a par with it, then the mortgagor must retain the estate; if the mortgagee is not to have just a list of powers, then he must have an estate; but there is only one sort of estate, so he must have that sort; therefore he must have a lease: and since the mortgagor also has a term, then it must be a sub-term. A very long sub-term: say 3,000 years. But this would be possible even if freeholds were restored. Therefore the mortgagor had no need of protection via a reinforced equity of redemption, therefore Gregory's calculus could be dropped. Hence Cherry could combine his old mentor Wolstenholme's basic scheme with the Bar Council's preference for the terminology of legal estates and equitable interests. Cherry's instinct notwithstanding, Scott's committee could not simply report 'wait'. All that business about Trustee Acts and perpetually renewable leases was way outside its terms of reference. So, with evident misgivings, the subcommittee recommended another mega-bill: a Cherry version of Wolstenholme as mediated by Underhill, plus the Lincoln's Inn set of bills, plus reforms to the registered system.[19] Underhill's clause 1 had been kept, but as Schuster was quick to see,[20] it was now just empty noise.[21]

One unheralded innovation emerged from the subcommittee: radical revision of joint ownership of land.[22] The common law allowed a choice of forms in private transactions: joint tenancy and tenancy in common. Under the first the co-owners comprised, as it were, a single owner with a single title to the property, such that on the death of one co-owner the survivors were taken to constitute that same single owner. With a tenancy in common each co-owner was rather like a separate shareholder: on the death of one tenant in common his share would

---

[19] 'Report of Sub-Committee', LCO3/44 (Schuster was nominally a member, but did not sign).

[20] 7th meeting, see n. 6 above.

[21] Entails, not being recognized by equity, were effectively abolished by Underhill's clause. This shocked even him, and on his assertion that conveyancers would reinvent them in long-winded form, a new rule, now Law of Property Act 1925, s. 130, was enacted allowing personalty to be entailed: Topham, *The Law of Property Acts 1925*, 3. I cannot reconcile this with what seems to have been the common understanding that entails of money could easily be achieved via the equitable doctrine of notional conversion.

[22] 6th, 7th, 8th, and 9th meetings, see n. 6 above; 'Memorandum' by Alfred Topham (at Scott's request), LCO3/44.

be inherited as his will directed. So whereas a joint tenancy would eventually metamorphose into the individual ownership of the survivor, a tenancy in common had a tendency to fragment, as each share could be the subject of individual dealing and subdivision. Further, on each such sub-dealing that share or sub-share would acquire its own title, so that if the land as a whole was to be sold or mortgaged the title to it would have become more complex with the passage of time. None the less, it is clear enough that tenancy in common was the preferred tenure for co-owners, as it is today in other common-law jurisdictions.[23] Throughout the inordinately long investigations into title registration and real property law over the previous decades co-ownership was just about the one aspect that had not been publicly raised as a problem, save in one respect. This concerned the action of Partition, by which one co-owner could compulsorily terminate the co-ownership by applying for a judicial sale. Some lawyers, though by no means all who considered the question, thought that process costly and cumbersome.[24] Accordingly The Law Society's pre-war bills had proposed that co-owners might instead use summary procedure to acquire court-appointed trustees for sale with overreaching powers.[25] But in later versions they dropped the idea, saying that it merited a bill to itself.[26] Nothing was said about it during the Royal Commission's inquiry, or during the discussion of Haldane's bills. Yet now the subcommittee proposed that tenancy in common be abolished as a common-law tenure. Henceforward co-ownership would have to take the form of a joint tenancy, though the land could be held on trusts

---

[23] e.g. Joshua Williams, *Principles of the Law of Real Property* (19th edn., 1901, by T. C. Williams), 139; *Jarman on Wills* (5th edn., 1893), ii. 1123; but abolition was proposed by Thornhill, (1889) 5 *LQR* 11. The common form in conveyances to joint owners was 'as tenants in common and not as joint tenants'. For the USA see *Powell on Real Property*, ed. R. M. Powell and P. J. Rohan, vol 4 A, chs. 49, 50, 51. For Canada, *Anger and Honsberger's Law of Real Property* (2nd edn., 1985, by A. H. Oosterhoff and W. B. Rayner), 789–90. There is a depressing insularity to the discussion between Thompson and Prichard, (1987) 51 Conv. 29, 273, 275.

[24] W. Gregory Walker, *The Partition Acts 1868 and 1876* (1876); (1922) 154 HCD (5th ser.) 139–42, 161–2, 165–7; 155 HCD (5th ser.) 388, 391; (1919–20) 64 *Sol. Jo.* 319, 723; (1920–1) 65 *Sol. Jo.* 8, 166. See Raymond Cock, [1982] Conv. 415.

[25] Conveyancing Bill 1906, cls. 12, 13, (1906) HCP i. 561.

[26] Conveyancing Bill 1910, Memorandum, (1910) HCP i. 223.

for persons as tenants in common in equity. Those trusts, however, would have to be trusts for sale—in which the trustees/joint tenants had a duty to sell the land.

It is not easy to unravel the reasons. Underhill's public defence of the proposition raises more problems than it solves. 'I do not think I fully realized [the question's importance] until I became one of the conveyancing counsel to the Court, on whom the duty falls of examining various titles of tenants in common where property is the subject of an action for partition or sale.'[27] If so it is legitimate to question the frequency of the problem, even if his measure of its seriousness once arisen is accepted. And questioned it was. But since the issue had been absent from the Royal Commission's deliberations there was merely anecdote, not empirical evidence. Yet it is clear that Cherry, Russell, and Trower did see tenancy in common as a problem, so much so that there was little articulation of what it was. Secondly, Underhill's explanation of the solution to the problem is very puzzling:

It is by no means uncommon to find the equitable title split into 50 or 60 parts, most of them mortgaged, and some of them settled, and the elusive legal estate so hidden as to be almost beyond the wit of man to discover. Where this is the case, nothing less than an action will suffice to cut the Gordian knot, and when (as frequently happens) the property is small—a few houses or a small farm—the costs of the necessary enquiries leave little to be divided between the unfortunate beneficiaries.[28]

Perhaps so: but in this example it appears that a trust already exists—so how would imposing a statutory trust make a difference? Perhaps it is because a statutory trust (be it trust for sale or settlement) would enable a sale to be made without court consent, a privatization of the sale process as it were, so that court fees would be saved. But Underhill's emphasis was equally upon the costs of the process needed to sort out the entanglement of multiple interests, which would remain untouched by his new structure. Both these criticisms were raised, but neither was ever answered.[29] Nor was a more subtle

---

[27] (1920) 37 *LQR* 107, 116.
[28] Ibid.
[29] See materials cited in n. 24 above.

objection properly tackled: in a conveyancing context, fragmentation of the legal estate is a problem only if there is difficulty in discovering the whereabouts of the fragments, which would be most likely where the tenancy in common arose on a death. But the Land Transfer Act 1897 had required land to devolve via an executor or administrator who must then convey legal title to the successors by regular legal document, leaving an easy documentary trail. So the problem would be diminishing, as indeed Alfred Topham acknowledged in his memorandum on the question to the subcommittee. Many roots of title would predate that Act, but the subcommittee also proposed to reduce the required period for investigating title to thirty years, which would further alleviate the difficulty. On the other hand, with the assimilation of intestate succession, such that intestate primogeniture would finally be abolished, more tenancies in common might arise. Yet in Kent, the one county whose local tenure already required partible intestate succession, the local law society thought the resulting tenancies in common unproblematic.[30] Seen as a conveyancing problem it is a puzzle. Close scrutiny of 'The Line of Least Resistance' suggests that Underhill himself had been content with some variant of The Law Society's proposal, and that his advocacy of the trust for sale reflected simply his wish for the package to be accepted.[31]

The conveyancers' first stab at a solution to whatever they thought the problem to be was to bring the tenancy in common under the provisions of the Settled Land Act.[32] In that way there would be someone with the statutory powers to overreach equitable interests on a sale, thereby making good title. But who should have those powers? A majority of the co-owners by value, was the first proposal—who would nominate the neces-

[30] Hohler, 154 HCD (5th ser.) 166–7; Memorandum of Kent Law Society, LCO2/448, and Cherry's reply, ibid. Cherry was particularly abusive about the Kent secretary: LCO2/449, Cherry to Birkenhead, 23 Feb. 1922. Underhill thought the probable increase in tenancies in common after the intestacy reforms important, LCO2/443, Underhill to Schuster, 9 Mar. 1920.

[31] See esp. p. 32, where it is unclear whether he is making one point or two. The sentence beginning 'That procedure . . .' was inserted later. His example in that paragraph is very close to Cherry's, see n. 32 below.

[32] For this para. see Records of 6th, 7th, 8th, and 9th meetings, see n. 6 above; Topham's 'Memorandum', n. 22 above. Cherry's example was given at the 9th meeting.

sary trustees. But suppose, said Benjamin Cherry, settled land devised to, say, a dozen daughters in tail equally as tenants in common, with cross-remainders in tail, and that some of their shares had been sub-settled, and others mortgaged . . . it would be just as difficult to decide who had the powers as it is now to effect a partition. Far better to use a trust for sale, which also passed good title, and vest the fee in an arbitrary number of trustees, or the Public Trustee perhaps. But since the situation that seems to have bothered the conveyancers involved a combination of an inheritance tenancy in common and land already settled, this trust for sale was to be machinery only. The trustees for sale were to have only the management powers provided by the Settled Land Act that they would have had if that Act's machinery had proved more amenable. And so it came to pass.

The main committee acquiesced, though why is anyone's guess. One member had his own reasons. When the plan became public Brickdale wrote to Schuster doubting that a problem existed.[33] Rare cases, of course; but he had met no difficulties, and if any did arise registration would cope perfectly satisfactorily with them in future, as it had done in the past. Why, on his investigations into continental registration systems he had come across a title divided into millionths, but it took only half an hour for the local registrar to sort it out. Schuster silenced him:

I may of course be unduly impressed by my own circumstances. I have the misery to be the owner of an undivided share in a block of buildings in Manchester which is already owned in forty sections and will on the occasion of the next death run into hundreds. The difficulty of managing the property and dealing with the tenant is immense. It is almost a commercial impossibility to effect necessary improvements, and the lawyers' bill year by year swallows up an enormous proportion of the gross rental. There is no difficulty in the title . . .[34]

3.   Unsurprisingly the Land Acquisition Committee's report in November 1919 endorsed the priorities settled by Haldane and

---

[33] LCO2/443, 'Lord Cave's Objections and Observations Thereon', 8 Mar. 1920.
[34] LCO2/443, Schuster to Brickdale, 9 Mar. 1920.

the Royal Commission.[35] Title registration needed improvement before extension beyond London, but, as the Royal Commission had said, extension was a national matter not suitable for something as parochial as a county council's veto. But on the other hand, solicitors' fees were not excessive, and had not even been so when the 1882 scale was introduced; a system of private conveyancing should be devised that would give them the advantages of a modernized law presently enjoyed by the Registrar so that they could attempt to better him in fair competition. The Committee's working assumption had been that there would be a two-year trial period, followed by an inquiry; though who should be entitled to call for the inquiry was contentious. Cherry had attended several of the Committee's meetings, and his influence on the Report is obvious. He promised that he could produce a version of Haldane's bill shorn of complexity, without novel terminology, and without the cumbrous register of cautions and inhibitions for beneficial interests. The Committee accepted; there was no other way in which a bill could be produced within the time allotted.[36]

Yet though the bill was available and had been seen at least by the subcommittee, it was not published until a month after the Report. Scott knew that the Committee had exceeded its brief by including so much on trustees, intestacy, and the like, and though he assented to the Lincoln's Inn *coup* he did so on the basis that the Committee need not confer its public blessing on what had become another mega-bill.[37] So the Report just sketched the bill in general terms, though disclosing the innovations concerning mortgages and joint ownership. But Underhill's 'Line of Least Resistance' was appended, rewritten a little from the original version, giving the impression that his had been the philosophy adopted. This caused some trouble, especially as when the bill was first published it did still retain Underhill's first clause.

The Report promised, and the bill[38] provided, a short list of legal estates and interests. The fee simple and the term of years

---

[35] *Fourth Report of the Acquisition and Valuation of Land Committee*, (1919) HCP xxix. 89.
[36] Ibid., para. 24.
[37] Record of 9th and 13th meetings, see n. 6 above.
[38] Law of Property Bill, (1920) HLP v. 323.

would be legal, but everything else would be equitable only, and those were listed to make doubly sure. Moreover, the manner of creation of equitable interests was stipulated— essentially they needed trusts for sale or settlements, with very limited exceptions. Where land was settled the fee simple would vest in the limited owner. On the whole, only legal things would concern a purchaser on a sale. Between the purchaser and equitable interests a 'curtain' was to fall shielding them from his view. They were internal matters only, not his business, and hence things into which he did not have to inquire. His conveyancing costs would thus be kept down, and with the list of relevant matters so short the chance of a difficulty arising that might need really expert help was greatly reduced. More will be said about the curtain later. Whereas the Wolstenholme/ Haldane bills had provided protection for beneficiaries through registration of cautions and inhibitions, Cherry proposed instead that no transaction should defeat their interest unless the resulting purchase money were paid to two trustees or to a corporation. It had been a commonplace that trustee fraud virtually only arose where a single trustee had the title. The gist of the bill was the same as Haldane's, the same as Wolstenholme's, and much as the 'Institute' and the Bar Council had wanted in 1913.

Among those to take fright at Underhill's 'somewhat violent proposals' was Haldane, who was surprised that the Committee had taken them seriously.[39] It had not; and Haldane was disabused by Cherry, who from this time on made it clear that clause 1 would never be allowed into law.[40] 'The Line of Least Resistance' was not a contribution to serious law reform in his eyes.[41] Muir Mackenzie, a friend of the late Sir Philip Gregory, must have queried whether such a departure from the Haldane bill was really necessary, because Cherry wrote soothing him too: Sir Philip would have approved it all, he said.[42]

[39] LCO2/443, Haldane to Birkenhead, 22 Jan. 1920.
[40] LCO2/443, Cherry to Schuster, 22 Jan. 1920; [B. Cherry], draft 'Reply to the Institute's Report', LCO2/444, 27 July 1920, paras. 2, 18.
[41] LCO2/443, Cherry to Muir Mackenzie, 23 Feb. 1920, a most informative letter.
[42] Ibid. Gregory died in 1918; obit., (1918–19) 63 *Sol. Jo.* 36.

4. Some of the lawyers' proposals caused lay controversy.[43] The abolition of copyhold raised disputes about the costs of buying out manorial incidents, compensation for loss of stewardships, custody of manorial court records. Mineral rights were difficult, as were rights of common, though the latter were an addendum not originating with the lawyers. Some proposals united lawyers' and lay interest, notably the abolition of the county council veto on extensions of compulsory title registration, to which we will return. But in the professional press and amongst the Lincoln's Inn conveyancers it was Part I of the bill, containing the proposed structural changes to real property law, that caused the trouble.

The *Solictors' Journal* had not thought much of Underhill's technique.[44] He was 'looking at what can be done without any great effort rather than the perfection of the thing done,' it said, his solutions 'a mere device'. But since he had evidently persuaded the Committee, the *Journal*'s conclusion was pessimistic: 'it may be that this is the best that can be done, and that leading conveyancers of the present day are willing to have their names associated with make-believe legislation of this kind.' When the bill appeared the *Solicitors' Journal* took no pains to hide its disappointment. It thought it short on principle and long on facile devices. Why could we not have a code, it asked? If estates were to be abolished, why could not the code be couched in terms of ownership of land itself? Why cannot mortgagees simply have a charge? Why must simplifying principles always get cluttered up with so many detailed alterations and amendments of technical points of conveyancing law, the effect of which is invariably to *increase* the quantity of legal rules? Can there really be no break away from the continuous cycle of amendment and re-amendment of the Settled Land Act, the Trustee Act, and the Conveyancing Act? When, please, will we get a 'well-thought-out and arranged scheme of statute law'? Why do we never start by looking at the numerous extensive reforms of conveyancing achieved in the colonies? It acknowledged the purpose, that private conveyancing should be able to

---

[43] Details are in PRO LCO2/443–9, esp. 447. Cherry negotiated a separate bill for mineral royalty owners, ibid., 449 *passim*.

[44] For this para. see: (1919–20) 64 *Sol. Jo.* 203, 219, 249, 286, 320 (praise), 373, 408, 439, 632 (axe); cf. (1920–1) 65 *Sol. Jo.* 598.

compete with registration on equal terms pending a final decision, and it recognized too that the forms instituted by the bills might achieve such simplicity of practice that registration might be halted. It once even congratulated the Lord Chancellor on this 'well devised measure'. But its heart was with Cyprian Williams and the codifiers. If this was the best that could be done, 'the next reformer will come with a very sharp axe'.

The Bar Council delegated its consideration of the bill to a special committee of the conveyancers' 'Institute', afforced by a couple of its own representatives.[45] One of these, Malcolm Macnaghten, became intermediary between 'Institute' and Lord Chancellor's Office as the battle lines were quickly drawn. His own sympathies were much the same as the *Solicitors' Journal's*. 'I trust that you will carry your registration proposal,' he wrote to Schuster. 'I only wish I could understand Part I.'[46] He had seen Williams's 1912 bill, which he did find intelligible. But alas, it was a difficult bill, Williams would not get on with Cherry, and he apparently regarded the present bill as the outcome of a corrupt bargain between Law Society and Registrar, a remark which Macnaghten did not understand but which he recognized as foreclosing co-operation.[47] Major Hills, as he had become during the war, agreed to support the bill in the Commons, but hankered still for the sort of thoroughgoing assimilation scheme he had proposed to both Royal Commission and Scott's committee.[48] The Law Society was anxious for some bill to pass, and when asked, would say that it supported this one whole-heartedly.[49] But it was taking Cherry's word for its effect; it

---

[45] Its report is reprinted at (1919–20) 64 *Sol. Jo.* 741; copy at PRO LCO2/444. It was the work of a special subcommittee, since four members of the regular committee helped draft the bill: LCO2/450, Cruikshank to Schuster, 20 May 1920, where a further report is appended.

[46] LCO2/450, Macnaghten to Schuster, 15 Oct. 1920; see also LCO2/445, Macnaghten to Schuster, 10 Aug. 1920, where he complains that Part I ought to be made intelligible to ordinary people.

[47] Dr Offer makes a lot of this remark, (1977) 40 *MLR* 505, 516.

[48] LCO2/447, Longmore to Schuster, 20 Apr. 1921; (1922) 154 HCD (5th ser.) 124. Hills's memorandum is at LCO3/43.

[49] Anxious: LCO2/445, Trower to Schuster, 27 July 1920; support: LCO2/445, Schuster to Trower, 28 July 1920 (2nd letter); 'Statement', LCO2/446, 9 Mar. 1921; LCO2/448, *passim* (against the Land Union). Its preference had been for Underhill: 'Sir W. Trower's Memorandum', LCO2/43; 'Preliminary Report of Land Transfer Committee of the Law Society', ibid., 21 Mar. 1919.

never went as far as showing enthusiasm for the text,[50] nor did anyone else. The bill was just unprincipled; in the words of the *Solicitors' Journal* it was opportunistic.[51]

It is unfortunately necessary to consider the bill in some technical detail. One cannot understand either the opposition it aroused, the ensuing compromise, or the peculiarities of the modern law without it. After Underhill's clause 1, clause 2 provided the short new list of things legal. Leave clause 3 for a moment. Clause 4 introduced a second major theme, the limitation of equitable interests. It is here reproduced in a paraphrased and simplified form:

(1) After the commencement of this Act, an equitable interest in or over land shall only be capable of being created by means of:

    (*a*) a declaration of trust of the proceeds of land held on trust for sale; or

    (*b*) a settlement; or

    (*c*) a statute—but unless the land is held on trust for sale the effect shall be that the land becomes settled land, with the statute acting as the settlement; or

    (*d*) a deposit of documents; or

    (*e*) a covenant or agreement restrictive of the user of the land, capable of affecting a purchaser with notice thereof.

(2) And, in particular, subsection (1) shall apply to:

    (*a*) interests in tail;

    (*b*) conditional, base, and determinable fees;

    (*c*) interests under executory devises etc.;

    (*d*) interests created under a springing or shifting trust;

    (*e*) interests for life or pur autre vie;

    (*f*) undivided shares in land;

    (*g*) any interest created by a will;

    (*h*) all estates, interests, or charges in favour of an infant in or over land, as well as all other interests in land nor capable of being created under this Act as legal estates.

(3) Attempts to bypass these restrictions shall operate only as

---

[50] LCO2/446, Cherry to Schuster, 15 Dec. 1920.
[51] (1919–20) 64 *Sol. Jo.* 249; and cf. ibid. 220.

agreements to give effect to the transaction by means of a trust for sale or settlement, and a purchaser shall not be concerned with them provided that any capital money arising on the transaction is paid to trustees.

(4) All this is subject to the express savings in Part I . . .

among which were those carried over from previous bills and still retained in the 1925 Act: persons acquiring interests by limitation or prescription, persons entitled to interests by virtue of possessing documents of title, and, relegated now to the status of a mere saving, the interests of any person 'in possession or actual occupation of land to which he may be entitled in right of such possession or occupation'.

Even this is a lot to swallow. But swallowed it was, with a Parliamentary Joint Select Committee established to scrutinize the bill being content merely to tidy up the loose ends.[52] In particular, it elaborated clause 4 by adding a new subclause making its reach even clearer:

4(4) Where an equitable interest arises by way of estoppel, lien or otherwise by operation of law. then if the land is subject to a trust for sale, the equitable interest shall attach to the proceeds of sale in like manner as if created by a trust affecting those proceeds, but where there is no trust for sale the equitable interest shall take effect as if the same land had been limited by a settlement, and the land shall be deemed settled land.

On a sale of land subject to a trust for sale or settlement, a purchaser would take free from equitable interests provided that he paid the purchase money to two trustees or to a corporation. For a settlement, the transaction had also to be within the limited owner's Settled Land Act powers. Schuster and The Law Society wanted these expanded to include all powers of an absolute owner, but the conveyancers had said no.[53]

We can return now to clause 3. In part it was transitional, sweeping existing equitable interests into the regime introduced by clause 4. But its subclause (3) was a future-looking catch-all:

---

[52] Report of the Joint Select Committee on the Law of Property Bill, (1920) HLP viii. 199; repr. (1919–20) 64 *Sol. Jo.* 631. Membership is listed at ibid, 351, and included Haldane, Buckmaster, Muir Mackenzie, and Hills.

[53] 7th meeting, see n. 6 above; 'Preliminary Report of the Land Transfer Committee of the Law Society', PRO LCO3/44, 21 Mar. 1919.

(3) In every case where, at the commencement or by virtue of this Act, there is no trust for sale (either created independently or by virtue of this Act) the estates, interests and charges which are or have by this Act been converted into equitable interests shall take effect as if the same had been limited by a settlement, the land shall be deemed settled land, and the instrument (if any) creating [them] shall be deemed the settlement . . . and, where necessary, trustees of the settlement shall be appointed . . .

There were further subclauses designed to ease the passing of title to purchasers, then the clause ended by excluding restrictive covenants from its scope, and anticipating the general savings contained at the conclusion of clause 4. Clauses 3 and 4 together were called by some commentators 'the universal curtain', and one can see why.

Two things can be said about this bill. First, its regime was all-embracing. Secondly, the style was quite different from Gregory's, who had taken pains to spell out directly in Haldane's bill not only what property interests could exist but also what could be done with them and what were the effects of their interaction in the various transactions henceforward to be permitted. This bill had no such clause spelling out the effect of all its provisions, nor did it speak in principles. Instead it used formulas. It did not explain how trusts for sale, settlements, or deemed-leaseholds operated, beyond stating their effect in just one context; it just recited words that would make them do so. It did not provide fall-back principles to help guide later generations in difficult or novel situations. Instead it was legislation by reference: if real property is a nuisance, deem it to be something that is not a nuisance; if equitable interests are a nuisance, deem there to be devices for getting rid of them. But in each case the 'something' or the 'device' already existed either in the law or, at least as often, simply in Lincoln's Inn conveyancing practice. No wonder Macnaghten felt out of it.

Outright opposition came from the 'Institute'[54] and, crucially, from Viscount Cave, a Law Lord and sometime senior Conservative politician. Cave had criticized Part I at second reading

[54] See report, (1919–20) 64 *Sol. Jo.* 741; copy at PRO LCO2/444.

stage.[55] He disliked all these trusts; he saw no harm in life estates; he feared that trustees provided less protection than the bill's sponsors thought—did not we all know about the numerous frauds perpetrated by trustees of stocks and shares? He disliked all those artificial trusts for sale: he thought that existing co-ownership law worked reasonably well. He hoped that these points of principle would be considered by the Joint Select Committee. But they had not been, so when the bill was recommitted to the Lords[56] Cave moved an amendment to omit the whole of Part I. Birkenhead, the Lord Chancellor, said at once that he supported him (internal departmental negotiation had reached no conclusion).[57] Haldane and Buckmaster were quick to protest: Part I was the essence of the bill, the heart and substance without which it was not worth proceeding; perhaps other ways *could* be found of reforming the law, but that was always true—whichever course was adopted there would always be people to press for a different one. Muir Mackenzie lamented the long hours he had spent on the bill, to the detriment of his health. But Birkenhead was unmoved: a change of this magnitude needed more widespread assent than it had got. He agreed that the bill was worthless without Part I, but hoped that further discussions with the 'very able gentlemen with whom Lord Cave has been co-operating' would produce a new one that would be acceptable. The amendment carried without a division. The *Solicitor's Journal* applauded the outcome, saying truly that Haldane had only himself to blame for the waste of the Joint Select Committee's time. He had been its chairman; it could and should have considered these matters of principle.[58]

Dr Offer thinks the motivation economic, seizing upon an exasperated outburst from Cherry.[59] The new law would be so simple that the conveyancing barristers would be put out of work. Well, perhaps they believed that, though there is no evidence either way. Cherry did not: in the same letter he wrote

[55] (1920) 39 HLD 270 ff.
[56] (1920) 41 HLD 486 ff.
[57] LCO2/443, Brickdale: 'Lord Cave's Objections and Observations Thereon', 8 Mar. 1920; Underhill to Schuster, 9 Mar. 1920; LCO2/444 (whole file).
[58] (1919–20) 64 *Sol. Jo.* 680.
[59] Offer, (1977) 40 *MLR* 505, 516, quoting Cherry to Schuster, LCO2/444, 22 July 1920.

(and not to one of the brotherhood) that there would be plenty for them to do.[60] And such an explanation would not fit Cave. He had been a conveyancer in his youth,[61] but that is no reason for his favouring the 'Institute' rather than Cherry & Co., who had drafted the bills and were themselves conveyancers. Cave got so quickly off the mark that he looks to have been reacting purely personally at first; and his opposition no doubt intensified when the Joint Select Committee which scrutinized the bill did not ask him to appear before it—slighting for a member of the Royal Commission. In the eyes of Christopher Addison, Minister for Reconstruction and a politician poles apart from him, Cave habitually saw difficulties not apparent to anyone else;[62] and, if anything, as negotiations with him continued over Part I he became even more obdurate.[63] I expect that he did co-operate with the 'Institute', but the conveyancer he used to formulate his main point of opposition was not a member of its committee, it was Edward Benn, a conveyancer who hitherto had been part of Cherry's team and who reverted to that role later.[64] Eventually Birkenhead nominated Benn to represent Cave in a small group instructed to find a compromise, Haldane to umpire.[65] The 'Institute' was excluded.

Since the bill represented a *coup* by a very small group of conveyancers it is unsurprising that those excluded took against it. Malcolm Macnaghten and Arthur Underhill thought the committee of the 'Institute' united only in opposition.[66] Some

[60] Cherry, ibid. Conveyancers as a separate subset faded away after 1925: Underhill (1935) 51 *LQR* 221, 222 n.; Lincoln's Inn did not become noticeably emptier.

[61] He edited George Sweet's *Concise Precedents in Conveyancing* (3rd edn., 1884), and *Gale on Easements* (6th edn., 1888; 7th edn., 1889).

[62] Christopher Addison, *Politics from Within* (1924), ii. 244 and *passim*.

[63] LCO2/445, Cherry to Schuster, 28 Oct. 1920; and cf. ibid., Benn to Cherry, 29 Oct. 1920; Cave to Birkenhead, 14 Nov. 1920.

[64] LCO2/445, Cave to Birkenhead, 4 Aug. 1920. Benn's Memorandum is reprinted in (1919–20) 64 *Sol. Jo.* 694, copies at LCO2/444 and LCO2/458; its para. 15 states his law-reforming credentials. Cherry took his memorandum very seriously: LCO2/445, Cherry to Schuster, 9 Aug. 1920 (detailed memo in reply), ditto, 15 Nov. 1920.

[65] LCO2/445, Schuster to Cherry, 16 Nov. 1920, implying that Birkenhead had backed Cherry.

[66] LCO2/444, Macnaghten to Schuster, 25 Apr. 1920; LCO2/445, ditto, 5 Aug. 1920, 13 Aug. 1920. He always emphasized the good faith of the 'Institute'. LCO2/444, Underhill to Schuster, 1 May 1920; LCO2/445, Underhill to Cherry, 29 July 1920. Also LCO2/444, Cherry to Schuster, 26 Apr. 1920.

members wanted a more ambitious, principled, assimilation scheme; some opposed so as to block the extension of compulsory registration; and some were simply very conservative—Cherry unkindly called them the grandmothers.[67] Their criticisms were as far-reaching as Cave's, but unlike him they had no easy access to Birkenhead. After arduous and often acrimonious exchanges of memoranda, Cherry wore them down, partly by relentless countering of their arguments and partly by challenging them to produce a better scheme.[68] This divided them and exposed their unwillingness to commit the time needed—indeed, they protested to Schuster that to expect them to be legislators was unreasonable.[69] Cave was a more powerful man, and at first seemed to object to everything in Part I. But Cherry learned from Benn that if he gave up the 'curtain', which had a wide unpopularity among conveyancers, Cave would let him keep everything else of value.[70] The 'deemed leasehold' clause had been destined for abandonment all along, so now was as good a time as any to surrender it. Mortgage by long lease was kept, so too was the abolition of legal tenancies in common, though the new co-ownership system was less obviously part of a coherent whole now that the universal curtain had gone. This compromise became the 1921 bill[71] and eventually the Law of Property Act 1922.

'That Part I of the Bill of last year was as bold an innovation as was desired we are not prepared to say,' wrote the *Solicitors' Journal* in judgment,[72] 'that the present bill falls far short of the reform of real property law which is urgently required we can

---

[67] LCO2/444, Cherry to Schuster, 20 May 1920. Apart from Part I their target was the reform of intestacy—ditto 23 June 1920; Underhill to Cherry, 15 July 1920; LCO2/448, Cherry to Schuster, 25 July 1921. (Cherry's remark, meant unkindly against the conservative conveyancers, was, of course, gratuitously offensive to women.)

[68] LCO2/445, *passim*.

[69] LCO2/445, Cruikshank to Schuster, 28 July 1920, 30 July 1920.

[70] LCO2/445, Cherry to Schuster, 28 Oct. 1920; Cherry was most reluctant, proposing merely a 'rearrangement' of Part I: ditto, 15 Nov. 1920. For 'unpopular' see ibid., Underhill to Cherry, 29 July 1920, Newsom to Schuster, 5 Aug. 1920; but cf. John Lightwood to Cherry, ibid., 4 Sept. 1920. Benn himself approved the principle, but thought the clauses incomprehensible, ibid., Macnaghten to Schuster, 5 Aug. 1920.

[71] Law of Property Bill, (1921) HLP iii. 1.

[72] (1920–1) 65 *Sol. Jo.* 409. Cherry's attempts to influence the *Sol. Jo.* (LCO2/445, Cherry to Schuster, 9 Aug. 1920) did not deflect it for long.

say with much confidence.' 'Mr Underhill's scheme was not put forward as a sufficient reform, but as giving the most that was practicable.' Now whatever theoretical coherence it had had was gone.

The major target of this criticism was the new clause 3, the substitute for the universal curtain. Clause 4 was gone, so nothing now said that all life interests and all tenancies in common had to subsist behind trusts for sale or settlements. Nor had the catch-all clause 3(3) survived. Its replacement said something quite different:

3(3)(iii) where the legal estate affected thereby is not subject to a trust for sale or a settlement, then, if the estate owner conveys his estate to a corporation, or to two or more individuals approved either by the persons in whom the equitable interests or powers aforesaid are vested, or by the court, upon trust for sale with or without power to postpone the sale, such equitable interests and powers shall, according to their priorities, have the like protection as if created or arising by means of a primary trust affecting the proceeds of sale and the income of the land until sale.

And even where there was a settlement or trust for sale created under this section, overreaching in at least some circumstances would be conditional on the consent of the equitable owner concerned. So not only had the universal curtain gone, but beneficiaries were sometimes being given a priority over purchasers that they had not enjoyed under the first bill. In addition the new clause contained an innovation: newly created restrictive covenants, equitable easements, and estate contracts[73] would require registration at the Land Registry if they were to bind purchasers, and local land charges would in future be registered there too. It concluded with the same savings for persons in possession, limitation interests, and the like that had been excluded from its precursor.

All in all this was a very considerable climb-down by Cherry. Further, the clause was drafted in excruciatingly difficult style— almost as though it was designed to conceal what had happened. The *Solicitors' Journal* thought it a horror, scarcely com-

---

[73] Not an innovation. Previous practice to protect a contract intended to remain executory for longer than usual was to issue a writ and then register a *lis pendens*: Sir Benjamin Cherry, *The New Property Acts* (1925), 47.

prehensible even to experts and far beyond the wit of laymen. It 'will impose on private conveyancing a heavy handicap in its competition with registration',[74] because far from overreaching being universal, it often now depended upon the prior establishment of an *ad hoc* settlement or trust for sale. None the less it became law. But it had to wait a year. In 1921 the compromise bill was pushed through the Lords but would have sunk in the Commons.[75] The Land Union threatened to upset the other compromise reached, on compulsory registration, discussed below. Kent and Hampshire Law Societies belatedly found fault with various provisions previously approved by The Law Society and the Associated Provincial Law Societies. There was general grumbling that for a bill of such importance too little time had been left for Commons consideration. Birkenhead withdrew it. Cherry and Schuster did a deal with the Land Union. Cherry soothed the law societies and, at last, the bill became the Law of Property Act 1922.

5.   For Brickdale obviously, Birkenhead and Scott probably, the point of the exercise was to extend compulsory registration of title.[76] On the whole the barristers on Scott's committee had not disagreed, but Trower for The Law Society had. The official plan, which Trower did not seriously contest at this stage, was to restore the position that would have obtained under the 1897 Act if the last-minute deal with Yorkshire had not been necessary. So whereas under that Act an extension order could be made only on request from a county council, the 1920 bill provided that the Privy Council could propose an extension. In practice, of course, that meant the Registrar in conjunction with the Treasury. A county council or local law society could then demand an inquiry, but the Lord Chancellor, who then had to consider the question, was not obliged to abide by its recommendation. He must however lay his proposed Order before both Houses of Parlia-

[74] (1921–2) 66 *Sol. Jo.* 345; similarly (1920–1) 65 *Sol. Jo.* 412.
[75] For what follows see: PRO LCO2/447, 448 *passim*; (1920–1) 65 *Sol. Jo.* 543, 564, 787; (1921–2) 66 *Sol. Jo.* 425 (Leeds LS); (1921) 44 HLD 648 ff., 965 ff.; 45 HLD 310. Both Haldane's side and Cave thought the new Part I's only virtue was that it was a compromise. Cave continued to grumble even after becoming Lord Chancellor: (1922–3) 67 *Sol. Jo.* 159, 174.
[76] 10th to 17th meetings, see n. 6 above.

ment under the 'positive laying' procedure, whereby both had to give their approval before the measure became law. No such Order was to be made in the first three years after the bill was passed. If an area asked for extension of compulsory registration, then an Order could be made after due notice had been given and any representations considered.

First off the mark to protest was the West Riding of Yorkshire, which had earlier sent a representative to plead its special case to Scott's committee.[77] Brickdale, though he professed his inability to understand these northern people, journeyed to Leeds to reason with them but returned empty-handed. They were more arrogant than even he had expected, he told Schuster in dismay.[78] But the Riding's concerns were parochial, and a deal was done whereby financial compensation would be forthcoming if the local deeds registry were replaced by a title registry. Vague promises were given about a local title registry office, but the Treasury ensured that they stopped well short of promising local control.[79] Once the bill was published, however, several other county councils protested, and opposition quickly coalesced. Dr Offer sees it as aroused at the solicitors' behest.[80] To me the papers he uses are inconclusive because they contain only the opinions of Cherry and Schuster to that effect. It was in their interest to claim to see just one opponent with one set of financial interests rather than two with complementary interests, especially since Parliament might be expected to disregard opposition if it could be pinned on the solicitors. On a later occasion Cherry similarly alleged that lawyers' manipulation lay behind opposition from the Land Union. After it had been quelled he acknowledged that its equating bureaucracy with socialism had actually been the cause.[81] On the other hand it is

[77] 9th meeting see n. 6 above; Memorandum of Yorkshire Union of Law Societies, LCO3/45; LCO2/450, *passim* (Mar. 1920 onwards).

[78] LCO2/450, Brickdale to Schuster, 17 May 1920, 31 May 1920; Schuster to Brickdale, 19 May 1920. Brickdale's public service ethic stopped him seeing that the issue concerned power (ibid., Brickdale to Schuster, 25 Mar. 1920), so Yorkshire bluntness shocked him.

[79] LCO2/450, esp. Schuster to Brickdale, 19 May 1920; Law of Property Act 1922, s. 183(6), (7).

[80] (1977) 40 *MLR* 505, 518, and sources cited.

[81] LCO2/447, Cherry to Schuster, 18 Mar. 1921; LCO2/448, Cherry to Schuster, 17 June 1921; LCO2/449, Cherry to Birkenhead, 23 Feb. 1922; but see materials at n. 66 above.

certainly true, as Dr Offer says, that once The Law Society had reached agreement with the Lord Chancellor it quickly got the County Councils Association to withdraw its opposition.

The Lord Chancellor won the first round of this contest. In July 1920 Viscount Galway's amendment to maintain the *status quo* was defeated by government whipping.[82] But since on that very night Part I had fallen on Cave's amendment, the bill was withdrawn anyway. The Law Society moved quickly to obtain a better deal for itself.[83] What it got was another compromise. The three-year embargo on compulsion orders was extended to ten, but the positive laying procedure was dropped. To stop a draft Order becoming law, once having been presented to Parliament, would now take an express motion from one House or the other. Such was the clause included in the 1921 bill. But no sooner had it been introduced than the Land Union announced its opposition to registration and began to campaign against it.[84] Cherry blamed his arch-enemy in the 'Institute', George Cruikshank, and looked to the solicitors for help.[85] They did what they could, but another deal was necessary and another year lost. In return for dropping their opposition the Land Union achieved the restoration of the positive laying procedure, duly written into the 1922 bill. This it seems was Cherry's achievement, through the agency of Brickdale and Liddell.[86]

'Brickdale and I are, as you know, the greatest of friends,' wrote Cherry to Schuster, '. . . at the same time he would be the last person to claim any special knowledge of the general law of conveyancing . . .'.[87] Curiously though, Brickdale seems to have been marginalized within the Lord Chancellor's office, even

[82] (1921) 41 HLD 512 ff.; LCO2/450, Schuster to Lord Hylton, 10 July 1920, 12 July 1920; Hylton to Schuster, 11 July 1920.

[83] LCO2/445, Trower to Schuster, 30 July 1920. For related issues see ibid., Cherry to Schuster, 28 Oct. 1920 and ensuing correspondence; the compromise is relayed by Schuster to Cherry at LCO2/446, 17 Dec. 1920.

[84] LCO2/447, 448 *passim.*

[85] See n. 81 above; LCO2/447, Trower to Schuster, 8 Apr. 1921; Schuster to Trower, 20 Apr. 1921. There is so much evidence in LCO2/447 and 448 that The Law Society stood by its compromise that I decline Dr Offer's implication that it, Cherry, and the Land Union were acting collusively.

[86] LCO2/447, Cherry to Schuster, 4 May 1921.

[87] LCO2/447, 21 Apr. 1921.

where he obviously did have expert knowledge. Nothing he suggested seems to have come to fruition and, as far as can be told, in negotiations with solicitors, the Land Union, and Yorkshire interests Schuster's was the dominant voice. Brickdale had gone along with the proposed two-year embargo; and he had even resisted a suggestion that compulsory registration be extended to transmission on death.[88] But at the slightest sign of backtracking from the solicitors he was urging a five-year plan for national compulsory registration, now apparently a necessary part of any 'land for the people policy'.[89] When that failed he badgered Schuster to get the Lord Chancellor to cajole Surrey, Kent, Sussex, Essex, and Hertfordshire voluntarily into the registered system. Schuster had to tell him to stop alarming their friends.[90] Though convinced that only solicitors blocked his way, Brickdale was so anxious to regain the initiative from the county councils that he offered a new fee structure in return, under which lay persons using the Registry would pay substantially higher fees than those employing solicitors.[91] 'He is certainly an enthusiast,' wrote Macnaghten, bemused.[92] But unlike Cherry he did not get his way.

Dr Offer sees Cherry as The Law Society's tool.[93] It was he who 'casually' mentioned to Schuster as early as April 1920 that The Law Society would settle for a ten-year embargo.[94] That plus his willingness to draft amendments for The Law Society 'side' while being the 'government's draftsman' is sure proof for Dr Offer that Cherry was a Law Society cuckoo in the Lord Chancellor's nest. And he implies that Cherry had a grievance for not yet having been paid. I do not see it like that. The point about payment is obviously bad. Cherry's very extensive preparatory

---

[88] 4th meeting, see n. 6 above.

[89] LCO2/450, Brickdale to Birkenhead, 11 Oct. 1920, in response to the speech of LS President C. H. Morton, (1920–1) 65 *Sol. Jo.* 8.

[90] LCO2/450, Brickdale to Schuster, 7 Apr. 1921; Schuster to Brickdale, 9 Apr. 1921.

[91] LCO2/450, Brickdale to Birkenhead, 11 Oct. 1920.

[92] LCO2/450, Macnaghten to Schuster, 15 Oct. 1920.

[93] (1977) 40 *MLR* 505, esp. 511, 517–20.

[94] LCO2/444, Cherry to Schuster, 26 Apr. 1920; also Underhill to Schuster, 1 May 1920. Dr Offer tars Underhill with the same brush, but is wrong to say that his article in the *LQR* in 1920 was commissioned. Instead, after writing it, Underhill sent a copy to Birkenhead asking for comments (there were none, of course): LCO2/443, Underhill to Schuster, 9 Mar. 1920.

work was done with Russell and others in the hope that an opportunity would present itself.[95] They were working for themselves, not for the government. From April 1920, after the successful second reading in the Lords, Cherry became a perpetual source of reference for Schuster. All queries were simply forwarded to him, and his memoranda in reply were routinely incorporated into departmental correspondence. And he was paid.[96] Yet that does not make him a government employee, nor even the government draftsman—Liddell was that. Cherry acted throughout as a freelance, and in all his letters that is how he presents himself. Nor do I think that Dr Offer's assumption that there were sides is right, save on the registration point. Yet here, unless we are to believe him a systematic liar, Cherry saw the future as Brickdale's. He had said as much to Scott's committee,[97] and when Lord Birkenhead looked set to frighten the Law Society out of their compromise by aggressive pro-Registry talk, he wrote warningly to Schuster:

We must be careful about showing that the ultimate goal is registration of title. When the bill is thro' we can talk as much as we like, till then let's talk of *both* systems being on trial.[98]

In 1922 he was pressing Schuster to find high-calibre replacements for long-standing Registry staff about to retire. 'For ten years after the Bill gets thro' the time will be crucial.'[99]

To understand Cherry we need to appreciate that even at this late stage he saw that 'registration' could come in several varieties. One of Scott's tactics while trying to lead his committee nearer the registration goal was to present it as inevitable but hold the type of registry out for negotiation. The solicitors' only choice, he would have them believe, was between a 'ministerial Registrar and a bureaucratic system'.[100] The former would leave

[95] LCO2/449, Cherry to Birkenhead, 23 Feb. 1922—consequent, of course, on Haldane's bill. But for Dr Offer Haldane is a conspirator too.

[96] LCO3/443, Schuster to Muir Mackenzie, 5 Mar. 1920; Muir Mackenzie to Schuster, 6 Mar. 1920.

[97] 10th meeting, see n. 6 above; his proviso was that the Registry should not cramp transactions by stereotyping them.

[98] LCO2/446, Cherry to Schuster, 15 Dec. 1920 (2nd letter).

[99] LCO2/449, 28 Mar. 1922.

[100] 13th meeting, p. 6 (see n. 6 above); also 15th meeting.

substantial skilled work in their hands. Schuster's firmness with Brickdale over registered mortgages is consistent with such a strategy, though it may be coincidental. The question arose because the Royal Commission had recommended that the Registry should play virtually no part in mortgages of land beyond recording them, the major work being done by deeds off the register. Haldane had modified that to the extent that one option for a lender would be a mortgage by registered charge, which could be done entirely by registered documents: no deeds, no need for solicitors. Brickdale had pleaded with Scott's committee to make registered charges the only form of mortgage for registered land.[101] When he failed he tried twice again with Schuster, so important a function was it.[102] Schuster told him to stop being a nuisance.[103] Brickdale believed that only a solicitors' plot stood against him, but Cherry gave an alternative explanation, that 90 per cent of mortgages were paid off without sale or foreclosure, so needed protection only via notices or cautions. He none the less promised to word his next edition of *Prideaux's Precedents in Conveyancing* so as to head off solicitors from using these 'protected' mortgages where inappropriate and to the Registry's detriment.[104] A registry with a strong recording function was part of Cherry's vision of efficient conveyancing within an independent professional structure. It was he who moved the registration of local land charges into the Land Registry, followed shortly afterwards by restrictive covenants.[105] So much work was thereby promised that Brickdale mooted the immediate establishment of district registries.[106] So, if mortgage business came to be shared between solicitors and Registry, and if the conveyancing step in a land transaction were made so simple that it could be done by solicitors' clerks, be the land

<hr>

[101] 14th meeting, see n. 6 above; Brickdale's Memorandum on Mortgages, LCO3/45; Hill's Memorandum supported him, LCO3/43.

[102] LCO2/443, Brickdale, 'Lord Cave's Objections and Observations Thereon', 8 Mar. 1920; LCO2/447, Brickdale to Schuster, 23 Mar. 1921.

[103] LCO2/443, Schuster to Brickdale, 24 Mar. 1921.

[104] LCO2/443, Cherry to Schuster, 29 Mar. 1921; Schuster to Brickdale, 31 Mar. 1921.

[105] 15th meeting, see n. 6 above; LCO2/450, Brickdale to Schuster, 17 Apr. 1920. He later added puisne mortgages: LCO2/763, Cherry to Schuster, 9 Apr. 1924.

[106] Brickdale to Schuster, ibid.

registered or unregistered, but if the contract step in a sale remained in solicitors' hands, then the package of reforms might be more attractive to The Law Society than anything else on offer. Whatever were to happen later, land law would have been reshaped as he had wanted. This I believe was Cherry's strategy.

When the 1922 Act was safely passed, Cherry wrote to Birkenhead.[107] The reason the law societies gave us whole-hearted support, he said, was that they realized that without such a structural reform of land law they would not stand a dog's chance in any inquiry into the desirability of extending compulsory registration. 'This gave us the opportunity of amending the general law so as to fit in with registry practice.' Us? Me. He had been the dominant figure throughout. He had been the one to work out compromises with interest groups, draft special accommodations for them, set one law society against another, manipulate intermediaries, massage vanities, and even arrange for friendly MPs to help his bill on its way.[108] When challenged by rivals he had derided them. To give his bill the presentation he thought suitable he had jealously fought off bids from Brickdale to prepare the necessary speeches and memoranda for the politicians,[109] just as he had brushed Underhill aside.

6.   As you know, there was an Act called the Law of Property (Amendment) Act, 1924. That was an Act with a great

---

[107] LCO2/449, 23 Feb. 1922.

[108] Compromises: LCO2/445, Cherry to Schuster, 28 Oct. 1920 (Leeds LS) and subsequent correpondence; LCO2/447, Cherry to Schuster, 4 May 1921 (Land Union); LCO2/448, 449 *passim* (Kent and Hants. LSs); LCO2/449, *passim* (Land Union, again). Accommodations: LCO2/444, Cherry to Schuster, 20 May 1920; for royalty owners see LCO2/449, Cherry to Schuster, 14 Dec. 1921, 26 Jan. 1922, 28 Feb. 1922, and *passim*. Intermediaries: LCO2/447, Cherry to Schuster, 21 Mar. 1921; and cf. LCO2/445, Cherry to Schuster, 9 Aug. 1920 (re. *Sol. Jo.*). Law Societies: LCO2/449, Cherry to Schuster, 2 Nov. 1921. Vanities: LCO2/449, Cherry to Birkenhead, 23 Feb. 1922. MPs: LCO2/449, Cherry to Schuster, 22 Feb. 1922; Hurst to Schuster, 21 Mar. 1922. Derided: LCO2/445, Cherry to Schuster, 4 Aug. 1920 (Benn), ditto 9 Aug. 1920.

Schuster once recognized Cherry's tendency to advocacy by withholding from further circulation a memorandum by Cherry which he thought evaded the point, LCO2/449, Schuster to S.-G., 27 May 1922; and cf. the complaint that a memorandum he prepared was 'argumentative', LCO2/764, Graham-Harrison to Schuster, 1 Aug. 1924.

[109] LCO2/447, Brickdale to Schuster, 21 Apr. 1921; LCO2/448, Brickdale to A.-G., 6 July 1921.

number of schedules, and one which it was almost impossible to understand, and I do not think that anybody except
those who drew [it] up ever read it.[110]

It was this Act which was consolidated by the better-known Law
of Property Act 1925, and it was the next step in Cherry's
achievement. In it he restored some of what had been lost to
Cave, though not all—Cave was Lord Chancellor,[111] he did not
trust Cherry's word,[112] and care had to be taken to ensure that
although the phrasing differed, the substance of the compromise
could plausibly be said to remain. So the dreadful clause 3 of the
1922 bill was rewritten as the cryptic section 2 of the 1925 Act,
still lacking the universal curtain to which Cave had taken such
successful objection, but implying a curtain none the less. The
newly expanded system of registration of estate contracts,
restrictive covenants, and the like was consolidated into a
schedule that became the Land Charges Act, and was completed
by the last-minute addition of mortgages that had not been
accompanied by a deposit of title documents with the lender.[113]
Though there was no explicit curtain, the minute enunciation of
equitable interests in the Land Charges schedule was thought by
Alfred Topham, a member of the Consolidation Committee, to
stand virtually in its stead.[114] It was at this time that the proviso
to section 4 of the Law of Property Act 1925 reappears. Forbidding the creation of novel forms of equitable interest, it originated
in Haldane's bills.[115] In 1920 it had been unnecessary, since the
universal curtain swept all equitable interests of whatever
description into its proposed regime. Absent from the 1922 Act it
returned unannounced to supplement the Land Charges Act;
the closest Cherry could get to defying Cave. Only one part of
Cherry's strategy unwound a little. He had hoped to boost the
Registry and to simplify unregistered conveyancing by lodging

---

[110] Topham, *The Law of Property Acts 1925*, 43.
[111] Haldane replaced Cave as Lord Chancellor on 23 Jan. 1924, Cave returning
on 7 Nov.
[112] LCO2/763, Cherry to Schuster, 18 Oct. 1923.
[113] LCO2/763, Cherry to Schuster, 9 Apr. 1924. Cherry saw this as a mere
recording function, *The New Property Acts*, 33.
[114] Topham, *The Law of Property Acts 1925*, 11.
[115] Real Property and Conveyancing Bill 1914, cl. 79(1) ((1914) HLP vii).

all recording registers at the Registry. But local land charges registers had had to be moved back to the custody of local authorities, the technical difficulties of centralizing them were too great.[116] They remain a blight on conveyancing to this day.

A couple of points of principle were not settled until this late stage, priorities of mortgages, for example. And Edward Benn even persuaded the Committee to reinstate mortgage by charge as an option—a reform which after all this time still provoked conservative hostility from Underhill and Topham, though Cherry became belligerently favourable.[117] All sorts of little points were altered. Brickdale's new overriding interest protecting the rights of persons in actual occupation was civilized, for example, by giving the purchaser a defence of 'actual inquiry'. Topham could see no point in the clause anyway, given that short-term leaseholders were protected by other clauses.[118] And whereas the 1922 Act enabled overreaching by payment of purchase money to any corporation, now only trust corporations would qualify. Topham again had his doubts. The definition incorporated from the Public Trustee Rules included any company listing trustee business in its Memorandum, and that was no protection at all.[119] It was tightened only in 1926.[120]

All these amendments, and everything else in that bill, were prepared in private by Cherry, using whatever helpers he chose and seeking whatever confidential advice he wanted from barristers he could trust.[121] The same teams then did the easier job of breaking down the new revision, as yet unapproved, into a series of consolidation bills. In October 1923 when the task was nearly over, Cherry asked Schuster for a consolidation committee, just to vet the bills for approximate fidelity to the parent

---

[116] Cherry, *The New Property Acts*, 47–8; Registrar Stewart-Wallace tried again in 1934: PRO LAR1/50, Stewart-Wallace to Schuster, 2 Mar. 1934; Cherry kept his enthusiasm for a centralized recording register: LAR1/49, Cherry to Schuster, 9 May 1929.

[117] Cherry, *The New Property Acts*, 59–60; Topham, *The Law of Property Acts 1925*, 82, but cf. 105; Arthur Underhill, *A Concise Explanation of Lord Birkenhead's Act 1922* (1922), 97; id., *The New Conveyancing (1925)*, 68.

[118] Topham, *The Law of Property Acts 1925*, 140.

[119] Ibid. 57.

[120] Law of Property (Amendment) Act 1926, s. 3.

[121] LCO2/763, Cherry to Schuster, 17 May 1923 [filed as though 1924].

Act.[122] He may not have told Schuster about the size or scope of the Amendment Act, and he clearly intended that it be slipped through as an uncontroversial 'facilitating' measure, as it was. He got his committee. It was chaired by a new face, Mr Justice Romer, but otherwise it was the old gang: Cherry, Russell, Liddell, Topham, Benn, and Underhill (who was a member only by accident, being meant as a reserve for Russell who was wrongly thought to be too ill to serve).[123] The solicitors were excluded, being soothingly told that the thing was technical and would demand a lot of time.[124] After initial hesitation Romer agreed to work the amendment bill and the consolidation bills in tandem so that 'no-one will at any time hereafter be able to shew that any of the provisions of the Consolidation Bills are not justified.'[125] When Cave threatened to undermine the plan by bringing in the consolidation bills seriatim Cherry urged the dispatch of Cave's old ally Benn to him to make him see sense. Liddell supplied the arguments and Cave was persuaded.[126]

Only the timetable could not be massaged; there was no room in the 1924 session.[127] In part this was Cherry's fault, since his amendment bill was much longer than the printer had expected. Liddell apologized to Schuster,

Cherry has thought it necessary, or at any rate advisable, to set out whole chunks of the Consolidation Bill where they differ considerably in form from the existing law though not intended to make any change; e.g. it is not proposed to alter the law embodied in the Statute of Frauds but the provisions [re-enacting it] have been set out at length. This was done with a view to expediting proceedings before the Consolidation Committee and so that it should not be necessary to justify before that committee the changes of language which were introduced.[128]

[122] LCO2/763, ? Schuster to Lord Chancellor, 15 Oct. 1923.

[123] LCO2/763, *passim*; Topham was probably the 'Chancery expert': Schuster to Romer, ibid., 16 Oct. 1923.

[124] LCO2/763, Schuster to Trower, 8 Dec. 1923. Trower seems to have been Schuster's permanent correspondent at the LS, even though no longer President.

[125] LCO2/763, Romer to Schuster, 29 Oct. 1923; draft, Cherry to Muir Mackenzie, June 1924.

[126] LCO2/763, Schuster to Liddell, 16 Oct. 1923; Liddell to Schuster, 18 Oct. 1923; Cherry to Schuster, 18 Oct. 1923.

[127] LCO2/763, Schuster to Trower, 15 May 1924.

[128] LCO2/764, Liddell to Schuster, 1 Dec. 1924; for printing problems, Schuster to Birkenhead and Cave, 8 July 1924. The example adds spice to *Grey* v. *IRC* [1960] AC 1.

By implying to Parliament that the Amendment Act facilitated consolidation, but telling the Consolidation Committee that it should where necessary be taken to change the law, Cherry effectively avoided public scrutiny.[129]

This delay was a setback, because another one was necessary further down the pipeline. To change the practice of conveyancing, books had to be written explaining the Acts and providing new forms and precedents. Cherry solved the problem by persuading Haldane, briefly returned as Lord Chancellor, that the bills should be introduced at the end of the 1924 session even though not proceeded with.[130] Thus publicized, the texts became available to the expositors. They needed to be: 'viewed from the proper angle, and in the right light, a dim outline of the [1925 Acts] was discernible through the mists of [the 1922 Act],' but not clearly enough for even experts to have been confident.[131] One man however had had a head start. G. C. Cheshire, who began work in January 1924. His former tutor, Sir John Miles, had a month or so before discussed with his wartime colleague Liddell how important it was for a book to be written solely on the new system, uncluttered with accounts of the changes from the past.[132] The consolidating bills should be the basis of such a book, he said. Cheshire was encouraged to write his book by Miles, his first edition exactly fitting that description, and I suspect that Miles arranged for him to have advance copies of the bills. This would explain how he, a novice with no conveyancing experience, stole a march on Harold Potter, the only other academic to attempt a major work.[133]

Cheshire shared the job of domesticating the legislation with

---

[129] Report of the Committee on the Law of Property Consolidation Bills 1924, Cmd. 2271, (1924) HCP xi. 363; note the lax terms of reference.

[130] LCO2/764, Cherry to Schuster, 23 July 1924; Schuster to Cherry, 25 July 1924. The books were vital to the introduction of a new system. The columns of the professional journals and correspondence files in the LCO are ample proof that even experts could not understand the bills unaided.

[131] *Key and Elphinstone's Precedents in Conveyancing* (12th edn., 1926, by F. Trentham Maw and H. W. Reynolds), preface.

[132] LCO2/763, Liddell to Schuster, 31 Oct. 1923. Miles was tutor at Merton College, Oxford, where Cheshire had been an undergraduate. Cheshire's *The Modern Law of Real Property*, (1st edn., 1925), preface, p. vii, acknowledged his encouragement.

[133] Harold Potter, *The Modern Law of Real Property and Chattels Real, Founded on the Fifth Edition of Goodeve's Real Property* (1929).

Cherry himself and with Topham, both of whom gave a series of lectures to practitioners. They were published in the *Solicitors' Journal* and reprinted in book form.[134] Topham incorporated a sketch of the legislation into his bar finals book.[135] All three men wrote in generalities, suggesting that the 1925 Act's 'curtain' was indeed universal, that there were indeed sections saying that no life tenancies could exist outside the Settled Land Act, and that all co-ownership did indeed fall subject to the regime of trusts for sale, as though Cave's amendment had never happened. One solicitor in Cherry's audience spotted the gap in the co-ownership provisions, but he was authoritatively brushed aside.[136] Only in 1959 did someone try again.[137] So legal education in the burgeoning law faculties and the professional cram schools taught that what ought to have been was, and Cherry's scheme became practical law even if the Acts themselves were incomplete. His own practitioners' books, and those of his rivals, provided the forms for professional use and the technical explanations necessary for rare cases. Finally, there were new national Conditions of Contract based upon the new Acts, settled by Cherry and carrying his blessing, but marketed exclusively by and for law societies.[138] What had been accomplished was a complete professional system.

[134] Topham, *The Law of Property Acts 1925*; Cherry, *The New Property Acts*. Topham's is much the better.

[135] Alfred F. Topham, *The New Law of Property* (2nd edn., 1925) (a continuation of his earlier *Law of Property*).

[136] Cherry, *The New Property Acts*, p. 124, q. 17—in modern form, is there a trust for sale in *Boland*? Cherry said yes, citing the Law of Property Act, s. 34, and discounting s. 36. He clearly regarded the Settled Land Act, s. 36 as applicable only to settled land: p. 26. Though the precise circumstances of *Boland* could not have been foretold, the general issue of 'secret trusts' was discussed at length, e.g. pp. 113 ff. More doubt is expressed in Alfred Fellows, *Everyday Points in Practice under the Law of Property Acts* (1928), 96, q. 2 [repr. from the *Sol. Jo.*]. S. 34 is an unlikely hero, having started life merely as a tidying-up provision, tucked away in a schedule and parasitic upon the universal curtain.

[137] R. E. Megarry and H. W. R. Wade, *The Law of Real Property* (1st edn., 1959), 404–5.

[138] Cherry, *The New Property Acts*, 84; Topham, *The Law of Property Acts 1925*, 110; 'monopoly': (1925–6) 70 *Sol. Jo.* 234. The *Law Journal*, edited by Lightwood, was very critical ((1925) 60 *Law Jo.* (1018), and T. C. Williams treated them disdainfully: *The Contract of Sale of Land* (1930) *passim*. Cherry revised them in 1928, and a new set was issued in 1934, after his death in 1932: (1935) 79 *Sol. Jo.* 485. These conditions are not the same as the 'default' terms issued by the Lord Chancellor under Law of Property Act, s. 46, 1925 SR & O (no. 779) 883.

9

Retrospect and Epilogue

1. The state recruited mainly from the bar, judges great and minor, the law officers, inspectors permanent or *ad hoc*, even so-called Solicitors to government departments, and whether the posts were new or old. This was a perennial complaint from law societies. Lord Cairns in 1875 had thought doing without district registries preferable to staffing them with solicitors. Of the seven First Class Clerks brought into the Land Registry in 1911, the men who did the really skilled work, barristers numbered six and solicitors one.[1] Putting it differently, barristers permeated the state machinery far more effectively than solicitors did,[2] hence continuing Law Society enthusiasm for a Ministry of Justice that might provide a second chance. Excluded from the state by the bar's superior status the solicitors remained overwhelmingly a private sector profession. If the state then went into the business of providing services, the most that could be hoped was that it would act as though it were a rival professional formation, allowing solicitors the chance to compete—as Johnson urged in 1874, Lake at the turn of the century, and as clearly happened over trusteeships at that same time.[3] Or, to put that point differently, the sort of state that the leaders of the solicitors could most easily tolerate, and hence the one they would actively seek to achieve, was one

---

[1] Sixth Report of the Royal Commission on the Civil Service, (1914–16) HCP xii. 1, evidence of J. S. Stewart-Wallace, qq. 54651 ff. His evidence generally is a spectacular example of the equation discussed by Perkin, see n. 5 below:

liberal education + professional qualification + individual merit (should) = lucrative and prestige-bringing career.

[2] Cf. pressure brought by the Solicitors' Managing Clerks Association for posts in the Registry to be opened to its members: (1912–13) 134 *LT* 18.

[3] Concerning separation of funds. For details see Harry Kirk, *Portrait of a Profession* (1976), 100 ff., though he does not make the link; for that see e.g. (1904) 133 HCD 186, 355 ff.

that behaved like a rival but essentially accommodating profession, itself adopting the conventions of professionalism—on advertising, for example.[4]

In his recent magisterial study of the rise of professional society in England since 1880, Harold Perkin advances a model of professional behaviour that fits the solicitors well.[5] Curiously he himself thinks this true of only half his analysis, the half that explains only what the solicitors stood to lose from title registration. His analysis, presaged by Avner Offer, is that solicitors, like professions generally, extracted a 'rent' from society by operating techniques of market closure which generated a monopoly for their services. But if we see title registration as necessitating either the creation of an independent sub-profession or the expansion of the general civil service, then we still have to explain how the solicitors won out for long enough to neuter the threat registration entailed. A part of the answer is simply that registration could come in unthreatening versions. That is how it had been conceived by Wilson, and how it lived on under the general rubric of the 'ministerial' registrar.[6] For only a relatively short period did the Registry envisage itself as the universal conveyancer.

But that is not the whole answer. Regrettably Dr Offer privileged title registration from critical examination, and he is followed in that by Professor Perkin. This seems to have concealed from Professor Perkin just how close was solicitors' conformity to his model of professional behaviour. He stresses that professionals, to constitute a profession at all, must succeed in persuading the rest of society that their 'property' is morally justified. This they do by asserting its usefulness—Perkin's central point indeed is that professional property is advanced as contingent, not as absolute. And then they assert their own merit by emphasizing their qualifications, usually educational. This is exactly how the solicitors conducted their defence. They did not deny their monopoly, they asserted it and justified it. First they detailed their qualifications, which they were forever

---

[4] See e.g. the strong claim by Robert Ellett, a veteran ILS council member: (1912) 133 *LT* 166.

[5] *The Rise of Professional Society* (1989, pbk. edn. 1990), esp. chs. 1 and 4, where Dr Offer's work is generously acknowledged.

[6] For a late formulation see e.g. (1912) 133 *LT* 188 (ILS Council annual report).

striving to increase—for new entrants, that is. Then they
adduced empirical evidence of their accomplishments: the
speed and flexibility of the land transactions they mediated,
their constant and successful efforts to reduce costs, their
confidentiality, the fiduciary duties they owed their clients,
their access to local expert advice from other solicitors in distant
regions, the gratuitous collateral benefits they conferred upon
landowners by negotiating with bodies such as the excise
commissioners and the Inland Revenue or by standardizing
contractual conditions.

One consequence of a profession's success in market closure
is obviously that its fees then become based upon professional
self-evaluation. Professor Perkin argues that professions tend to
justify the prices they fix by reference to the remuneration of
other professions, so that a pay 'equity' develops, stratified by
assertions of relative merit—a calculation combining a small
element of usefulness with a larger measure of 'qualification'.
This too was part of solicitors' defence against the Registry. To
assertions that conveyancing was too expensive they juxtaposed
the charges habitually made by estate agents and accountants,
men who were always said to be less well qualified and less
well disciplined but who charged at least as much.[7] Taken
together, their defence is a long way from the primitive Ludd-
ism that Dr Offer describes. It is an appeal to what Professor
Perkin sees as the prevailing ethic of the day. To that extent
resistance to registration at least swam with the tide.

The argument that title registration was an inadequate substitute for professional virtues could be put easily enough, and
was. But for a long time it had the intrinsic weakness that it was
mere prediction, vulnerable to portrayal as sour self-interest.
This is why the 1908–11 Royal Commission was so important;
for the first time there was some real evidence. And it convinced
at least the lawyers that the Registry was not likely to do the job
markedly better than solicitors (and it is worth interpolating
that they were not pre-selected to do the Registry down.) Of

---

[7] e.g. (1899) 34 *Law Jo.* 700 (Hastie). In some earlier versions the comparison
is tacit—'taxes' on solicitors are enumerated, with the correct implication that
rivals do not bear them: e.g. (1844) 38 *Leg. O.* 444. Those imposts, however,
contributed to the value of the 'property' (e.g. (1888–9) 33 *Sol. Jo.* 413) and could
be used to justify its retention: (1889–90) 34 *Sol. Jo.* 121.

course, today we have far more evidence. We know, for example, that in 1987 the Registry was coining money hand over fist but was prohibited by the Treasury from employing the staff needed to clear a backlog of 980,000 applications. It was taking four months to answer inquiries.[8] In 1985 a knowledgeable and sympathetic academic lawyer could still ask whether registration was a white elephant—concluding that it was not, but by a slight margin only.[9] And, *pace* Professor Perkin, even the old slogan that registered conveyancing can have land sold as cheaply as stocks and shares looks thinner in a Thatcherite world—special arrangements to insulate small investors from the usual brokerage charges had to be made when shares in nationalized public utilities and in the Abbey National Building Society were sold to the populace.[10] But inefficiency at the Registry cannot be a necessary truth. It will be put right sometime. So this part of the solicitors' argument was always vulnerable, even when combined with a strong assertion of their own virtues.

In part also it was a change in the job specification that saved the solicitors. It worked from two directions. A state interest in registration waxed in the 1880s but waned before the Great War. Title registration drifted back towards private law. Meanwhile the narrow 'land transfer' element in private conveyancing was supplemented. Contracts of sale, which originated in auction sales, spread into private transactions as a usual preliminary to the transfer, no doubt at the behest of solicitors. Localism in legal technique was stamped out by the uniformity inherent in the 1925 property legislation, but it had already reappeared in a different guise. Increasing municipal regulation of property required, or at least justified, extensive inquiries before purchase as to possible local authority charges, closing orders, plans for roads and so on. There was sufficient realization of this in 1911 for the Royal Commission to grant at least a temporary reprieve. Perhaps if the typical purchaser had remained as a small capitalist investor either the system would not have developed as it did or he would have been able to do

---

[8] 32nd Report of the Public Accounts Committee, (1987–8) HCP (no. 318).

[9] Roger Smith, [1986] *Current Legal Problems* 111.

[10] Perkin, *The Rise of Professional Society* (pbk. edn.), 136. The refutation is nearly as old as the claim itself, e.g. (1888–9) 33 *Sol. Jo.* 771 (Keen).

the work himself. But the small private landlord faded away, and the new owner-occupier would need help from somebody. That would mean solicitors, unless someone else made a positive bid.

Could the Registry have taken even this function on itself? Of course, if it did not simply stifle the development. But it would have to have been a super-Registry, expanding even on the grandest schemes of Lloyd George and Brickdale combined. Since such a registry would have had as its justification the benefits it gave to the state machinery, no amount of inter-professional analysis could have saved solicitors. To head off that possibility solicitors had to ally themselves with what Perkin calls capitalist property—absolute property free from state regulation—and fight the battle vicariously. They did this when they had to, but the argument swam against the tide and was used only as a last resort. It is, I think, a failure to listen carefully enough to the whole range of argument against the many facets of the varying registration schemes that led to Dr Offer's misdiagnosis. Small schemes were a boon not a threat; middling ones could with effort be accommodated. Big ones needed outside assistance, either to defeat them, or to reduce them to a manageable size.

My description fits the ILS nearly all the time, the *Solicitors' Journal* and the major regional law societies for most of the time. But it is possible that some solicitors did combine a professional characterization of their 'property' with the capitalist belief in its absolute sanctity. Sometimes the argument was opportunistic, as when used to remind Halsbury of a speech he had made deploring nationalization of capitalist property.[11] More deeply, however, such a crossover could stem from solicitors' self-perception as 'men of business', an appellation partly offensive against the bar but partly also descriptive of the work they did. There was obvious danger in the phrase. Though it was used time and again to differentiate solicitors from barristers both pure and bureaucratic, its indiscriminate usage against other occupational groups might undermine the claim to professional status. It was for this reason that the professional press was

---

[11] e.g. (1895–6) 40 *Sol. Jo.* 124. It was repeated frequently thereafter, but only against Halsbury personally.

assiduous in attributing solicitors' bankruptcies to 'non-professional' work wherever possible, with the warning that it would be better for everyone if building speculation and speculative company flotation were left to others.[12] Yet sometimes even the great men let the 'business' prevail over the 'professional'. Marshall's harassment of the ILS Council in 1892 is one example, and there was further embarrassment in 1906 when Liverpool ILS, always the most aggressively business-minded of the regional societies, voted that it saw no reason against solicitors conducting any 'honourable profession or business'.[13] The professionals' reaction came from the law society of nearby Manchester: it is important in maintaining our dignity and the confidence of the public that we stick to our own business and not encroach on others'.[14] This was an isolated and extreme example, but the fault line was always there.

The claim that solicitors provided a complete business service in conducting land transactions was an important element in fending off bureaucratic rivals. How could it be maintained together with the assertion of special qualifications justifying a monopoly of just a part of that service? One solution was for solicitors collectively to operate behind companies. Insurance was the earliest example—the professional journals encouraged the flotation of insurance companies by solicitors for solicitors, subsequently carrying detailed reports of their annual meetings.[15] Later, when it seemed that trust companies or the Public Trustee might cream off business from solicitors, the Law

---

[12] e.g. (1859–60) 34 *LT* 17. For individual examples see (1901) 36 *Law Jo.* 351 (Fuller), ibid. and 413 (Joseph); (1900–1) 110 *LT* 541 and (1901) 111 *LT* 33 (Warner). Bankruptcy reports for these years portray a very wide range of business and investment activity by solicitors, much of it obviously hazardous.

[13] (1905–6) 50 *Sol. Jo.* 684.

[14] Ibid.

[15] e.g. Solicitors & General Life Assurance Co., (1846–7) 8 *LT* 104, (1860–1) 36 *LT* 366, 373, Law Union Assurance Co., (1858–9) 32 *LT* 134. The index entry for 'Law Societies' in (1855) 25 *LT* reads: 'Equity & Law Life Assurance Society; Juridical Society; Law Life Assurance; Law Property & Life Assurance Society; Liverpool Law Society; Metropolitan & Provincial Law Association; United Law Clerks; Yorkshire Law Society'. See too the remark below concerning the ILS and the annual *Law List*. The *Law Times* once proposed that local solicitors form limited liability companies to do debt-collecting work in competition with 'sham lawyers': (1854–5) 24 *LT* 2. The tradition of reporting these annual general meetings continued, e.g. Law Union Fire and Life Assurance Company, (1889–90) 34 *Sol. Jo.* 366, Law Life Assurance Society, (1902–3) 47 *Sol. Jo.* 322.

Guarantee and Trust Society moved to meet the threat.[16] A newcomer, as lawyers' enterprises went, its directors none the less included many of the big names of the day; Osborne Morgan was a shareholder. Its objects enabled it to issue fidelity bonds to secure private trustees and also to act as trustee itself. In its latter role it could offer security, while leaving discretionary decisions to a private co-trustee. Its annual general meetings were reported in the *Solicitors' Journal* and an advertisement for it appeared on the cover of the very first number of The Law Society's house journal.[17] Thus the profession owned stakes in what might turn out to be rivals—as today's newspapers have bought into local radio. Eighteenth-century solicitors had driven the scriveners out of conveyancing; in 1888 their descendants formed The Solicitors' Law Stationery Society Ltd. to drive them out of law publishing.[18] A form of co-operative, all its shareholders and a majority of its directors had to be practising solicitors. Its annual reports proudly recorded co-operation with local law societies right into the computerized world of the 1970s. This was the company that published the Conditions of Contract drafted by Cherry and available only through local law societies.

This commercial involvement is important for two reasons. First, it enabled solicitors collectively as a profession to compete in other markets while formally appearing not to do so. The individual solicitor was not printing law stationery or underwriting insurance. If professionals were needed in that work they were used—but employed ultimately by the solicitor-shareholders. The narrowly 'legal' monopoly could then be defended without fear of counter-attack. Secondly, the readi-

---

[16] Objects: advertisement at (1888–9) 33 *Sol. Jo.* 307; close association with solicitors: (1893–4) 38 *Sol. Jo.* 258, where Lake, Henry Leigh Pemberton, Pennington, Thomas Rawle, and Henry Roscoe appear as directors. Its main business turned out to be guaranteeing risky mortgages, especially those on flats and on licensed premises; it collapsed in 1909: (1908–9) 53 *Sol. Jo.* 326, (1909–10) 54 *Sol. Jo.* 109, (1909) 128 *LT* 143. It had earlier hit technical difficulties in acting as co-trustee: *The Law Guarantee and Trust Society (Ltd.) and John Hunter* v. *The Bank of England* (1890) 24 QBD 406.

[17] e.g. (1902–3) 47 *Sol. Jo.* 301; (1903–4) *Law Society's Gazette*, no. 1, front cover.

[18] Kirk, *Portrait*, 127–8; (1970) 114 *Sol. Jo.* 393, 893–4, 979; (1971) 115 *Sol. Jo.* 233, 489, 497; (1972) 116 *Sol. Jo.* 353, 360, 382; (1973) 117 *Sol. Jo.* 338.

ness with which solicitors formed these commercial companies cemented them the more firmly in the private sector.

Participation in law-making was obviously sought as an enhancement of status, which it conferred both directly in itself through official recognition of the participators' importance and indirectly through appearing as voluntary altruistic behaviour. And it was obviously in their interest that law, seen as a type or as a system, should retain its structural characteristics—for to replace it with some other normative system would be for a new profession to supersede their own. Hence one reason for dislike of official discretion and of 'rule-making'. But one should not neglect the individual satisfaction gained from law reform. The legal professions can be scholarly professions—obviously so for the senior consultant barristers, but also from time to time for a great number of lesser practitioners. The correspondence columns of the legal press always contained ingenious analysis of novel and difficult legal questions raised by solicitors otherwise anonymous. Supersession of that sort of system would be felt as a spiritual loss, just as the writings of today's legal historians sometimes betray regret at the passing of the common-law system itself, lost in a welter of statute and that same official discretion.[19] Unsentimental economic historians may find it embarrassing, or even naïve, but law is a thing that can be loved. The Fields, the Cooksons, the Lewises, the Johnsons, the Wolstenholmes, the Cherrys, were not in it just for what they could get out of it.

But the first collective expression of these aspirations, the Law Amendment Society, rested on doomed premises. Lawyers were not an estate that could transcend class or politics.[20] Law was not a unified entity with a conceptually coherent content. Their ministry of justice was a phantom. Suitably the LAS folded itself gently into the Social Science Association, which saw 'measures', legal or otherwise, as means to social ends, and was a body unable to resist affinity to just one of the great

---

[19] J. H. Baker, *An Introduction to English Legal History* (3rd edn., 1990), 79–81; S. F. C. Milsom, *Historical Foundations of the Common Law* (2nd edn., 1981), vii and 80–1; and cf. Milsom, 'The Nature of Blackstone's Achievement', (1981) 1 *Ox. Jo. LS* 1, 3.

[20] For lingering hopes that they may be, see (1853–4) 47 *Leg. O.* 117, 138, 289, 354.

political parties. In 1886 the pincers of mass democracy and a professional civil service squeezed it out too.[21]

The legal professions were not integrated into government, but remained as lobbyists on the outside. When government needed technical services—and that is how they were seen—it would buy them *ad hoc* from barristers or from permanent employees who would be kept in a service grade with access to policy-making barred. Or sometimes it would consult, with barristers individually and with solicitors through their professional bodies. But for solicitors that meant that consultation did indeed tend to be through their professional bodies. A Cookson or a Field could obtain independent standing via the LAS, but their successors could not. Indeed, there is a nice coincidence in the timing of the Law Amendment Society's demise in 1863. Just three years later the ILS made a symbolically significant first appearance in the front section of the annual *Law List*, where dwelt the professions' governors and the élite. Hitherto it had skulked at the back of the book with the benevolent societies, insurance offices, and the like that offered services to practising lawyers. The resulting equation of solicitors' law reform with their professional bodies did not matter if a government accepted their own societal view, as did Cairns in the early 1880s. But if it did not the tensions became very obvious. Desirable internal reforms could be blocked. Benjamin Lake's position was embarrassingly ambiguous: a negotiator for the Law Society, thus for all solicitors, but personally persuaded of the virtues of registration. There was only one institutional hat he could wear. If there had still been a Law Amendment Society to which he and like-minded solicitors could have decamped, it is possible that a full range of legislative proposals, polished by debate, would have been available to any Lord Chancellor receptive still to 'law reform'.

As it happened such a Chancellor seeking ostensible neutrality could turn only to the individualists of Lincoln's Inn. Any one of them would do a tolerably good job, but there was no way in which detailed estimates could be obtained and submitted to professional scrutiny in advance. Or, better perhaps,

---

[21] Lawrence Goldman, 'The Social Science Association (1857–1886): A Context for Mid-Victorian Liberalism', (1986) 101 *EHR* 95.

there was no forum which could have that task already performed in advance for a Chancellor whose time-frame was dictated by the intervals between general elections. The drafting of the 1925 property legislation was in that sense inevitable. One expert or another would be the only one seated when the music stopped—and it turned out to be Benjamin Cherry. But his product carried only his personal imprimatur, hence the possibility always of a wrecking amendment—from Cave, so it turned out. He even had to provide the bureaucratic momentum needed to push what ought to have been a departmental bill through Parliament. In the absence of a Ministry of Justice there was no department. And though Cherry performed heroically between 1922 and 1924 to retrieve his vision from Cave's sabotage, anyone who reads the statutes knowing their history can see the scars clearly enough.

2. It was conceivable in the immediate aftermath of war that the nature of the contest between solicitors and Registry might have shifted irreversibly in the latter's favour. If socialist housing had replaced the private market, Brickdale's bureaucratic land transfer methods might have meshed well with whatever central or local authorities replaced the private landlord. The stake solicitors had in private transactions through their negotiating of contracts, preparing auctions, and, to a diminishing extent, finding sources of finance would have been useless if private transactions declined. But it did not happen, and the Scott Committee's tacit assumption was correct, that the private market would remain dominant, within which solicitors and registrar would compete over price.

In 1919 the Lord Chancellor agreed to a 33⅓ per cent increase in solicitors' fees in contentious business, consequent on the post-war explosion in wage rates.[22] The Law Society had not asked for an increase in the conveyancing scale, no doubt for good political reason. Instead more subtly it had sought to make 'free contract' outside the scale a more practicable option for solicitors.[23] That had always been allowed under the Solicitors Remuneration Act, but carried the onerous rider that the bill

---

[22] RSC (Solicitors Remuneration Rules) 1920 (no. 630), 1919 SR&O ii. 471 n.
[23] (1918–19) 63 *Sol. Jo.* 649 (LS annual report).

must be itemized, which The Law Society now asked to be removed. But the Orders achieved, though they did increase the charge per item by 33⅓ per cent, applied only to uncompleted transactions, not to mainstream sales or mortgages.[24] At the same time the conveyancing fee scale for Northern Ireland was increased by 50 per cent.[25] The Law Society still kept very quiet. Only in 1922 did it seek a rise, which came finally in 1925: 33⅓ per cent.[26] Dr Offer is scandalized,[27] but need not be. Prices were indeed falling in 1925, but only from their very high post-war levels, and there had not yet been a down-turn in wages. Using 1914 to equal 100, the wages index (all occupations) had stood at 75 in 1882, and cost of living at 102. In 1925 the figures were 196 and 175 respectively.[28] In the depths of the Depression they fell to 183 and 140, but an Order in 1932 took account of that by reducing the 1925 Order's scale increase from 33⅓ per cent to 20 per cent.[29] The full amount was restored in 1936.[30]

So viewed simply as figures there is nothing remarkable here. Dr Offer recounts that during the Scott Committee's deliberations Trower, for The Law Society, suggested that a fee reduction might be possible if Cherry's plan were adopted. And he regards it as another example of Law Society duplicity that fees were instead increased. It is hard to tell what the meeting itself made of it, since its discussion of comparative costs fizzled out when Brickdale was discovered once again to have been biasing the data in his own favour—this time by basing his projections of Registry costs on pre-war figures.[31] Trower's offer, if that is what it was, seems not to have been repeated. Cherry hoped

[24] Solicitors Remuneration Act General Orders, 1919 SR&O (no. 1878) 461; 1920 SR&O (no. 1015) ii. 687.
[25] 1920 SR&O (no. 1457) ii. 688.
[26] Solicitors Remuneration Act General Order, 1925 SR&O (no. 755) 1441.
[27] 'The Origins of the Law of Property Acts 1910–1925', (1977) 40 *MLR* 505, 521.
[28] B. R. Mitchell and Phyllis Deane, *Abstract of British Historical Statistics* (1962), 344–5.
[29] 1932 SR&O (no. 940) 1634.
[30] 1936 SR&O (no. 326) ii. 2512.
[31] Land Acquisition and Valuation Committee, Record of Proceedings, 15th meeting, PRO LCO3/42. Dr Offer does not record this, being content with Brickdale's initial presentation: Offer, 'Origins', at 513.

that the scales could be reduced.[32] Yet, oddly, we have only Cherry's word for it that as things stood only a reform such as his would save the solicitors from being caught between a politically unacceptable fees rise on the one hand and increasing skimping of necessary investigation of title on the other.[33] It was in his interest to claim importance for his scheme, and it is surprising that there is no independent confirmation that this dilemma was real. One would expect Brickdale to have been making similar allegations of shoddy practices among solicitors if it were true.

Brickdale was Dr Offer's hero, and he regards his successor Stewart-Wallace as a lesser man for conceding solicitors a fees increase for Registry business in 1925, and getting nothing in return.[34] Brickdale would have done no better; power was no longer the Registrar's but the Remuneration Committee's, of which he was just one member. The Order also assimilated the structure of fees for Registry business to that for traditional conveyancing. Thus a separate charge was allowed for negotiating a sale—which included drawing the contract —and this served to integrate solicitors into Registry practice, and Registry practice into solicitors'. A work-sharing arrangement was emerging. It is symptomatic of the shift of lawyerly emphasis from conveyance to contract that Cyprian Williams, who was preparing a post-1925 edition of *Vendor and Purchaser*, should have interrupted his work to bring out a new book wholly devoted to 'the contract of sale of land'.[35]

Stewart-Wallace was sensitive to the change.[36] In 1934 The Law Society asked him to agree to an increase in solicitors' fees for Registry business. He tried first to bargain: an increase in

[32] Sir Benjamin Cherry, *The New Property Acts* (1925), 101.

[33] LCO2/445, Cherry, 'Law of Property Bill: Replies to Mr Edward Benn', 25; LCO2/443, 'Law of Property Bill Memorandum', 5—attributed to Cherry by Dr Offer, rightly I think.

[34] Offer, 'Origins', 521. Solicitors Remuneration (Registered Land) Order, 1926 SR&O (no. 2) 1224; reduced by 1932 SR&O (no. 941) 1636, restored by 1936 SR&O (no. 327) ii. 2513. To Dr Offer's references add PRO LAR1/97, Stewart-Wallace to Cherry, 30 Oct. 1924.

[35] T. C. Williams, *The Contract of Sale of Land* (1930). He died in 1932, shortly after Cherry; there is an affectionate tribute at (1932) 74 *Law Jo.* 229, probably by John Lightwood, who finished off the final edition of *Vendor and Purchaser*, published in their joint names in 1936.

[36] For this paragraph see the correspondence in PRO LAR1/96.

exchange for a promise not to seek an inquiry if he proposed an extension Order. The Law Society demurred, so Stewart-Wallace set out the position as he saw it. He was not hostile to solicitors. If an extension came, and with it an increase in Registry business such that its own fees could be reduced, he would allow solicitors' fees to rise to take up the balance. And if solicitors' overheads had risen he would allow their Registry fees to increase in line with any increase for unregistered conveyancing. But they were seeking a comparative advantage for unregistered over registered conveyancing, which was part of a continuous hostility towards him. Drop that, and he would be co-operative. Already he gave a pro-forma letter to inquirers at the Registry suggesting that lay persons use a solicitor and saying that the Registry itself did not fill that role. If the fees gap closed too much he would be unable to continue pushing lay persons in this way, and he would expect institutions such as building societies, land developers, and large builders to cut solicitors out.

The Registry was gaining ground. In 1933 the Lord Chancellor's Office cleverly established a committee chaired by Lord Tomlin to inquire whether the procedure for extending compulsory registration was adequate, and whether Middlesex would be a suitable first step.[37] The Law Society's opposition was of the weakest sort imaginable, merely that there should be no extension without evidence of local popular demand.[38] During his fees negotiation with The Law Society, contemporaneously with this inquiry, Stewart-Wallace for the first time sensed that The Law Society expected title registration to win.[39] Sure enough, when the draft extension Order for Middlesex was promulgated The Law Society decided not to exercise its power to call for an inquiry.[40] Only two localities, Eastbourne and Hastings, had voluntarily adopted compulsory registration for their areas, but there had been a steady flow of inquiries, and

[37] Land Transfer Committee Report, Cmd. 4776, (1934–5) HCP x. 395. By asking the question hypothetically the LCO flushed out the opposition and neutralized it.
[38] Law Society, 'Memorandum on Compulsory Registration of Title', LAR1/50; (1934) 78 *Sol. Jo.* 453 (LS annual report).
[39] LAR1/96, note by Stewart-Wallace, 3 Dec. 1934.
[40] (1935) 79 *Sol. Jo.* 482, 485 (LS annual report).

voluntary registrations of individual titles outside compulsory areas were numerous, especially from counties bordering London.[41] At an earlier inquiry by Lord Tomlin into Registry practice, Stewart-Wallace had been highly praised even by solicitors for the administrative improvements he had made.[42] These coped so well with the building boom that although the Registry was flooded with work the time taken per transaction actually fell, costs were reduced, the Registry paid off the remaining debt on its own building, and the Treasury was able to appropriate over £300,000 accumulated surplus from the insurance fund.[43] To cap it all, when the work became so heavy that the Land Charges department had to be relocated on a nearby site, the move was accomplished over a weekend with no disruption to business. The *Solicitors' Journal* lauded the Registrar's 'high administrative ability . . . an example of how a Government Department ought to be run'.[44] There were one or two rearguard skirmishes by local law societies after 1945, but the outcome was in no doubt.[45]

Behind Stewart-Wallace's veiled threat to The Law Society was the possibility that if it maintained its hostility institutional users of the Registry would develop their own legal departments, bypassing independent solicitors. Gone was Brickdale's claim that any businesslike individual property-owner could do his own registered conveyancing. It may always have been an extravagant boast. Brickdale, as Cherry said, was not much of a conveyancer, nor had he ever been in business. But there may be other reasons for the shift in emphasis. In its evidence to the

---

[41] Eastbourne and Hastings: PRO LAR1/97; inquiries: LAR1/49 *passim*; LAR1/182–91, esp. 188.

[42] Report of the Land Registration Committee, Cmd. 3564, (1929–30) HCP xv. 539; LAR1/49, *passim*.

[43] *Report of the Chief Land Registrar to the Lord Chancellor on H.M. Land Registry for the Financial Year 1931–32* (HMSO, 1932); the time taken for first registration was down to 5.6 days, from 6.3 the previous year and 24.8 in 1920; costs per registration had been halved since 1921–2, and fees reduced twice in the last six years. See also the *Report* for 1935–6. Land Registration Act 1936, s.4; and see the supportive debate at (1936) 312 HCD 148 ff. Cherry and Brickdale had both anticipated that the indemnity fund would be worked as a source of revenue, without demur: LCO2/443, Cherry to Schuster, 11 Feb. 1919.

[44] (1936) 80 *Sol. Jo.* 355, 356. For the building boom see Mitchell and Deane, *Abstract*, 239.

[45] Kirk, *Portrait*, 143.

second Tomlin Committee The Law Society emphasized the
increased importance of the contract stage in a transaction as a
reason why registration touched such a small part of a conveyancing transaction that local people might not think compulsory
registration worth the bother.[46] Special pleading of course, but
it maintained a mystique which would deter laypersons. Secondly, the sort of property-owner Brickdale probably had in
mind may have been an endangered species. The private
landlord was being squeezed by fiscal policies and on/off rent
controls, and though he was to some extent being replaced by
public authorities who would employ their own legal staffs,
they would not be bodies which did much buying, selling, or
mortgaging after the initial acquisition.[47] Owner-occupation of
houses was growing rapidly, extending ownership into social
strata unaccustomed to large business transactions. Perhaps a
big builder would employ a solicitor to do all the legal work for
the initial purchasers of his houses, but on a subsequent sale
such a new house-owner would really have no choice but to use
a solicitor. It is possible, speculatively, that a similar process
was at work with agricultural land. When much of that was
concentrated in the hands of traditional land-owning families,
it is conceivable that their estate offices might have come to
handle their own registered conveyancing, at least after first
registration. But the land sales of the early 1920s broke up these
big estates, spreading ownership across a far wider spectrum
than before. Where could a former tenant, now the owner of
his freehold, turn but to the local solicitor?

Perhaps the crucial institutions were the building societies,
and once a spokesman for them did hint to The Law Society
that they might start employing their own full-time solicitors.[48]
But he admitted that it was a very remote threat. Building
societies were changing, but not in the direction the Registrar
envisaged. The pre-war pattern had been for each small local
society to use a retained solicitor, who would charge the

[46] Law Society, 'Memorandum on Compulsory Registration of Title', LAR1/
50; (1934) 78 *Sol. Jo.* 453 (LS annual report).

[47] John Burnett, *A Social History of Housing, 1815–1970* (1978), chs. 8, 9.

[48] J. B. Leaver, 'Building Societies and the Legal Profession', (1933) 77 *Sol. Jo.*
710, a paper given to a LS annual provincial meeting. Unattributed statements
in this paragraph are from this paper and the ensuing discussion.

purchaser/borrower for the legal side of the mortgage, but on a society scale much lower than the Remuneration Order's. — Whether he also handled the purchaser's dealings with the vendor, and if so at what price, was not a matter that aroused concern. It became one in the thirties. Some building societies which had become national in their operations designated particular solicitors in various localities as authorized to do work for them. Solicitors excluded from the panel were jealous. Further, as a speculative building boom got underway, some builders and building societies combined to offer inducements to purchasers, fuelling a competitive spiral with their rivals. One such inducement was free or cut-price conveyancing, loudly advertised. But it was dependent, of course, on the purchaser/borrower using a panel solicitor, who would thereby gain a competitive advantage. After complaints from The Law Society in 1930, building societies themselves stopped advertising cheap conveyancing, but that did not prevent builders from doing so, even where the estate in question was being partly financed out of building society capital. So in 1934 The Law Society took up the question with the National Association of Building Societies, the outcome being the Solicitors' Practice Rules 1936.[49] These prohibited all solicitors from allowing themselves to be held out, directly or indirectly, as offering conveyancing services at below the local scale in force where the land was situated, or at less than two-thirds of the Remuneration Order scale where there was no such local scale. Rather than employing a full legal staff, even the big building societies continued using local solicitors on an agency basis.

In these various ways solicitors stayed in conveyancing. Registration became as Wilson and Cookson had intended it to be, a private law matter giving public benefits ancillary to a profession, a century after Wilson had first written. The only part of their vision unrealized was that they had wanted law societies to gain prestige through proposing it.

3. 'He was not a profound scholar, but he was extraordinarily industrious, meticulously accurate in details, courageous in his

---

[49] (1934) 78 *Sol. Jo.* 448 (LS annual report); (1936) 80 *Sol. Jo.* 515, 516 (LS annual report); Solicitors' Practice Rules, 1936 SR&O (no. 1005) ii. 2509.

advocacy of law reforms. . . .' David Hughes Parry's appreciation of Cherry describes his Law of Property Act too.[50] Today's
'leading' cases are difficult exactly because of Cherry's preference for rule over principle. *Williams & Glyn's Bank* v. *Boland*[51]
reaches the only possible answer compatible with Cherry's
insistence on the primacy of the two-trustee rule,[52] but it was a
close-run thing. He had not told us *how* he thought trusts for
sale gave their protection, only *when*. *City of London Building
Society* v. *Flegg*[53] is another example. How faithfully Lord
Templeman follows Cherry's concealed lifeline to the safe haven
tucked away in the Trustee Act.[54] But how difficult it was to
make sense of the guarantee of occupiers' rights proclaimed in
the Law of Property Act. Unlike Haldane, Cherry had not
worked this through as a principle, nor said what is to happen
if principles clash.[55] Occasionally he did slip on points of detail.
In *Ives Investment* v. *High* Lord Denning divined, or perhaps
remembered, exactly what Cherry had meant by 'equitable
easement',[56] but when it came to fitting proprietary estoppel
into the statutes the court was left to its own imagination. Yet it
had been added to the 1920 bill by an amendment of which
Cherry must have known.[57] Perhaps this is one occasion where
Cave's destruction of the universal curtain has left a mark.

If so it is most unusual. *Shiloh Spinners* v. *Harding* is, I think,
the only case in which a judicial attempt explicitly to re-create
the curtain has been rejected,[58] but generally courts have acted
as though it existed. *Boland* itself restores the lost provision that
all tenancies in common, however arising, must subsist behind

---

[50] (1932) 174 *LT* 196. I cannot find corroboration of the *LT*'s statement at p.
206 that Cherry's early career was as a Parliamentary draftsman.

[51] [1981] AC 487.

[52] Cherry, *The New Property Acts*, e.g. p. 30; p. 124, q. 17 is directly in point.

[53] [1987] 2 WLR 1266.

[54] Cherry, *The New Property Acts*, 50. He thereby surreptitiously reinstated a
principle he had been forced to drop when proposed directly: see above, Ch. 8
n. 70 and accompanying text.

[55] I have found no discussion anywhere of the rule that became Law of
Property Act, s. 14.

[56] *Ives (E. R.) Investment Ltd.* v. *High* [1967] 2 QB 379; Cherry, *The New Property
Acts*, 47; cf. *Wolstenholme and Cherry's Conveyancing Statutes* (11th edn., 1925, by
Sir B. L. Cherry, J. Chadwick, and J. R. Perceval Maxwell), i. 585.

[57] See above, p. 296.

[58] Russell L. J., [1972] Ch. 326, reversed [1973] AC 691.

a trust for sale.[59] And courts have been quite undaunted by the disappearance of the clause saying that all life estates had to exist behind a settlement. Sections 1 and 2 of the Settled Land Act have been turned on their head to do the job, their structure and their logic being ignored so as to achieve an end compatible with the textbook view of what ought to be.[60]

So, up to a point, textbooks have provided the policies that had to be dropped from the earlier bill, and the Acts have supplied the rules. Cherry's system continued more or less intact into the late 1980s, like the professional structure for which it was intended. Missing from it were the principles from which new rules can be generated. Like his lectures to The Law Society in 1925, his statutes are not texts, they are a compendium of answers to particular questions. When the questions changed, as they did when owner-occupation combined with the economic emancipation of women to fuse new social forms of co-ownership, Cherry's Acts were hopelessly inadequate. The reason was not that the social forms were new, it has been a commonplace that law changes to meet new social forms, rather that in importing the trust for sale for one purpose Cherry thought that he had done all that was needed. So courts have had to struggle with competing characterizations of the situation—is it 'trusts for sale', and if so how much of the law of trusts does that import? Or is it 'co-ownership', a continuation of the pre-1925 law? Or is it a wholly new situation—'family property'? Or should solutions be found by analogy to contract?[61] In this conundrum trusts for sale alone carry statutory weight, making the absence of statutory principles all the more unfortunate. There have been conveyancers with academic interests since Cyprian Williams was passed over, Potter

---

[59] At least at C.A. level, [1979] Ch. 312, *pace* W. J. Swadling, (1986) 50 Conv. 379; and see Ch. 8 n. 136.

[60] The latest in this well-known line of cases is *Ungurian* v. *Lesnoff* [1989] 3 WLR 840, and note Russell L. J. (again) in *Dodsworth* v. *Dodsworth* (1973) 228 *Estates Gazette* 1115. The point was noticed, and doubt expressed, in J. P. H. Cookson, *Further Points in Practice under the Law of Property Acts* (1931), 98, q. 7 (repr. from the *Sol. Jo.*). Wolstenholme and Cherry's *Conveyancing Statutes* (11th edn.) also thought an instrument necessary before the Act applied, acknowledging one tiny exception to the curtain principle: ii. 27, note to Settled Land Act, s. 1(1).

[61] *Bull* v. *Bull* [1955] 1 QB 234; *Dennis* v. *McDonald* [1981] 1 WLR 810, [1982] 2 WLR 275; *City of London Building Society* v. *Flegg* [1987] 2 WLR 1266 (Lord Oliver).

and Hargreaves in particular. But they had no institution within which to promote critical law reform, even if they had wanted to. Only very recently has the Law Commission even begun to discuss principles of property law with a view to law reform of more than the narrowest incremental sort,[62] having for a long time simply reiterated the textbooks' policy of promoting unencumbered sales. In doing so it happily perpetuated the view that sales were the problem, whereas in fact mortgages were and always have been. Meanwhile academic articles have rediscovered problems well known half a century ago, and statute has hurriedly made good problems long ago foretold.[63] It is as though in the meantime nobody was bothered; an answer had been found to a little local difficulty. In the age of Law Commissions, when the law-reform business has become international, there has been no export market for Cherry's work.

[62] Esp. Law Commission, nos. 158, 'Third Report on Land Registration' (1987); 181, 'Transfer of Land; Trusts of Land' (1989); and 188, 'Transfer of Land; Overreaching; Beneficiaries in Occupation' (1989).

[63] Esp. the influential article by S. M. Cretney and G. Dworkin, 'Rectification and Indemnity, Illusion and Reality', (1968) 84 *LQR* 528; and see generally, Roger Smith, 'Land Registration: White Elephant or Way Forward?' [1986] Current Legal Problems 111. My own 'The Proper Narrow Scope of Equitable Conversion in Land Law' (1984) 100 *LQR* 86 comes into this category. The need for Law of Property Act 1969, s. 25, an important reform, was apparent long ago—Alfred F. Topham, *The Law of Property Acts 1925* (1926), 46, 61.

Appendix: Some Land Registry Statistics

TABLE 1. *Fees, salaries, and expenses*

Year ending 31 March	Salaries & expenses (£ s. d.)	Fees (£ s. d.)
1863	—	64. 5. 0
1864	8,331	133. 0. 0
1865	4,900	411. 15. 0
1866	5,030	1,275. 5. 0
1867	5,280	1,689. 15. 0
1868	5,440	1,253. 15. 0
1869	5,470	1,479. 4. 6
1870	5,490	1,315. 8. 0
1871	5,570	1,081. 8. 0
1872	5,310	589. 17. 0
1873	5,330	723. 0. 0
1874	5,350	632. 13. 0
1875	5,370	598. 0. 0
1876	5,398	596. 6. 0
1877	5,414	815. 15. 0
1878	5,418	776. 14. 0
1879	5,418	989. 9. 6
1880	5,418	793. 17. 0
1881	5,428	883. 13. 0
1882	5,421. 2. 6	840. 3. 10
1883	5,426. 17. 3	1,016. 1. 0
1884	5,424. 17. 11	852. 14. 4
1885	5,417. 11. 7	835. 19. 9
1886	4,957. 10. 5	892. 7. 5
(1) 1887	2,917. 15. 4	800. 12. 9
1888	2,876	763
(2) 1889	2,939	1,186
1890	3,375	3,828
1891	3,429	3,670
1892	3,495	3,726

TABLE 1. *(cont.)*

Year ending 31 March	Salaries & expenses (£ s. d.)	Fees (£ s. d.)
(3) 1893	6,433	16,250
1894	6,817	14,809
1895	7,166	16,257
1896	7,387	17,224
1897	7,750	20,139
1898	7,863	20,262
(4) 1899	11,949 [5,000]	21,844 [2,203]
1900	18,830 [16,000]	35,206 [17,647]
1901	38,393 [32,800]	53,802 [37,600]
1902	43,160 [37,600]	61,706 [44,150]
1903	54,317 [46,573]	64,190 [47,929]
1904	57,521 [47,935]	67,384 [49,179]
1905	58,904 [49,085]	62,042 [44,830]
1906	62,963 [52,470]	62,264 [45,390]
1907	58,659 [50,000]	54,957 [38,186]
1908	54,048 [44,919]	51,352 [35,920]
1909	50,780 [40,270]	47,703 [33,155]
1910	50,181 [40,019]	53,889 [40,192]
1911	48,966 [38,288]	52,037 [38,800]
1912	49,556 [39,299]	54,338 [41,565]

[1] Registrar Follett died during this year, and was not replaced until 1891.
[2] Land Charges Act 1888 came into force on 1 Jan. 1889.
[3] The Land Registry acquired the Middlesex Deeds Registry on 1 Apr. 1892.
[4] The figures in [ ] represent the Registrar's estimates of the expenses and fees attributable to work done under the Land Transfer Acts 1875 and 1897.

Sources: 'Account of Receipts and Expenditure in Land Registry in Year Ended 31st March', HCP, annual; also (1882) HCP (334) liv. 171.

T A B L E 2: *Business*

(*a*) 1863–1886

Year ending 31 Dec.	First registrations	Transfers (all)	Mortgages	Others	Removed	Total	Total estates on register
1863	8	2	1	—	—	11	
1864	8	1	1	—	—	10	
1865	48	39	11	10	—	108	
1866	105	106	37	31	3	282	
1867	40	116	90	42	3	291	
1868	66	229	172	70	4	541	
1869	38	214	130	82	8	472	
1870	29	159	98	77	2	355	
1871	7	220	70	52	19	368	
1872	33	190	97	69	12	401	
1873	7	163	99	86	4	359	
1874	5	176	60	72	1	314	
1875	4	173	83	96	3	359	
1876	16	230	83	117	14	460	
1877	22	233	104	118	13	490	
1878	18	270	143	147	7	585	
1879	10	282	133	143	8	573	
1880	8	258	147	161	16	590	
1881	16	247	171	186	14	634	2,580
1882	14	246	219	150	19	648	
1883	6	266	207	172	11	662	
1884	6	244	195	155	15	615	
1885	8	254	123	151	7	543	
1886	4	209	133	150	5	501	

Appendix

There appear to be no published figures for the next two years. When they resume, the format is different.

(b) 1889–1911

Year ending 31 Dec.	First registrations	Trans-fers (all)	Mortgages	Recon-veyances	Leases	Other	Total	Estates on register
1889	29	234	–	208 –	47	37	555	3,530
1890	26	357	–	304 –	18	70	775	
1891	38	301	142	52	43	26	602	
1892	34	345	192	96	48	27	742	
1893	32	357	232	121	48	50	840	
1894	18	398	263	101	34	69	883	4,236
1895	18	405	236	165	61	37	932	
1896	13	525	291	153	93	38	1,113	
1897	8	490	201	156	353	130	1,338	
1898	17	549	238	137	87	91	1,119	5,021
1899	2,954	805	1,235	170	132	280	5,576	8,255
1900	11,368	1,475	4,630	297	572	1,336	19,678	19,885
1901	16,077	2,834	7,671	734	1,278	2,746	31,340	36,469
1902	15,838	3,978	7,849	1,342	1,734	3,963	34,704	52,994
1903	15,126	5,010	8,693	1,841	2,266	5,079	38,015	68,891
1904	13,926	5,401	8,434	2,114	2,108	5,655	37,638	83,732
1905	14,229	6,634	8,649	2,813	2,199	9,379	43,903	99,168
1906	11,258	6,111	6,120	2,490	1,963	9,120	37,062	111,686
1907	10,187	6,181	6,216	2,539	1,622	9,382	36,127	122,954
1908	9,689	5,788	8,447	2,841	1,477	5,829	34,671	133,755
1909	7,161	5,519	8,180	3,027	1,393	5,577	30,857	141,795
1910	6,841	5,930	6,729	3,276	1,396	4,685	28,830	149,329
1911	6,791	5,725	6,549	3,339	1,289	4,796	28,489	156,972

(c) *Land Charges Act and Middlesex Deeds Registry Business*

Year ended 31 Dec.	Land Charges Act			Middlesex Registry	
	Registrations	Official searches	Personal searches	Registrations	Searches
1889	977	1,597	9,315		
1890	496	1,848	11,953		
1891	473	2,381	12,740		
1892	520	2,600	14,477	38,995	15,926
1893	530	3,066	14,785	38,362	15,176
1894	549	2,699	14,833	39,878	15,936
1895	466	2,705	18,440	40,589	17,199
1896	566	3,146	23,710	47,702	20,945
1897	513	3,027	25,659	49,160	21,708
1898	605	3,731	28,276	52,292	22,838
1899	523	3,571	29,206	47,560	21,835
1900*	981	3,771	30,618	36,518	20,047
1901	1,599	5,314	35,012	35,558	20,023
1902	1,510	5,284	36,247	34,455	19,927
1903	1,540	5,419	38,901	37,346	21,013
1904	1,627	4,858	37,624	36,260	19,239
1905	1,657	4,974	36,886	35,742	18,915
1906	1,670	4,891	36,038	33,852	17,478
1907	1,628	4,469	36,071	32,763	16,868
1908	1,608	4,027	33,727	30,456	15,286
1909	1,491	5,632	33,563	29,824	14,020
1910	1,543	5,212	31,362	27,777	12,909
1911	1,489	5,686	30,410	26,774	12,248

* Land Charges Act 1900.

Sources: 'Returns' of Land Registry work under various titles in HCP: 1882 (334) liv. 171; 1887 (228) lxvii. 141; 1895 (463) lxxxi. 343: 1899 (304) lxxix. 267; then annually to 1903; then 1906 (276) xcix. 271; 1908 (154) lxxviii. 227; 1911 (212) lxiii. 325; 1912–13 (319) lxviii. 341.

TABLE 3. *Overview of the Land Registry, 1862–1911*

| Year ending 31 Dec. | Title Registration | | Titles on register | Land Charges | | Middlesex Registry | | Outgoings (£) | Fees (£) |
	First registrations	Dealings		Registrations	Searches	Registrations	Searches		
1862									506
1863	8	3						12,006	
1864	8	2							
1865	48	60						4,998	1,059
1866	105	177						5,218	1,587
1867	40	251						5,400	1,363
1868	66	475						5,463	1,423
1869	38	434						5,485	1,356
1870	29	326						5,550	1,140
1871	7	361						5,375	713
1872	33	368						5,325	690
1873	7	352						5,345	655
1874	5	309						5,365	607
1875	4	355						5,391	597
1876	16	444						5,410	761
1877	22	468						5,417	786
1878	18	567						5,418	936
1879	10	563						5,418	843
1880	8	582						5,426	861

Year									
1881	16	616							5,423	851
1882	14	644							5,424	972
1883	6	656							5,425	894
1884	6	609							5,420	840
1885	8	535							5,073	878
1886	4	497							3,428	824
1887			2,580						2,887	772
1888									2,923	1,080
1889	29	526	3,530	977	10,912				3,266	3,168
1890	26	749		496	13,801				3,416	3,710
1891	38	564		473	15,121				3,479	3,712
1892	34	708		520	22,277	38,995	15,926	5,699	13,119
1893	32	808		530	17,851	38,362	15,176	6,721	15,169
1894	18	865	4,236	549	17,532	39,878	15,936	7,079	15,895
1895	18	914		466	21,145	40,589	17,199	7,332	16,982
1896	13	1,100		566	26,856	47,702	20,945	7,659	19,410
1897	8	1,330	5,021	513	28,686	49,160	21,708	7,835	20,231
1898	17	1,102	8,255	605	32,007	52,292	22,838	10,928	21,449
1899	2,954	2,622		523	32,777	47,560	21,835	17,110 [13,250]	31,866 [13,786]
1900	11,368	8,310	19,885	981	34,389	36,518	20,047	33,502 [28,600]	49,153 [32,612]
1901	16,077	15,263	36,469	1,599	40,326	35,558	20,023	41,968 [36,400]	59,730 [42,513]
1902	15,838	18,866	52,994	1,510	41,531	34,455	19,927	51,528 [44,330]	63,569 [46,984]

TABLE 3. *(cont.)*

Year ending 31 Dec.	Title Registration			Land Charges		Middlesex Registry		Outgoings (£)	Fees (£)
	First registrations	Dealings	Titles on register	Registrations	Searches	Registrations	Searches		
1903	15,126	22,889	68,891	1,540	44,320	37,346	21,013	56,720 [47,595]	66,586 [48,867]
1904	13,926	23,712	83,732	1,627	42,482	36,260	19,239	58,558 [48,798]	63,378 [45,917]
1905	14,229	29,674	99,168	1,657	41,860	35,742	18,915	61,948 [51,624]	62,209 [45,250]
1906	11,258	25,804	111,686	1,670	40,929	33,852	17,478	59,735 [50,618]	56,784 [39,987]
1907	10,187	25,940	122,954	1,628	40,540	32,763	16,868	55,201 [46,189]	52,253 [36,487]
1908	9,689	24,982	133,755	1,608	37,754	30,456	15,286	51,597 [41,432]	48,615 [33,846]
1909	7,161	23,696	141,795	1,491	39,195	29,824	14,020	50,331 [40,082]	52,343 [38,433]
1910	6,841	21,989	149,329	1,543	36,574	27,777	12,909	49,270 [38,721]	52,500 [39,148]
1911	6,791	21,698	156,972	1,489	36,096	26,774	12,248	49,409 [39,046]	53,763 [40,874]

Note: Fees and outgoings are estimates for calendar years, calculated from the financial years in Table 1 above. Figures in [ ] represent fees and outgoings attributable to the Land Transfer Acts, calculated in the same way.

Select Bibliography

A. B., *A Letter to the Solicitor-General on the Landed Estates Bill* (1859); repr. (1859)

ABEL, RICHARD L., *The Legal Profession in England and Wales* (1988).

ABEL-SMITH, BRIAN, and STEVENS, ROBERT, *Lawyers and the Courts* (1967).

ADDISON, CHRISTOPHER, *Politics from Within* (1924).

ARNOLD, ARTHUR, *Free Land* (1880).

BAR COMMITTEE *Land Transfer* (1886).

—— *Annual Statement, 1887.*

—— *Annual Statement, 1889.*

(see also under General Council of the Bar.)

BARRY, E. ELDON, *Nationalisation in British Politics* (1965).

BENTHAM, JEREMY, *Lord Brougham Displayed* (1832).

—— *Collected Works: Correspondence*, vi and vii, ed J. R. Dinwiddy (1984 and 1988); viii and ix, ed. Stephen Conway (1988 and 1989).

—— [Review of Humphreys], (1826) 6 *Westminster Review* 446.

BEYNON, HELEN, 'Mighty Bentham', (1981) 2 *Jo. Leg. Hist.* 62.

BLYTH, EDMUND KELL, *The German and Austrian Systems of Land Transfer and their Application to England* (1892).

BRODRICK, G. C., *English Land and English Landlords* (1881).

BURNETT, JOHN, *A Social History of Housing, 1815–1970* (1978).

CAMPBELL, ENID, 'German Influences in English Legal Education and Jurisprudence in the Nineteenth Century', (1959) 4 *Univ. of W. Austr. LR* 357.

CAMPBELL, JOHN, *Lives of the Chancellors* (1847)

CARR, SIR C. T., *A Victorian Law Reformer's Correspondence* Selden Society lecture, (1955).

CHAMBERLAIN, JOSEPH, *The Radical Platform: Speeches* (1885).

—— *Speeches*, ed. Charles W. Boyd (1914).

—— *et al.*, *The Radical Programme*, ed. D. A. Hamer (1971).

CHERRY, B. L., *The New Property Acts* (1925).

—— and MARIGOLD, H. W., *The Land Transfer Acts* (1899).

CHESHIRE, G. C., *The Modern Law of Real Property* (1st edn. 1925, and subsequent edns.).

CLEARY, E. J., *The Building Society Movement* (1965).

COCKS, RAYMOND, C. J., *Foundations of the Modern Bar* (1983).

—— *Sir Henry Maine* (1988).

COLLINI, STEFAN, WINCH, DONALD, and BURROW, JOHN, *That Noble Science of Politics*, (1983).

CORNISH, W. R., and CLARK, G. DE N., *Law and Society in England, 1750–1950* (1989).

DART, J. H., *The Law of Vendors and Purchasers* (6th edn., 1888, by W. Barber, R. B. Haldane, and W. R. Sheldon; 7th edn., 1905, by B. L. Cherry, G. E. Tyrell, A. Dickson, and I. Marshall).

DAUNTON, MICHAEL J., *House and Home in the Victorian City* (1983).

DAVIDSON, CHARLES, *Concise Precedents in Conveyancing* (2nd edn., 1845; 4th edn., 1852).

DREWRY, GAVIN, 'Lord Haldane's Ministry of Justice', (1983) 61 *Public Administration* 396.

EMY, H. V., *Liberals, Radicals and Social Politics, 1892–1914* (1973).

FELLOWS, ALFRED, *Everyday Points in Practice under the Law of Property Acts* (1928).

FIELD, EDWIN WILKINS, 'Law Reforms', 39 *Westminster Review* 205 (1843).

FOSTER, R. F., *Lord Randolph Churchill* (1981).

FREEDEN, MICHAEL, *The New Liberalism* (1978).

GARVIN, J. L., *The Life of Joseph Chamberlain* (1935).

GENERAL COUNCIL OF THE BAR, *Annual Statement, 1897–98*.

—— *Annual Statement, 1914*.

GEORGE, HENRY, *Progress and Poverty* (1879).

GILBERT, BENTLEY B., *David Lloyd George: A Political Life* (1987).

—— 'David Lloyd George: The Reform of British Land-Holding and the Budget of 1914', (1978) 21 *Hist. Jo.* 117.

GREENWOOD, G. W., *A Manual of the Practice of Conveyancing* (1856).

HAMER, D. A., *Liberal Politics in the Age of Gladstone and Rosebery* (1972).

HARDCASTLE, MRS, *Life of John, Lord Campbell* (1881).

HART, H. M., and SACKS, A. M., *The Legal Process* (tentative edn., 1958).

HAWKINS, FRANCIS VAUGHAN, *Optional Mobilisation of Land: A Scheme for Simplifying Title and Land Transfer* (1869).

—— *The Title to Landed Estates Bills and the Solicitor General's Speech Considered* (1859).

HAZLITT, WILLIAM, *The Registration of Deeds in England: Its Past Progress and Present Position* (1851).

HENNOCK, E. P., *Fit and Proper Persons* (1973).

HEUSTON, R. F. V., *Lives of the Lord Chancellors, 1885–1940* (1964).

HOGG, J. E., *Treatise on the Law Relating to the Ownership and Incumbrance of Registered Land* (1906).

HOLDSWORTH, SIR W. S., *A History of English Law* (1922–52).

HUMPHREYS, JAMES, *Observations on the Actual State of the English Law of Real Property with the Outlines of a Code* (1827).

HUMPHRY, JOSEPH THOMAS, *The Registration of Assurances Bill: Its Peculiar System and Practical Consequences Considered* (1853).

ILBERT, SIR COURTENAY, *Legislative Methods and Forms* (1901).

JAY, RICHARD, *Joseph Chamberlain: A Political Study* (1981).

JENKINS, T. A., *Gladstone, Whiggery and the Liberal Party, 1874–1886* (1988).

KAY, JOSEPH, *Free Trade in Land* (1879).

KER, H. C. BELLENDEN, *On the Reform of the Law of Real Property* (1853).

—— *The Question of Registry or No Registry Considered* (1830).

—— *Shall we Register our Deeds?* (1853).

KEY, T., and ELPHINSTONE, H. W., *Precedents in Conveyancing* (5th edn., 1897; 9th edn., 1909).

KIRK, HARRY, *Portrait of a Profession* (1976).

KOSS, STEPHEN, *Asquith* (1976).

—— *Lord Haldane: Scapegoat for Liberalism* (1969).

LAWRENCE, N. T., *Facts and Suggestions as to the Law of Real Property* (1880).

(INCORPORATED) LAW SOCIETY, *Memorandum of the Land Transfer Committee of The Law Society on the Lord Chancellor's Bills* (1914).

—— *Memorandum on Officialism* (1905).

—— *Remarks on the Present Situation in Regard to Compulsory Land Registration* (1907).

—— *Report of the Special Committee on Malpractice* (1900).

—— *Report of the Special Committee on Solicitors' Practice* (1907).

—— *Some Reasons Against Registering Land at the Land Registry* (1906).

—— *Statement on the Land Laws* (1886).

LEAVER, JOHN, 'Building Societies and the Legal Profession', (1933) 77 *Sol. Jo.* 710.

LEWIN, T., *The Law of Trusts* (12th edn., 1911, by C. C. M. Dale and G. A. Streeten).

MACKAY, H. W. B., *An Apology for the Present System of Conveyancing* (1870).

MANCHESTER, A. H., *Modern Legal History* (1980).

MARSH, PETER, *The Discipline of Popular Government: Lord Salisbury's Domestic Statecraft, 1881–1902* (1978).

MARTIN, DAVID, 'Land Reform', in Patricia Hollis, ed., *Pressure from Without in Early Victorian England* (1974).

MEGARRY, R. E. and WADE, H. W. R., *The Law of Real Property* (1st edn., 1959).

[MOORE, JOHN], *Observations on the Proposed Registration of Deeds, with reference more particularly to the Pamphlet of William Hazlitt, Esq., by a Country Solicitor* (1851).

MORGAN, SIR GEORGE OSBORNE, *Land Law Reform in England* (1880).

MURRAY, BRUCE K., *The People's Budget, 1909–10* (1980).

OFFER, AVNER, *Property and Politics, 1870–1914* (1981).

—— 'The Origins of the Law of Property Acts 1910–1925', (1977) 40 *Modern Law Review* 505.

PARRIS, HENRY, *Constitutional Bureaucracy*, (1969).

PERKIN, HAROLD J., *The Origins of Modern English Society, 1780–1880* (1969).

—— *The Rise of Professional Society* (1989, 1990).

—— 'Land Reform and Class Conflict in Victorian England', in J. Butt and I. F. Clark, eds., *The Victorians and Social Protest* (1973).

—— 'Professionalism, Property and English Society since 1980' (Stanton Lecture, University of Reading, 1981).

POLDEN, PATRICK, 'The Public Trustee in England, 1906–1986', (1989) 10 *Journal of Legal History* 228.

PRICE, SEYMOUR J., *Building Societies: Their Origin and History* (1958).

Prideaux's Precedents in Conveyancing (21st edn., 1913, by B. L. Cherry and R. Beddington).

PUE, W. WESLEY, 'Guild Training vs Professional Education: The Committee on Legal Education and the Law Department of Queen's College, Birmingham in the 1860s', (1989) 33 *American Journal of Legal History* 241.

ROACH, JOHN, 'Liberalism and the Victorian Intelligentsia', (1957) 13 *Cambridge Historical Journal*, 58.

ROUTH, GUY, *Occupation and Pay in Great Britain* (1st edn., 1965).

ROWLAND, PETER, *The Last Liberal Governments* (1971).

RUBINSTEIN, J. S., *The Land Registry Fiasco: The Reign of King Stork* (1907).

RUDDEN, BERNARD, 'A Code too Soon', in P. Wallington and R. M. Merkin, eds., *Essays in Memory of Professor F. H. Lawson* (1986).

SADLER, THOMAS, *Edwin Wilkins Field*, (1872).

SCULLY, VINCENT, *The Irish Land Question, with Practical Plans for an Improved Land Tenure and a New Land System* (1851).

—— *Mutual Land Societies, their Present Position and Future Prospects* (1851).

—— *Occupying Ownership: Ireland*, ed. V. Scully the younger (1881).

SEWELL, HENRY, *A Letter to Lord Worsley on the Burdens Affecting Real Property, with Reasons in Favour of a General Registry of Title* (1846).

SHAEN, MARGARET JOSEPHINE, *William Shaen: A Brief Sketch* (1912).

SHAW-LEFEVRE, Sir George, *English and Irish Land Questions* (1881).

SPRING, DAVID, *The English Landed Estate* (1963).

SPRING, EILEEN, 'Landowners, Lawyers and Land Law Reform in Nineteenth Century England', (1977) *American Journal of Legal History*, 40.

STEPHEN, SIR JAMES FITZJAMES, 'The Laws Relating to Land', (Feb. 1886) 6 *National Review*.

STEWART, JAMES, *On the Means of Facilitating the Transfer of Land* (1848).

—— *Suggestions as to Reform in Some Branches of the Law* (1842; 2nd edn., 1852).

SWEET, GEORGE, 'Impediments to the Transfer of Land', in *Papers read before the Juridical Society*, iv (1874).

THOMPSON, F. M. L., *English Landed Society in the Nineteenth Century* (1963).

TOPHAM, ALFRED F., *The Law of Property Acts 1925; A Series of Lectures* (1926).

—— *The New Law of Property* (2nd edn., 1925).

UNDERHILL, ARTHUR, *Change and Decay* (1938).

—— *A Concise Explanation of Lord Birkenhead's Act 1922* (1922).

—— *The New Conveyancing* (1925).

—— 'Lord Birkenhead's Law of Property Bill', (1920) 36 *Law Quarterly Review* 107.

—— 'Lord Haldane's Real Property and Conveyancing Bills', (1914) 30 *Law Quarterly Review* 35.

—— for 'The Line of Least Resistance' see *Fourth Report of the Acquisition and Valuation of Land Committee*, (1919) HCP xxix. 89, appendix.

VINCENT, JOHN, *The Formation of the Liberal Party, 1857–1868* (1966).

—— ed., *Disraeli, Derby and the Conservative Party: The Political Journals of Lord Stanley, 1846–1869* (1966).

WAKEFIELD, EDWARD THOMAS, *The Feasibility of Constructing a New System of Registering Title Deeds* (1853).

WILLIAMS, JOSHUA, *Letters to John Bull on Lawyers and Law Reform* (1857).

—— *Principles of the Law of Real Property* (from 1845; 2nd edn., 1849; 19th edn., by T. Cyprian Williams, 1901).

—— 'On the True Remedies for the Evils which Affect the Transfer of Land', in *Papers read before the Juridical Society, 1858–1862*, ii (1862).

WILLIAMS, PETER HOWELL, *A Gentleman's Calling: The Liverpool Attorney-at-Law* (1980).

WILLIAMS, T. CYPRIAN. *The Law of Vendor and Purchaser* (2nd edn., 1910).

—— ed., *[Joshua] Williams on Real Property* (19th edn., 1901).

W. R., 'Transfer of Real Property', (1845) 43 *Westminster Review* 373 (a review of Wilson's *Outlines* . . .).

WILSON, ROBERT, *Outlines of a Plan for Adopting the Machinery of the Public Funds to the Transfer of Real Property: Respectfully Inscribed to the President and Council of the Society for Promoting the Amendment of the Law* (1844).

WOLSTENHOLME, EDWARD PARKER, 'Simplification of Title to Land: An Outline of a Plan', in *Papers read before the Juridical Society, 1858–1862*, ii (1862).

—— and Turner, R. O., *The Conveyancing Acts 1881 and 1874* (1882).
—— *The Settled Land Act 1882* (1883).

Official papers

Real Property Commissioners, Reports: (1829) HCP x. 1; (1830) HCP xi. 1; (1831–2) HCP xxiii. 321; (1833) HCP xxii. 1.

Select Committee on Copyhold Enfranchisement, (1837–8) HCP xxiii. 189.

Select Committee on Burdens on Land (Lords), (1846) HLP xxii. 1.

Select Committee on Fees in Courts of Law and Equity, First Report, (1847–8) HCP xv. 1.

Select Committee on the Investment of the Savings of the Middle and Working Classes, (1850) HCP xix 169.

Select Committee on Official Salaries, (1850) HCP xv. 179.

Commission on Registration and Conveyancing, Report, (1850) HCP xxxii. 1.

Letter from C. H. Bellenden Ker to the Lord Chancellor on the Cost of Registration of Assurances, (1852–3) HLP xxv. 687.

Select Committee on the Registration of Assurances Bill, (1852–3) HCP xxxvi. 397.

Commission on Registration of Title, Report, (1857, 2nd session) HCP xxi. 245.

Commission on the Operation of the Land Transfer Act . . . and the Registry of Deeds for the County of Middlesex, Report, (1870) HCP xviii. 595.

Registration of Title (Australian Colonies), (1872) HCP xlii. 499.

Select Committee on Civil Service Expenditure, Second Report, (1873) HCP vii. 391.

Select Committee on Land Titles and Transfer, evidence, (1878) HCP xv; Report, (1878–9) HCP xi. 1.

Commission on Agriculture, evidence, (1881) HCP xvii. 1; Final Report, (1882) HCP xiv. 1.

Select Committee on the Conveyancing Bill, (1882) HCP viii. 259.

Select Committee on the Yorkshire Land Registries Bill and the Yorkshire Registries Bill, (1884) HCP xvi. 593.

Memorandum Accompanying the Land Charges Registration and Searches Bill, (1888) HLP v. 255.

C. F. Brickdale, *Report on Observations of the Law Society on the Land Transfer Bill*, (1894) HLP xi. 453.

Select Committee on the Land Transfer Bill, (1895) HCP xi. 1.

[C. F. Brickdale], *Land (Registration of Title) (Germany and Austro-Hungary)*, C. 8139, (1896) HCP lxxxiv. 85.

Memorandum to the Land Transfer Bill, (1897) HLP vi. 1.

Report of the Registrar of the Land Registry on the First Three Years, etc., Cd. 111, (1902) HCP lxxxiii. 595.

Select Committee on the Housing of the Working Classes Act, (1906) HCP ix. 1.

Land Registry Return of Work, (1906) HCP xcix. 271.

Report of the Registrar of the Land Registry for the Years 1902–1905, Cd. 3132, (1906) HCP xcix. 279.

Royal Commission on the Land Transfer Acts, First Report, Cd. 4510, (1909) HCP xxvii. 733; Second and Final Report, Cd. 5483, (1911) HCP xxx. 1.

Explanatory Statement as to the Lord Chancellor's Bills, (1913) HLP vii. 439.

Memorandum on the Real Property and Conveyancing Bills, (1913) HLP ix. 45.

Commission on the Civil Service, Sixth Report, (1914–16) HCP xii. 1.

Report of the Machinery of Government Committee, Cd. 9230, (1918) HCP xii. 1.

Fourth Report of the Acquisition and Valuation of Land Committee on the Transfer of Land in England and Wales, Cmd. 424, (1919) HCP xxix. 89.

Joint Select Committee on the Law of Property Bill, Report, (1920) HLP viii. 199.

Committee on the Law of Property Consolidation Bills, Report; Cmd. 2271, (1924) HCP xi. 363.

Report of the Land Registration Committee, Cmd. 3564, (1929–30) HCP xv. 539.

Report of the Chief Land Registrar to the Lord Chancellor on H.M. Land Registry for the Financial Year 1931–32 (HMSO, 1932).

Report of the Land Transfer Committee, Cmd. 4776, (1934–5) HCP x. 395.

Public Accounts Committee, 32nd Report, (1987–8) HCP (no. 318).

Index